MEN OUT OF FOCUS

The Soviet Masculinity Crisis in the Long Sixties

MARKO DUMANČIĆ

Men Out of Focus

The Soviet Masculinity Crisis in the Long Sixties

UNIVERSITY OF TORONTO PRESS
Toronto Buffalo London

ISBN 978-1-4875-0525-7 (cloth)
ISBN 978-1-4875-3185-0 (EPUB)
ISBN 978-1-4875-3184-3 (PDF)

Library and Archives Canada Cataloguing in Publication

Title: Men out of focus : the Soviet masculinity crisis in the long sixties /
Marko Dumančić.
Names: Dumančić, Marko, 1979– author.
Description: Includes bibliographical references and index.
Identifiers: Canadiana (print) 20200286226 | Canadiana (ebook) 2020028634X
| ISBN 9781487505257 (cloth) | ISBN 9781487531850 (EPUB) |
ISBN 9781487531843 (PDF)
Subjects: LCSH: Masculinity in motion pictures. | LCSH: Masculinity in
popular culture. | LCSH: Men in motion pictures. | LCSH: Men in popular
culture. | LCSH: Motion pictures – Soviet Union – History – 20th century. |
LCSH: Masculinity – Soviet Union – History – 20th century. | LCSH: Men –
Soviet Union – Identity – History – 20th century.
Classification: LCC PN1995.9.M34 D86 2020 | DDC 791.43/65211–dc23

This book has been published with the help of a grant from the Federation
for the Humanities and Social Sciences, through the Awards to Scholarly
Publications Program, using funds provided by the Social Sciences and
Humanities Research Council of Canada.

University of Toronto Press acknowledges the financial assistance to its
publishing program of the Canada Council for the Arts and the Ontario
Arts Council, an agency of the Government of Ontario.

**Canada Council   Conseil des Arts
for the Arts   du Canada**

ONTARIO ARTS COUNCIL
CONSEIL DES ARTS DE L'ONTARIO

an Ontario government agency
un organisme du gouvernement de l'Ontario

Funded by the   Financé par le
Government   gouvernement
of Canada   du Canada

Canadä

To my mother, Vera Dumančić,
who always helps me see things clearly.

Contents

Illustrations

Acknowledgments

The inspiration for this project came in the very distant mid-1990s when my family moved to the United States from Zagreb, Croatia. I read an article on how 1980s and '90s gay urban subcultures shaped heterosexual masculinities. I was fascinated by the idea that masculine identities were fluent, dynamic, and interdependent. This concept made such a deep impression on me that it followed me to Connecticut College, where I discovered a passion for history (thanks to Professor Alexis Dudden) and Russian studies (thanks to professors Sofie Efimovna Pais, Andrea Lanoux, Marijan Despalatović, and Eleanor Despalatović). As an undergraduate, I conceived of a thesis, of which I am only mildly embarrassed now. I was so taken with the promise of this research that I wanted to pursue it in graduate school.

At UNC–Chapel Hill the inimitable Don Raleigh took a chance on me and this idea of mine. I am not sure I can ever repay him for all he has done while serving as my adviser. Besides being a one-of-a-kind mentor, he showed me kindness and compassion every step of the way. Starting with our very first meeting in Hamilton Hall, Don has become a trusted friend and confidant. Louise McReynolds made this project infinitely better in two ways. First, her approach to cultural history inspired me to dig deeper and explain myself more eloquently. Second, she pushed me to be more thoughtful, nuanced, and deliberative in my gender analysis. Although not "officially" one of my advisers, Paula A. Michaels shepherded this project and shaped my professional career. She opined on everything from book chapters to job letters with a keen eye, sage advice, and infinite wit. Paula remains a role model, a comrade, and a force of nature.

During a year-long research trip I met three people who proved central to the evolution of *Men Out of Focus*. As a native Muscovite, Mikhail Stakanov became my guide through the labyrinth that is Russian culture. His eclectic and erudite familiarity with Soviet cultural tropes helped me glean aspects of the Soviet ethos that would have otherwise remained hidden from (my) view. At RGANI, archivist Liudmila Ivanovna Stepanich did her utmost to make sure I procured the documents I needed to bring my project to fruition. As a great film aficionado herself, she told me fabulous stories about sixties movie stars, controversial film scenes, and Soviet fan culture. I wish I could have shared this book with her before she passed away, since it is, in no small way, a reflection of the conversations we shared. Finally, Juliane Fürst added depth and colour to the archival research we engaged in. Juliane had a way of asking the most incisive questions to get to the heart of what my book was addressing. I consider myself lucky to have benefited from her ingenious cast of mind.

And where would we be without our nearest and dearest? My grandparents, Marija and Mirko Crmarić, lived the kinds of lives that epitomize for me the values of ceaseless hard work, modesty, and perseverance. Since childhood, my sisters Katja and Marija have given me unconditional support when I doubted myself the most. My uncle and aunt, Žorž and Snežana Crmarić, housed and fed me when I came to Washington, D.C., to take advantage of the Library of Congress European reading room. Their hospitality helped me write some of the toughest parts of this book. Fran Wacht stands out as the person who taught me to enjoy the craft of writing and proves, yet again, that our high school teachers are often the most important people in our intellectual lives. I often find that I don't deserve my friends: Violet Anderson, Addie Cheney, Zara Martirosyan, Alex and Adrianne Jacobs, Gabriella and Sam Toossi, and Scotti Branton. To imagine completing this book without them is to imagine arriving at the finish line and not seeing the very group that made the journey an exciting adventure.

Although writing a book manuscript can be a lonely task, I was lucky to have a support group of fellow scholars: Marc and Susan Eagle, Tammy Van Dyken, and Nicolette Bruner. Occupying various sections of Spencer's coffeehouse in downtown Bowling Green, Kentucky, we kept one another inspired and accountable as we pursued our projects. To prove it takes a village to write a book, I must confess that the credit for the title goes to my fabulous colleague and friend Robert Dietle. Beth Holmgren and Chad Bryant shrewdly encouraged me to consider the effect that the Polish and Czechoslovak film industries exerted on Soviet filmmaking. Without their input, this book would have lacked a transnational viewpoint. Of the colleagues I met later in my career, few have left as deep an impression on me as Amy E. Randall. Her reflections on the fatherhood chapter were often more trenchant than the chapter itself. At least two chapters of this book have been made better by the collective wisdom of the Midwest Russian History Workshop. Specifically, Christine Evans, Deborah Field, John Randolph, Christine Varga-Harris, and Roshanna Sylvester offered the kind of encouragement that mattered the most in moments of self-doubt. Western Kentucky University's terrific history graduate students – Shelley Spalding, Maja Antonić, Morgan Baxter, and Allie Crume – helped proofread the entire manuscript and present my ideas more precisely.

Approaching a publisher was a harrowing prospect for me. I consider myself lucky that Stephen Shapiro played the role of Virgil in my publication odyssey. Unfailingly prompt, considerate, and meticulous in his responses, he made the process thoroughly enjoyable and rewarding. The two anonymous reviewers went above and beyond in providing me with concrete ways of improving the manuscript. Both reviewers generously donated their time and expertise to understand what I aimed to accomplish and then gave me the tools to get to the destination faster and more effectively.

I owe a great debt to both the UNC Graduate School at Chapel Hill and WKU's History Department. The former funded both my research travel and the completion of my PhD work; the latter defrayed costs associated with the publication of the monograph. I am humbled and endlessly obliged to them for the crucial support they lent me.

My partner, Nathan Parker, ought to receive a plaque commemorating his saintly patience for witnessing the vicissitudes of completing this book. Perhaps more importantly, he preserved my sanity by gently reminding me of what matters most at the end of day.

Finally, this book is dedicated to my mother Vera. To her, I owe everything. Her decision to move to Boston and start a new chapter for our family was not the easy path but it was brave and worthwhile. To this day, my mother teaches me the importance of a positive mindset and a fighting spirit. She remains my anchor, my compass, and my guiding star.

MEN OUT OF FOCUS

The Soviet Masculinity Crisis in the Long Sixties

Soviet Men in Need of Saving?

Are Soviet men facing a crisis? Do men require protection? These two seemingly innocuous questions, posed by demographer Boris Urlanis in his 1968 article "Protect the Men!" (*Beregite muzhchin!*) evoked passionate responses.[1] The op-ed started a mass media storm and set the stage for the gender debates of the 1970s and '80s. Urlanis's exhortation became a shorthand for the late Soviet-era "battle of the sexes" and is, to this day, used any time a male-related issue comes to the fore. When he first deployed the term in the summer of 1968, Urlanis intended to sound an alarm about the existential calamities facing Russian men. He pointed to a higher infant mortality rate among male children and discussed the fact that the average male lifespan was eight years shorter than that of women. To Urlanis, the causes of this disparity seemed self-evident: men suffered higher rates of alcoholism, committed suicide in larger numbers, and more frequently suffered fatal injuries at work. He recommended that the country open "male clinics" (*muzhskie konsul'tatsii*) to offer prophylactic services to men. Besides presenting the data, Urlanis made the case that "saving men" was in everyone's interest, especially women's. He warned: "The predominance of male mortality means hundreds of thousands of 'splintered' families and hundreds of thousands of women who lose all the benefits of a normal family life." He also believed this to be of crucial importance to unmarried women: "If you save men, then all the girls will find life companions."[2]

   While no one objected to his demographic data, many wondered aloud about the causes of this "masculine malaise" and the most appropriate solutions. Almost immediately, fiery polemics broke out about men's behaviour, their status in society, and their treatment of the "fairer sex." *Literaturnaia gazeta* (*LG*) readily gave voice to those who contended that men should be denied sympathy because they were victims of their own negligence. These commentators insisted that the so-called crisis facing men had little to do with environmental factors and was, in fact, self-inflicted. Larisa Kliachko, a prominent journalist, was the first to reject Urlanis's diagnosis, noting that she spoke not only for herself but also for the thousands of women who had written to reject Urlanis's call to action. She averred that it would be much better for men to take some personal responsibility for their predicament than to expect a free lunch. Without mincing words, Kliachko argued that men themselves were to blame for the higher/earlier mortality rates they faced. By any statistical indicator, men were self-destructive: they boasted sky-high rates of smoking, alcoholism, and hospitalization due to injury.[3] She contended that while men indeed lived shorter lives, women's quality of life was poorer because of innumerable professional, societal, and domestic obligations. They faced a higher incidence of malignant tumours and were disproportionately affected by various diseases of the circulatory system. She not so subtly implied that men were contributing to women's ill health by being absent in pursuit of the next hedonistic high. Most of all, Kliachko objected to what she perceived as Urlanis's blackmail approach to recruiting women to his cause: "To exert a strong influence on impressionable women, the scientist resorts to intimidation: 'If you do not take care of the men, you will remain without suitors.'" Between the lines, she seemed to be pondering women's true predicament: with suitors like that, who needs marriage? Kliachko's journalist colleague, Ada Baskina, amplified the criticisms of Urlanis's article by pointing to an experiment involving two groups of squirrels. It turned out that the squirrels who were made to run in a hamster wheel outlived their sedentary counterparts. Baskina declared that Soviet men could learn something from the diligent rodents and should apply their energies to helping around the house: "Wouldn't this reduce the time for drunkenness, and maybe even for smoking? And wouldn't it be nice if they came home to a happy spouse rather than a wife who was irritated that he had, once again, showed up at the doorstep black-out drunk?"[4] By all (published) indicators, it seems clear that *LG*'s female audience had turned a deaf ear to Urlanis's call to "protect the men," countering that men would do well to follow the example of their female compatriots, who had proven themselves to be the stronger, not just the fairer, sex.[5]

The "pro-male" side of the debate retorted that Kliachko and Baskina's supporters had it all wrong and declared that men were suffering disproportionate physical, mental, and emotional harm because they played a colossal role in the functioning of Soviet society.[6] Their dismal health and overall dissatisfaction with life had more to do with the undue burdens placed on men than with their wilful desire to engage in self-destructive behaviour. M. Barovich, an engineer from Moscow, blamed a range of factors, from urbanization to desk jobs to family obligations, as the chief culprits of men's early mortality. Given men's multiple and overlapping obligations to employer, family, and state, Soviet men had no opportunity to engage in exercise or physically strenuous activity, something Barovich maintained men were born to do.[7] In a similar vein, a pilot from Minsk argued that overrepresentation in dangerous occupations that involved machinery – mining, truck driving, marine occupations, and the like – exposed men to undue physical hazards. He concluded: "Men are dying because even the most advanced technology is far from perfect."[8] But machines and desk jobs were not the only problems; some pointed an accusatory finger at men's spouses. For example, a comedic sketch appeared in *Izvestiia* in response to Urlanis's article to show that men needed to be protected *from* women rather than *by* them. This piece described the nerve-wracking process a man must endure to obtain a custom-made built-in wardrobe just to please his wife's whims. Tormented by his hectoring mate and bloodsucking craftsmen, he suffers a nervous breakdown as an outsider forced to participate in a consumer-driven nightmare.[9] The sketch intimated that a domestic life filled with "comforts" decreed by the missus is the road to an early grave.

Those who believed the Soviet men faced a genuine crisis also often objected to the mocking tone of the opposing side. Implicit was a sense of betrayal by "modern women," who, like Kliachko and Baskina, doubted the authenticity of men's problems. In response, they posited that there was nothing wrong with the "separate but equal" doctrine and that helping around the kitchen would hardly improve men's lot anyway since the true source of their plight lay elsewhere. One reader expressed directly the idea that the two sexes occupied separate spheres: "Improving women's health will do little to lengthen men's lifespans."[10] In general, the "masculinist" side identified systemic problems, such as urban isolation, family pressures, dangerous technology, soulless consumerism, and women's callousness as causes of men's predicament. The responses exhibited knee-jerk reactionism defined by a muted nostalgia for simpler times when women were dutiful, labour manual, youth deferential, domestic obligations minimal, and one's worth measured by story-worthy exploits rather than office or paycheque size.

Although one side portrayed men as victims of an urban, industrialized, and consumerist society while the other painted them as reckless deviants undeserving of compassion, both sides agreed on two

Figure I.1. "Protect the men!" (1968).

things. First, men, as a group, required attention, if not help. Second, change in gender relations was a must. Even those who saw men as the "stronger sex" argued for an intervention. One Orel doctor, who supported Urlanis's call for men's clinics, thought of men as an at-risk group: "The question of male vulnerability [*uiazvimost'*] has for a long time interested science."[11] The notion that men required supervision resulted in visuals depicting them as infantilized creatures in need of babying. A cartoon in *Literaturnaia gazeta* that accompanied the 1968 debate and a 1982 comedy that took Urlanis's phrase as its inspiration and title, both imagine grown men as mollycoddled babies (Figures I.1 and I.2). The press continued to satirically promote the idea that men required protecting and represented the supposedly stronger sex as showing signs of arrested development.[12] Although specialists insisted this matter be treated as a serious demographic and medical issue, the discussion often focused on determining how men had come to be so helpless and which sex benefited most from the post-Stalinist reforms.[13]

Figure I.2. Film poster for *Protect the Men!* (1982).

As has been pointed out, this debate chronologically belongs to the late Soviet era since explicit discussions about a masculinity crisis evolved over the course of the 1970s and '80s, during late socialism.[14] *Men Out of Focus*, however, makes the case that the road to Urlanis's article and to the notion that Soviet men had entered crisis mode began in the early 1950s and was hidden in plain sight on the nation's movie screens. Urlanis had coined a term that captured the popular imagination, but the crisis itself emerged over the course of the 1950s and '60s. This book makes visible the polemics about problematic masculinity models pervading Soviet cinema and the popular press between 1953 and 1968, a period I dub "the long Soviet sixties." During those fifteen years, filmmakers built stories around male protagonists who felt disoriented in a world that was becoming increasingly (sub)urbanized, rebellious, consumerist, household-oriented, and scientifically complex. The dramatic tension of much of sixties cinema essentially revolved around the male protagonists' inability to navigate the challenges of post-Stalinist life. Mass consumerism generated fears of selling out.

Women's and youth's demand for independence meant surrendering control. The scientific revolution stirred fears of the unknown and unknowable. Being a father seemed to be tougher than ascending Mount Everest. The renegotiation of men's standing in the post-Stalinist order was an uneven and messy affair that began in the early 1950s and culminated in the publication of Urlanis's article in the summer of 1968, by which point the male malaise had acquired a diagnosis and become publicly recognized.

The sixties masculinity crisis was rooted in the large-scale changes the post-Stalinist leadership had launched. Throughout the 1950s and '60s the Soviet government initiated ambitious efforts to bring about a modernity that could, in a single move, reward its population for its Second World War sacrifices, distance itself from the Stalin era, and display the Soviet Union's superiority over the West. In addressing the legacy of the Second World War, Stalin's death, and the Cold War, the Party leadership reconfigured the core Stalinist traditions and practices. Starting in 1953, the post-Stalinist leadership began pushing for a modernity defined by mass consumerism, (sub)urbanization, technological revolution, and the democratization of the public space so as to more substantively include youth and women.

By transforming material life, Nikita Khrushchev's and Leonid Brezhnev's policies caused a shift in interpersonal relations and altered expectations for normative male behaviour. It remained unclear, however, what type of masculine identity could build a system capable of winning the Cold War while remaining true to the principle of peaceful coexistence. It seemed that without combat, women, as "consumers-in-chief," were on the front lines of this ideological battle. The Party set out to distinguish the Soviet Union from the United States, yet it was competing against its ideological opponent on parallel tracks and measuring its standing in the race using the enemy's consumerist metrics. It is not for nothing that the debate between Nikita Khrushchev and Richard Nixon took place in a kitchen and that the First Secretary repeatedly insisted that the Soviet Union would overtake the United States in the per capita production of meat, milk, and butter. The Cold War was, in key and obvious respects, about bread and butter issues. Just like they had in wartime, Soviet men were expected to fall in line with the new direction the authorities articulated. As the 1950s progressed and the sixties, as a distinct era, took shape, questions arose whether Soviet men were up to the task of surpassing the United States by manifesting the kind of domesticated, consumerist, and hypertechnological *"dolce vita* modernity" envisioned by post-Stalinist leaders.

The modernization processes set in motion by Khrushchev explain a great deal not only about Soviet masculinity but also about the sixties as a period more generally. Emphasizing post-Stalinist modernization efforts more directly integrates the Soviet experience with the broader European one and allows for a comparative investigation. After Stalin's death, Soviet society confronted the same (existential) conundrums that plagued societies across the continent:

- Could men adjust to the postwar emphasis on domesticity? Could they cease being absent or distant disciplinarians whose relationship with their children was mediated through the mother? Could they be flesh-and-blood fathers without jeopardizing their patriarchal privilege?
- Had crimes of the state committed during the 1930s and '40s impugned an entire interwar generation of "fathers" and made them unfit to lead the postwar generation of "sons"?
- Was mass consumerism promoting the loss of individualism and the economic ascendancy of women? Were men becoming soft from all the modern gadgets and conveniences?
- Were scientific advances depriving individuals of initiative and accountability? Did scientists control technology, or vice versa?

Overall, Soviet directors – as well as their European and American counterparts – imagined their male compatriots as besieged on a number of fronts and/or unable to address some of their own key deficiencies. Men's commitment to their biological offspring remained in question throughout the period. In the Soviet Union this anxiety formed the epicentre of many social dramas, expressing itself through the trope of runaway fathers and abandoned single mothers. Marriage proved no less tricky to navigate than fatherhood. Sixties protagonists often "lost" in romance because they engaged in the game of love without fully understanding the "modern" courting rules. As a result, they fell victim to avaricious *femmes fatales* who turned men into unwitting enablers of a female-driven consumerist economy. Soviet heroes could not expect much support from youth either, for "the sons" saw "the fathers" as Stalin's heirs and therefore as unfit to provide true guidance. Celluloid protagonists also proved no more successful in mastering new scientific and technological frontiers. They were prevented from achieving their goals by party ideologues who were as clueless about science as they were dedicated to toeing the party line. Even when party officials did not get in the way, technology – either unruly robots or invisible but lethal radiation – turned scientists into victims. In short, sixties filmmakers, journalists, party officials, and ordinary citizens worried openly about the state of men at least a decade before Urlanis's article even though they did not yet refer to it as a crisis.

Movies are an obvious forum for examining and contesting the post-Stalinist "masculine condition." Official statistics on yearly ticket sales demonstrate that in 1950, there were around 1 billion visits to the cinema throughout the Soviet Union; by 1957, 3 billion.[15] This increase was even more dramatic in the non-Russian republics. In Kazakhstan, attendance more than tripled from 33 million spectators in 1950 to 113 million in 1956, and in Ukraine, the numbers more than doubled from 212 million to 540 million during that same period. Indeed, moviegoing was Soviet citizens' favourite leisure activity. A 1963 survey found that 77.3 per cent of the respondents attended the movies at least several times a month and that 44.8 per cent went at least several times a week.[16] When asked how they usually spent a weekend, 48.8 per cent reported moviegoing as their main weekend leisure activity.[17] Cinema was twice as popular as entertaining guests or visiting friends and three times more popular than reading.[18]

Many of my conclusions about Soviet masculinity after 1953 are based on multiple types of evidence. I draw on materials gathered at the Archive of Literature and Art (RGALI) as well as the Archive of Contemporary History (RGANI). The relevant archival sources I utilize are recently declassified censorship records, transcribed meetings of the Cinematographers' Union, and transcripts of conversations that followed public film premieres. I have also researched the fifteen-year run of two key Soviet film periodicals: *Cinema Art* (Iskusstvo kino), which was intended for movie industry professionals, and *Soviet Screen* (Sovetskii ekran), which was aimed at the broad moviegoing audience. Informing my readings of films are also articles and reports from the most widely circulated dailies such as *Pravda*, *Izvestiia*, *Sovetskaia kul'tura*, and *Literaturnaia gazeta*. Finally, throughout the book I utilize cartoons that appeared in the popular satirical magazine *Krokodil*, because their visual tropes reflected people's shared experience of the cinematic medium. This wide range of sources has allowed me access to various voices: from party officials to ordinary film fans, from directors to journalists, novelists, and literary critics. By weighing archival and published sources equally, I reconstruct the complex cultural ecosystem in which cinema operated.

The diverse sources allowed me to identify the most popular as well as the most controversial motion pictures to investigate. Out of the hundreds of Soviet productions during this fifteen-year period, I viewed eighty-three that each sold more than 20 million tickets and/

or attracted significant attention from the press and Party officialdom. Since low ticket sales may have been a reflection of the state's lack of support (evident in the small number of copies produced and/or restricted distribution), I also relied on the yearly readers' poll conducted by *Sovetskii ekran*. Readers of that magazine mailed in their ballots to determine the "people's choice awards" for various categories, including best domestic and foreign films and the year's best actors and actresses. Of the eighty-three films I selected for viewing, around forty had won people's hearts or hit it big at the box office, or they had been heavily censored because they were deemed too controversial.

Collectively, the films discussed in this book serve as an X-ray of a society emerging from Stalin's early Cold War freeze and struggling to make sense of its historical moment. *Men Out of Focus* is a story about masculine figures on the silver screen, a commentary on the directors who made them, and a portrait of a society reacting to new productions. Celluloid heroes projected onto the screen embodied the filmmakers' own fears and evoked strong responses from moviegoers. Soviet filmmakers did not have complete control over the production, distribution, and reception of their films, and the movies I discuss here testify to their attempts to negotiate postwar norms and values by reforming the Soviet film industry. As one would expect, sixties directors were not uniform in their actions: some embraced modernization while others expressed angst about the rapidly changing world. All of them, however, were invested in reflecting their own version of the sixties, be it as an era of hopeful possibilities or an era of false turns. This book also delves into audience responses to the films. Even when the press did not record moviegoers' voices and opinions about particular films, I acknowledge their power by tracking ticket sales and letter-writing campaigns, as well as the yearly "people's choice awards" opinion poll in *Sovetskii ekran*. I also acknowledge the average Soviet citizen by situating the films in the context of more general conversations about the day's major issues as reflected in newspapers, magazines, and professional journals.

Before proceeding, I offer a couple of caveats regarding my use of the term "masculinity crisis." I agree that the notion of a "gender crisis" has been "overworked to the point of semantic collapse."[19] At the same time, the public square and closed-door debates I have unearthed indicate clearly that Soviet masculinity had entered a period during which Soviet citizens found it hard to predict what would come next for the country's men. Rather than perceiving a gradual transformation, contemporaries wondered aloud whether masculinity, as they knew and understood it, could survive the demands of post-Stalinist modernization. As the responses to Urlanis's article tell us, the existential dread about the future of Soviet men did not appear overnight; the vocabulary, tropes, and even imagery framing the "protect the men" debate had been circulating for at least a decade prior to 1968. I deploy the word *crisis* deliberately, to capture sixties popular culture's preoccupation with men's vulnerability, be it perceived or real. For many Soviet observers, the crisis was real; for many others, it was not. There are hundreds of sixties films, movie reviews, and public debates that do not concern themselves at all with gender issues. That said, the trope of "soft masculinity" operated in a complex cultural ecosystem of competing masculine tropes. Overall, the period's film productions clearly indicate that anxieties about men's inadequacy left a profound mark on sixties culture and an enduring legacy for subsequent periods.

Although principally a critical study of Soviet masculinity, *Men Out of Focus* comments on three distinct dimensions of postwar Soviet history. First, it reframes the Khrushchev and early Brezhnev eras as a single, coherent period. This chronological demarcation is helpful not only because it bridges the Khrushchev era and the first quarter of Brezhnev's rule but also because it reframes the periodization of Soviet sociocultural history based on gender considerations.

Second, *Men out of Focus* demonstrates that debates about sixties masculinity were neither chronologically nor geographically bound. The disenchantment with postwar mid-century modern life in the Soviet Union paralleled masculine discontent in Europe and the United States. Although primarily a study of a particular historical context, this book also offers insights into how masculine ideals function across space and time.

Finally, I conceptualize the cinematic sixties as a part of the global New Wave movement and explain how parallel cultural and ideological reforms taking place across Europe enshrined documentary realism as the primary mode of understanding contemporaneity. Aside from its documentary characteristics, the New Wave can be characterized by protagonists who struggled to figure out how to live authentically by avoiding the bogeymen of postwar modernization: conformity, uniformity, and hypocrisy.

The Soviet Sixties as an Age of Anxiety

Often dubbed "the Thaw," the Khrushchev era (1956–64) has been the focus of much historical scholarship since the early 1990s. Questions dominating the study of the period scrutinize whether Khrushchev's haphazard de-Stalinization drive signalled a decisive and substantive turn away from Stalin's authoritarian ethos or masked a Stalinism redux. Current scholarship on the 1950s and '60s takes into account a number of groups to determine the extent to which the post-Stalinist system purged itself of Stalin-era impulses and practices; some of the population factions include intellectuals,[20] the urban middle class,[21] women,[22] youth,[23] and Gulag returnees.[24] These studies make clear that the sensibility, mentality, and praxis of the late Stalin era had not vanished into thin air. On the contrary, as Juliane Fürst argues persuasively, postwar Stalinism in key ways defined the outlines of late socialism. In particular, the dislocation created by the Second World War caused generational ruptures as well as sociocultural practices that formed the foundation of the Khrushchev and Brezhnev eras; late Stalinism thus saw the emergence of a fledgling consumer society, the birth of youth countercultures, and the rise of a Soviet middle class.[25] Moreover, as Polly Jones reminds us, de-Stalinization's impacts can be considered ambiguous at best. De-Stalinization remained a contested process that presented Party members and the general populace with a dilemma to resolve: how to determine whose prerogative it was to direct and control societal change. The results of de-Stalinization proved equally equivocal as the Party's attempts to strengthen the Soviet system through reform "led to the paradoxical combinations of liberalism and conservatism, iconoclasm and preservation of Stalinist norms."[26]

Although I agree that a hard and fast division between postwar Stalinism and the Thaw did not exist, I ultimately concur with Denis Kozlov and Eleonory Gilburd's assertion that "to speak meaningfully about continuity and change during the Thaw, it is insufficient to measure these years against the Stalin epoch."[27] If postwar Stalinism provided a foundation and impetus for Thaw-era reforms, then Khrushchev's modernization imbued the reconstruction of Soviet society with substance and direction. Just a decade after Stalin's death, immense changes were apparent in the lives of Soviet citizens. In the way they dressed,[28] spoke,[29] entertained themselves,[30] travelled,[31] related to technology,[32] and understood the world around them,[33] Soviet citizens were perceptibly different. The Soviet Union of the late 1960s was not the same place it had been twenty years earlier. *Men Out of Focus* builds on the scholarship detailing the foundational alteration of Soviet life after 1953 to bolster the notion that post-Stalinist reforms substantively transformed the action scripts and mental frames of Soviet citizens. In the process of forming itself in opposition to Stalinism, the Thaw created an alternative version of Soviet modernity and subjectivity.[34]

To signify the uniqueness of the period, I opt to discuss Soviet society within the framework of the long Soviet sixties rather than the Thaw.

This choice is justified by the fact that contemporaries identified the emergence of a distinct sixties generation: the *shestidesiatniki*, that is, the people of the sixties. Although the concept of a sixties generation has a long lineage (the term was employed as early as 1960),[35] the concepts of Soviet sixties and "socialist sixties" are relatively recent. Western scholars began employing this terminology in the early 2010s as they began investigating the era's global and international dimensions. Sheila Fitzpatrick, for instance, questions the notion that two separate sixties existed, one in the Soviet Union and the other in the West.[36] Similarly, Denis Kozlov and Eleonory Gilburd advance the idea that Europeans of the 1950s and '60s on both sides of the Iron Curtain responded to common concerns with similar if not identical answers and in ways that transcended the Cold War divide.[37] Anne E. Gorsuch and Diane P. Koenker observe that even as the so-called Second World aimed to develop an alternative modernity, "the socialist world was not a singular world, separate from what was happening elsewhere."[38]

Men Out of Focus dovetails with existing scholarship on the Soviet sixties but emphasizes more heavily the similarities between East and West, showing how postwar modernization in the West and post-Stalinist modernization in the Soviet Union affected the male segment of the population. Although I acknowledge cultural specificities and idiosyncratic responses within the Soviet Union, I shed light on the fact that filmmakers on both sides of the Iron Curtain felt compelled to chronicle the predicaments facing men in industrialized societies. My emphasis on the commonalities between the two blocs echoes the "convergence system theory" that emerged in the 1960s and '70s. A decade and a half after the Second World War, a number of Western sociologists and economists opined that the two blocs' likenesses outweighed their differences.[39] In 1960, four labour economists hypothesized that industrialism, rather than capitalism, would shape international institutions into a common mould. I do not entirely concur with the idea of convergence but agree that during the 1950s and '60s, the modern, bureaucratized, and industrialized state became a common denominator for the two superpower adversaries. This welfare state, which promised to usher in an affluent age, bred unrealistic expectations among the citizenry for the postwar quality of life and served as a driver for counterculture movements.[40] In both East and West, widespread discontent with the "good life" – either having too much or not enough of it – came to be expressed as a masculinity problem. K.A. Cuordileone's statement about the state of American masculinity applies equally well to the post-Stalinist context: "The ailments that plagued mid-century men, at least as far as they were diagnosed by experts and social critics, paralleled expressions of a wider cultural malaise and anxiety in the 1950s."[41] Thus the unease about a consumerist, technologically advanced, (sub)urban, and statist modernity, as mirrored in a masculinity crisis, should figure prominently in any narrative about the long sixties. Sixties moviegoers' worries about the passing of the autonomous male indicate that broad elements of Soviet society harboured reservations about the country's direction even while celebrating Sputnik, revelling in trips abroad, and enjoying access to a wider range of consumer goods.

The beginning of the Soviet sixties and the rise of widespread pessimism is notoriously tricky to pinpoint in time. While the political and cultural Thaw has a relatively clear chronology that more or less follows the trajectory of de-Stalinization or Khrushchev's office term, the sixties, as a distinct epoch, have a more ambiguous starting point, depending on the author's thematic focus. I begin the story with Stalin's death in 1953 because it both enabled the reform-minded processes that began in the late 1940s and allowed for a reconsideration of what it meant to be a Soviet man. As John Haynes's and Lilya Kaganovsky's studies of Stalin-era cinema demonstrate, Soviet masculinity could not be imagined without Stalin since it was Stalinist discourse that created a "patriarchal" language, a unitary language spoken by unified subjects, with as little room for ambiguity as possible.[42] With the death of the man to whom no other man could compare, it finally became possible to build alternative masculine forms. By 1954, slowly but surely, new masculine models had begun to emerge on Soviet silver screens. Urlanis's article demonstrates that by the summer of 1968 the crisis had been called out and named. The Soviets invaded Czechoslovakia to crush the Prague Spring just as the debate about Soviet masculinity was taking place on the pages of *LG*. It is telling, however coincidental, that the crisis of confidence in the system and that of the country's men evolved simultaneously.

The last two decades of the Soviet Union and the first decade of the post-Soviet era stand out as a time when men's problems become a matter of state concern. The war in Afghanistan, rising unemployment, sky-high divorce rates, and a catastrophic mortality rate all contributed to the impression that men's condition had reached the level of a national emergency.[43] If men faced an uncertain future during the sixties, the masculinity crisis reached pandemic levels during the 1980s and '90s. So concerned were the Soviet authorities about men's precarious position that during *perestroika*, Mikhail Gorbachev asked women to stay at home to fulfil their familial and marital obligations as the economy contracted.[44] Vladimir Putin's reign has breathed new life into the

masculinist project, with Putin himself playing the lead role.[45] Very
much in the vein of Stalinist idealized subjectivity, Putin-era cultural
politics advocate for resolve, sobriety, and (obedient) virility as key
markers of Russian masculinity. Although seemingly an idiosyncratic
development, the Putin-era project can be seen as an attempt to address
the masculine crisis that Urlanis pointed to in the distant summer of
1968. For Putin, as for Urlanis, the fate of the country's men is inseparable from the fate of the nation as a whole.

Sixties Masculinity, or, The Return of the Superfluous Man

The Soviet sixties were, in some ways, a time of optimism. Khrushchev had proclaimed that the country's main goals were to surpass
the United States in per capita production by 1970 and to achieve communism by 1980. In Pittsburgh on 24 September 1959, he declared: "We
have a very popular slogan in our country right now – 'catch up with
and overtake the United States.'"[46] He made this slogan an ideological
mantra at the Twenty-Second Party Congress in 1961, where he predicted that the "current generation will live under Communism."[47] De
spite the public optimism, a range of cultural and political authorities –
including Khrushchev himself – fretted that the country lacked a
masculine ideal that matched the country's improving situation. As
the sixties advanced, both professional and lay commentators became
increasingly critical of the period's film protagonists, considering
them poor role models for tackling the challenges facing the nation.
It seemed to many that the men on the silver screen were not the sort
who could respond effectively to the call to build communism by 1980.
Numerous articles and opinion pieces demanded that Soviet artists
provide more Hercules and less Hamlet, more action and fewer "to be
or not to be?" reflections. In 1958, for example, the highly decorated
aviator B.F. Gofman complained that the movie industry no longer inspired viewers. He recalled how moved he and his friends had been
by the 1939 movie *Destroyers* (Istrebiteli). He pointedly admonished
film professionals in the audience that if they kept failing to create
"real" heroes, "eventually there will be no one inspired enough to fly
to the moon."[48] Five years later, the situation remained unchanged,
and even Khrushchev noted that few films were being made that were
capable of mobilizing the masses to communism and a decisive victory
over the Americans. During a speech delivered to Soviet writers and
artists on 8 March 1963, the Soviet premier criticized M. Khutsiev's
1962 movie *Lenin's Guard* (Zastava Il'icha) in particular. Khrushchev
excoriated the movie's three main protagonists: "They were shown as

men who know neither why nor how to live. And this during our time when we're building Communism, guided by the Program of the Communist Party! ... No, our society cannot rely on men like that; they are not fighters who will remake the world."[49] Three months after Khrushchev made his feelings known, the chairman of the Party's ideological commission, L.F. Il'ichev, used the Plenum of the Central Committee to accuse the film industry of showcasing ideologically unsuitable protagonists. He griped that even in movies about the Great Patriotic War (i.e., the Second World War), Soviet soldiers look "more like victims than self-assured and manly fighters against fascism."[50] Il'ichev warned artists that the misuse of government resources in the ongoing struggle against bourgeois ideology would be professionally reckless. After all, if the country was to surpass the United States, reflective and vacillating protagonists were counterproductive at best and subversive at worst.

The quotations above testify to the fact that concerns about a masculine lack were shared widely at the highest level of government. There existed a widespread concern that the movie industry was retreating from the revolutionary, masculinist, and martial ethos that had defined much of the 1930s and '40s. Though the Great Leader was persona non grata, many openly called for a return to the Stalinist model of subjectivity. On and off screen, Stalin-era individuals had been expected to radiate heroism by fulfilling the revolutionary cause. Thus, in their diaries and personal writings, Soviet citizens of the time expressed an active desire to refashion themselves into revolutionary subjects and turn themselves into proactive builders of a socialist utopia.[51] Since the mandated aspiration consisted of not only "speaking Bolshevik" but also thinking and acting Bolshevik, the Soviet person was expected to "see reality in its revolutionary development – to focus on those aspects of reality that provided evidence of history moving forward."[52] As Stalin-era diaries testify, some individuals earnestly and self-consciously sought to conform and become fully integrated into state-sponsored systems.[53] Soviet directors post-Stalin reversed course on this cultural mandate after Khrushchev exposed the Great Leader as a false idol. Sixties protagonists thus became more interested in the journey than in the destination and questioned the existence of a shared national ideal. Their search was often labelled "Hamletism" (*gamletizm*). Sixties heroes were men perpetually in search of meaning. Many artists saw doubt as a necessary antidote to the decades of Stalinist authoritarianism, but others rejected critical reflection as too passive and defeatist, particularly in the context of escalating Cold War tensions. An analysis of the experience of Soviet men as presented in popular films and then interpreted by various social groups indicates that contemporaries responded to sixties modernization and the changing position of Soviet men with anxiety and uncertainty.

My characterization of men's roles in terms of nervous apprehension amid shifting expectations complements the two main works on post-Stalinist masculinity while adding a different angle. Erica Fraser and Claire McCallum both explore the ways in which sixties culture addressed military topics in a postwar setting. McCallum notes that between 1945 and 1965 visual culture had stripped away "the elements traditionally associated with the military hero – his courage, his fearlessness, his willingness to perpetrate violent acts in the line of duty."[54] Not until the mid- to late 1960s did visual culture begin to deal more honestly with the realities of the Second World War. Fraser points out that during that same period, "government agents sought to clarify and reinforce notions of masculinized Soviet fortitude that they feared were undermined by high male casualties and women's service in the war."[55] While officials busied themselves with fashioning the meaning of masculinized service in a postwar world, a number of postwar developments worked against this mission: the population's profound weariness of war, a bourgeoning peace movement, and the "growing plurality in postwar society that offered young men the option of locating their identities, and authority, in non-martial categories."[56] Fraser and McCallum both elucidate the precarious position of martial spaces after 1945, with McCallum emphasizing that "by the 1950s ... the focus was on regeneration and family life, and Leninist ideals were retrospectively reconfigured to fit this more domestic vision of Soviet society."[57] Although *Men Out of Focus* does not specifically scrutinize the legacy of the Great Patriotic War, it captures a related contemporary phenomenon: the fear that Soviet men had become soft and that the boundary between genders was growing ever more porous. The sources I analyse affirm McCallum's and Fraser's conclusions but locate the source of anxiety not in the negotiation of the Second World War's repercussions but in the challenges of modern life, which, rather than proving Soviet men's ability to overcome obstacles, underscored their feebleness and marked them as unworthy inheritors of the country's wartime legacy.

The figure of the earnestly inquisitive but indecisive male figure whose (lack of) heroism is defined by (perpetually) delayed action was not, however, unique to the 1960s or specific to the Soviet Union. *Men Out of Focus* centres on the sixties in the Soviet Union, but it also considers masculinity from a longitudinal and transnational perspective. Russian imperial masculinity and post–Second World War masculinity in Europe and the United States faced similar kinds of pressures attending modernization, and in both situations, concern emerged about men's standing in society. Although clearly distinct, the upheavals that followed both Russia's nineteenth-century industrialization and the West's 1950s economic boom generated fears that men could not rise to the challenge, disoriented as they were by seismic changes taking place. As a result, nineteenth-century Russia and the long sixties in twentieth-century Europe and the Soviet Union can both be viewed as times of "superfluous masculinity."

In many ways, the superfluous man of the 1960s represented the return of a masculine type from a century before, when the country took on its modernization mission and Russia's artists responded by recalibrating their relationship with the state. Ivan Turgenev brought the term "the superfluous man" (*lishnii chelovek*) into wide use with the publication of his 1850 *The Diary of a Superfluous Man* (Dnevnik lishnego cheloveka).[58] The superfluous man combined seemingly contradictory characteristics; some writers saw him as brave but apathetic, while for others he combined cowardice with high moral standards. Central to most expressions of male superfluity in the nineteenth century was the "hope that somewhere in the universe there exists a beautiful truth that will give his life meaning and purpose, and that this will eliminate the vicious pain of feeling useless on this earth."[59] The most extreme example is the title character of Ivan Goncharov's 1859 novel *Oblomov*. He lives on the income of an estate he never visits and preoccupies himself mostly with daydreaming. Oblomov spends most of his time lying in bed thinking about what he will do when (and if) he gets up (Figure I.3). Contemporary literary critic Nikolai Dobroliubov argued that Oblomov was "a sign of the times" and that Oblomovism was a national scourge whose main symptom was the absence of action. He averred: "The feature common to all these men is that nothing in life is a vital necessity for them, a shrine in their hearts, a religion, organically merged with their whole being, so that to deprive them of it would mean depriving them of their lives." Decades later, Lenin described Goncharov's protagonist as emblematic of all the country's problems: "The old Oblomov has remained, and for a long while yet he will have to be washed, cleaned, shaken and thrashed if something is to come of him."[60]

Notwithstanding Lenin's project to reform Oblomov-like men out of existence, Oblomovism resurfaced in Russia after Stalin's death. For instance, in *Lenin's Guard*, director Khutsiev showcases a protagonist whose quest to identify life's meaning hits a dead end in a most unusual way. The scene to which Khrushchev himself objected features a fantastical and Hamletesque reunion between Sergei and the ghost of

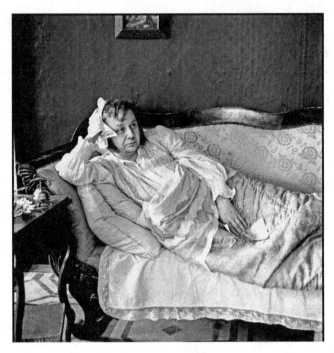

Figure I.3. Oblomov as superfluity embodied in the film *Oblomov* (1980).

his father, who died during the Second World War when he was only twenty-one. Sergei, who is struggling to determine life's purpose, urges his father to reveal exactly how one should live. The father responds with a question: "How old are you?" And when the son tells his father he is twenty-three, the latter retorts: "Well, I am twenty-one. How am I supposed to help you?" And then the ghost vanishes. The idea that there are no ready-made answers and that men have to make it through life unmoored from the Great Mission became the defining feature of sixties masculinity. That there could be a link between the middle-aged aristocratic Oblomov and the young working-class Sergei sent a chill down Khrushchev's spine because it meant that traces of Oblomovism could be found in the postwar era. Sergei rarely mimics Oblomov's reclining poses, but the multiple scenes in which he aimlessly wanders around Moscow at night while reciting Mayakovsky's verses point to a similar contemplative calm that masks inaction. In a scene in which Sergei convalesces in bed, he resembles Oblomov not only in posture but also in attitude as he asks his friend about life's real meaning (Figure I.4). Surely, he wonders, there's more to life than checking off

Figure I.4. Sergei in *Lenin's Guard* (1962), in an Oblomov-like reclining pose.

all the right boxes: working, preparing for university, contributing to society. He finds himself to be so proper, such a square, that he feels himself becoming not a man, but a poster boy for the Soviet way of life. These doubts paralyse Sergei throughout Khutsiev's film.

Of course, there are limits to this parallel, because aristocratic privilege, which was so central to the image of superfluous masculinity of the 1860s, could not be applied to the men of the 1960s. However, what bound together these two iterations of masculine superfluity was the hero's evident aimlessness and attendant search for meaning in a world that could not offer definitive answers – not even from fathers who inhabited the great beyond. Characters like Sergei professed no ideology, but this meant in effect that they rejected the state-sanctioned one, and this led Soviet authorities to brand them as nihilists. The rejection of ideology in search of "authenticity" was an ideological position in its own right.

Men Out of Focus demonstrates that this de-ideologized masculine type was not geographically bounded – a dedication to realism was the order of the day across Europe and the United States. The world view of Soviet sixties heroes mirrored, for example, the perspective of Jimmy Porter in John Osborne's 1956 play *Look Back in Anger*: "I suppose people of our generation aren't able to die for good causes any longer. We had all that done for us, in the thirties and the forties, when we were still kids ... There aren't any good, brave causes left." Jimmy, like Sergei in *Lenin's Guard*, eschews the existence of "good, brave causes," yet at the same time, he expresses his sense of uselessness by howling in anger rather than engaging in contemplative calm. Although their reactions differ, both young men find themselves unmoored, their battles having been fought and won by their fathers in the Second World War. It is also appropriate to compare young Sergei with the combative Jim Stark in 1955's *Rebel Without a Cause*: "Boy," he says, "if, if I had one day when, when I didn't have to be all confused, and didn't have to feel that I was ashamed of everything ... if I felt that I belonged someplace, you know?" It's clear from Sergei's conversation with the ghost of his deceased father that he, like Jim, feels an acute sense of displacement and confusion. The sixties on both sides of the Iron Curtain generated a range of types of young superfluous men who were angry or confused because they lacked a Cause, with a capital C, believing that it had been won by the preceding generation.

But men who had survived the war, "the older generations," were in no better position to realize themselves as men because "the system" expected them to conform. Had Sergei's father returned alive from the war, it is likely that he would have been depicted as a Soviet version of the iconic "man in the grey flannel suit." Surviving the Second World War did not prepare veterans to outmanoeuvre the career yes-men who dominated the corporate and bureaucratic mazes, or to guard against the consumerist world dominated by women, or to even defend themselves against threats posed by nuclear energy and robotics. Tom Rath, the hero of Sloan Wilson's 1955 novel *The Man in the Gray Flannel Suit*, reflects on the shallowness of his career prospects after returning from the war: "I could get a job in an advertising agency. I'll write copy telling people to eat more cornflakes and smoke more and more cigarettes and buy more refrigerators and automobiles, until they explode with happiness."[61] As much as Tom, as a thirty-something former paratrooper, wishes to avoid the rat race, he finds himself unable to resist the magnetic pull of the postwar order: "It seemed as though all I could see was a lot of bright young men in gray flannel suits rushing around New York in a frantic parade to nowhere. They seemed to me to be pursuing neither ideals nor happiness – they were pursuing a routine. For a long while I thought I was on the sidelines watching that parade, and it was quite a shock to glance down and see that I too was wearing a gray flannel suit."[62] Henry Tanner, the chief of *The New York Times* bureau in Moscow, remarked in 1964, the year of Khrushchev's ouster, that men in grey flannel suits were running the Soviet Union.[63] Describing the top Party leaders after Khrushchev, he remarked:

"These are the new-style Soviet manager-politicians and executives, the efficient organization men equivalent to the industrial managers and organization men of the West – 'the Communists in gray flannel suits,' as one diplomat recently called them." For those who faced the possibility of selling out to "the man," superfluous masculinity akin to Hamlet's or Sergei's could appear redemptive because it implied a conscience. This reflects a world view found in many Czechoslovak New Wave films, which directly confront the pressures to repress individuality and the go-along-to-get-along mentality. Miloš Forman's 1963 film *Black Peter* presents a sequence of seemingly insignificant events in the life of a sixteen-year-old supermarket trainee named Peter. He is stuck in his job, unable to spend his afternoons by the pool, talking to his friends, and flirting with girls. Instead, he must spend his days dealing with his boss's controlling management system and his father's incessant nagging. Be they alive or dead, fathers clearly had no answers for their sons.

Thus the superfluous men had two defining characteristics. First, they were moral because they refused to conform and abhorred hypocrisy. Second, they rebelled not because they had a cause but because they lacked one. Their instinctive urge was, quite simply, to question everything. As much as their rootlessness placed them above the faceless yes-men in grey flannel suits selling out for the material trappings of a respectable middle-class existence, superfluous men lacked a clear system of values, which became a problem when they had to face the vagaries of the postwar order. As such, they often fell prey to the machinations of the political system, manipulative women, and even devious robots. They were vanquished without ever having believed in anything. They could not be martyrs. The superfluous man was a Soviet-specific trope, but he shared fundamental traits that were evident in the cinematic output of the West. The long reach of this masculine trope testified to the profound reconfiguration of men's socioeconomic roles on both sides of the Iron Curtain.

Thaw Cinema: Europe's Forgotten New Wave

Albeit in a more understated way, the new generation of Soviet directors participated in some of the most innovative trends in European filmmaking since the 1920s. Like their European colleagues, who set out to revolutionize their conservative national film industries throughout the late 1940s, '50s, and '60s, Soviet reformist filmmakers battled against the ossified practices characteristic of Stalinist cinema. Declaring "sincerity" as their guiding principle and rejecting

the pretentiousness that was so typical of Stalinist productions, reformist sixties directors approached their craft in much the same way
as Italian, French, and British directors. In each of those three Western
European countries a group of rebellious young filmmakers declared
war on big commercial studio productions. Postwar Italian directors
criticized the domestic "white telephone cinema" (*cinema dei telefoni
bianchi*) that imitated Hollywood films of the 1930s.[64] Young French
filmmakers mocked the old-fashioned *cinéma de papa* – "Dad's cinema" – throughout the 1950s. The up-and-coming 1950s British
filmmakers ridiculed British productions for being "snobbish, anti-intelligent, emotionally inhibited, willfully blind to the conditions and
problems of the present, and dedicated to an out-of-date, exhausted
national ideal."[65] Following the lead of Italian neorealists, who continued to influence European and Soviet filmmaking long after the
movement's zenith in the late 1940s, postwar directors across Europe
rejected elaborate studio productions. Instead, they focused on the
everyday, paying particular attention to the troubles and pain that
people faced in their daily lives. They chipped away at the pillars of
interwar society – at its blind obeisance to family, official authority,
class hierarchy, and national pride.[66] Collectively, these movements
were labelled the "New Wave," in that they washed away the staid
cinematic and sociopolitical conventions that had dominated cinema's turbulent interwar years.

Aesthetically, post-Stalinist motion pictures – as well the New Waves
that emerged in Britain, France, Poland, and Czechoslovakia – were
clearly influenced by Italian neorealism. The Italian movement exercised a strong influence on the Soviet movie industry after 1953, due
in no small part to the fact that the neorealist directors' aim to discredit
glitzy Fascist aesthetics mirrored the efforts of Soviet filmmakers to
invalidate Stalinist pageantry.[67] Vittorio De Sica, the leading figure of
Italian neorealism, declared that the movement had been born out of
"an overwhelming desire to throw out of the window the old stories of
Italian cinema, to place the camera into the mainstream of real life."[68]
To capture "real life" as it happened, neorealists adopted a specific set
of filmmaking practices: "a preference for location filming, the use of
nonprofessional actors, the avoidance of ornamental mise-en-scène, a
preference for natural light, a freely-moving documentary style of pho-
tography."[69] As they focused on ordinary people and their everyday
lives, Soviet filmmakers had to defend their new aesthetics tooth and
nail against charges of pessimism and even of "slandering Soviet reality." The Soviet New Wave's detractors saw its aesthetics as an un-
ambiguous depoliticization of socialist art. In the West, the neorealist

approach could be defended because it focused on the working class and was rooted in leftist politics; in the Soviet Union, the New Wave style was vulnerable to charges of ideological deviationism and bourgeois extravagance. Instead of imbuing the exploits of ordinary workers with historic importance, the Soviet New Wave directors focused on their heroes' disjointed stream of consciousness and their angst-ridden attempts to make sense of their place in the world.

No less provocative than their European counterparts, the Soviet New Wave's superfluous heroes drew in ticket sales of up to 20 million. Some productions were so controversial they were nearly banned – for example, M. Khutsiev's film *Lenin's Guard*. Their popularity owed much to the fact that depicting daily life with documentary realism was such a radical reconfiguration of Soviet cinematic experience. Yet as with any novelty, audiences eventually grew accustomed to, and then bored with, stories that focused more on psychology than on action. Despite the productions' popularity and lucrativeness, the Brezhnev administration rejected artistic experimentation after the Prague Spring. The New Wave nonetheless left an indelible mark on 1970s and '80s Soviet movie industry production; an end to documentary realism did not lead to a rebirth of Stalinist monumentalism.

The cinematic New Wave in the Soviet Union has, until recently, been loosely defined, encompassing various films as well as different chronologies. Film scholar Steven P. Hill first employed the term "Soviet new wave" in a 1967 article that described the era's dynamic innovations.[70] Although Hill divides the movement into two generations of directors (the ones born in the 1920s and those born during or shortly after the Second World War), he does not describe its distinguishing characteristics. The concept reappeared in print in 1981, when newspaper columnist Richard Grenier noted the appearance of Brezhnev-era envelope-pushing productions; he addressed a broad range of films, from auteur Georgian director Sergei Paradzhanov's 1965 *Shadows of Our Forgotten Ancestors* to Nikita Mikhalkov's 1980 adaptation of *Oblomov*. Overall, though, Grenier found Soviet cultural output depressing: "Soviet films [that] merit any attention at all have been as scarce as Kohinoor-size diamonds, freak works that somehow slipped through the net."[71] Almost ten years later, Herbert Marshall discussed the idea of a Soviet New Wave by reflecting on what Soviet critics termed "difficult films," which included the work of auteur filmmakers of the late 1960s and early 1970s, such as S. Paradzhanov and A. Tarkovskii. Like Grenier before him, Marshall understood opposition to the state as a defining characteristic of the New Wave: "Thus the basic sin of the new school and all of its artists is that they do not arrange things into class categories, but into human categories, and the Party is always at odds with this idea of humanism, this 'bourgeois' humanism, this 'abstract' humanitarianism."[72] Until the Soviet Union's collapse, analyses of the New Wave were few, and focused on films and directors who had run afoul of the Party or the cultural establishment.

It was not until the late 1990s and early 2000s that Soviet productions of the 1950s and 1960s received the kind of attention that reflected the complexity of the Soviet New Wave. The reconceptualization of post-Stalinist cinema began in 1996 with Vitalii Troianovski's edited essay collection *Thaw Cinematography*. Relative to Hill, Grenier, and Marshall, Troianovskii expanded the limits of the movement chronologically and thematically, arguing that the cinematic Thaw stretched from the early 1950s to the early 1970s and that it radically reconfigured Soviet film's aesthetics, value system, and social role.[73] Russian film scholars in Troianovskii's volume also challenged the Manichaean perception of Soviet filmmakers as enlightened crusaders battling the spiritually corrupt state bureaucracy. Rather, they charted the artists' paradoxical relationship to state ideology and structures. Instead of inhabiting a place outside of Soviet culture, even the most iconoclastic films artists played a part in generating it.

Soviet sixties cinema has been rediscovered in the West, and there have been many recent retrospectives about the "forgotten Soviet New Wave." Film critic Ian Christie has gone so far as to wager that 1950s and '60s Soviet productions will "elicit admiration, and a realization that the aesthetic ferment of that decade was much richer and more profound than any Western New Wave, including France's."[74] Although Soviet cinema remains largely peripheral to studies of global New Wave movements, including those that focus on Brazil, Mexico, Iran, and Japan,[75] Russian and Western scholars of Thaw cinema have made a strong case that experimental post-Stalinist productions hold up well against their international counterparts both stylistically and conceptually.

Josephine Woll, Aleksandr Prokhorov, Oksana Bulgakowa, and Tim Harte, among others, have brought Thaw-era cinema into the limelight as part and parcel of a global new wave movement.[76]

The chronological markers for the Soviet New Wave vary,[77] and a consensus does not exist as to which directors belonged in it. In this monograph I have in mind a very broad definition that encompasses films featuring an explicit gender politics. As a work of cultural history, *Men Out of Focus* privileges productions that challenge accepted social norms, regardless of how avant-garde or experimental their visual style. Considering that New Wave filmmakers' change in style was driven by an ideological perspective, my own selection of films is based on the productions' gender politics. Anxiety and uncertainty about men's standing is, at its core, an ideological and political stance and in that sense was a central characteristic of New Waves across the continent. My strategy is inspired by Geneviève Sellier's critique of the French New Wave.[78] Sellier argues that gender relations were the primary subject of the almost all-male cast of French "new wavers," who, despite *appearing* modern in their attitudes and revolutionary in their aesthetics, in fact reinscribed patriarchal norms within their films. Although there now exist excellent gender analyses of Thaw cinema, most of them focus on the two auteur female directors – Larisa Shepit'ko and Kira Muratova. Less attention has been paid to the gender politics of male Soviet filmmakers.[79]

By discussing the gender politics of the Soviet New Wave, I aim to make visible the ways in which the predominantly male film industry openly wrung its hands about how post-Stalinist modernity threatened the gender status quo. If (in Sellier's interpretation) French new wavers valorized men in terms of their social, professional, and family identity, their Soviet counterparts saw their compatriots as failing in all those categories. In this way, the Soviet movement resembled the one formed by postwar directors in Italy, Britain, Poland, and Czechoslovakia, who viewed their nation's men as underperforming. Ewa Mazierska's conclusion that Czech, Slovak, and Polish cinema "is populated by defeated men" applies equally well to the cinematic production of Italy.[80] Perhaps no better Italian example exists than Vittorio De Sica's 1948 *Bicycle Thieves*. The narrative centres on a poor working man whose only means of economic sustenance – a bicycle – is stolen from him and who hunts for it unsuccessfully over the course of one day. A 1949 *New York Times* review observed that the film addressed the "isolation and loneliness of the little man in this complex social world that is ironically blessed with institutions to comfort and protect mankind."[81] In the British New Wave of the late 1950s and early 1960s the much more pronounced anxiety and sense of defeat came from a perceived "loss of the soldierly prowess which made Britain 'Great.'"[82] In all these various national contexts, New Wave cinematic output defined itself by zeroing in on men and finding them wanting, defeated, passive, and, ultimately, out of focus.

To make visible the challenges that sixties New Wave directors perceived Soviet men to be facing, the core chapters of this book examine depictions of Soviet men in different arenas: as fathers, as role models for postwar youth, as romantic partners, and as architects of the nation's scientific future. These four thematic chapters are bookended by a chapter that explains the origins of the crisis of masculinity and a chapter that pans out to show how the crisis reflected a broader European postwar phenomenon. The book's epilogue discusses the legacies of sixties celluloid masculinity; although out of the limelight by the early 1970s, the figure of the superfluous hero continued to (re)appear in the films of late socialism.

Chapter One

What Was Stalinist Masculinity and Why Did It Change?

During the almost three decades of Joseph Stalin's reign, the Red screen depicted virile, square-jawed, and unambiguously upright male heroes. As products of Stalinist cultural politics, hypermasculine film heroes popularized hierarchy, obedience, and uniformity as core national ideals. Despite Khrushchev's de-Stalinization campaign, 1930s and '40s gender paradigms persisted into the post-Stalinist period, and Stalin-era protagonists endured as aspirational models. Vasilii Chapaev, the gruff, tough, and fearless Civil War captain, continued to be trotted out as a paragon of manhood for men of all ages. That he gritted his teeth throughout the surgical extraction of a bullet lodged in his skull in complete silence exemplified his physical and mental fortitude. Famed Civil War hero Pavel Korchagin was another positive hero whose fate remained entrenched in popular imagination long after Stalin's death. Despite being blind and bedridden, Korchagin remained eager to make the ultimate sacrifice. His mutilated body and impaired senses took centre stage in two feature films (in 1942 and 1956) and a TV miniseries (1975).[1] Finally, there was Aleksei Mares'ev, the Second World War fighter pilot, who continued fighting the Nazis even after both his legs had to be amputated below the knee. Although these cinematic supermen loomed larger than life, submission and martyrdom defined their male subjectivity. Their epic stature notwithstanding, they were cogs in the great Stalinist machine, admittedly the most visible ones.

As calls for greater authenticity in Soviet art grew louder in the early and mid-1950s, it seemed that Stalin-era mythic masculinity would fall by the wayside. This is exactly what writer V.M. Pomerantsev called for in his December 1953 article "About Sincerity in Literature." In criticizing S.N. Boldyrev's novel *The Decisive Years* (Reshaiushchie gody) in particular, Pomerantsev argued: "One cannot believe in the characters in this book. The hero is a superhero. He is planned out, premeditated, made up, and schematic."[2] Yet even as the intelligentsia began to develop more realistic and spontaneous models of masculinity, there emerged calls to resurrect yesteryear's idols. In his 1961 address to the Cinematographers' Union, veteran scriptwriter and Stalin Prize winner A.Ia. Kapler lamented: "It seems to me that the scale of ideas, the scale of heroes has shrunk beyond recognition. Take, for example, the concept behind either the 1930s heroes Maksim or Chapaev and you immediately notice the philosophical weightiness that stands behind those figures! A return to such grand proportions and grand affect is indispensable for us."[3] During the same union meeting, noted playwright A.D. Salynskii exclaimed: "Give us a hero already – a real hero who mobilizes people and does not depress them."[4] These filmmakers were not advocating for the Stalinist aesthetic to be restored wholesale; rather, they were promoting a return to the scale of Stalinist heroism.

The popularity of foreign film heroes among Soviet moviegoers lent their arguments additional weight and urgency. In 1963, for example, cinema critic V.I. Tolstykh and his colleagues fretted about the popularity of *The Three Musketeers* both inside and outside the movie theatre.[5] They recalled how the legendary 1934 film *Chapaev* had profoundly affected their lives. Because of that blockbuster, an entire generation played "Reds" and "Whites": all boys wanted to grow up to be just like the title hero. Tolstykh commented: "Somewhere along the line we forsook the [cinematic] traditions of the 1930s and 1940s." Several participants agreed with Tolstykh. One exclaimed, "Nowadays all the children want to be musketeers"; another added, "Because there's nothing else offered."[6] That same year, art critic R.N. Iurenev expressed his nostalgia for S.A. Gerasimov's 1936 film *The Fearless Seven*, which told of an expedition of young explorers braving the inhospitable Arctic and ultimately subjugating it to human will: "Gerasimov admirably expressed the romanticism that defined my generation's desire to conquer new lands, dominate the Arctic, and break world records in flight distance and speed."[7] Another prolific cultural critic, N.N. Klado, asked how one could possibly compare contemporary "heroes" to the film icons of the past; he felt that the Red Army commander Chapaev and the brave pilot Mares'ev, unlike post-Stalin heroes, would serve as masculine role models for centuries to come.[8]

Although the superfluous hero instilled a great deal of public anxiety among government spokespersons and artistic intelligentsia, flawed sixties celluloid masculinity persisted as a prominent feature of the cultural landscape. Filmmakers were drawing movie heroes to scale largely as a consequence of the humanization of the Soviet system following the excesses of Stalinism. In 1956, Stalin's successor, N.S.

Khrushchev, denounced the Great Leader's tyranny and his personality cult at the Twentieth Party Congress. Khrushchev not only exposed Stalin's abuses of power and his crimes against innocent Party members but also made a mockery of how the former despot had used the arts to embellish and distort historical events. In Khrushchev's polemic, films served as incriminating evidence: "Stalin loved to see the film, *The Unforgettable Year of 1919*, which portrayed him on the steps of an armored train, where he was practically vanquishing the foe with his own saber."[9] Khrushchev's jaw-dropping speech lampooned the Father of the People, claiming that he rarely saw even his own "offspring," let alone bonded with them. He declared that Stalin "knew the country and agriculture only from films. And these films dressed up and beautified the existing situation in agriculture. Many films depicted *kolkhoz* life with tables collapsing under the weight of turkeys and geese. Evidently, Stalin thought that it was actually so."[10] Khrushchev challenged the way filmmakers depicted the Soviet Union's past and present, urging them to present contemporary realities in truer colours. In a direct call to action, in a May 1957 speech Khrushchev described earnest Bolsheviks as those "who weigh real conditions and potentialities of their actions, who are unafraid of difficulties, who never conceal contradictions, and who are able openly and honestly to tell their people the truth, bitter as it may sometimes be."[11] With these sentiments, Khrushchev legitimized a "thawing" of Soviet cultural life and signalled an expansion of political and artistic freedoms.

Although Khrushchev's pronouncements proved crucial to the reinvention of Soviet masculinity, they should be seen as only one element of a much broader phenomenon. After all, Khrushchev's rule is known today for its frequent ideological zigzags and reversals. Had the Party Secretary's views been decisive, the sixties film industry might have eventually (re)produced Chapaevs, Korchagins, or Mares'evs. But instead of reinventing Stalinist masculinity for the sixties, filmmakers focused on offering new notions about what it meant to be a man in a scientifically complex, predominantly urban, mass-consumerist society. Five principal factors allowed directors to move away from Stalinist tropes and examine the New Soviet Man from a less heroic angle. First, the draconian censorship system that had crippled the film industry for two decades slowly came undone as the Party leadership insisted that the film industry increase production. The number of films being released escalated from dozens to more than a hundred per year, and the censorship apparatus could not adequately supervise this increased output. Filmmakers seized on this development to assert their artistic visions and the industry's prerogatives. Second, the green light to begin organizing the Cinematographers'

Union in 1957 further ensured the industry's relative autonomy. Directors, scriptwriters, and actors jointly defended motion pictures that faced official condemnation by the censors. The activism of the Cinematographers' Union members, which crossed generational lines, ensured that the day's most controversial celluloid heroes reached audiences nationwide. Third, the newfound confidence of film professionals mirrored an equally vibrant homegrown film fan culture, which encouraged moviegoers to express a sense of ownership over their cinematic experiences. The biweekly *Sovetskii ekran*, one of the country's most popular magazines, served as a high-profile vehicle for moviegoers' voices, making their demands impossible to ignore. The unionized filmmakers and the highly active fan base together created what can only be called the golden age of Soviet cinema. Fourth, rather than going at it alone, the country's film professionals participated in a much broader, intelligentsia-driven push to de-Stalinize the population's perception of Soviet realities. Finally, essential to the deconstruction of Soviet masculinity was the rising authority of sociological research. The marketing of films to particular groups marked a radical shift in how films were made. By the mid- to late 1960s, film critics were claiming that every movie had its target audience. This strategy illustrates the rejection of the notion that a standardized, one-size-fits-all masculinity could appeal to all strata of the population. Stalinist cinema had created uniform movie heroes who embodied values of universal appeal; post-Stalinist ideologues and directors began filming with the intention of attracting specific audiences. In the sixties, the government's emphasis on cinema's profitability gave audiences a central role in determining which heroes, which genres, and which narrative lines most closely corresponded to national tastes and sensibilities.

Naturally, movie industry professionals and the artistic intelligentsia did not all respond uniformly to de-Stalinization, nor did they all have analogous experiences of sixties modernization. As a political and social category, the intelligentsia comprised men and women of various educational levels, life experiences, economic strata, and age groups. Even the artists and intellectuals who supported the state's modernization agenda did not always see eye to eye about the nature of the reforms or how best to partake in the socio-economic changes occurring in the country. These caveats notwithstanding, there existed a discernible core group of artists and filmmakers who shaped the broad outlines of sixties culture by arguing that it was imperative to take a critical and documentary approach to contemporary phenomena. The sixties cultural system, as a reaction to de-Stalinization, offered space for Soviet filmmakers to advance the notion that New Soviet Men were slowly becoming victims of circumstance and of the caprices of the powerful.

The Beginning of the Soviet Film Renaissance

Evgeny Dobrenko points out that Stalinist masculinity resembled spectacle more than it did personalized narrative; he observes that in Stalin-era cinema "there is no individual fate, there is no element of everyday life, there are no human relationships, and psychology is absent. Characters do not speak, but orate; passions are not experienced, but played – as in Greek tragedy – and they die here, as in operas, after long monologues on fighters' shoulders, in open fields, on burial mounds."[12] Boris Groys recognized a similar lack of flawed individuality in Stalinist heroes, arguing that they were more akin to deities than to humans: "In and of themselves the positive and negative heroes have no external appearance, because they express transcendental demiurgic forces."[13] Indeed, central to Stalinist masculinity was the rejection of realism and a full embrace of romanticism. Stalinist movie heroes denounced facts, technical realities, and objective limits as a cowardly excuse for passivity. Literary and celluloid protagonists overcame all obstacles that a bureaucrat – tethered to facts and commonly accepted standards – viewed as insurmountable.

This romanticized version of heroism did more than represent a product of a particular ideological expression; it was also rooted in the idiosyncratic film production process that had evolved during the Stalin era. Ideas about how the movie industry was supposed to function and how it ought to approach its propaganda mission had a direct bearing on the kinds of masculine models it produced. The Stalin-era model of production, which emphasized extensive censorship and centralized planning, gave rise to an iconographic masculinity defined by an absence of individual psychology.

As early as 1922, V.I. Lenin advised the first People's Commissar of Enlightenment A.V. Lunacharskii that "you must always remember that of all the arts the most important for us is the cinema."[14] Stalin echoed Lenin's sentiment at the Thirteenth Party Congress in 1924, stating that "cinema is the most important means of mass agitation. Our task is to take this matter into our own hands."[15] Although it began in the early 1920s, the strict control of the film industry did not begin in earnest until the Communist Party declared socialist realism the official artistic standard at the Congress of Soviet Writers in 1934, which chronologically corresponded with the invention and proliferation of "talkies." As an artistic policy and a way of thinking about Soviet reality, socialist realism accentuated the positive and the epic, portraying the human condition as it could and should be. Socialist realism came to be defined as "a combination of the most matter-of-fact, everyday reality with the most heroic prospects."[16] Stalin's chief cultural commissar at the time, A.A. Zhadnov, noted in his speech that "Soviet literature must be able to show our heroes, must be able to glimpse our tomorrow." Initially intended for literary works, socialist realism soon became obligatory for all artistic endeavours. Cinema became directly affected by this policy since the Soviet Union had begun producing and implementing its own sound technologies in 1931. As sound became more widespread, so did the censorship of movie scripts. With the advent of "talkies" in Soviet cinematography and with the increased stress on socialist realism as official artistic policy, the state censorship organ, *Glavlit*, began restricting the relatively laissez-faire creative licence that scriptwriters had enjoyed during the 1920s. Despite the censorship apparatus that hamstrung scriptwriters and directors, Stalinist films enjoyed considerable popularity, for Soviet filmmakers adopted many of Hollywood's strategies and techniques to make motion pictures both instructive and entertaining.

Boris Shumiatskii, the head of *Soiuzkino* from 1930 to 1937, declared that in order to be politically effective, filmmakers must create "cinema for the millions." Keenly aware that audiences must be catered to, he argued: "If the public is not interested in the picture that we produce, it will become boring propaganda and we shall become boring agitators."[17] And while some Party officials criticized Shumiatskii for outdoing Hollywood in the scale and glitz of films made during his tenure, the appeal of the motion pictures he supported was undeniable.[18] Movie heroes, who became increasingly uniform in their epic stature, their grand acts of bravery, and their bombastic rhetoric, boosted the appeal of Stalinist films. For instance, *Chapaev* sold 30 million tickets in 1934 and Mares'ev's 1948 biopic *A Story of a Real Man* (Povest' o nastoiashchem cheloveke) sold 34.4 million. Crowds flocked to enjoy their favourite heroes over and over, watching them tread confidently toward a mythic reality that was, according to the tenets of socialist realism, in the making, looming in the not-so-distant future.

The creation of a reality populated by supermen was a delicate political task as Stalin became increasingly paranoid and his restrictions on culture intensified. Throughout the 1930s, '40s, and early '50s, film projects dragged out for months or years and could be terminated at any point along the way due to the overvigilant caprices of one or another censoring committee. Iosif Manevich, who was a scriptwriter during the 1930s, remembered the arbitrary process of rejecting ideologically unsuitable films. He commented: "Writers, directors, editors would work for a year on a project, only to find out unexpectedly that their labor was in vain even after the script had been approved, rehearsals had begun, and some scenes had been already filmed."[19] As even a cursory examination of statistics reveals, this strategy made little economic sense. In 1935, thirty-four movies were shelved, costing the movie industry 13 million rubles. The following year, 17 million rubles were wasted after fifty-five productions were deemed unacceptable for release.[20] By the late 1940s, the average number of days required to complete a motion picture was 423. By comparison, British, French, and American films never took more than 240 days to shoot.[21] Such interference slowed down production and inhibited creativity. Central planning had been intended to increase the film industry's productivity, yet production levels declined steadily throughout the 1930s.[22] The industry was releasing more than one hundred features annually at the end of the 1920s; by 1932, that figure had dipped to seventy; by 1934, to forty-five. For the rest of the Stalin era it never again reached triple digits. In 1951 only nine motion pictures were released.[23] Meanwhile, the British and French film industries were producing around one hundred movies every year, and the American industry five to six hundred.

New productions were crippled by the censorship apparatus, and meanwhile, old movies were in constant danger of being pulled from circulation for even the smallest ideological faux pas. For instance, Vladimir Shneiderov's 1935 movie about the dog Dzhul'bars, the Red Army's most famous canine, was banned in 1938 because the background of one scene featured a portrait of the head of the secret police, Genrikh Iagoda, who had been shot as a spy and an enemy of the people. This ideological witch-hunt led to a dismal situation in the national repertoire; by 1937, around five hundred previously produced films had been shelved, not to be seen again until after Stalin's death in 1953 or even after M. Gorbachev's rise to power in 1985.[24] In 1951, audiences could watch a meagre forty-six movies throughout the year: twelve Soviet and twenty-two East European ones, as well as twelve Western ones that had been captured during the Second World War.[25] These statistics demonstrate how intolerant, indeed paranoid, the Stalinist system had become of films and narratives it considered subversive. Central to Stalinist hegemony was the policing of meaning and of alternative social visions as embodied in the movie heroes' appearance and actions.

Stalin had assumed control over the movie industry, inserting himself as producer, director, and screenwriter as well as ultimate censor. He suggested titles, ideas, and stories, worked on scripts, lectured directors, coached actors, ordered shoots and cuts, and released movies for distribution.[26] Shumiatskii regularly conducted private screenings for Stalin and Politburo members late at night and into the early morning. Between May 1934 and January 1937, he recorded conversations that took place before and after these screenings.[27] These documents illustrate how seriously the head of state and those closest to him approached the question of mass entertainment. These late-evening conversations reveal how these men consciously manipulated the technical aspects of the cinematic medium to construct and relay particular impressions and meanings.

When one surveys the Stalinist ideological and artistic system, it becomes clear that the film industry was powerful in terms of the control it imposed on the artistic process but also singularly ineffective at getting products to moviegoers. By the late 1930s, to justify their anemic production figures, bureaucrats had developed a theory of "masterpieces." They argued that since too much money was being wasted on movies that were economically unprofitable and/or ideologically unsound, the state should invest more resources in fewer projects that would guarantee satisfaction on both fronts. Tightened censorship (i.e., *more* tightened) meant that every script and every production was closely inspected by four or five different bodies simultaneously.[28] The resulting movies were "masterpieces" of socialist realism that self-consciously enshrined official theories as absolute truths. The ideological control of meaning left directors unable to improvise beyond the narrow confines of the officially sanctioned reality, which was supposed to be cast in exclusively romantic and positive tones.

Moreover, the few scripts that dealt with permissible topics were given to ideologically trustworthy filmmakers to the detriment of younger ones. It is no surprise that, in the last several years of Stalin's rule, the few moviemakers allowed to work produced only one genre: historical biography. Movie screens were populated only by great men – admirals, generals, scientists, writers. And even these were not accounts of individuals so much as depictions of types that stood in for ideas central to the regime's priorities.

Despite its concerted efforts, the rigid Stalinist system undermined its own mission between 1948 and 1952, when foreign titles the Red Army had captured during the Second World War flooded the country's cinemas.[29] These so-called trophy films were supposed to offset the financial losses caused by the anemic domestic output.[30] Based on Claire Knight's research, eighty-six trophy films (mostly of American and German provenance) were approved for release, and they played to packed houses in the four years prior to Stalin's death.[31] Based on available (albeit incomplete) box office data, foreign titles sold 27.5 million tickets per film while Soviet movies sold 23.6 million tickets per film.[32] The relative imbalance in favour of stolen imports had a lot to do with the massive popularity of the Tarzan series, which included *Tarzan the Ape Man* (1932), *Tarzan Escapes* (1936), *Tarzan Finds a Son* (1939), and *Tarzan's New York Adventure* (1942). Mark Edele, Juliane Fürst, and Oksana Bulgakowa all reflect on how trophy features in general and the brawny, loincloth-clad Johnny Weissmuller in particular created and expressed generational chasms in the making. Fürst comments that young Soviet audiences applied their own desires and opinions to Tarzan's persona, "turning him – the semi-primitive of the jungle – into a counter-icon for the strict, rule-bound Stalinist society in which they lived."[33] According to Bulgakowa, the exposure to unfamiliar preverbal physiognomic experiences offered by in trophy films influenced even bodily motion, such as manners of walking and sitting, thus severing the younger generation from the world of their parents, who had been raised on Stalin-era "masterpieces."[34] In his recollections of the period, the exiled poet Joseph Brodsky went so far as to claim that "the four Tarzan films alone did more for de-Stalinization than all Khrushchev's speeches to the Twentieth Party Congress and beyond."[35] In a similar but less dramatic vein, historian Sergei Kapterev observes that Hollywood features showcased in the final years of Stalin's reign "prepared the ground for Soviet society's transition to more open forms of everyday existence and intellectual life."[36] The trickle apparent under Stalin would turn into a flood under Khrushchev and Brezhnev, when non-Soviet visual references, fashion trends, and cultural cues became so commonplace as to be integral to the Soviet cultural fabric.[37]

Propelled by processes of the high Stalinist era, the film industry experienced a revolution in the fifteen years following Stalin's death. Its source was cinema's rising independence and ability to assert its own agenda. The industry's autonomy arose for the most part due to the exponentially growing number of movies produced and released. In 1951, for example, the Soviet Union produced only thirty films, and of those, only six were feature films. By 1956, only three years after Stalin's death, the film industry had completed 113 movies, 85 of which were feature productions. After 1958 the number of domestic feature films made each year would never fall below triple digits. The Stalinist system had been designed to closely monitor the filming of no more than thirty "masterpieces," so the upsurge in production left the censorship apparatus ill- equipped to deal effectively with the avalanche of new projects. The film industry's productivity also led to growth in the censorship apparatus. In the early 1950s only seventy people were employed in the Ministry of Culture's Central Committee for the production of films; by 1963 the newly established Committee on Cinematography employed four hundred workers to regulate directors and movie studio production plans. The number of officials continued to grow, and by the 1970s around seven hundred officials were "managing" Soviet cinema.[38] Considering the anemic nature of the film industry in the five years prior to Stalin's death in 1953, its revival appears even more stunning. It began as early as 1954, as historical biographies came to be excluded from future production plans and their low attendance figures ensured that these Stalinist remnants would quickly disappear from neighbourhood movie theatres as well. New movies were earning upwards of 90 million rubles, whereas Stalinist celluloid biographies of "great men" consistently ranked at the bottom of the profitability scale, never making more than 20 million rubles.[39] With the decisive elimination of the "great man" biopic genre from the national repertoire, the film industry signalled a decisive turn toward depicting versions of masculinity drawn to scale.

Vasil'evskaia no. 13: An Island of Artistic Freedom

Throughout the sixties, filmmakers maintained a level of autonomy not only because of a weakened censorship system but also because of a strong sense of camaraderie. Unlike the Writers' Union or the Musicians' Union, both of which had been created by official decree, film workers never formed a professional association under Stalin. In 1957, some of the greatest names in the Soviet film industry – M.I. Romm, I.A. Pyr'ev, E.I. Gabrilovich, Iu.Ia. Raizman, and many others – invested their time, efforts, and reputations to organize the Cinematographers' Union.

Working out of Vasil'evskaia no. 13, the union's official headquarters, veteran and up-and-coming directors worked to establish a unified front against political interference, defending one another's works from ideological watchdogs. Although the union was not officially established until November 1965, its organizing committee (*orgkomitet*) brought together the most capable, energetic masters to negotiate the day's most controversial feature films. Led by Ivan Pyr'ev, the nascent professional organization strengthened cinema's semi-sovereignty at a time when Khrushchev's unpredictable reforms had left censors without coherent and consistent guiding principles.

The Cinematographers' Union was all the more dynamic because young, innovative directors were beginning to fill its ranks. M.M. Khutsiev, A.A. Tarkovskii, V.M. Shukshin, K.G. Muratova, L.E. Shepit'ko, G.N. Chukhrai, and other new talent brought novel stories and perspectives to national screens. Whether or not they had been directly impacted by the horrors of Stalinism and the Second World War, directors born in both 1920s and '30s committed themselves to reflecting critically on

Soviet realities, both past and present. Sixties directors bonded through a shared sense of social responsibility.[40] Grigorii Chukhrai recalled: "When we came back from the war, we were completely changed. We felt that now everything can be substantially different. And this was noticeable in motion pictures made by my generation. Our older colleagues, having survived the war, also hoped for better things. They too were trying to build a better life in the way that they could."[41] Indeed, veteran filmmakers encouraged young directors to focus on their contemporaries in depicting postwar realities. S.I. Rostotskii, opposing Stalinist dogma on hierarchical authority, boldly stated: "A student will never surpass his teacher if he copies him instead of defying him."[42] Crossing generational differences, Soviet moviemakers dedicated themselves to examining Soviet realities in ways that deviated from the party line. At the same time, sixties cinematic discourse involved more than a social and political critique of official policies; it was also a candid and open-ended exploration of contemporary lives. The artistic intelligentsia's keen sense of mission (evident in their biographies) drove them to create films that were equal parts expressive and transformative.

The fruitfulness of these intergenerational interactions was especially evident among filmmakers, whose community was even more tightly knit than those of other artists. For instance, three of the day's most prominent and controversial directors – Romm, Chukhrai, and Khutsiev – individually and jointly helped define the basic outlines of the Soviet New Wave. Born in 1901, Romm had participated in the Bolshevik Revolution, the Civil War, and the Second World War. The seminal events in Soviet history punctuated his biography to the same extent that his oeuvre defined the nation's cinematography and culture. In fact, Romm won five Stalin Prizes between 1941 and 1951.[43] His Stalin Prizes notwithstanding, after 1954 Romm remade himself into an uncompromising advocate for social justice. He got into hot water with his 1965 documentary film *Ordinary Fascism* (Obyknovennyi fashizm) because it implied that there existed little difference between Hitler's regime and Stalin's. According to oral testimonies, Mikhail Suslov, who served as the unofficial chief ideologue of the Party from 1965 until his death in 1982, invited Romm to his office to discuss the documentary and asked the director point-blank: "Mikhail Il'ich, why is it that you do not love us at all?" (*Za chto vy nas tak ne liubite?*). Meanwhile, the arch-conservative novelist Vsevolod Kochetov indirectly attacked Romm's "anti-Soviet" bent; his 1969 novel *What Do You Want?* (Chego zhe ty hochesh?) imagines a contemporary reception of *Ordinary Fascism* in the following way: "I recently saw a doc about fascism. If only you saw how it presented the issue! Cunningly, I swear! It seems to be about

Hitler, but it hints at us ... a little bit here and a little bit there. Naturally there's laughter in the hall; people are not idiots and understand what's really going on."[44] And Romm did not hide behind Aesopic language in advancing his point of view; he was one of the twenty-five intellectuals who signed a 1966 open letter protesting Brezhnev's moves to rehabilitate Stalin's legacy.[45] Sergei Linkov, one of Romm's mentees, recalls that Romm blended high-mindedness with accessibility to all who sought his help. In Linkov's recollection: "Romm rejected and hated anything that humiliated a person, deprived them of their dignity, their individuality and inner freedom – any freedom. Mikhail Il'ich was absolutely accessible to all. Everyone could call, ask for a meeting. He never refused anyone."[46] Besides being a world-class filmmaker, Romm exerted an incomparable influence on sixties filmmaking by mentoring a new generation of exceptionally talented practitioners who would leave a mark on both Soviet and world cinema.[47]

One of Romm's most renowned protégées was G.N. Chukhrai. Like Romm, Chukhrai grew up under Stalin, his first vivid memories being of the collectivization drive in Ukraine. Born in 1921, Chukhrai was thirty-two when the Great Leader died, and he had an accurate image of Stalinist oppression. However, it was his wartime experiences that figured most prominently in his world view and served as his main inspiration.[48] As his wartime memoir makes clear, his service at the front allowed him to grasp the artifice and narrowness of Stalinist propaganda. For instance, he rejected the Stalin-era interpretation of heroism: "The guy who was lucky enough to destroy a tank and get featured in the newspaper is no more of a hero than the unlucky fellow who died trying to do the same."[49] Chukhrai's movies about ordinary but honest and likable soldiers affected the ethos of the long 1960s in much in the way that Romm's *Ordinary Fascism* shaped the moral debates of the era. Chukhrai's 1961 masterpiece *Clear Skies* (Chistoe nebo) was the cinematic equivalent to *One Day in the Life of Ivan Denisovich* in that it featured a Second World War pilot unjustly accused of collaborating with the Germans simply because he had survived the war as a POW. Chukhrai bravely overturned the idea that Stalin ruled justly and pushed back on the Stalinist hypermasculine model. It is no surprise then that Chukhrai was one of thirteen signatories of a 1966 open letter to the Central Committee Presidium that opposed the creeping restoration of Stalin's reign. Not mincing words, Chukhrai and the co-signatories argued that "Stalin's rehabilitation – in any form – would be a disaster for our country and for the whole cause of communism."[50] This anti-Stalinist attitude shone through the Chukhrai's films as they defined sixties culture.

Four years Chukhrai's junior, Khutsiev lived through the horrors of the war but did not participate in it, finishing his directorial degree in 1950. Having lost his father to the 1937 Great Purge, Khutsiev adopted a more uncompromising attitude toward authority. Khutsiev had far less personal attachment to the Soviet state than Romm or Chukrai. While openly admitting that he thought highly of some Stalinist block-busters,[51] he challenged the basic tenets of socialist realism in his films. Khutsiev pithily encapsulated his lifelong creative manifesto in 1966: "The main goal of the artists should be to help moviegoers live their life but not flatter them."[52] This approach – honouring "real life" and giving moviegoers the straight goods – transcended filmmaking and constituted a political attitude, evident in the fact that, like Romm, Khutsiev signed the 1966 letter to Brezhnev objecting to Stalin's rehabilitation. If Romm and Chukhrai were able to push through their more controversial films because of their (wartime) service to the state, Khutsiev was frequently not so fortunate. The authorities viewed the young director and most of his films with suspicion. Had it not been for the support of figures of Romm and Chukhrai's stature as well as the Cinematographers' Union, it is likely that younger directors like Khutsiev would have had their work harshly edited or shelved. The older generation's political and cultural capital ensured that the voices of Khutsiev's generation were heard. Romm recollects defending Khutsiev and Chukhrai from Khrushchev, arguing publicly that the First Secretary had misunderstood the essence of the offending scene in which the father's ghost refuses to give council to his confused son.[53] Although Khrushchev remained unconvinced, Khutsiev's film was eventually released, and the young director continued to create, eventually becoming one of the most celebrated Russian filmmakers. Such was the power of a tightly knit community united in a common cause.

On the very evening that Romm and Chukhrai defended Khutsiev at the famous meeting of the Central Committee with the artistic intelligentsia, they also pleaded with Khrushchev to not close the union's fledgling *orgkomitet*. Romm had it on good authority that the Central Committee would soon release a decree eliminating the union and transferring its responsibilities to the Ministry of Culture. On that stressful night on 12 December 1962, Romm and Chukhrai argued passionately in front of Khrushchev, pointing out that the professional association was financially self-sustaining and that it remained ideologically trustworthy. In a typically melodramatic fashion, Khrushchev asked the assembled audience: "You know, comrades, the moviemakers have broken our ranks. You see, we had essentially already eliminated their union but after hearing them we thought maybe we should leave them be for now?" After the gathered artists collectively called out "Let's leave them be!,"[54] Khrushchev relented, and the union lived to fight another day for the interests of envelope-pushing moviemakers like Khutsiev.

Besides securing the release of "difficult" domestic movies, the union ensured film professionals access to international features and contacts with the broader cinematic world. A 1965 Cinematographers' Union report on the association's cooperation with international delegations in 1964 illustrated a vibrant exchange. Over the course of 1964, 236 members of the union went abroad to visit other movie studios, international film festivals, and professional conferences. Significantly, 136 of them visited capitalist countries while 100 went to socialist countries. That same year, the union welcomed twenty-seven delegates from Western Europe, including the United Kingdom, Italy, West Germany, and France.[55] Even when they could not leave the Soviet Union, directors could familiarize themselves with the latest industry developments at the Soviet national repository of domestic and foreign films (Gosfil'mofond), which enjoyed active cooperation with similar agencies abroad. The noted sixties director A. Mitta recalled: "During the 1950s, when no one could watch any foreign films, Gosfil'mofond gave us, the students of the Cinematography Institute, the opportunity to familiarize ourselves with the masterpieces of world cinema."[56] The renaissance of Soviet cinema deepened through the exchanges Khrushchev established with the United States and other Western countries, ensuring a steady diet of international fare for Soviet filmmakers and viewers alike.[57]

By defending outside-the-box directors and by promoting international features, the Cinematographers' Union ultimately "splintered the concept of Soviet cinema" to include "very disparate phenomena: large-scale directorial projects, socially engaged films, Bildungsromans, auteur cinema, and a substantial number of average, little-known Soviet melodramas."[58] With the proliferation of cinematic genres on Soviet screens and the increased visibility for international features came exposure to alternative modes of masculinity. As the beginning of this chapter made clear, non-Soviet characters became household names. There was no shortage of non-Soviet models of masculinity to be had: from cowboys (John Wayne, Yul Brynner, Steve McQueen) to musketeers (Gérard Barray), from rebels (Zbigniew Cybulski, Alain Delon) to debonair charmers (Cary Grant, Gregory Peck). Despite the hand-wringing and protestations regarding the Soviet male's vanishing act, sixties filmmakers, buttressed by the strength of their union, experimented with the look, feel, and narrative arcs of popular films.

Sincerity as a Call to Arms

However committed they were to one another, Soviet film professionals could not have advanced the controversial domestic and international productions had they not been part of a broader conversation on the direction of Soviet art that had begun to take shape in the early 1950s. Playwright Nikolai Virta's article in *Sovetskoe iskusstvo* launched what would turn into a campaign against the "no-conflict theory."[59] Virta and others attacked those dramatic works that had been prevalent during high Stalinism, which featured "conflict" where the good competed against the better, and which highlighted the decent protagonist struggling against an even more wholesome hero. Another turning point was the 1952 publication of Valentin Ovechkin's collection of narrative sketches *District Routine* (Raionnye budni), which reflected on *kolkhoz* life in a realistic and critical manner. So radical was the appearance of Ovechkin's sketches in the context of late Stalinism that Aleksandr Tvardovskii, the editor of the liberal literary journal *New World*, later compared it to Aleksandr Solzhenitsyn's 1962 groundbreaking work *One Day in the Life of Ivan Denisovich*, the first novel to discuss life in the forced labour camps. Tvardovskii wrote: "Solzhenitsyn, incidentally, outstanding as he is, is not unique or unprecedented in our literature. We should not forget the courage of Ovechkin's *District Routine* which appeared in *Novyi Mir* as early as 1952 and marked a turning point."[60] Ovechkin criticized party leaders in the countryside, arguing that they concerned themselves only with the fulfilment of the plan and bothered themselves little with the well-being of workers, thus drastically reducing the initiative and productivity of the *kolkhoz* workers. The sketches began a literary trend that demanded that Soviet literati pay more attention to the supposed trivialities of life and to the individual's inner life.

The publication of V.M. Pomerantsev's article "About Sincerity in Literature" in December 1953 continued to disparage the frequent glossing over of the problems of daily life. The literary critic accused Soviet literature of being more a sermon than a confession. Criticizing S. Boldyrev's novel *The Decisive Years* in particular, Pomerantsev argued: "All we get is a too-well-known story line, completely bereft of emotional resonance, and flavoured with a hero embodying the cult of personality."[61] According to Pomerantsev, such books, which predominated during the Stalin era, committed what in literature was the cardinal sin: insincerity. Pomerantsev used Ovechkin's sketches as a prototype against which he measured other works such as Boldyrev's. Pomerantsev criticized both the "embellishment of reality" (*lakirovka deistvitel'nosti*) and the dehumanization of Soviet heroes. He argued with an imaginary Soviet author:

Remember how your mechanic from the machine-tractor station dreams
about a girl who has caught his eye – about how together they might re-
pair the inventory? Did he really get married only for this? Does he really
have his machine shop at home, too?! Or your miner, exclaiming: "I really
want to use the lengthened bore-holes! I wish the weekend would end
sooner!" Where did you find such a mole, who spends all his time digging
underground? Or the speech of a character in another one of your novel-
las, talking to his wife who had stolen a can of milk from the farm! That's
the kind of language they use at meetings or in prosecutors' speeches during cases of theft, but not in face-to-face conversations between people.[62]

Thus Pomerantsev's article asked Soviet artists not only to pay closer
attention to the darker side of life, but also to refrain from idealizing the
Soviet hero, and to depict him instead as a person of flesh and blood,
capable of reflection and error. Though Pomerantsev's thoughts were
criticized intermittently for two years following the publication of his
article, his ideas became central to how artists in general and filmmakers in particular approached their subjects.

The phrase *lakirovka deistvitel'nosti* was not unique to the sixties.
Stalin-era writings also frequently denounced stereotypes or clichéd
images in literature and art. The term gained currency in the early
1930s; in the previous decade the term *lakirovka* referred almost exclusively to the lacquer used in theatrical productions or paintings. A
version of the following statement typified conversations about 1930s
and '40s Soviet art: "We are hostile to the varnishing of reality. As it
addresses the achievements of socialist construction, literature must
not forget about our weaknesses, about the difficulties on the road to
socialism, about our unresolved problems as well as the ugly legacy of
capitalism. Literature is obliged to separate the wheat from the chaff."[63]
In the Stalinist context, to "unvarnish" social ills meant to unmask enemies of the people; the phrase was a call to vigilance and deployed as a
cudgel against all who spoke against the regime. By contrast, the 1950s
and '60s artists and commentators used the same phrase to denote an
artist's obfuscation of sociological reality. The phrase was no less ideologically charged in the sixties than it was under Stalin, but its function
had been reversed; instead of the government using it to set its agenda,
artists employed it to criticize the deficiencies in the Soviet system. The
project of capturing an unvarnished version of Soviet reality became
inseparably tied to accurately characterizing the post-Stalinist version
of masculinity. The ultimate litmus test for this project proved to be
not Party authorities but Soviet audiences, who made their opinions
known through a vibrant film fan culture.

"A Jury of Many Thousands": The Mighty Sixties Film Fan Culture

Soviet moviegoers responded enthusiastically to the eclectic and glo-balizing repertoire, forging a vocal and independent fan culture in the process. The vehicle for the moviegoers' varied and fluctuating inter-ests became the biweekly fan magazine *Sovetskii ekran* (*SE* hereafter). Over the course of the 1960s, *SE* became increasingly viewer-centred, and it used its sky-high number of subscribers to fend off complaints about its lack of ideological focus. Initially available to only 200,000 lucky subscribers in 1957, it quickly turned into the nation's most pop-ular magazine; by 1966 it had a press run of more than 2.6 million.[64] Subscribers did not always use *SE* to glean critical insights into particu-lar movies; often, they simply cut out photographs of their favourite actors and actresses to decorate their walls.[65] As such, *SE* could be de-scribed as a lifestyle magazine, which explains its soaring subscription numbers and a reading audience that cut across gender, generational, national, and socio-economic lines.

Central to the magazine's popularity and indeed to the creation of a distinct Soviet fan culture was the magazine's annual survey of the most popular film productions and performers, launched in 1959. As the only barometer of popular preferences (besides ticket sales), the *SE* viewers' choice awards became a source of prestige in the movie industry. What had begun as a modest experiment to determine the year's favourite Soviet film turned into a notable event in the life of the country, not just the industry. The annual contest was especially mo-mentous in the Soviet system because not all movies enjoyed the same distribution; a movie's officially assigned category determined both the number of copies it merited and whether it would be shown locally or nationally. Thus, though few movies were actually shelved during the 1950s and '60s, many "problem" movies suffered cripplingly restrictive distribution. So the *SE* survey could act as a corrective to the often ar-bitrary decision-making of the studios or the ministries. For instance, 15 per cent of *SE* subscribers who saw M. Khutsiev's controversial 1966 movie *July Rain* (Iul'skii dozhd') voted it the year's worst film while 10 per cent considered it the year's best. As a result, despite its limited circulation and negative press, the contentious production continued to attract attention. Equally notable were the absences from the top-ten list. For example, S. Iutkevich's 1957 film *Stories about Lenin* (Rasskazy o Lenine) and L. Kulidzhanov's 1963 Lenin-inspired *The Blue Notebook* (Siniaia tetrad') not only were poorly attended (11 million and 8 million tickets sold, respectively) but also failed to make it onto the *SE* chart. Al-though *SE*'s survey did not provide a representative sample, composed as it was of around 40,000 self-selected movie enthusiasts under forty, it complicated the authorities' long-standing practice of pronouncing unqualified and definitive judgments about the Soviet people.

Extremely popular with readers from the start, the viewers' choice awards developed even further so as to reflect audience preferences. By 1966 the *SE* staff had begun differentiating the respondents' age, sex, occupation, educational level, and place of residence. By 1968 the survey had expanded in scope and size: around 45,000 ballots were cast for best Soviet and foreign films as well as for top actors and actresses at home and abroad.[66] The enthusiasm for the survey was evident in the fact that entire families, *kolkhoz* collectives, army units, and apartment complexes voted together on one ballot. These collectives would use a single ballot, but each individual's vote would be recorded separately. Consequently, the total number of votes for a given film was usually much higher than the total number of surveys received. And since the number of survey forms was limited, some movie theatres and cinema distribution centres would voluntarily copy and reproduce the official *SE* survey, circulating it to moviegoers and even designating a special post office box where all the responses could be collected locally.[67] Although critics also weighed in with their choices once the results were announced, it was clear that the popular vote was more relevant than the opinions of the respected few. Filmmaker Grigorii Chukhrai echoed this sentiment when he received the *SE* viewers' choice award for the best film of 1961: "To tell you the truth, I do not have total confidence in the reviews of professional critics. After all, twenty people could be wrong; their evaluations could be based on a number of extraneous factors. But a jury of many thousands cannot be swayed in a similar way."[68]

The general moviegoing audience was keen to see and vote for international stars and features no less than they were for homegrown talent. In fact, Soviet viewers became so accustomed to imports from Europe, Hollywood, Mexico, Egypt, and Bollywood that in the early to mid-1960s, the top ten list of fan-favourite films, actors, and actresses always included at least one non-Soviet entry. Considering the consistent exposure to international films, it is not surprising that imports regularly sold between 20 and 40 million tickets, often outselling Soviet films, just as they did in the late Stalin era. For instance, around 5 per cent of Georgia's population saw the generally popular 1961 Russian feature *Nine Days of a Year* during the first year of its release while 53 per cent went to see the French hit movie *The Three Musketeers* during the same period.[69] In the Uzbek capital of Tashkent the situation was similar. Movie theatres showed the 1960 Hollywood western *The Magnificent Seven* a total of 170 times and the 1955 musical *Oklahoma!* 50

times, while a domestic contemporary classic, *Ballad of a Soldier*, was shown only 11 times during the same year.[70] This state of affairs was all the more frustrating given that Soviet authorities on average released six times more copies of Soviet films in the republics. For example, in 1963 the Latvian Republic received 419 copies of the most recent fifty Soviet productions and only 64 copies of the ten newly imported foreign movies.

Despite this distribution strategy, cinemas in the Latvian capital, Riga, screened twice as many Western motion pictures as Soviet films.[71] Soviet viewers frustrated Party functionaries in voting with their feet for "frivolous entertainment"; they also posed a challenge to Soviet filmmakers, who aimed to bring about a fundamental turn away from the Stalinist mentality with their reflective heroes. Moviegoers passionately defended their right to choose which movie to watch and which heroes to admire. One reader asserted her autonomy by rejecting the negative reviews of professional film critics: "Your job is to reflect the audience`s point of view like a mirror, rather than put words into our mouths."[72] New Wave directors adeptly manoeuvred around institutional and bureaucratic barriers, but they could not fully master the commercial side of the movie business; superfluous men as protagonists rarely broke box office records and were unable to compete against the two crowd-pleasing juggernauts: Hollywood and Bollywood. Thus by the late 1960s moviegoers were openly asserting their independence and becoming ever more active arbiters of popular taste. The rise of surveys, both informal and scientific, gave moviegoers an additional platform for advancing their causes.

Soviet Sociology and the Death of the "Average Viewer"

A 1964 article in *SE* opened with this line: "At the end of the day, does anyone know what really goes on in a moviegoer's head?"[73] That question reflected the movie industry's growing preoccupation with understanding the psychology behind moviegoing trends. From the late 1950s onward, those involved in film production in particular and cultural politics in general struggled to understand the mentality of the "average moviegoer." The country's ballooning movie theatre repertoires, which offered around 150 foreign and domestic releases a year, made a more "scientific" approach to audience preferences imperative. This effort involved not only quantifying moviegoers' (dis)likes but also plumbing the psychology that underpinned consumer choices. The unparalleled popularity of foreign blockbusters among Soviet viewers propelled studies on consumer behaviour. However hesitantly,

Party authorities and movie industry officials began investigating how to lure Soviet viewers away from foreign blockbusters and attract them to domestic productions, debating questions central to this mission: Why do Soviet citizens go to the movies? Why do moviegoers choose one film over another? What factors determine the success of a film?

Although seen as necessary, sociological studies on moviegoing trends generated controversy because of the implicit assumption that audiences were the ultimate judge of a film's ideological value and artistic merit. In other words, by fixating on moviegoer's opinions, this type of research made the success of a film dependent on audience approval rather than official pronouncements. In contrast to the Stalin era, when the party acted as the unchallenged representative and executor of the people's will, Khrushchev-era populism ensured that a film's fate was tied as firmly to box office profits as it was to reviews in Party publications. The voice of the people could no longer be easily evaded. A contemporary sociologist expressed this sentiment bluntly: "It is foolish when some film critics arrogate to themselves the exclusive right to speak in the name of the people ... The people are not a faceless mass with identical tastes."[74] In effect, public opinion polls exposed the heterogeneity among the populace and undercut the Party's tendencies toward monolithism.

However unpalatable to artistic and ideological authorities, the populist paradigm entrenched itself in public consciousness as sociological research once again became a valued and even fashionable discipline.[75] After a twenty-year moratorium on sociological research under Stalin, at the Twentieth Party Congress the Party leadership declared sociological research indispensable to the country's modernization project.[76] Although conservative officialdom still viewed sociology with suspicion and saw it as threatening the status quo, the first cohort of post- Stalin sociologists were able to test long-established truisms about Soviet society. Sociologists of culture and leisure in particular began challenging long-held conventional wisdom on audience reception and moviegoing practices.

The movie industry's efforts to reconceptualize its relationship with the viewer led to the promotion of sociological research aimed at understanding "consumer behaviour." Soviet sociological studies, founded as they were on a rational and scientific approach to film distribution and propaganda, were intended to reduce the vague generalizations that had long mired debates on the nature of moviegoing. Scriptwriter Kh.N. Khersonskii observed that individuals who spoke their mind about films or moviegoing practices often "channelled" the opinions and feelings of "the people," claiming to speak on their behalf. Insisting that no one can generalize about the opinions of millions of moviegoers, he suggested a "cardiogram of the movie hall," that is, some kind of strategy that would help determine the factors that affect audience reception.[77]

In an effort to produce films that were both profitable and ideologically sound, the Soviet movie industry increasingly turned to sociological research to determine how audiences chose which films to see and how they reacted to them. After the mid-1960s, sociological research into moviegoing patterns analysed both quantitative and qualitative aspects of the viewing experience; although empiricists at heart, Soviet sociologists also wanted to understand the psychological dynamics behind the numbers. The resurrection of the sociological discipline relegitimized a profession that had been defunct since the 1930s; it also amounted to a call to think about Soviet reality in a new way. Reflecting on the renaissance of Soviet sociology in the 1950s and '60s, sociologist G.S. Batygin concluded: "By reinterpreting society, sociologists reformed the contents of Marxist social doctrine as well as the style and language of science, creating new social symbols and standards."[78] The impact of sociological research on the movie industry was no less profound than it was on the perception of Soviet society overall.

Research for a full-length monograph that addressed the sociology behind moviegoing and the movie experience commenced in 1963, led by one of the country's first sociologists of culture, Lev Naumovich Kogan. This research, conducted in the Sverdlovsk region in the Urals, took four years to complete and was, according to Kogan, a response to two related assumptions about cultural sociology. First, Kogan felt that sociological research on moviegoing had, up to that point, been plagued by methodological infelicities, resulting in dubious conclusions and ineffective policy recommendations. Second, Kogan fought against the widespread viewpoint that empirical research was ill-equipped to add to theoretical studies of popular tastes. Thus his work not only represented a regional case study of local moviegoing trends but also validated approaching the question of audience reception within a sociological framework. Kogan argued for his methodology in no uncertain terms: "The value of theoretical discussions diminishes manifold if it is based on a priori assumptions instead of studies of concrete, lived experiences."[79]

Kogan and his colleagues formulated four main goals for their ambitious project: to determine the level of interest in cinema for various demographic groups; to elucidate factors that influenced moviegoers to choose one movie over another; to ascertain how certain films become blockbusters; and to understand what role film protagonists play in attracting moviegoers to films. To ensure representativeness, the research team resorted to random, systematic, and stratified sampling and utilized both written surveys and oral interviews. In striving for representativeness, Kogan and his co-workers divided his sample into social groups (blue-collar workers, peasants, the intelligentsia, students, white-collar workers, pensioners, and stay-at-home moms) as well as according to age and education. It was their contention that there was significant variation within social groups that required careful consideration if their results were to adequately reflect the diversity of Soviet audiences. In other words, Kogan's study conceptualized the viewer as being motivated by multiple factors simultaneously; it took into account moviegoers' identity (age, gender, education, and social class) as well as external factors (distance to movie theatre, the comfort of the movie theatre, the diversity of film offerings, TV ownership). This approach allowed Kogan to advance the notion that the "average viewer" (*srednii zritel'*) does not exist in practice and that each genre, each film, has a target viewer and target audience (*kazhdaia gruppa fil'mov imeet "svoego" zritelia, "svoiu" auditoriu*).[80] By differentiating social groups and advocating for multiple interest groups, Kogan legitimated the multifunctionality of both films and celluloid masculinity. If each film had its target audience, then by extension, each hero had his target group.

Kogan's research highlighted the seemingly endless variety of factors that shaped Soviet citizens' moviegoing experiences and determined how they judged a film. For instance, the results showed that, although most of those surveyed chose films randomly rather than intentionally, the respondents' motivation to go to the movies depended, more often than not, on their level of education. Generally, the higher their education level, the more selective and thoughtful their rationale for visiting the movie theatre in the first place.[81] Individuals' visits to the screen were motivated more by chance than by clearly defined reasoning; furthermore, different demographic groups held different notions of what they wanted to see. Kogan's study showed the disparate demands the sexes and age groups held regarding cinematic themes and genres.[82] Men preferred science fiction and thrillers; women were drawn to musicals and fairy tales. Both sexes, however, preferred comedy above all and expressed a desire to see more humour on Soviet screens. Whereas the gender discrepancy was no surprise, the revelations about generational patterns were much more revealing – and worrisome – since they flew in the face of official rhetoric on youth. Only 5 per cent of 16- to 25-year-olds expressed interest in seeing films about the Civil War, and only 10 per cent wanted to see more films about the Second World

War. Youth were much more interested in movies about the present day (34 per cent) and love (26 per cent).[83] Moreover, compared to other age groups, the 16- to 25-year-olds paid less attention to movies about rural life.

The diversity in audience preferences led the researchers to conclude that the movie industry should produce and distribute films with specific audience contingents in mind, going so far as to suggest that the industry would be much more effective in promoting its motion pictures if it could predict which geographic districts and demographic groups were most likely to secure a film's (financial) success. While Kogan and his team realized that some heroes and films garnered an enormous following despite demographic or locational particularities, they argued that such productions were the exception and that a more pragmatic approach was required for the great majority of motion pictures. Radical in the Soviet context, this proposal essentially advised a marketing approach to moviemaking, one that grasped that producing a film was pointless unless there was a target group to "consume" the product.

The variety the study identified in terms of why audiences went to the movies and what genres/topics they preferred was equally obvious in the respondents' attitudes toward celluloid heroism. Kogan concluded that there was no foolproof formula for creating a universal hero: "The analysis of the statistics once again demonstrates that a formula for creating a positive hero does not exist and cannot exist. Heroes are as varied as are our lives."[84] At the beginning of his chapter on celluloid heroes, Kogan declared the "problem of the movie hero" to be the most important in "considering the interrelationship between the screen and the viewer."[85] The issue of cinematic heroism was important to the research since sociologists posited that protagonists relayed social, moral, behavioural, and aesthetic norms and ideals.

Unlike previous surveys, which had limited themselves to asking respondents which hero was their favourite, Kogan's study took pains to examine how and why audiences related to some heroes while rejecting others. In an effort to understand the psychological aspect of identifying and connecting with movie heroes, Kogan devised two sets of survey questions.[86] One set was geared toward understanding the kind of relationship viewers had with movie heroes; the other sought to identify how audiences responded to particular types of heroes. The first set asked respondents to state whether they put themselves in the hero's shoes during a viewing, whether they emulated their favourite hero, and whether their favourite heroes had, at any point, helped them change, make a decision, or look at life differently.

The second set gauged the type(s) of heroes viewers preferred: ideal heroes, ordinary heroes, heroes in the vein of musketeers/cowboys, or all three types of heroes equally. Respondents were also asked to state whether they preferred foreign protagonists over Soviet heroes or regarded them equally.

Although the responses to these questions were valuable, the questions themselves were even more revealing in that they exposed the researchers' assumptions about masculinity.[87] First, they phrased heroism in exclusively masculine terms. All the examples the pollsters provided and reported revolved around male protagonists. Second, researchers assumed that a viewer's response to a protagonist reflected their age or educational level rather than evidence of a particular hero's impact. In other words, the survey's architects thought of celluloid heroism as working according to a certain set of invisible rules – that is, that there was a logic to how viewers, based on their identity, deconstructed and experienced the heroes they watched. Third, the fact that the survey offered three types of heroes – ideal, ordinary, and musketeer/cowboy-like – demonstrated the researchers' conviction that positive heroes could be defined by multiple characteristics. To prove their point, Kogan's team discussed the fact that G. Kozintsev's 1965 *Hamlet* appealed to Soviet moviegoers as much as A. Saltikov's rough and gruff *kolkhoz* chairman E. Trubnikov. On the face of it, the reflective Danish prince had little in common with a volatile Second World War veteran who restored a *kolkhoz* in the immediate postwar period through merciless but effective tactics. Nonetheless, Kogan poetically hypothesized that Hamlet's and Trubnikov's popularity lay in the force and harmony of their thoughts and actions.

The last two assumptions about on-screen protagonists were particularly significant, for they undercut the socialist realist model of the ideal hero as it had been presented during Stalinism. A complex but uniform set of signs and symbols that defined the hero was no longer tenable; nor was an extremely limited range of plots. Men's fates and identities could now be expressed in a number of ways, for different audience contingents responded differently to specific types of masculine leads. The movie hero's effect, in other words, was both constrained and enabled by the viewer's identity; only heroes with a certain *je ne se quoi* could reach the widest range of moviegoers.

Kogan's research proved valuable but remained underutilized. By 1971, sociology's "golden age" had passed and only conservative research that supported the party's narrow agenda received funding. Because the research published in the late 1960s showed a growing disparity between official propaganda and social realities, the Communist

Party concluded that the empirical findings obtained by Soviet sociologists had dubious scientific value. As sociologists continued to expose the gap between Marxist theory and Soviet realities, the authorities only approved research that would unequivocally reflect the superiority of the socialist system.

Moreover, instituting Kogan's findings would have required a substantial reorganization (i.e., commercialization) of the movie industry, film distribution channels, and local theatre operations. Even so, Kogan's conclusions as they related to targeting films to particular audiences became an accepted theorem in professional discourse.[88] During late socialism, movie industry professionals continued to refine his central premise that each film had its own target audience and that moviegoers responded to films based on their age, education level, and occupation.

Kogan's research on differentiated audiences had profoundly affected notions of how celluloid masculinity functions. The notion that filmmakers could replicate, for instance, Chapaev's singular fame and popularity slowly dissipated. Chapaev, Korchagin, and Mares'ev were now seen as discrete episodes, products of a particular time and place; no longer were they seen as providing universal formulas for constructing an ideal masculinity for the mythical "average viewer."

Conclusion

Once Khrushchev threw the first stone at the glass house of Stalinism, it proved difficult to contain the damage, for the Soviet symbolic order now needed to be reconfigured to address new ideological realities. This change affected not only how filmmakers portrayed masculinity but also how they conceptualized the perspective from which they filmed it. Unlike Stalinist heroes, whose ultimate goal was to integrate into a homosocial hierarchy by becoming self-disciplining subjects, post-Stalinist protagonists sought to independently and idiosyncratically come to terms with a world they perceived as alien and sometimes threatening. Although central to this project, Khrushchev's de-Stalinization drive was not wholly responsible for the new kinds of heroes populating movie theatre screens. By the early 1960s, the First Party Secretary was worried about the state of the film industry. During an 8 March 1963 meeting with the artistic intelligentsia, he noted in an uncharacteristically subdued fashion: "It is very disconcerting to see so many second-rate movies on Soviet screens. These films induce sleepiness, boredom, and melancholy with their dull plots and unexciting styles."[89] Khrushchev's gripes notwithstanding, sixties filmmakers took seriously the call to depict an unvarnished version of Soviet reality.

As film professionals strove to capture contemporary realities in a documentary fashion, cinema became an unapologetic witness to a rapidly changing world in which men felt increasingly alienated and helpless. The next four chapters demonstrate that sixties directors often found their male compatriots wanting as romantic partners, fathers, role models to youth, and supposed masters of science and progress. These flawed heroes could not have reached audiences had it not been for five interdependent factors: a weakening censorship regime, a Cinematographers' Union committed to its members' artistic licence, a vibrant film fan culture, the intelligentsia's strong commitment to reverse Stalinist policies, and, finally, a rise in sociological research. Taken together, these factors allowed directors to fashion versions of masculinity that stood in sharp contrast to that of Stalinist supermen à *la* Chapaev. The "unvarnished" celluloid masculinity of the sixties represented a denunciation of Stalinist romanticism and focused instead on men as men. In the course of this process it became evident that perhaps men of the post-Stalinist era were not equipped to go boldly where no man had gone before.

Chapter Two

Being a Dad Is Not for Sissies

The 1959 feature *Life Passed Him By* (Zhizn' proshla mimo), which sold around 27.5 million tickets, showed Soviet critics that audiences craved the thrills of a whodunit.[1] The unique aspect of *Life Passed Him By* was its authentic *noir* feel. Dark alleys, ominous city shadows, creepy hallways, growling black cats, a damsel in distress, and a hardened criminal come together to mimic the feel of a classic American *film noir*. At the centre of the plot is a gruff thief and murderer named Shark (Akula), who escapes a labour camp and returns home to wreak havoc among his former partners, who have in the meantime taken the straight and narrow path. In no mood to become a boy scout in his thirties, Shark mercilessly hounds, threatens, and intimidates anyone who crosses his path. Clearly, the director had no intention for the audience to sympathize with the anti-hero, and it seems until the very end that this hardened criminal is irredeemable. At the very last moment, however, Shark has a change of heart. The moment of penance comes when he confronts his former mistress and partner in crime and meets a son he didn't know he had. His former mistress, Ninka, never told Shark he had become a father; she had told the boy his dad was a famous sea captain who was on in a long transoceanic voyage. Appeals to self-interest, marital responsibility, romantic affection, and universal values had all failed to convince Shark to mend his ways; only the fact that he is a father now makes him see the light. As one Soviet film critic observes, the son converts the father: "He is no longer the same Shark, a cold and cynical individual from the beginning of the movie; the new Shark has very little in common with his former self."[2] Although Soviet reviewers did not believe that a lifelong criminal like Shark could reinvent himself after a lifetime of misdeeds, they did not call into doubt that an encounter with one's child could fundamentally better a man.[3] Shark is so moved by the idea of being a father that he decides to return

Figure 2.1. A boy domesticating a hardened criminal in
Life Passed Him By (1959).

to the penal colony and serve out his time, wishing to return to his son
as an honest man. Indeed, in this short scene, Shark's gruff demeanour
disappears; even his face softens, his prominent facial scar no longer his
most distinguishing feature. For a brief but transformative moment, the
hardened criminal looks like an ordinary dad engulfed in his son's stories (Figure 2.1). This short but crucial interaction introduces a theme
central to the sixties cultural landscape: children in general, and sons
in particular, are necessary – as in Shark's case – to "domesticate" men
and unearth their hardwired nurturing instincts.

   That men were expected to embrace paternal instincts as innate was
made most overtly in movies addressing out-of-wedlock pregnancy and
the hot-button topic of abortion. Though plots centring on unplanned
pregnancies were meant to be cautionary tales for young women, their
most direct targets were licentious males, the era's playboys and Cas-
anovas. In sixties films the anti-hero responsible for impregnating his
unwed partner usually either abandons the girl completely or aggressively "encourages" her to abort the pregnancy, expecting that the court

of public opinion will, despite the occasional wagging finger, ultimately condemn the female partner for her carelessness.[4] Desperate and with nowhere to turn, the heroine is seemingly left with only one choice. But the narrative then introduces a champion ready to shoulder the responsibilities of childrearing with her. These films elevated nuclear families to a superior social unit and brandished the male citizen as its nucleus. Single-mother families were treated positively in films and combated the stigma associated with single motherhood, but it was clear that the cultural cachet lay with family units headed by men. These stories were the post-Stalinist version of the Cinderella story. The ultimate takeaway was that single mothers should not be shunned but pitied, and that in helping them, men were realizing their essential social and personal identity – that of being a caring father, a proactive citizen, and a decent human being. So culturally dominant was the commitment to familial harmony that films effectively destigmatized "non-traditional families." Blood no longer counted for much; men were defined in terms of their ability to take up the difficult duties of parenthood regardless of their child's genetic make-up. These films challenged the notion that only biological parents could provide the best care. In a truly democratic fashion, one could choose one's family based on shared values and temperament.

Besides serving as an ennobling influence, parental duties played a central role in realizing a man's identity; that is why so many Soviet films of the 1950s and 1960s divide a man's life into two stages: pre- and post-fatherhood. A man who did not have a genuine, caring, and involved relationship with his offspring had not actualized himself fully. This perspective on paternal responsibility was new to Soviet cinema. If Stalinist fatherhood was wedded to mirroring the party's ideological prerogatives and divorced from lived experiences, then post-Stalinist cinema reversed that trend. Soviet filmmakers brought paternity to the foreground so that on-screen dads no longer appeared as aloof and distant semi-deities *à la* Stalin. After Khrushchev's secret speech, dictatorial father-figures on the silver screen came to be read as allusions to Stalin, the problematic "father of the peoples." Directors maintained that simply the presence of a man was insufficient; a man needed to be attentive in dealing with his offspring. Although the ideological symbolism attached to fathers and father-figures was not lost, and although the Party continued to promote a paternalistic attitude, films of that era made it clear that fathers are made, rather than born, and that being a flesh-and-blood dad is no easy job. While fatherhood, biological or otherwise, was central to postwar masculine identity, it was not a guaranteed right and could be lost if the father played a secondary role in the adult–child dyad. In a reversal of the Stalinist model, adults needed the idealistic innocence of children more than children needed the experiential wisdom of adults. If men wanted to become effective fathers, they needed to support rather than lead and to listen rather than boss around; the model rejected hierarchical relationships and prioritized partnerships as an ideal.

The drama, comedy, and tragedy of films on fatherhood rested on the fact that protagonists found the "paternal condition" a *terra incognita*. Thus, a significant number of Soviet filmmakers turned their attention to absent, indifferent, or negligent fathers. No mere allegory or symbolism, these films mirrored the era's preoccupation with deadbeat dads as a lived reality. Newspapers and journals often featured human interest stories about men who refused to fulfil their familial obligations. According to media accounts, even when men discharged their marital duties, they often made poor fathers who were largely distant from and/or uninvolved in familial affairs. In a range of popular publications such as *Izvestiia*, *Krokodil*, and *Pravda*, men were often shamed for ignoring their childrearing responsibilities. Because the media and specialists popularized the notion of the sexes as "separate but equal," there was no way for a man's role to be substituted. Consequently, commentators worried that without proper masculine role models, boys would grow up to be "less than." Following already established Stalin-era patterns, sixties discourse often associated a child's poor academic performance and/or hooliganism with an absent father and weak family ties.[5] The causal link that people perceived between fatherlessness (*bezotsovshchina*) and deviant adolescence was a prominent source of anxiety throughout the sixties.

In pondering men's ability to realize themselves as fathers, Soviet directors arguably commented on a postwar phenomenon Mie Nakachi ingeniously calls a "government-sponsored sexual revolution." If cataclysmic dislocations and separations facilitated casual sexual relations during the war,[6] then the 1944 Family Code codified sexual promiscuity into law.[7] Worried about the demographic catastrophe that was likely to ensue because millions of fertile men had died in combat,[8] Stalinist legislation absolved men of any financial or legal responsibility for children fathered outside marriage. In this way the government encouraged men to have as many illicit liaisons as they could, promising to financially support unmarried mothers but forbidding them from naming the father on the birth certificate. These measures bore the hoped-for results. In the late 1940s and throughout the 1950s, out-of-wedlock births accounted for 15 to 20 per cent of all births.[9] As economist and gender historian Elizabeth Brainerd concludes: "Rather than strengthening the family as intended, the 1944 Family Code appears to have weakened the family and reduced the likelihood that men would marry."[10] Thus the Stalin-era pronatalist measures weakened men's commitment to marriage and family, spawning a generation of men who had few reasons to consider fatherhood relevant to their identity. The films analysed here can be seen as an attempt to reconstitute the traditional family after the sexual libertinism of the late Stalin era.

Adding to fears about the stability of Soviet families was the growing divorce rate. The reported annual divorce rate for the Soviet Union as a whole rose from 0.6 to 2.8 per 1,000 between 1955 and 1966. By the 1970s the Soviet divorce rate was second only to that of the United States.[11] Significantly, one local study reported that while between 10 to 25 per cent of women initiated divorce because of the husband's lack of participation in housework, men initiated divorce because they missed their autonomy, the company of other men, and alcohol.[12] Although open to interpretation, these statistics suggest that postwar libertinism continued to exert its influence among a segment of the male population well into the sixties. In short, a cross-section of the male population experienced difficulties adjusting to middle-class respectability and empathetic fatherhood.

Sixties films placed a higher premium on fatherhood because skyrocketing abortion rates had brought into sharp relief that men failed to show up when it mattered most. After abortion became legal in November 1955, the procedure became the principal mode of birth control, for contraceptives were very hard to come by.[13] By the mid-1960s, "8 million abortions were registered in the USSR, that is, about 150 abortions for 100 live births."[14] Alarmed by these statistics, the pronatalist regime launched an anti-abortion campaign that targeted both men and women. Amy Randall shows that this massive propaganda effort "helped to domesticate Soviet masculinity" by promoting abortion "as a husbandly concern and fatherly matter."[15] Whereas up until the early 1950s "the Soviet regime largely emphasized men's procreative role and defined masculinity primarily by what men did in the public sphere," by the early 1960s official discourse promoted "the idea that the yearning for fatherhood is instinctual."[16]

Sixties visual culture aimed to construct an idealized version of the father-figure. This calls into question Zhanna Chernova's provocative idea that the Soviet "government utilized laws and its control of the economy to oust men from the family and alienate them from fatherhood."[17] Chernova contends that between 1944 and 1968 men were "freed by law from almost all duties to women and children" as well as excluded "from the emotional side of parenting."[18] While frequent public complaints about deadbeat dads make clear that many men took advantage of governmental *policy*, sixties *culture* propagated the exact opposite: a fatherhood ideal based on emotional availability and engagement with offspring. The evidence presented in this chapter supports Sergei Kukhterin's and Helene Carlbäck's oral histories that investigate the dynamics between Soviet-era fathers and their children. Carlbäck's research suggests that despite a cultural double standard, men "seem to have spent large parts of their leisure time at home," with some of the informants sharing stories about fathers "sometimes feeling guilt for not having been sufficiently present and involved."[19] Kukhterin's respondents similarly "recalled having what they called warm and positive relations with their fathers during the Soviet era."[20] This is not to say that the "involved fatherhood model" dominated during the post-Stalinist period. As contemporary surveys indicate, the era featured conflicting expectations for how men were supposed to "perform" their spousal and parental duties; while some believed it was high time for men to actively participate in household life, others considered any kind of domestic activity contrary to men's "true nature."[21] The divided popular expectations notwithstanding, cinema specifically and sixties visual culture more broadly showcased fathers in a range of roles "that far outstripped the rather narrow representations of paternity of the late Stalin era."[22]

The ideological and sociological prerogatives of the post-Stalin era consequently created a cultural moment that reconfigured how Soviet fatherhood – and by extension, masculinity – was discussed and understood. Even while the 1944 Family Code prioritized birth rates over the preservation of the nuclear family on a policy level, the day's cultural scripts insisted that men, as gendered subjects, could not realize themselves fully unless they embraced their paternal instincts. The sixties fatherhood crisis happened not because men had been excluded from the emotional side of parenting but because they had failed to measure up to the fatherhood ideal that sixties films advanced.

The Sixties Fatherhood Crisis

The Soviet press was no stranger to discussing issues relating to family life. In terms of both reproduction and upbringing, the Soviet authorities had, since the time of Anton Makarenko, designated parents as responsible for the correct upbringing of future Soviet workers: "The family is the primary cell of society, and its duties in childrearing derive from its obligations to produce good citizens."[23] In the mid-1960s, however, the Soviet press turned up the volume on the various ways in which men in particular refused to engage in family affairs. Although women were hardly blameless in the eyes of Soviet commentators, their sins paled in comparison to those of fathers, who were often seen as erring too much on the side of carelessness and benign neglect.

Brazen and cruel infidelity, blatant indifference to domestic affairs, and utter ineptitude seemed to be the markers of the 1950s and '60s Soviet "family man." Their sins were many, but particularly egregious were those of men who forced their partners into dangerous abortions or who refused to acknowledge paternity after impregnating their girl-friends. For instance, in 1959, *Literaturnaia gazeta* reported on the case of a woman who died after undergoing an illegal abortion. The reporter was aghast that only the quack doctor and his shady sidekicks were punished when most of the blame lay with M., a man who had, through lies and deceit, seduced and impregnated the trusting maiden – only to then push her into the unsanitary and unnecessary procedure. While the expectant mother was dead, the criminal was free to go about his business, encouraged to commit more of the same heinous acts.[24] The reporter makes clear that this was not simply a legal issue; it was also a moral one that was necessary to resolve as Soviet society inched toward communism. The article insisted that there could be no communism without justice in the realm of family law and that men needed to be held responsible for their role in marital and familial affairs.

There was also no shortage of articles about men abandoning their partners either during or immediately after pregnancy. A particularly stunning account appeared in a 1953 issue of *Krokodil*. It told the story of a thirty-eight-year-old – Aleksei Ivanovich Titov – who married six times in ten years, leaving each wife after she gave birth. And he clearly had a type: a financially secure and employed female who had a room or apartment of her own, preferably in an urban setting. Each of the mistresses was eventually left to care for the child single-handedly, her only recourse being the people's courts. Meant as a wake-up call, the cautionary tale was intended to alert naive Soviet maidens to the dangers of Casanova types who lived only to satisfy their earthly ap-petites at the expense of others.[25] Although meant to shame Titov, the author made it clear that the wronged women should not count on the law enforcement authorities to help them locate deadbeat dads and make them pay up. Runaway dads *à la* Titov remained a social ill well into the 1960s; the cover of the November 1965 issue of *Krokodil* shows a young couple running away from a maternity ward, waving to the nurse cradling a newborn. The man shouts to the nurse: "Leave the child to the care of the state." Whether he is eloping with his wife or

Figure 2.2. "Leave the child to the care of the state!" *Krokodil* 32 (1965): cover.

Figure 2.3. "So long! We have nothing left in common!" *Krokodil* 34 (1965): 14.

mistress is unclear (Figure 2.2). In the following issue of *Krokodil* was a cartoon depicting a similar dynamic: a male bluebird tells his female companion guarding a stroller filled with chicks: "So long! We have nothing left in common!" (Figure 2.3).[26]

Even when not denying their families financial support and thereby condemning their children to the stigma of illegitimacy, Soviet men were portrayed as negligent in discharging their parental duties in a

Рисунок Г. ПИРЦХАЛАВА.

— Это же место для детей.
— А я с ребёнком.

Figure 2.4. "These seats are reserved for children ..." *Krokodil* 15 (1955): 12.

Figure 2.5. "Dad, go get us a half-liter bottle!" *Krokodil* 34 (1957): 7.

range of areas. For instance, a 1955 cartoon exemplified how men often used children as props. A woman on an overcrowded tram admonishes a man for hogging a section reserved for children; he points to his standing daughter and responds that he is, in fact, with a child (Figure 2.4). The notion that sons eventually mirror their fathers was embodied in a 1957 cartoon that showed that alcoholism is inherited and indeed becomes worse from one generation to the next and that fathers have the power to stop the vicious cycle by example (Figure 2.5).[27]

Figure 2.6. "Please come back when my wife's home." *Krokodil* 6 (1965): cover.

Krokodil readers encountered a similar tableau ten years later on the magazine's February 1965 cover, which featured a situation in which a father assumed zero responsibility for his son. The building superintendent brings a misbehaving boy to his doorstep and asks the father: "Is this your son?" The father, sporting a comfortable caftan, cigarette in hand, flippantly comments: "Yes, but come by another time. The wife is not at home" (Figure 2.6). The Peter Pan complex was not the only explanation commentators dished out to explain men's dereliction of paternal duties; the Party and political ambition were to blame as well. One cartoon points the finger at the political duties men had to discharge in order to climb the social ladder. A toddler points to a man's photograph, and the mother none too happily explains: "That's your daddy. He has a lot social obligations [*obshchestvennykh nagruzok*]. You will see him when he takes a vacation" (Figure 2.7).[28] Whether out of selfishness, careerism, or sheer obliviousness, it was clear that by the end of the Khrushchev era there was a sense that men were actively, regularly, and unabashedly recusing themselves from their caretaker roles.

The roots of the sixties debates on fatherhood – especially those involving runaway dads and illegitimacy – are most properly viewed as a reaction to the Soviet Family Law Code of 1944, which recognized only registered marriages and the offspring of those marriages.[29] In case of divorce, the 1944 law essentially made men financially responsible

Figure 2.7. "You will see him when he takes a vacation." *Krokodil* 6 (1965): 7.

exclusively to women with whom they had a registered marriage. Similarly, the law made men accountable only to children they had fathered in registered marriages. Children born into "common marriages" were, in the eyes of the state, considered out-of-wedlock, and men could not be made to pay alimony – even in cases where they openly acknowledged paternity. Although the courts made a show of making men responsible for monetarily supporting their legally recognized offspring, it was notoriously difficult for local and regional authorities to enforce, let alone guarantee, regular alimony payments.

Between 1944 and Stalin's death in 1953, *Izvestiia* and *Literaturnaia gazeta* in particular carried stories that featured deadbeat dads who either kept changing their places of residence in order to avoid the very short arm of the Soviet law or bemoaned the fact that the legal and criminal systems were too uncoordinated, or divested from locating and prosecuting miscreant fathers.[30] Few, however, doubted the soundness of the law itself; the assumption underlying these discussions was that the 1944 Family Code would prove effective only if those engaged in its enforcement did their jobs and only if the broader collective brought its ire to bear upon the offenders of decency.[31] In 1947 the Soviet Union's justice minister, internal affairs minister, and attorney general all reported to the Presidium of the Supreme Soviet of the USSR on the poor job that regional and republican courts were doing at helping mothers

and ex-wives track down men who owed alimony. The report indicates
that the courts were shirking their responsibilities for the most insignificant reasons. For instance, sometimes the judges refused to accept
applications on the grounds that the plaintiff (customarily the ex-wife)
did not, or could not, indicate the address of the individual who was
not paying alimony; thus instead of assisting aggrieved mothers, the
courts enabled the very deadbeats they were supposed to apprehend.[32]

There was even a sense that the courts and the police actually admired deadbeat fathers, who were so skilled at outrunning the system
that they never paid a kopeck of alimony in their lives.[33] Despite these
clear deficiencies, the *Pravda* editorial board continued to support the
law, all the while inviting readers in a 1948 editorial to call "welfare
kings" to task and to "bring down the force of the collective wrath
upon these moral freaks, abominable remnants of a hateful past."[34] By
1952, fathers shirking their responsibilities to their families had become
so prevalent that two words became commonplace in 1950s Soviet
newspaper parlance: runaway father (*otets-beglets*) and "welfare king"
(*alimentshchik*).[35]

Women were placed in an unenviable position not only because official institutions did not dedicate resources to locating deadbeat dads,
but also because there was no real punishment for evading the law.
Although the law technically foresaw a prison sentence for men who
shirked their parental duties, the families would generally ask the
judge not to demand imprisonment since a jailed man cannot make alimony payments. Deadbeat dads, although generally useless, had more
potential value free than behind bars.[36] The law created a situation in
which runaway fathers could continue to operate without any kind of
meaningful intervention.[37] Thus while the official propaganda insisted
that fatherhood be central to a man's identity, the lived realities showed
that men were less likely to choose that path because there were so few
restrictions on men's movement and choices, allowing men to become
libertines and flâneurs.[38]

A year after Stalin's death, newspapers slowly began to question the
soundness of the 1944 Family Code itself, rather than the mere appli-
cation of it. Discussing the ongoing reformation of laws in the Tajik
Republic, the justice minister, H. Nazarov, observed that there existed
plenty of complications in the attempts to codify marriage and family
law. He concluded that even though the law should not go to the opposite extreme of allowing easy marriage and divorce, it still required
change since it had outlived its purpose. He argued that it was time to
return to decrees signed by Lenin, which did not distinguish between
children born in registered and "common" marriages.[39] For the next

ten years, the press often featured commentary arguing that the 1944 marriage law had not caught up to the realities on the ground and that it contradicted communist morality.[40]

After 1953 the concern shifted from alimony payments to actually ensuring that men would play a meaningful and positive role in the lives of their charges. For instance, in 1956, a *Literaturnaia gazeta* article argued that the 1944 law needed to be changed because it was telling young men they had absolutely no responsibility for the children they fathered outside of registered marriages. It also reflected on the fact that the law contradicted Leninist edicts that insisted men and women have equal rights and responsibilities. The author held that it was much more important that no child be considered illegitimate in the eyes of the law since the label of illegitimacy brought unfair pressure upon the mother and stigmatized the child.[41] Yet at the same time, the law made it very difficult for men to assume their duties and be recognized as legal fathers. A poem in a 1961 edition of *Krokodil* spoke to the issue of men who, for whatever reason, could not obtain a divorce. The poem's protagonist's former wife refused to grant him a divorce. As a result, his children were illegitimate in the eyes of the law and his new wife was considered to be a single mother, even though they had clearly formed a household and shared an extended family.[42]

By the early 1960s the call to put an end to runaway fathers had grown louder as Soviet experts in the fields of education and psychology insisted that fathers were not just necessary but irreplaceable. Since the Soviet press and experts on child development cleaved to the notion that men and women had fundamentally different roles to play in raising a child, it was impossible to know how exactly the child, especially a male child, would develop without a male authority figure. As one writer noted: "Only when a man and woman correctly understand their innate nature and responsibility, their union will be true, and they will build the kind of rich and beautiful relations that characterize happy families."[43] The author contended that boys would grow up to be men and fathers; to be adequate heads of households, they needed to be trained to fulfil this role. The solution was not so much to give women the ability to not perform housework by building new cafeterias or by mechanizing domestic work; rather , it was to teach men and women how to assume their "natural roles." Thus men needed to be raised to learn that their highest priority in life was not to measure their masculinity in terms of sexual escapades, but to assist the weaker sex. According to this author, fatherhood was about a sense of repaying a social debt by reaffirming a societal gender balance based on essentialized gender roles.

But this public conversation about assuming parental roles was about more than just fathers as such. There was a broader concern that men had abrogated their responsibility to mentor boys in general, preoccupied as they were with either affairs of the state or the pursuit of carnal pleasures. For instance, N. Kvashnin, a specialist at the Moscow Regional Institute of Teachers' Training, complained that schools lacked male teachers. He opined that women could not be expected to provide young boys with the kind of advice that is based on the experience of being a man.[44] Men did not work with boys because nurturing and mentoring youth carried less social cachet than being an engineer or geologist.

A noted educator, L. Kovaleva, similarly observed that too often Soviet culture – particularly literature – celebrated sacrificing family relations for professional advancement. Kovaleva criticized Soviet authors for forgetting that raising a family was as important a social responsibility as building a hydroelectric damn or a factory – and no less complex. It was not enough for a child to be part of an orderly, clean, and educated working-class family unit; raising a child also required plenty of patience and warmth. Interestingly, all of Kovaleva's examples focused on fathers, who considered work their primary and only responsibility and pushed familial responsibilities onto their wives. Kovaleva warned that men should avoid two major sins characteristic of Soviet fatherhood: being despotic, and substituting material welfare for emotional care. A child (always a son in Kovaleva's narrative) would become either a "yes-man" if the father was too authoritarian or an egotist if he attempted to make up for his lack of attention with gifts. A father who did not talk to his son as an equal and who was not emotionally present could neither expect his son to have an adult relationship with him nor expect him to become a fully functioning member of Soviet society. Much of the press on fatherhood in the 1950s and '60s came to view fatherhood as an integral part of family life. If in the 1930s and '40s fatherhood was measured by the value a man added to the state economic system, the two decades following Stalin's death redefined fatherhood as a crucial ingredient to ensuring that the next generation of men would be autonomous, confident, socially minded leaders.[45]

By discouraging parallels between fatherhood and economic output, Kovaleva was inverting the production myth of masculinity that had defined the Stalinist era. Often, she wrote, the hero abandoned his family, believing that he was the only one who could deal with the problems facing the particular region/factory/collective farm. She quoted from A. Antonov's short story "Alenka" in which the protagonist rationalizes leaving his sick wife and two children in the following manner: "I left because I understood that besides me, no one here can do my job." Kovaleva criticized this logic because it implied that anyone could assume the hero's familial and spousal responsibilities whereas the protagonist was uniquely equipped to handle his job. Not only were his domestic responsibilities secondary to him, but (so it was implied) domestic life could and would sort itself out without his presence. Kovaleva, however, made the case that no one could replace a father, since fathers are singular and unique; any job will get done because specialists, unlike fathers, are interchangeable and replaceable. The idea that fathers are irreplaceable certainly guided filmmakers' depictions of them. However, the dramatic – and occasionally comedic – tension in Soviet movies on fatherhood was based on the notion that irreplaceable did not also mean deeply flawed.

Where Do Dads Come From? Masculinity and Out-of-Wedlock Children

Thaw-era films were not afraid to confront extramarital sexual relations, adultery, single motherhood, and abortion.[46] While a few of these films were patently moralizing and patronizing, most of them treated a variety of hot-button issues with compassion and open-mindedness. When raising thorny social and personal issues, filmmakers ultimately resorted to straightforward solutions, usually by reinforcing the sanctity of the nuclear family. It is evident from the era's films that there was a clear stigma attached to women who decided, or were forced to, raise a child on their own. Postwar films put a human face on single mothers but stopped short of portraying their lifestyle as ideal, or even viable, in the long term. As fatherhood came to serve as kind of civilizing institution in the postwar period, these films presented the nuclear family as beneficial for the woman and necessary for the man. It was not the out-of-wedlock pregnancy in and of itself that caused controversy (though it remained shameful) but the fact that the mother and child lacked a male presence. The filmmakers did not insist that the biological father take responsibility; any well-intentioned and upstanding man might step in and, in doing so, make himself whole. The family structure was as important for the male characters as it was for their female companions.

A script about the final days of the Second World War reflects on the social opprobrium single mothers faced. The war began on the very Sunday the heroine was supposed to marry her fiancé, by whom she had gotten pregnant. Over the course of the war, however, he goes missing. The bride remains a bride-to-be. As a result of this tragedy, she becomes a mother to an "illegitimate" child. In a conversation with a stranger, she reflects on her situation:

"They registered my son under my maiden last name. But am I the only
   one in this position?"
She waved her hand and gloomily smiled.
"Not a widow and not a wife. To my father I am a camp follower and
   to all others a single mother [*mat'-odinochka*]. Ha. Single mother. Of
   course, I hear much worse."
"That is terrible," agreed Rozhkov.
"Never mind. I will wait. We, women, we know how to wait."[47]

This exchange underscores the limited options available to women who
bore children out of wedlock. The judgment of neighbours, co-workers,
and even family members weighed heavily on women who, for whatever reason, became single mothers. In many scripts, the plot revolved
around men who callously abandoned women they had impregnated,
knowing that the court of public opinion would rule in their favour while
the responsibility – and shame – would be placed squarely on the woman's shoulders. The directors of the 1950s and '60s often returned to this
scenario because it lent itself well to a script full of tension and, possibly,
catharsis. Although postwar films aimed to humanize the single mother
and to contextualize her position, they nonetheless clearly extolled the
nuclear family as the ideal basis for societal harmony. Similarly, celluloid
heroines tended not to be able to navigate life's turbulent waters and parenthood on their own; the true heroes of the narratives were men who
had come to their rescue and married them, thus saving them from the
open or indirect contempt of their narrow-minded social milieu. In that
sense, films involving single mothers were actually more about the male
protagonists, who were given the opportunity to display both their valour and their moral compass. These films shamed men who built their
lives around bachelorhood and playboy values, while promoting family
values as central to the postwar order and postwar masculine identity.

    Positive depictions of single motherhood were not exclusive to the
post-Stalin era. In fact, we encounter the prototype for heroines of the
Thaw cinema in the 1953 film *Marina's Fate*. This film was significant
because Soviet authorities nominated it for the Cannes Film Festival's
Grand Prize and because it proved highly popular, selling around
38 million tickets. Its significance also lay in the fact that it amplified
the calls to humanize Soviet cinema. In 1953 the deputy director of the
"thick journal" *Novyi mir*, A. Tarasenkov, defended filmmakers who
took it upon themselves to focus on the personal and leave the production theme in the background. He averred that "Love, jealousy, friend-
ship, family life, motherhood, and fatherhood – all of these can serve
as wonderful material to showcase the ordinary person and their rich

inner world."[48] As with most Stalinist fare, the plot is rather straightforward. The film begins with a personal tragedy: the protagonist's husband, Terentii, demands a divorce from Marina, claiming that he has intellectually surpassed her and that he cannot possibly take her with him to Kyiv, where he has spent the last three years studying agronomy and attending graduate school. He disparages her by saying: "In the time I have been away, I have become an agronomist, while you're still harvesting beets. You are not evolving while I am constantly advancing; I have committed my life to science ... And what will become of you if you move with me to the city? Cultured people – academics and professors – will be visiting me. What on earth will you have to talk to them about?" Although humiliated, Marina agrees to the divorce and rededicates herself to her studies and her work, eventually earning the title "Hero of Socialist Labor," which was the highest award for exceptional achievements in national economy and culture.

Marina's Fate established two tropes that would endure into the post-1953 period. First, filmmakers promoted a positive prototype of a caring single mother abandoned by a callous male partner. The reviews of the film set up the contrast between the two partners, calling attention to Marina's selflessness: not only does she raise their daughter single-handedly while studying and working, but she also shares her salary with the husband, successfully putting him through school. Although he claims all the success for himself, it is clear that he could not have graduated without Marina's financial assistance and without her commitment to being a single parent for three full years. Second, the film advances the trope of the runaway husband and father. Film reviewers saw the husband for what he was: an egoist, a careerist, and a pathetic philistine.[49] Under the cover of respectability Terentii chases after the pleasures and ease of city life; he has mooched off Marina and the *kolkhoz* for three years and now that she is no longer useful, he is no longer interested. Instead, he pursues the daughter of a famous academician and agronomist.

Although it introduces new themes of single motherhood and deadbeat dads, the film remains didactic in its resolution; as the *Iskusstvo kino* reviewer points out, the film is weighed down by the "genre of production" and the idea that the collective will always come to the rescue.[50] After the betrayal, Marina continues to play the role of the long-suffering but resourceful single mother. Like the heroines of Second World War films, Marina endures and finally triumphs over the treason of the man she was closest to. She does so not only because she is capable of deep and honest feeling but also because she ties her destiny to the interests of the people. In the words of the *Iskusstvo kino* reviewer: "The unhappiness of her personal life forces Marina to love her work even more, to find comfort, and eventually happiness, in her *kolkhoz* collective." In this way the movie connects the production theme, so central to socialist realism, to her personal life. Celebrated Soviet actress Lidiia Sukharevskaia noted shortly after the premiere of *Marina's Fate* that although the heroine's life path was indeed shared by many Soviet women, the moviegoer does not get a sense of her psychology. Sukharevskaia wonders: "Why did Marina agree to the divorce so easily? How did she feel about being a single mother? How did she view her husband's new love interest?"[51] Indeed, the film does not seek to understand Marina as an individual, as a woman, and as a single mother; instead it shames men who do not take marital and familial duties seriously while telling unwed mothers to pour their energies into their work.

Films after *Marina's Fate* would make it clear that personal and romantic fulfilment cannot be replaced with meeting production quotas. Film critic Nina Zorkaia puts this dynamic in very concrete terms. "It is not credible to portray a scene in which a single mother exits the maternity ward and is relieved upon seeing the joyous faces of her co-workers. This scenario's not credible because no collective, no matter how helpful and friendly, can substitute the child's father."[52] In short, by the end of the decade swapping out professional activity for personal fulfilment could no longer pass for convincing – at least according to Zorkaia. The issue of national economy and production did not disappear after 1953, but the emphasis certainly shifted. By the late 1950s the construction site, the mine, and the *kolkhoz* field had become backdrops for the personal drama of the protagonists. This shift in focus proved essential to re-examining the trope of fatherhood. Rather than simply maligning men who were unwilling to assume the duties of marriage and parenthood and urging women to seek solace in collective labour, post-Stalinist cinema became more interested in considering what goes into making good fathers.

A shift could already be seen in the 1954 film *Big Family* (Bol'shaia sem'ia), which examines out-of-wedlock relations much more directly and does not in any way tie them to economic or ideological issues. Although in some ways a traditional Stalinist production featuring a large ensemble cast and lots of pathos about the uniqueness of Soviet working-class culture, *Big Family* distinguishes itself by unambiguously tying masculinity to paternal responsibility. The epic, dedicated to showcasing three generations of shipyard workers – the Zhurbins – pauses to consider the story of a young woman, Katia, who falls for a man who fancies himself a refined but misunderstood poet. The

Figure 2.8. *A Person Is Born* (1957). The lonesome fate of a single mother.

26 million moviegoers who watched *Big Family* witnessed the story of an impressionable and status-conscious young woman who is seduced by a man who is morally and psychologically similar to Marina's Terentii. During their courtship, she becomes pregnant. Certain that her paramour will welcome the news, she joyfully announces her pregnancy, only to hear him insist she have an abortion. Like Marina, she immediately grasps that she has been taken in by his glossy surface, beneath which hides a rotten core. Katia's beau is, of course, free of any responsibility, since under the 1944 Family Code he never registered his relations with his sweetheart. Their relationship over, the heroine abandons hope and reconciles herself to being a single mother.

However, in a *deus ex machina* moment, the most handsome and charming of the Zhurbin sons – played by the period's heartthrob, Aleksei Batalov – proposes to her and promises her domestic bliss. Where the law failed, the moral core of a young blue-collar worker saves the day. What makes the situation interesting is that Katia is never shamed for her pregnancy and chastises herself only for not having seen her paramour for who he really was. Also, both Prince Charming and the damsel in distress initially have doubts about the arrangement. He is uncertain whether he should be responsible for another man's child; she believes herself to be unworthy of his attention. Nonetheless, the two overcome their doubts and plunge into uncharted waters. The success and official approval of the film gave Soviet directors a green light to unabashedly embrace scripts that condemned failed fathers and celebrated selfless father figures without scrutinizing single motherhood as such.

Just as *Big Family* was playing in the movie theatres, the script for *A Person Is Born* (Chelovek rodilsia) was being developed. However, it was not until 1957 that it reached the screen. The long road from concept to realization had partly to do with the fact that the topic was rather controversial. It dealt much more directly with the issue of extramarital affairs than *Big Family*, in that the heroine – Nadia, a freshly minted high school graduate – becomes pregnant without getting married (Figure 2.8). Her suitor, Vitalii, aggressively encourages her to abort the pregnancy, but she refuses. Relying on the kindness of a stranger and co-worker Gleb, the heroine eventually marries and settles into familial bliss.

The straightforward plot clearly hit a nerve; according to newspaper reports, actress O. Bgan, who played Nadia, received hundreds of letters from single mothers asking for advice and counsel.[53] Precisely because the film proved so popular, film reviewers, audience members, and social commentators wondered aloud who was actually responsible for Nadia's predicament and whether it was right to let women believe that men would marry women who had been foolish enough to become pregnant without having gotten married first. For instance, film critic S. Rozen argued in his review that it was essential to get to the bottom of why Nadia found herself pregnant and alone. How had Vitalii gained Nadia's trust? Rozen posited that the scriptwriters, directors, and actress should have reflected more thoroughly on the extent to which Nadia was responsible for having become a single mother. He posed a hypothetical question: "What exactly happened in Nadia's life? Is Vitalii exclusively to blame for her and her baby's misfortune, or is she equally as responsible?"[54] The most interesting aspect of Rozen's review is that he defended Vitalii in response to the many commentators who argued that he, rather than Nadia, ought to be blamed. Rozen was pushing back on the seemingly prevailing popular expectation that the male partner should assume responsibility for the woman he had impregnated.

For the rest of the decade, *A Person Is Born* was invoked repeatedly in the press as a high point in Soviet filmmaking. Clearly, both audiences and Party officials had turned a corner on the expectation that single mothers ought to be shunned; now they were promoting the notion that men should take responsibility for their decisions and behaviour. *Krokodil*, too, seemed to confirm that men were the root of the problem:

Figure 2.9. "His life path." *Krokodil*, 3 (1958): 8–9.

a 1958 cartoon shows the well-trodden path of a Soviet dandy who en-snares one woman after another.[55] The cartoonist does not blame So-viet institutions that simplify marriage contracts and dissolutions or inherent male–female differences. Instead, the Soviet male is the central perpetrator of the vicious cycle, which the artist titles "His Life Path" (Figure 2.9).

This dynamic is central to 1962's *Introduction to Life* (Vstuplenie), which was popular not only at home – it attracted 14.1 million viewers – but also on the international film festival circuit – it won the Special Jury Prize at the 1963 Venice Film Festival and was nominated for a Golden Lion. The film centres on the consequences of the Second World War and the fates of Leningraders in exile, but its emotional attention focuses on a young man, Volodia, and his mother, whose name is never uttered. While the youth's life is largely governed by his mother's choices (of men), the mother's is ultimately decided by the youth's clear sense of right and wrong.

As the film begins, Volodia and his divorced mother are fleeing Len-ingrad at the start of the Second World War for a provincial town deep in Russia's interior. There, the mother begins dating an army captain and Volodia finds a job outside of town in order to find his own lodg-ings and give his mother and her new love interest some space and privacy. When the mother becomes pregnant, however, the captain abandons her without marrying her, and it is up to Volodia to save the day. Being a divorcée and having borne a child out of wedlock, Volodia's mother is shunned: she cannot find a collective apartment where she is not continually harassed for her "loose morals." She is also on the verge of losing her job because she cannot find child care for her newborn, and she is continually making mistakes at work because of exhaustion. Volodia's plan is simple: he will travel back to Leningrad and persuade his biological father to ensure his mother a Leningrad residency permit, a job, and access to child care.

The scene between father and son is tense. The father emphatically rejects every possible reason why he should help his ex-wife. Volodia, however, insists on it till the end, and prevails. What is striking about the film, then, is that the "happy ending" is tied less to the war's end than to securing shelter for a woman who has been persecuted by her own community for having borne a child out of wedlock. It is evident from the reviews that Volodia's mother's heroism during the war consisted in persevering in the face of society's cruelty toward unwed mothers even while she was contributing to the war effort. The film argues that women who bear children out of wedlock are victims of circumstance rather than flawed individuals deserving of persecution and re-education. At the same time, *Introduction to Life* presents unwed mothers as requiring rescue, whose salvation depends on men fighting for their cause. One review focused on Nina Urgant's character in particular, arguing that this woman represented "a type of woman that one meets often in life and infrequently in art."[56] The crux of this judgment was that she had been redeemed by her maternal character and by her selflessness during the war, during which she, like her compatriots, sacrificed her health and well-being. Her "sin" therefore was redeemable because of her general feminine kindness (Figure 2.10). At the same time, the pregnancy was a marker of her internal weakness, which could be redeemed by the charity of a moral man.[57]

Arguably, the most popular film of the 1950s and '60s about single motherhood – one that definitively captivated the public – was 1966's *Women* (Zhenshchiny), featuring an all-star cast of female protagonists; it attracted 36.5 million viewers and became the sixth most popular movie of the year. *Women* follows three generations of women who have three things in common: they are rural newcomers to Moscow, they all work in a furniture factory, and they are all single mothers. The eldest, Ekaterina, is a widow who lost her husband in the Second World War and had to raise her son on her own. So committed is she to doing so that she decides not to date, fearing it would spoil the parental bond. Although clearly selfless and well-intentioned, the film portrays

Figure 2.10. Volodia's mother as an object of derision in *Introduction to Life* (1962).

her decision to remain single despite numerous marriage proposals as misguided. By not remarrying, she denies her son the chance to grow up with a male presence in the household and becomes overly possessive. The stoic and principled Ekaterina becomes a kind of mentor to Dusia, a fellow villager who comes to Moscow as a nanny. Soon, they are living and working together in the factory. Their bond is challenged, however, after Dusia has an affair and has an abortion. Faced with remaining childless as a result of the botched surgery, she turns her attention to acquiring baubles and plans to travel abroad, all in an attempt to fill her childless life with meaning. Finally, the two women mentor Dusia's niece, Alia, who moves to Moscow to financially support herself and her out-of-wedlock child.

The three women are brought together once Ekaterina's son Zhenia falls for Alia and wishes to marry her. Ekaterina is opposed to the match based on the fact that Alia is a single mother and a factory worker who will get in the way of Zhenia's professional advancement. A lengthy review in *Pravda* accused the proud mother of three cardinal sins: motherly egoism, maternal jealousy, and spiritual philistinism.[58]

The reviewer made it clear that Alia's only mistake was placing her trust in the wrong man, arguing that her overall character should not be defined by one miscalculation. Addressing all young single mothers, the film critic declared that *Women* showed that having a child out of wedlock does not preclude a happy personal life. Thus, ultimately, this film was – despite its title – less about women's relationships than about a romantic courtship that overcomes obstacles. In reporting audience reactions to the film, the reviewer focused on the positive reaction of the female moviegoers, who also saw *Women* as a compelling love story. One moviegoer was reported as saying: "Thank you for a good movie about true love. One often hears that true love doesn't exist but in this movie you see real love and you believe in it." *Women* cultivated the belief that educated, cultured, and successful men can and will fall in love with "fallen women" who have offspring out of wedlock.[59] It accomplished this by making single mothers sympathetic heroines whose maternal devotion made them deserving of male affection and marriage proposals.

Women was ultimately one in a long sequence of Soviet films postwar films that strove to normalize out-of-wedlock pregnancy. Although Soviet filmmakers generally evaluated single motherhood positively, the most satisfying resolution was generally one in which a man saved the day and created a nuclear family. The humanization of out-of-wedlock pregnancies was consistently paired with the idea that it is not just desirable but morally imperative for men not to shirk their masculine responsibility to care for their sweethearts even when, or, especially when, the offspring is not theirs. As the ensuing section shows, the notion that fatherhood is not biologically determined would become a pronounced trend in 1950s and '60s Soviet cinema.

Blood Is Not Thicker Than Water: Fatherhood as a Social Construct

A whole host of films showed that fatherhood was not solely a biological category and that fatherhood involved a unique set of skills. The message was therefore mixed: all men could *technically* fulfil this role, but only a few were capable of following through. M. Ershov's 1963 film *Blood Relations* (Rodnaia krov'), which sold 40 million tickets and became one of the most watched movies of the year, poignantly shows the extent to which sixties cinema glamorized "ordinary" relationships and the positive effect that family life had on a man. In that sense, it provides a solid example of the era's idealization of paternal responsibilities while driving home the point that fatherhood was an essential ingredient of postwar masculinity.

This romantic drama begins during the Second World War, when Fedotov, a soldier on a ten-day leave, meets Sonia, a hard-working single mother of three who had fled the Baltic as the Germans advanced. The two fall in love during his brief furlough, and Fedotov returns to Sonia and her family after the war's end. *Blood Relations* in essence details Fedotov's evolution and maturation as a husband and father. At the beginning of the film, Fedotov is an ordinary Joe, a soldier like millions of others. By the end, it is evident that marriage and fatherhood have transformed him, providing him with meaning and structure in the postwar society. Fedotov's love for Sonia – a perfect stranger – and his willingness to be a father to her three children ultimately enable him to make a smooth transition from wartime to peacetime.[60]

However, two events shake up the family: Sonia's sudden death, and the unexpected reappearance of the children's biological father. Having heard of his ex-wife's death, the biological father comes to claim the children after years of absence and neglect. Fedotov has no option but to let the children decide their own fate. Two of the three children decide to stay with their stepfather, acknowledging that, despite their passports and despite the law, they feel tied to their adoptive parent by bonds stronger than blood. The motion picture offers an idealized depiction of postwar life, establishing marital and familial life as a stabilizing social force. More than a simple love story, the movie draws the outlines of the postwar "Soviet Dream." Like its American counterpart, the Soviet Dream included a picture-perfect nuclear family that never went wanting. It associated men more closely with family life; they were not just breadwinners or authority figures but also caregivers. Because the Stalinist regime was much more concerned with reconstructing the national economy in the immediate postwar years, the image of a warm and affectionate Soviet father did not dominate visual culture, although the final decade of Stalin's rule more closely associated demobilized men with domestic spaces.[61] By the 1960s, however, the regime's stress on material well-being offered fertile ground for the emergence of a celluloid hero whose masculinity and personal fulfilment were defined by the domestic sphere. *Blood Relations* thus captures the significance that both popular and official audiences attached to wholesome family life as the cornerstone for individual happiness as well as social harmony.

When the movie came out, the reviewers lauded Sonia and Fedotov's marriage as an accurate representation of all that was best about Soviet life. The union between a brave soldier and a hard-working worker struck a chord with reviewers. Critic G. Kremlev, for instance, opined that these protagonists did not distinguish themselves by appearance or deed from millions of other Soviet citizens; their appeal

Figure 2.11. Still from *Blood Relations* (1963). Fedotov living the "Soviet dream" with his wife Sonia.

and mutual attraction lay instead in their spiritual wealth.[62] Praising Sonia in her review, N. Ignat'eva accentuated the heroine's self-possession: "Sonia's charm is most likely the result of her calmness and her innate ability to experience even the most unexpected of events without losing her composure. She has it hard with three children, but you'll never hear her complain."[63] These traits attract Fedotov to Sonia as he readjusts to civilian life. Sonia eases Fedotov's transition back into peacetime so much so that his military past rarely emerges after demobilization. He seldom mentions his combat experience, his social life does not include other veterans, and the apartment shows no signs of military memorabilia; Fedotov's domestic and familial existence eclipses his wartime participation. For his part, Fedotov more than completes the family unit; he fulfils his paternal role so admirably that his stepchildren take him for their own father (Figure 2.11). Even more importantly, being a father proves to be less about blood lines and more about earning the title through purposeful and long-term dedication to the well-being of the children.

Blood Relations was one of a long string of films that elevated relationships between men and boys. Significant about these films is that the parenting, rather than the marriage, is what defines the adult male. In these scenarios women either are absent or play secondary roles; the real action happens between father and son, whether that relationship is biological or adoptive. Films like *Two Fedors* (Dva Fedora, 1958), *The Fate of a Man* (Sud'ba cheloveka, 1959), *Steamroller and the Violin* (Katok i skripka, 1960), *We Are Two Men* (My, dvoe muzhchin, 1962), and *I Bought Dad* (Ia kupil papu, 1963) present fatherhood as a redemptive, cathartic experience. Even when the shared times do not bring the two together permanently, being around the boy makes the adult re-examine his attitudes and behaviours and opt to change for the better. Collectively, these movies advance the notion that parental roles are the true gateway into adulthood and a purposeful life.

A range of films partly overturned the trope of male socialization that had reigned supreme since the revolutionary years. Eliot Boreinstein points out that 1920s post-revolutionary literature "constructs the myth of a new, masculinized society" in which "domesticity and traditional femininity have no place."[64] Soviet writers like Isaak Babel, Iurii Olesha, and Andrei Platonov were dedicated to creating a "world without women" in which homosocial communities constituted the ideal and "the masculinization of the new Soviet society is underscored by the family's replacement with all-male structures."[65] Lilya Kaganovsky's work builds on Borenstein's research to show that the exclusively male microcosm continued to dominate Stalinist popular culture. In this culture, however, the male protagonists had to negotiate Stalinism's contradictory impulses: an insistence on the absolute mastery of nature, and absolute submission to Stalin. Consequently, maimed, paralyzed, and amputated bodies proved the heroes' dedication to the Great Leader. As Kaganovsky puts it, the ideal man was at once "committed to the cause, yet chained to his bed" – he was "visionary yet blind."[66]

Post-Stalinist cinema continued to privilege male bonding and pointedly excluded women from these connections. Women remained "the point of exchange" rather than subjects in their own right; as in Stalinism, women in post-Stalinist culture served "as the means by which men work out their relationships of admiration, identification, jealousy, rivalry, and envy."[67] At the same time, the principal bonds now were *not* between male adults but between men and boys; moreover, the hierarchy became reversed in that boys were now instructing the seasoned and weathered men. These movies thus suggest that men can skip marriage and romance and find their true identity by cultivating relationships with male youth, whom they essentially adopt as their own. Unlike their Stalinist predecessors, who proved their masculinity by sacrificing their bodies and senses, Thaw-era men had to focus on making themselves emotively whole and were encouraged to mature into adulthood by learning the lessons taught by children. The breaking of this 'father–son bond – be it literal or symbolic – was seen as tantamount to cutting oneself off from the collective and living a meaningless existence.

The most "extreme" case of this trend is the little-known *Children of Don Quixote* (Deti Don Kikhota, 1965). Although not in the pantheon of Thaw-era masterpieces, the film merits attention because it sold just over 20 million tickets. The action revolves around a humble but principled doctor, Bondarenko, who works in a maternity ward. His nickname Don Quixote stems from the fact that he is not only an idealist but also an active humanitarian. Over the course of the film, it becomes clear that he and his wife adopted three sons from the maternity ward after the mothers abandoned them. Significantly, the focus is not on the errant mothers but on the masculine model Bondarenko exemplifies. Furthermore, it is Bondarenko, rather than his wife, who is the architect of this unorthodox, all-male family structure. None too subtly, the film ends with Bondarenko adopting a fourth son. The essentially plotless narrative offers not so much a "message" as a prototype of a family unit that can reproduce itself ad infinitum and be taken on by people who seem naturally constituted to tilt at windmills.

Soviet directors were just as interested in investigating and exposing men who failed to come even close to Bondarenko's seemingly innate idealism. Il'ia Frez's *A Traveler with Baggage* (Puteshestvennik s bagazhom, 1965), which appeared around the same time as *Children of Don Quixote*, touchingly relays the story of Sevka Shcheglov, a boy travelling from the Altai region to the country's premier pioneer camp on the Black Sea. The main destination of Sevka's trip, however, is not Crimea, but Moscow. The boy takes advantage of a train layover in the nation's capital to seek out his biological father, Misha, who had abandoned him and his mother when the boy was about four years old. Sevka's mom tries to convince her son that his father was a sybarite who could never keep a promise, fancying himself a Byronesque figure. Even telling Sevka openly that his dad was a constant embarrassment does not dampen the lad's enthusiasm to find him, because he does not feel complete. Throughout the film, he imagines in great detail what his dad might look like and how they are likely to embrace as soon as they lay eyes on each other. Clearly projecting a romanticized ideal of a paternal figure, the movie sets up the viewer for Sevka's disappointment.

When he finally meets his long-lost father, Sevka does not immediately disclose his identity, in part because he hopes Misha will instantly recognize him as his own and in part because he wants to determine his dad's true character. The brief interaction leaves the young boy disheartened – his mother's description has proved accurate. A dashing playboy riding around the capital on a glitzy motorcycle, Misha is, worst of all, a liar. Once Misha learns that Sevka just came from the Altai region, he launches into a story that Sevka knows well, a story involving the father figure in Sevka's life: Stepan Pavlovich Chistov. Misha, however, reverses the roles, making himself into the hero who saved Chistov's life and lost his toes on the frozen steppe to frostbite. Unable to resist the urge to brag in front of the boy, whom he does not yet know is his son, Misha turns himself into something he patently is not: a selfless, caring individual. In reality, it was Chistov who suffered frostbite while searching for Sevka's wayward dad. While Chistov risked life and lost limb, Sasha was, unbeknownst to anyone, in the nearest town, enjoying a visiting circus troupe. This moment makes clear to Sevka that his fantasies were just that; vanished is any trace of the illusion that his father has reformed.

The final scene is both sobering and comforting. Catching his father in an outright lie, Sevka leaves for the train station without revealing his identity. But Misha's young neighbour lets slip the mysterious Siberian visitor's name. Realizing his mistake, the dad guns for the station, hoping to reach his son in time. Sevka, however, hides from Misha, and observes his prodigal father from a distance with binoculars gifted to him by Chistov so that "he could see further than his nose." Watching his father through the binoculars, Sevka can see him for what he truly is: a playboy who has never grown into a man. The final scene is not all bleak, however, since the boy has clearly learned from Chistov how to tell a true man from a false one.

If at the end of the war the term fatherlessness reflected the physical and literal absence of fathers, then by the 1960s it more properly referred to the moral scourge of deadbeat dads. Sixties directors focused on both sides of the paternal equation: on men who took up paternal duties, and on those who all too happily relinquished them. In no uncertain terms, filmmakers established a cultural trope according to which (surrogate) paternity brought untold rewards, while paternal negligence spawned nothing but grief for all parties involved.

Democratizing the Father–Son Relationship

Sons were necessary to fathers, but the opposite was not always true. In fact, the fathers in sixties Soviet cinema were often portrayed as helpless, callous, or clueless. Moviemakers often cast young protagonists as heroes who had the potential to cleanse the Soviet polity through their spontaneous energy, youthful enthusiasm, and unreserved candor.[68] These movies focused on the lives of Soviet youth and their perceptions of the world around them. This subgenre resisted the urge to advance hagiographic stories about exemplary Soviet youth; instead, they offered narratives about people still in the process of being formed, emphasizing their slow and often painful maturation. Notwithstanding the imperfections of the adolescent protagonists, it was generally the adults who were found wanting. The youth served as a kind of a corrective force, leaving the adults around them less corrupted and more genuine.

These movies reflected a culture that focused increasingly on its children's vantage point. Motion pictures celebrated childhood as expressively as did one of the most significant architectural undertakings of the period: the Pioneer Palace. The construction of that complex in Moscow's Lenin Hills began in 1958 and was completed in 1962. The palace and the grounds that surrounded it were staggering in size; the palace, set in 56 hectares (around 140 acres) of park, was twice the area of the Kremlin.[69] The ideas that underpinned the construction of this complex were tied to the process of de-Stalinization. Susan Reid comments: "The Pioneer Palace had the symbolic task of identifying Khrushchevism inextricably with the rejuvenation of the socialist project and the realization of the happy future through communist education, social and technological progress, and aesthetic modernization."[70] Moreover, the enthusiasm for this modernist compound was shared by the Party, Komsomol organizations, and the reformist intelligentsia alike. The complex as a whole lay bare a perception of childhood as a distinct and especially happy condition, "essentially *different* from adulthood."[71]

Filmmakers readily resorted to adolescent and pre-adolescent heroes because, as film critic A. Volkov succinctly argues, "'childhood issues' in so-called 'youth films' were employed continually as a cover for illustrating problems characteristic of the society as a whole.[72] Narratives that highlighted social problems but featured lovable protagonists sporting shorts and flip-flops or sandals alarmed the censors less and had an easier time reaching the screens. But these young protagonists become a cultural phenomenon not only due to political machinations on the part of the New Wave filmmakers, but also because the authorities saw children as a suitable symbol for the period, which in many ways represented a renaissance for the communist movement at home and abroad. Many directors thus took advantage of the official legitimization of childhood as a unique stage of human development to offer thought-provoking critiques about the country's sociopolitical system.

These motion pictures drew on the children's universe to express a philosophical stance regarding how adults could and should conduct themselves to achieve a more equitable social order. Filmmakers presented men and boys as partners, and their conversations and dealings reflected their parity. At the same time, it seems that the children, however helpless, provided actual support to their adult counterparts, offering them something more valuable: a sense of purpose and meaning. Once reformist directors began examining questions of authority and power from a child's point of view, the great myth of the Soviet family started to ring hollow; children's spontaneity and sincerity replaced grown-ups' uniformity and conformity. The child-hero enabled directors to raise the kinds of critical questions they could not with protagonists played by adolescents or grown men because the appearance of spritely, mischievous boys often disarmed even the most orthodox censor.

Among the series of movies that imagined childhood as a state in which an individual perceives the world in unmediated and unadulterated ways, the film *Little Sergei* in many ways serves as the prototype. *Little Sergei* reflects the subtlety with which directors used children as heroes to comment on the day's most sensitive ideological issues. This motion picture is especially poignant in portraying the relationship between the six-year-old Sergei and his new stepfather. The movie focuses on their burgeoning relationship and on ways in which the father and son are not so much at odds with each other, but nurture an interdependent relationship, providing each other with encouragement and opportunities for further growth.

The blockbuster movie *Little Sergei* was a sign of rapidly changing times. It was the first instance in the history of Soviet cinema that a very young boy played the protagonist. It was this six-year-old who attracted around 23.2 million viewers to movie theatres, following the immense success of Vera Panova's 1955 novel of the same title. In the decade that followed, *Little Sergei* would remain a staple in film critics' commentary; the movie quickly entered the official canon as an example of what Soviet films, especially those dealing with children, ought to aspire to. The memoir of the famed film critic Irina Shilova identifies one particular scene as expressing the quintessence of the Thaw. In it, the little protagonist reprimands an older gentleman visitor for offering him an empty wrapper under the pretence of giving him actual candy. Sergei asks the guest: "Mister, are you a jackass [*durak*]?" Shilova comments that "disregarding good etiquette, Sergei allowed himself to speak truthfully ... Honesty became the precondition for new relationships, a repudiation of lies and prejudice. The clarity of a child's *Weltanschauung* represented a foundation upon which one so badly wanted to recommence the construction of a new Soviet man."[73] The boy's honesty is captivating; his feelings unexplored but true; and his innocence charming.

Little Sergei first captured the attention of Soviet audiences when Panova's novella compellingly narrated several episodes from the life of this very small boy. Filmmakers G. Daneliia and I. Talankin, both of whom received their diplomas from the State Institute of Cinematography in 1959, created an equally captivating childhood on the screen by employing Panova's script adaptation. The two directors captured the world "from below," applying both innovative cinematography and imaginative dialogue. The movie, much like the novella, proved popular with audiences and critics alike. Critic M. Kuznetsov commented: "We can see, once again, all that surrounds us with a feeling of freshness, the initial sparkle that accompanied our discovery of the world, and this sensation does not leave us throughout the movie."[74]

This father-and-son story begins under skies of light blue, between lush meadows and along an unpaved village road. There, in that untarnished rural environment, lives a six-year-old boy by the name of Serezha. The film opens with him exclaiming, "I have a heart," as he tries to get the attention of his two older neighbours. This simple and straightforward declaration leaves the two neighbours unaffected, but the audiences suffer the first tender assault of the six-year-old charmer.

His sincere smile, his untidy blond hair, his watchful eyes, and his carefree movements demand full surrender. Daneliia and Talankin manoeuvre camera angles adroitly so that the viewer always has the benefit of the child's perspective, which allows for suspension of disbelief and gives full credence to his developing world view. Close-up shots of farm animals, panoramic shots of an endless horizon dotted with figures of children, and the view of adults from ground level together paint a grown-up world in which children have appropriated a small corner from which they can weave their influence.

Critics commented that one of the few shortcomings of the movie was its unconvincing portrayal of adults. Serezha, together with his neighbourhood buddies Zhenia, Lidka, Shurik, and Vas'ka, are much more compelling as they answer life's great questions than the grown-ups are as they address their daily concerns. Reviewer M. Kuznetsov considered the dramatic quality of the movie distinctive in that it is "transferred to the inside," to the depth of the child's soul.[75] Soviet literary commentators were generally quick to mention terms such as spirit, soul, and character, pairing them with verbs that imply formation, cultivation, and construction, ready to launch into a fervent discussion about the impending communist epoch. Serezha's demeanour and actions show him to be a man of the future, who will travel safely and confidently on the road to communism by "being receptive to all that is beautiful, intelligent, rightful, and benevolent."[76]

The space that the children occupy in Soviet ideology thus becomes paramount; these are the future builders of communism. For this undertaking, they are in need of models to help form their character so that they might recognize the value of tomorrow in the present. Throughout the film, mothers, aunts, and other female villagers prove to be either passive or inefficient exemplars of upstanding behaviour. Serezha's own world view begins to expand once his mother tells him he will have a father again. The new father figure represents the true beginning of the movie and allows for a singularly intimate look into how Soviet masculinity is forged.

Before Serezha's stepfather, Korostelev, arrives to his new family, Serezha composes various scenarios about the character of the newcomer from gossip, household commentaries, and events that foreshadow his arrival. The older neighbourhood kids inform him that Korostelev is the chairman of the local *kolkhoz*. A single suitcase and a hefty bundle of books are delivered as Serezha overhears a village woman telling his grandmother that the little boy certainly needs a father and concludes that "after all, someone needs to apply the belt." These small clues collectively sketch out a studious, stern, responsible Party man who subscribes to the 1920s revolutionary ideals of asceticism. As he beholds the new family member, Serezha casts a sceptical and fearful glance.

As timidity quickly transforms into curiosity, little Sergei, mimicking Korostelev's actions, asks him whether he will beat him with a belt if he misbehaves. Korostelev takes the boy's casually spoken apprehensions seriously, wanting them to come to an understanding "man to man." The accomplished collective farm chairman symbolically shares a smaller chair as he speaks with his stepson. By addressing Sergei on equal footing, Korostelev literally and figuratively creates an unaffected foundation for a common language that benefits both in the long run (Figure 2.12). Sergei's masculine role model demonstrates that power is not about punishment but about dialogue. Unlike Stalinist father-and-son relationships, the Khrushchevian extended family is conditioned by mutual support and understanding. At the end of the conversation, Serezha is promised a bicycle, which begins a series of novelties that Korosetelev brings into his life.

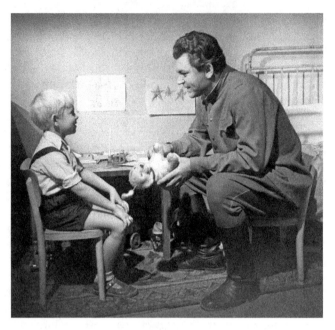

Figure 2.12. Still from *Little Sergei* (1960). Discovering the world together
and anew.

Besides bicycles, bus rides, stuffed monkeys, and eventually a baby
brother, Korostelev offers his stepson small but crucial lessons in life.
When a visitor gives Serezha a piece of candy that turns out to be an
empty wrapper, little Sergei matter-of-factly calls the guest a jackass.
His mother Mar'iana demands an apology and when it isn't promptly
forthcoming, grounds him for the rest of the day. When Korostelev arrives home later that evening, he good-humouredly disagrees with his
wife's reaction, amused that the boy had called the fool by his proper
name. The stepfather sides with his stepson's reaction referring to his
response as justified criticism (*spravedlivaia kritika*). Overhearing this,
Serezha falls asleep contented, sure of his future behaviour.

Korostelev's parenting techniques benefit Sergei: he has an instinctive feel for what masculine qualities are necessary for success in Soviet society. In approving of Serezha's actions, Korostelev censures
Mar'iana's emphasis on proper behaviour, for it would deny Serezha
his right to express justified criticism. Being a conscientious man, Korostelev wants Serezha to rebuke anyone who demonstrates unprinci-
pled behaviour. Minding one's manners in such circumstances would

achieve nothing but decorum, and being a communist man of vision, he is aware that widespread acceptance of a status quo simply so as not to offend anyone would impede the building of communism. Serezha might not have the vision at that moment, but Korostelev provides him with the tools and authorization to achieve it. At the same time, although this moment builds a stronger and more open relationship between the stepfather and his charge, it diminishes automatic respect for authority figures in general. The sixties model of filial relations embodied by Sergei and his stepfather is a far cry from stories about Pavlik Morozov, who denounced his father for supposedly forging and selling documents to enemies of the Soviet state. Even though Pavlik's central goal was to serve justice, his sense of right and wrong was strictly moderated by party dictums. Contrastingly, Serezha's ethics were directed by his own innate sense of universal right and wrong. As he himself declaims: I have a heart!

Korostelev not only gives Serezha the courage to express himself, but also sets an example. He is driven but not unreasonable. He is at the same time sensible and sensitive, warm but impartial, amicable but demanding. He denies himself sleep and meals but still manages to provide for the happiness of his family, giving both material goods and tender affection. As Serezha falls asleep on a couch in a conference room where his stepfather is meeting with a group of admiring workers, he comments to himself: "Of course he cannot eat. What would they do without him? When I grow up I'd like to become a *kolkhoz* chairman." Korostelev teaches Sergei the importance of communicating clearly and patiently, encourages him to speak his mind, supports him in employing justifiable criticism when necessary, and demonstrates that it is important to earn both the respect of co-workers and the affection of family members. All of these traits represent identity markers of post-Stalinist masculinity.

The stepfather, meanwhile, benefits from his stepson's example. As preparations to move to the city of Kholmogorod are under way, Serezha comes down with a fever, and the adults decide to leave him behind until he recovers. Serezha is devastated, and Korostelev tries reasoning with him, explaining the concept of duty and obligation (*Est' takoe slovo – nado*). The boy grasps the meaning of his stepfather's message because he has seen him living this very lesson at the *kolkhoz*. He respects and abides by his stepfather's wish and gives his word of honour (his manly word – *muzhskoe slovo*) that he will be brave and patient until they return for him. Little Sergei cannot, however, stop what he was doing all along – remaining faithful to the drumbeats of his heart. As the truck begins to pull away, Sergei turns away, head bowed and

eyes in tears. Suddenly, with a tearful face, Korostelev shouts out to
Serezha to collect his things and climb into the truck. As the mother
protests the decision, Korostelev resolutely responds that he simply
cannot leave the boy behind. As a *kolkhoz* chairman he has learned to
approach the needs of individuals with tact and balance those with societal demands. Serezha has taught him not only to listen to the voices
of others but to heed his own heart as well.

As the film ends, a jubilant Sergei sits next to his stepfather en route
to Kholmogorod. His trip is made possible by Korostelev's ability to
recognize the difference between the weighty "must," which guides the
dutiful actions within the collective, and the drumbeats of the heart
that give personal experiences value and meaning. Korostelev thus becomes the masculine paradigm of the early Khrushchev era since he
skilfully manages to satisfy his family's material needs while practising
the virtues of humility and modesty. As such, he, rather than Mar'iana,
represents the optimal example for Sergei. In the end, it is clear that
neither Korostelev nor Sergei could have developed without each other's mutual influence; the development of one is conditioned by the
presence of the other.

Conclusion

In 1957, Soviet cinemas showcased an allegorical and cautionary tale
about the powerful role fathers play in the lives of children. Sergei
Gerasimov, a giant of Soviet cinema, brought to life a Russian classic:
Gutta-Percha Boy. First published in 1883 by famed Russian author Dmitrii Vasil'evich Grigorovich, the short story was adapted into a movie
twice, in 1915 and 1957. The story is set in fin de siècle Russia and involves an eight-year-old orphan, Petia, who has been given to a circus
for training. His instructor is the harsh and cruel German acrobat Karl
Bekker, whose only motivational technique is corporal punishment.

Because of the boy's elasticity, he is given the nickname Gutta-Percha,
after a type of natural rubber tapped from trees. Becker keeps pushing
Petia to complete ever more complex and dangerous stunts; the clown
Edwards is the only one who shows the orphaned boy any sympathy
and attention. But the clown's affection is not enough to protect Petia
from Bekker's merciless ambition. In the final scenes of the film, Bekker forces the boy to perform an act he is unprepared to do. Petia slips
and falls to his death as the audience looks on. Clearly, the boy was
bendable but not unbreakable, and the force that broke him was the
cruelty of the world around him, embodied in the thoughtlessness of
his "guardian" Bekker.

Gerasimov's remake was meant to showcase the moral bankruptcy of tsarist society, which exploited its citizens and cared nothing for its most defenceless. Although set in the imperial era, the film offers two starkly different models of fatherhood, and it is evident that the authoritarian approach to parenthood leads to certain death. The caring Edwards, although unable to protect Petia from the brutality of the system, is nonetheless clearly elevated as a masculine model to emulate. Although the film was not a box office hit, it did encapsulate the Soviet cinematographers' prescription for ideal fatherhood. The essence of sixties paternity can be accurately expressed by modifying the famous Bette Davis quip on aging: "Being a dad is not for sissies." The films of the period made it clear that fatherhood, although expected, did not come naturally to Soviet men. Precisely because Soviet filmmakers framed fatherhood as a dramatic process, films of the time investigated it from a range of perspectives. How exactly did one become a father? Some films reflected thoughtfully on the social position of single mothers but also used them as a prop; the real focus was on coaching men to do the morally upright thing when another man couldn't or wouldn't. Other films emphasized the dangers of failing to fulfil parental duties. No medals were given out to dads who merely showed up; Soviet filmmakers expected their compatriots to foster real and meaningful relationships with their (male) offspring.

Regardless of the kind of scenario they focused on, Soviet filmmakers outlined a key set of criteria for effective fatherhood. First, the "condition of fatherhood" was elected rather than given. The biological fact of paternity was essentially irrelevant; fatherhood was defined in terms of the care and attention that fathers paid to their offspring. Also, this attention had to strike the right balance between guidance on the one hand and the capacity to listen and learn from the offspring on the other. A man without a family was incomplete, and so was a man who did not become a family man. But it was important that one be a family man in the full sense of that word: active, present, and thoughtful. Romantic and marital relationships were clearly important, but there was something distinct about fatherhood. Thus fatherhood, as an experience, was presented as an essential gateway into adulthood, in some senses more important than marriage. Fatherhood was more than an extension of a marital relationship; it also played a unique and specific role in the life of the adult Soviet man. Indeed, it was often more important for the father to listen to his son than vice versa. If in Stalin-era filmmaking men forged their character by taking the advice of an ideologically conscious and usually older mentor, then after Stalin filmmakers turned that model on its head, anticipating that men could learn a great deal from their protégés. But as the next chapter shows, fatherhood was ennobling only with regard to younger children. With offspring in their teens and twenties, the relationship was more acrimonious and tense, underscoring the limits of partnership between men and their adult sons and protégés. The generational conflict that defined the sixties globally also manifested itself in the Soviet Union. The fathers-and-sons conflict of the 1860s reappeared a century later and proved to be every bit as publicly contentious as the one that shook the imperial system.

Chapter Three

Fathers versus Sons, or, the Great Soviet Family in Trouble

One of the most (in)famous films of the Khrushchev era was M.M. Khutsiev's *Lenin's Guard* (Zastava Il'icha, 1962).[1] One scene became especially contentious. It featured an improbable reunion between the young protagonist Sergei and the ghost of his father, who died during the Second World War when he was only twenty-one. Sergei, who is struggling to determine life's purpose, asks for his father's advice on how to live. Although the son has no living memory of him, their exchange evokes genuine intimacy. In a moment of compassion, the father locks eyes with Sergei, making it clear that the advice comes from the heart (Figure 3.1). He then counsels him: "One must simply live." But when Sergei urges his father to reveal exactly how one should live, the father responds with a question: "How old are you?" And when the son tells his father he is twenty-three, the latter replies: "Well, I am twenty-one. How am I supposed to help you?" The ghost then vanishes.

The ideological campaign that N.S. Khrushchev galvanized against Khutsiev earned the movie its legendary status. Overnight, *Lenin's Guard* became the *enfant terrible* of the film industry, and for the next several years it was invoked at major political gatherings as an example of ideological immaturity *par excellence*. During a meeting with four hundred members of the artistic intelligentsia in the Kremlin's Sverdlov Hall in March 1963, Khrushchev vehemently objected that the film portrayed the father as incapable of guiding his son: "Will anyone believe that a father would not answer his son's question and wouldn't help him by advising him how to find the right path in life? ... The idea [of the scene] is to impress upon the children that their fathers cannot be teachers in life, and that there is no point in turning to them for advice."[2] Although Khutsiev and others, such as veteran movie director M. Romm, tried to emphasize the movie's expressed faith in the young to forge their own path, Khrushchev remained insistent that this kind of

Figure 3.1. The infamous father–son exchange in *Lenin's Guard*.

portrayal of intergenerational relationships contradicted Soviet reality. He protested that the father-and-son problem was slanderous because "there are no divisions between generations in Soviet socialist society."[3] Those words became a mantra repeated ad nauseam as a warning to other artists who might attempt to question the unbreakable ties that bonded Soviet generations.[4]

The regime considered depictions of generational dynamics fundamental to its domestic image; indeed, it viewed such depictions as a crucial aspect of the Cold War. On 18 June 1963, three months after Khrushchev had criticized *Lenin's Guard*, a Central Committee plenum yet again condemned the notion of generational conflict, describing it as patently anti-Soviet. In his opening speech, L.F. Il'ichev, the CPSU secretary in charge of propaganda, contended that the "enemies of socialism" were exploiting the fictitious discord between "fathers and sons" to weaken the Communist Party's mandate to govern: "Certain members of the intelligentsia ... have taken up the fabricated generational conflict and begun promoting it left and right, delighting our opponents. Our enemies think that the distorted representation of Soviet life will enable them to undermine the authority of party leaders ... and popularize anarchism."[5] Not only were Soviet scriptwriters and directors committing an ideological sin by depicting generational conflict, but they were also supporting "the imperialist cause" by disseminating "rotten Trotskyite ideas about the moral degradation of the older generation."[6]

Khutsiev's scene incensed the top leadership because it negated the official line that Soviet youth were tightly bound to the state's agenda and to the older generations' historic experiences. Khrushchev's announcement at the Twenty-Second Party Congress in 1961 that "the present generation will live under Communism" only strengthened the party's insistence that the younger generation see its aspirations as inseparable from official dictates. By this logic, Sergei, an exemplar of heroes who had been appearing on-screen since 1953, was now a liability since he had compromised the politically sacrosanct idea that the Party led a unified people in a generational relay (*estafeta pokolenii*) whose finish line was communism. The baton that Marx and Engels passed on to Lenin, and that Lenin then entrusted to the Communist Party under Stalin's leadership, was now to be surrendered to young men who knew Lenin only as a historic figure and who associated Stalin with the crimes he had committed.

Thus Khutsiev's scene – however much it embraced the spirit of de-Stalinization – provoked a strong reaction from Khrushchev because the young director was striking at two myths central to Bolshevik rule. First, he was implying that the party elders, tainted as they were by association with the Stalinist regime, should allow a modicum of popular self-governance and political autonomy. Second, by questioning the authority of the generation then in power, he was questioning the idea that men (should) define their gendered identity only under the guidance of a politically conscious father figure and only in a collectivist homosocial context. The father-and-son dialogue in *Lenin's Guard* simultaneously undermined state-sponsored views on the hierarchical nature of Soviet authority and challenged official ideals about the formation of masculine identity.

Khutsiev's film was a watershed moment in redefining post-Stalinist masculinity and its relationship to political authority. At the same time, it was also the outgrowth of a broader cultural and cinematic trend that had been critically re-examining and reformulating the Stalin-era generational trope ever since Khrushchev's secret speech.[7] After 1956, artists and commentators struggled to find new ways to confront the authoritarian principles that had led to Stalin's personality cult and reign of terror. The masculine experience and male relationships had served as central tropes of the Stalinist regime; now, sixties filmmakers were exploiting the same masculine tropes but inverting them in order to destabilize the official myth that had enabled the Stalin-era tyranny: the myth of "the great Soviet family."[8] This reductive myth, which identified the Party apparatus and Stalin as the exclusive producers and guardians of totalizing truths, had functioned as the structuring logic for Stalinist culture in general and for films in particular. Stalinist cinema promoted this patriarchal world view by featuring hardened, hypermasculine heroes whose initiation into the national body was directly linked to their obedience to an older, politically conscious father figure.[9] The simultaneous processes of achieving political maturity and realizing one's masculinity thus involved obeying hierarchy, becoming an unwavering champion of collective interests, and achieving victory in Stalin's or the Party's name.

This vision of a masculine and, by extension, national collective imagined Soviet citizens as dependent on the infallible leadership of the Party elders and ensured a clear sociopolitical division between those who produced knowledge and those who internalized it – that is, between wise fathers and their dutiful progeny. Hardly a nation of equals, the "great Soviet family" reserved its validation for men who followed the lead of their elders by willingly sacrificing themselves whenever necessary. Prompted by Khrushchev's denunciation of Stalin's personality cult, some directors, such as Khutsiev, began depicting more democratic relationships between men and sometimes inverted the hierarchical dynamics, making the progeny as wise as the elders (if not wiser).[10] No longer did celluloid heroes attain membership in the Soviet collective by dutifully following the lead of a politically conscious mentor.[11] The relationship between generations was becoming more egalitarian, and on occasion, younger male protagonists, like Sergei, achieved consciousness independently.

Alexander Prokhorov argues convincingly that the myth of the great Soviet family remained central to post-Stalinist culture but that the scale of the family unit had been reduced so that nuclear families stood in for the national whole. The previous chapter about paternity very much corroborates Prokhorov's thesis. But while sixties directors certainly drew families to scale, this chapter pushes back on the idea that the primary goal of Khrushchev-era narratives remained "the reconstitution and preservation of the nuclear family."[12] On the contrary, post-Stalinist culture emphasized disunity and conflict, between fathers and adult sons in particular, even as it celebrated "the generational relay" as an ideal. Here I echo Margaret Peacock's conclusion that a range of post-Stalinist films depicted "adults who had abdicated their responsibilities as parents and youth who had become ideologically disillusioned, abandoned, and devoted to the pursuit of personal goals over the needs of the state."[13] Moreover, fears about a generational chasm characterized literary life as much as they did the film industry. As Ann

Livschiz points out, "if for writers the Thaw meant expressing their desire to tell young people how to live, for young people, the Thaw meant expressing their desire not to have to listen."[14]

Anxieties about intergenerational rifts remained prominent not only because those rifts challenged the Soviet system's ideological and symbolic order but also because they reflected broader societal concerns. First, juvenile delinquency, a problem that had plagued the system since its inception, had shown no signs of abating, in part because Khrushchev and Brezhnev used hooliganism as a catch-all category for all manner of "antisocial" behaviour.[15] Although most convicted hooligans were adult men in their late twenties and thirties, juvenile hooliganism "often monopolized the attention of the authorities and mass media."[16] Second, the ongoing superpower conflict made the Party nervous about the war-readiness of its postwar generation. Peacock points out that "governments on both sides of the Iron Curtain took unprecedented legal steps to intervene in the lives of the young ... because it was thought by many that parents simply had no idea how to raise Cold War kids."[17] Concerns about hooliganism and the Cold War were themselves rooted in a panic about fatherlessness (bezotsovsh-china).[18] As I discussed in the previous chapter, the wartime demographic collapse and correlated gender imbalance[19] had resulted in thousands of single-mother households, which the public deemed inferior to nuclear families. In one story typical of the sixties coming-of-age genre, a single mother ponders the causes of her son's misbehaviour and concludes that she is powerless, for "a boy always needs a father, a good father."[20] Fears that Soviet boys would grow up without male role models at home were compounded by the skyrocketing postwar divorce rates, which rose by 270 per cent between 1955 and 1965.[21] As is evident from Khutsiev's scene, Soviet directors did little to allay these interrelated anxieties, but rather amplified them by parading unassertive and ineffective patriarchs across the silver screen.

But even the filmmakers' liberalizing attitude had its limits; throughout the 1950s and '60s the idea of a generational relay remained framed by patriarchal logic and cast in predominantly masculine terms. This is not to say that "daughters" did not feature in these discussions, but they appeared as secondary and supporting characters to the "sons." If the sons were the fathers' sidekicks, the daughters were the sidekicks' sidekicks. And though "daughters" might feature in a generational relay in a distant second position, the head of the relay was always a father, never a mother. Even Soviet artists invested in challenging the concept of a generational relay did not seem concerned to elevate the position of "daughters" or "mothers" in the power paradigm. Instead, they challenged the hierarchical nature of the power relations in Soviet society so as to allow "sons" a more prominent and independent role in public life. Even those artists who advocated greater autonomy for Soviet youth frequently defaulted to the hierarchical and exclusively masculine notion of the generational relay. As a result, any issue tied to generational conflict remained expressed in exclusively masculine terms.

The (Undeserving) Inheritors of the Generational Relay: Errant Sons in the Soviet Press

Since the generational relay was a key tenet of Soviet ideology, its mention in the press and popular culture remained ubiquitous from the mid-1950s onward. In the mid-1950s the term established a direct connection between veterans of the Civil War and the Second World War. By the late 1950s, "generational relay" alluded to generational re-lations more generally rather than being restricted to the military arena. For instance, in 1957, the fortieth anniversary of the Bolshevik Revolu-tion, *Pravda* boasted that three generations of Bolsheviks had built the socialist system; this deliberate integration of the postwar generation into the state-sanctioned national narrative spoke to the premium the Party placed on the Soviet youth delivering its promise.[22] The visual representation of the "generational relay" could be seen on the October 1958 cover of *Krokodil*, which featured a grandfather leafing through a photo album and bragging that three generations of his family – all seated around the dining room table and surrounded by material comforts – had participated in different All-Union Komsomol plenums.

The interconnectedness of generations sometimes stretched into Rus-sia's imperial past, as it did on a 1956 *Krokodil* cover, which featured Ermak, a sixteenth-century Cossack *ataman* who had started the Rus-sian colonization of Siberia, welcoming young Virgin Lands volunteers as the region's modern conquerors (Figure 3.2). Occasionally, the term was used ironically, as it was in a 1963 *Krokodil* cartoon, which mocked bad habits, such as gluttony and sloth, being passed down from father to son; the title of the drawing is "A family relay"[23] (Figure 3.3). By the early 1970s, however, the phrase was so ubiquitous that it had lost it concrete meaning.

Before it turned into a throwaway expression, the interpretation of "generational relay" remained central to presenting the harmony of the Soviet system. In official rhetoric, the social order worked as well as it did because young men willingly and unblinkingly followed the lead of their (male) seniors. For instance, Valentin Kataev, the founder and

Figure 3.2. "Welcome to the new conquerors of Siberia!" *Krokodil* 17 (1956), cover.

Figure 3.3. "A family relay." *Krokodil* 18 (1963): 6.

editor of the avant-garde journal *Youth* (Iunost'), related an anecdote from his 1958 visit to China: His hosts unexpectedly asked him to comment on Soviet youth. Tellingly, he conflated the activities of all the preceding generations into a string of heroic, exclusively male, feats: the October Revolution, the Civil War, the Five-Year Plans, the Second World War, and, finally, the Virgin Lands campaign. In all these victories, Kataev painted the Komsomol as the Party's indispensable, albeit still junior, associate.

Kataev's observation about the Civil War was one he would repeat for all the subsequent national triumphs: "Forever shall we remember the heroism of the young contemporary hero; he was a trusty partner to his father and elder brothers on all fronts of our people's revolutionary past."[24] Although the term relay implies a kind of equality, it was clear from public pronouncements such as Kataev's that the logic of the relay was to carry the baton without reflecting critically on the race or one's role in it. The younger brothers and sons in Kataev's metaphor were expected to follow the lead of their "fathers and older brothers" rather than take part in the event on an equal footing.

But not everyone agreed that Soviet youth should automatically be granted access to the relay; they contended instead that one's place in the race ought to be earned. While much of the official rhetoric described the great majority of Soviet youth as inheriting their fathers' legacy by default, some commentators (Second World War veterans in particular) pointed out that it was impossible for young people to fully appreciate the wartime struggles, from which they had been protected. They took this claim further to argue that because the older, wartime generations had sheltered them from the savagery of the most recent war, the postwar generation was now self-indulgent and irresponsible. For instance, Liubov' Kabo, a prominent novelist who had experienced the horrors of the Second World War first-hand, believed that those born during the war had grown up without principles because they had been spared the atrocities of combat. Speaking specifically about fourteen- to eighteen-year-olds born between 1941 and 1945, she averred that high school graduates knew about mortal danger and personal loss only from literature and hearsay. When it came to facing and overcoming obstacles, they usually opted for the easiest path. Kabo noted as well that Soviet youth romanticized concepts such as labour and hardship in their essays but had never endured true suffering. She suggested that to address this problem, young people should be compelled to engage in physical and manual labour rather than focus solely on their intellectual development.[25] Her critique echoed the sentiments expressed by Alexander Shelepin, a long-time member of the Central Committee

(1952–76), who declared at the 1954 Komsomol Congress: "It is wrong when some Pioneer leaders, Komsomol officials, and teachers tell the schoolchildren: 'Study hard and you're sure to become a scientist, an engineer, or a writer'– and fail to interest him in becoming a skilled workman, mechanic, tractor driver, or combine operator." He ended by arguing that the Komsomol must do a great deal more to instil in young people a "love of manual labor."[26] Implicit in these exchanges was the idea that young men and women had become emasculated during their schooling and required hardening in fields, in mine tunnels, and on factory floors.

Throughout the 1950s the leadership propagated a move away from middle-class respectability and toward working-class dignity. By the mid-1950s, the trope that youth were being coddled was becoming firmly entrenched. At the famous Twentieth Party Congress in 1956, Marshal Kliment Voroshilov outlined a very clear attitude toward Soviet youth, asserting that "the Party and the Soviet government shall continue to bring up young people to be ideologically and physically hard-tempered [zakalennoi]."[27] Unsurprisingly, even at the beginning of de-Stalinization Voroshilov was depicting a super-heroic youth that likely existed only on Stalin-era posters: young men and women mastering the most complex aspects of applied technology while also engaging in backbreaking physical labour on construction sites. *Krokodil* frequently put on display just how divorced Soviet youth were from Voroshilov's ideal. A 1956 cartoon titled "Art and Life" features a young artist's painting in which pigs are climbing up and down a tree. When a woman asks the bearded and eclectically dressed *artiste* how the animals got up there, the urbanite casually and non-ironically remarks: "I have no idea. I only heard that pigs feed on acorns" (Figure 3.4).[28] Thus the male youth is thrice removed from Voroshilov's masculine ideal: he shirks manual labour, lacks any practical knowledge, and has to be told how the "real world" operates. In this sense the *artiste* in the cartoon was delivering exactly what *Krokodil* specialized in throughout the sixties: a generational stereotype of young Soviet people.

The commentaries of Voroshilov, Shelepin, and Kabo should also be seen as part of a debate spurred by one of Khrushchev's pet projects: school reform. The fundamental shift proposed by this reorganization consisted of moving away from instruction performed at school toward a policy that linked schools with enterprises and that sought to involve pupils more directly in production processes. In essence, this law was an attempt to unify general and polytechnical education with industry.[29] Test-piloting of this restructuring began as early as 1954, and in December 1958 the law went into effect under the official title

Figure 3.4. "Art and Life." *Krokodil* 17 (1956): 4.

"On strengthening ties between school and life, and further developing public education in the country."[30] The country-wide implementation of the law was mandated by 1963. With the 1958 decree, an eleventh year was added to the ten-year school program, and these schools were renamed to reflect the addition of "production training" (*proizvodst-vennoe obuchenie*). Students were expected to achieve successive ranks and graduate with the ability to enter the production process as skilled workers. A 1954 poster, "You, too, will become a master of your craft," by V.V. Sur'ianinov, provided an idealized image of the school reform's end product: a youth (almost always male) learning directly from sea-soned (male) professionals and maturing as a citizen in the process. It is significant that the apprentice is depicted in the seconds prior to receiving judgment on his labour and, by extension, on his worth as a worker and a man-in-the-making. This is an obvious representation of a top-down relationship in which self-worth is achieved solely through the senior master's validation. Both the craft and one's masculinity thus become an apprenticeship (Figure 3.5). As with previous depictions of the

Figure 3.5. V.V. Sur'ianinov, "You, too, will become a master of your craft!" (1954)

generational relay, this transference of knowledge and expertise was rendered as exclusively male. Considering the emphasis on technical and manual labour and the conscious move away from academics, it is clear that Khrushchev saw youth, particularly young men, as having become too "soft" in classroom settings.

In the lead-up to announcing the controversial law, Khrushchev made a hard sell, often chastising Komsomol and non-Komsomol members alike. At the Thirteenth Komsomol Congress, eight months before the law went into effect, he chided youth for their condescending attitude toward labour and their expectation that everything would be done for them (*v gotovom vide*). Khrushchev made plain that he hoped hard work would cure two major social ills: youth riding the coattails of their parents (entitlement) and drunkenness/hooliganism. The Party Secretary warned that "sonnies and daughterlings must, by the virtue of their own labour, win the respect of people"[31] and not live at the expense of "mommies' and daddies'" reputation and connections. Regarding drunkenness, he observed that "there are among the youth such 'heroes' who boast of spending nights in drunk tanks, as if they went to the theater."[32] Khrushchev maintained that since there was no unemployment or exploitation in the Soviet Union, there was also no reason for a young man to poison his mind with alcohol. The two greatest sins of the young generation were indications that so much had been done for them that they had developed two opposite but equally dangerous habits: laziness/apathy and destructiveness/hooliganism. The Cold War cast a long shadow over Khrushchev's urging youth to work smarter and harder as he pronounced that "in the era of colossal competition between socialism and capitalism, the tempo of production is essential."[33] The First Secretary was implying that errant youth could cost the country the next war. Given all this, Article Six of the school reform law emphasized that "the most important task of teachers, parents and public organizations is to further improve students' behaviour at school, in the family, and on the street."[34]

Following the announcement of the 1958 decree, newspapers continued to feature stories about young people's misguided sense of individualism, attesting to the fact that school reform was very much necessary as a cure for wayward youth – most often depicted as young men. A 1959 *Krokodil* cartoon poked fun at a young man's unwillingness to serve in the far reaches of Siberia and Kazakhstan after graduation, "having eyes" only for Moscow.[35] In the left-hand frame, the fancily dressed youth – a *stiliaga*, or "hipster," in the parlance of the day – cannot read the optometrist's eye chart in which the words "Kazakhstan" and "Siberia" are most prominent, but discovers he has twenty-twenty vision for the word "Moscow" (Figure 3.6).[36]

Many commentators argued that the issue demanded more than fixing youths' behaviour and insisted that the problem was essentially moral and attitudinal. In 1960, David Zaslavskii, a journalist who was a fixture in the Stalinist literary and journalistic world and who had barely escaped the Stalinist anti-Semitic purges of 1953, denounced *stiliagi* as a particularly worrisome trend, describing them as "freaks who wore skinny pants," distinguished themselves with "their rickety legs," and sported "sheep's wool instead of a proper haircut on their brainless heads." Above all these dangers, Zaslavskii diagnosed indifference (*ravnodushie*) as public enemy number one. In Zaslavskii's opinion, "they are impossible to impress, inspire, or amaze because they have seen it all; they know it all because they know nothing."[37] The article warned that although these unimpressible youth were few in number, they could spread like weeds in a field. In the same vein as Zaslavskii, the Soviet press more generally often described the *stiliagi* lifestyle as a gateway to, and a reflection of, graver moral offences: egoism, asociality,

Figure 3.6. "A high school graduate at the optometrist." *Krokodil* 17 (1959): 11.

and ideological untrustworthiness. A 1963 *Krokodil* cartoon captured this persistent fear in featuring a *stiliaga* who, with utter disregard for his elders serving on the committee determining graduates' work placements, declares that he cannot possibly agree to being assigned to the "periphery" (Figure 3.7). Apparently without irony, he worries that the main hangout of the Moscow *stiliaga* crowd, Gor'kii Street, could not possibly survive without his presence. Visually, the distance between the young man and his elders could not be more pronounced – they are divided by two massive conference tables. Moroever, the Gor'kii Street fashionista has his back turned to the committee, barely deigning to look in their direction. It is obvious just how wide the generational chasm is.[38]

It was not uncommon to encounter the term "spiritual stiliagi" (*duhovnye stiliagi*) in the Soviet press as writers sought to identify those whose inconspicuous appearance did not reflect problematic attitudes. For instance, according to Vladimir Nemtsov, a noted science fiction writer, "everyone understands that even external imitation often leads to more dire predicaments. In pursuit of unsavory entertainment, a young person develops contempt for work, cynicism, as well as a general indifference."[39] Sixteen months later, Nemtsov upped the ante on his initial diagnosis, arguing that while his younger contemporaries might be familiar with, and even honour, rules of good behaviour, they were not true humanists. He argued that a young man can stand

Figure 3.7. "Me? Go to the periphery?" *Krokodil* 10 (1963): 5.

for a woman in public transport but lack something much more important: respect for women more generally. Nemtsov's broader point was that the postwar generation's flaunting of rules spoke to a broader issue: they had never internalized a moral compass that made social rules meaningful. The offspring had inherited socialist principles and learned them by heart, but they had never had to defend them. The point was not to make the youth memorize and abide by the rules, but to make them understand why the rules were established in the first place.[40]

Besides moralizing in the media, the authorities set out to coercively influence "youth's decision in its choice of dress, style of dancing, displays of love and affection and leisure pursuits," thus becoming even more proactive in curtailing youth autonomy.[41] Even as "Khrushchev unquestionably attempted to de-Stalinize Party and state attitude toward youth," Komsomol patrols, regular press harangues, and compulsory participation in massive public works projects intruded into ordinary young people's lives on a daily basis.[42] Despite the government's strong-arm tactics, some Soviet youth, inspired by Western and pre-Soviet norms, continued to fashion an idiosyncratic subculture with its own argot, clothing styles, and artistic sensibilities. The government's vigilance had much to do with the Khrushchev era's ever-expanding notions of what constituted hooliganism as an affront to Soviet values. As Brian LaPierre points out, the government's tough-love approach in prosecuting perceived deviants in practice served to resurrect "the post-Stalinist Soviet Union's frayed sense of social solidarity, ideological certainty, and moral superiority."[43]

By 1963, when Khrushchev rejected Khutsiev's representation of Soviet youth as featured in *Lenin's Guard*, the negative depiction of the postwar generation had become old-hat. A trope had emerged that Soviet youth were bookish nerds whose experience with physical labour was limited at best and who, as a result of being coddled, had given in to a range of moral and criminal offences: cynicism, hooliganism, slothfulness, and materialism. When Party propagandist-in-chief Il'ichev openly chided Soviet youth in June 1963, he was treading on familiar ground. In his famous speech in June 1963, Il'ichev provided two examples of wayward Soviet youth; the drunken reveller walking down the street pouring out obscenities in broad daylight, and the young man blasting music from his tape recorder and angering his entire neighbourhood. In Il'ichev's mind, these issues had nothing to do with the "right of the individual" or with "democracy." Soviet society, he declared, should declare war on feral egoism (*dikoe svoevolie*). Just in case the point was lost on anyone, Il'ichev underscored that "true freedom is not about ignoring the rules of the socialist order but about intentionally fulfilling them."[44] That *Krokodil* did not drop the ball in finding fault in young people's delusions of grandeur is evident in a cartoon titled "Self-advertising poet," which features a young poet declaiming (presumably) his own verses. His body serves as an advertising column plastered with posters reading "I about myself," "I, alone," "Me abroad."[45] In one fell swoop, the cartoonist has succeeded in ridiculing a slew of postwar youth's cardinal sins: narcissism, superficiality, effeminacy, uncritical worship of Western trends, and reverence for poetic idleness over manual labour (Figure 3.8). Clearly, these failings constituted an affront to ideological and gender rules.

The Stalin-era and wartime generations also doubled down on the prescription for the alleged crisis among Soviet youth: the advice and guidance of their elders. Il'ichev declaimed: "Sometimes young people do not receive good advice, and then make hasty conclusions, compensating their political immaturity with loud phrases and nihilistic posturing. All of our organizations and general public should take care

Поэт Саморекламов   Рисунок К. НЕВЛЕРА

Figure 3.8. "Self-advertising poet." *Krokodil* 5 (1963): 2.

of our youth and cultivate in every young person a deep respect for
the victories of their fathers and grandfathers, thus inculcating in them
proper ideological views on life, on society, on work, on the family." In
this, he seemed to have been rewording Article Six of the 1958 school
reform law: "The most important task of teachers, parents and public
organizations is to further improve students' behaviour at school, in
the family, and on the street." He insisted that the older generation was
indispensable to the younger and that it had a lot to offer Soviet youth:
vast experience, a belief system, fiery enthusiasm, revolutionary courage, integrity, and, finally, constant readiness to do socially beneficial
work.[46] Yet it seemed that in practice, fathers and grandfathers needed
to beg youth to participate in realizing the common good, as depicted
on the 1963 *Krokodil* cover. In this satirical scene, a variety of Komsomol,
Party, and factory leaders implore the young worker to "not shame the
collective" and to "overcome his shortcomings."[47] In an ironic reversal
of Sur'ianinov's 1954 poster "You, too, will become a master of your
craft!," and with clear allusions to iconographic images of a saint being surrounded by worshipers, the cartoon mocks the elders for surrendering their authority and for allowing the novice to call the shots

Figure 3.9. "We beg you to overcome your flaws." *Krokodil* 6 (1963), cover.

(Figure 3.9). Clearly, the generational relay was in trouble, even without Khutsiev's film.

Despite the frequent and vociferous denunciations of Soviet youth, the Party continued to, paradoxically, insist on the unbreakable bond between different age groups in the Soviet Union. Upon the return of cosmonauts Valentina Tereshkova and Valerii Bykovskii in 1963, Nikita Khrushchev declared that there could be no such thing as a conflict of generations in the Soviet Union, foreign reporters' claims to the contrary. Unlike in the West, Khrushchev argued, the Soviet generations were marching in unison down a common Leninist road.[48] And it was not just Khrushchev who kept denying that a conflict of generations existed. In an interview, the editor-in-chief of the journal *Novyi Mir*, A.T. Tvardovskii, argued that a conflict of generations was a figment of Western propaganda. Echoing Khrushchev, he maintained that the generations were unified in their goals; then he went even further, maintaining that the very notion of generations was redundant in the Soviet Union since all citizens, regardless of age, agreed on the nation's ideals and basic values.[49] Discussions of the generational conflict predominated in 1963 and 1964 and reverberated thereafter. In 1967, Konstantin Fedin, the First Secretary of the Soviet Union of Writers, recalled that "not too long ago, our ideological enemies propagated this nonsensical idea that in Soviet literature there existed a conflict between generations." In Fedin's mind, these foes were taking advantage of the "complexities of our spiritual life that accompanied the process of trying to overcome the personality cult."[50]

Official declarations about intergenerational harmony notwithstanding, there remained those who did not consider the issue resolved and who thought of the younger generation as not having proved their mettle. In 1967, poet Evgenii Vinokurov spoke about the division between those who had participated in the great cataclysm of their age and those that were born too late to do so. He opens his reminiscences by noting "how many generations of young people complained they were born too late, lamenting they had missed out on the most significant historical events."[51] According to Vinokurov, the Second World War had defined an entire generation of men, since "there exists a virility [*muzhestvennost'*] that is accessible but to a few." Considering that he was referring to the unquestionable unity and loyalty of soldiers as a brotherhood, it is clear that Vinokurov imagined a masculine utopia that was specific to his generation of male combatants. This kind of interpretation of the past, accessible to only one generation of men, embodied the quiet desperation of many sixties discussions of the postwar generational chasm.

The Brezhnev government, too, implicitly conceded that the proscribed guidance of the senior generations had proved ineffective in the face of Soviet youth's destructive tendencies.[52] Hooliganism among teenagers appears to have been widespread enough to merit the 28 July 1966 decree "On Strengthening the Liability for Hooliganism." The Presidium of the Supreme Soviet of the USSR set forth clear and severe punishments for acts of hooliganism and, in many instances, expanded them.[53] Although the legislation did not focus on teenagers per se, Article Fifteen specified punishments for juvenile delinquents, especially those between the ages of fourteen and sixteen and sixteen to eighteen. Whether the plenum worked with concrete data is uncertain, but it is clear that they considered these two age groups deserving of particular attention. In the aftermath of the announcement, *Krokodil* dedicated two of its 1966 covers to hooliganism, treating the phenomenon as an expression of postwar masculinity. In the June edition, two "sheepish" parents profess to the police that their son is a "lamb" and could not be guilty of hooliganism (Figure 3.10). The August 1966 cover shows a young Neanderthal figure encircled by an impregnable series of anti-hooligan laws (Figure 3.11). Clearly,

Figure 3.10. "Our little lamb." On the left, *Krokodil* 17 (1966), cover.

Figure 3.11. "Surrounded." On the right, *Krokodil* 23 (1966), cover.

a large enough portion of young Soviet men were viewed as a serious enough threat to public peace to make the Brezhnev cabinet need to appear tough on crime.

Ultimately, the Party wanted it both ways when it discussed Soviet youth, particularly young men. On the one hand, it depicted them as wholesome and committed future communists, marching in unison and offering obeisance to their fathers and grandfathers. On the other hand, it complained that Soviet youth were not only ignorant about the basic facts of life but also actively engaged in criminal activity, destroying collective property, and disturbing the peace. Although mutually exclusive, these contrary depictions achieved the same goal: the Party, and the older generation of men more broadly, portrayed themselves as deserving of unconditional support – either because the idealized youth willingly submitted or because the imperfect youth needed the firm guidance of those who knew better. Of the two depictions of Soviet youth, the imperfect one predominated. Yet at the same time, most of the period's films argued that youth's sense of being unmoored, disoriented, and eager to carve out a space of their own stemmed from their desire to redeem the sins of the Stalinist generation.

The Generational Relay That Wasn't: Fathers Who Cannot Lead

Khrushchev's denunciations of generational conflict in the Soviet Union upped the ante on discussions about the state of the nation's youth. But the notion that something was "off" with Soviet youth and the talk of a generational conflict preceded the hubbub surrounding *Lenin's Guard*, particularly in the arts and especially in film. Playwrights, writers, and filmmakers emphasized the independent-mindedness and idealism of the younger generation and the inability of the generations to find a common language. But rather than dismissing the elders wholesale, these productions moderated the strict hierarchy of the generational relay. They cast the older generation in the supporting role and asserted that it was imperative that young people autonomously uncover their life philosophy. They agreed (either out of conviction or for political expediency) that the Party had indeed unearthed immutable historical axioms, but at the same time they argued that youth needed to test these truths for themselves before they could wholeheartedly embrace them.

Perhaps official praise for Soviet youth's industriousness was at its apex during the Virgin Lands campaign, when around 300,000 teenagers and thousands of young adults rushed to help with yet uncultivated lands in parts of northern Kazakhstan and the Altai region of the RSFSR. Although this campaign was not exclusive to the postwar generation, it nonetheless acted as an unofficial public referendum on Soviet youth. Starting in 1954 and into the early 1960s, innumerable articles praised the industriousness of teenage and young adult volunteers, who undertook the quixotic task of conquering the so-called virgin and fallow lands.

This venture was intended to give Soviet youth their own crucible moment in Soviet history. If their grandfathers spearheaded the revolution and won the Civil War and their fathers vanquished Nazism, then the conquest of the Virgin Lands would/should be *their* epic achievement. All the conditions for romantic heroism were present: hard labour in adverse weather, construction of farms and homes from scratch, and the shattering of record-breaking production targets. On a practical level, the youthful volunteers, under the guidance of their elders, would solve the perennial problem of grain shortages as well as provide the postwar generation with the kinds of practicums Khrushchev's school reform envisioned.

Although this massive endeavour included both sexes, it was often cast as a primarily masculine project. Recruiting posters, although not featuring only men, very frequently depended on tropes generally associated with war: duty, sacrifice, national honour, and (male) camaraderie. Two posters stand out in this regard: V. Ivanov's "I will be proud of you" (1954) and A.G. Kruchina's "Demobilized soldiers! The Virgin Lands need our young hands!" (1960). The first poster references the parting of a mother and son, evoking the spirit of 1941, when millions of mothers sent their male offspring off to the front (Figure 3.12). Kruchina's poster, commissioned by the Defence Ministry, unambiguously depicts the Virgin Lands as a front in need of conquest as well as a field of battle on which postwar youth will be able to prove themselves worthy of their fathers' wartime legacy. With one hand on the tractor wheel and the other high in air, the uniformed youth evokes mobilization posters of the wartime era; having exchanged the tank for the tractor, the demobilized soldier is ready to take on the new mission.

The Soviet press was keen to capture men in uniform either on their way to "the front" of the Virgin Lands or on the agricultural "front lines." A 1960 photograph featuring soldiers in the wheat fields of Kazakhstan captures the all-male camaraderie as well as the spirit of (peaceable) conquest (*osvoenie*) the authorities were keen to sell to the public (Figure 3.13). These former soldiers set the martial tone expected of civilian participants. Even in an era of peaceful coexistence, wartime preparedness remained a potent cultural imperative.

Figure 3.12. "I will be proud of you!" (1954)

Figure 3.13. Soldiers on a wheat field during the Virgin Lands
development in Kazakhstan.

КРАСНА ВЕСНА ОТЛИЧНЫМ СЕВОМ

Figure 3.14. "Spring radiates with an excellent harvest." (1954)

Women, too, featured in this propaganda effort, but they were generally either absent or relegated to secondary positions. This dynamic is most evident in the recruiting posters from 1954, titled "Cultivate the Virgin Lands!" by V.M. Livanova. In this image women are included as active participants but follow the lead of their male peers as distant seconds. In general, when women are highlighted in Virgin Lands visual iconography, they are placed in a pastoral and bucolic setting, a context coded as female from the earliest days of Soviet visual propaganda (Figure 3.14).[54] Men, on the other hand, often stand next to, or are associated with, machinery and technology in general, for these are coded as tools of non-military conquest. For instance, in a 1954 poster by N. Tereshchenko, a young woman boasts of a plentiful harvest, abstractly personifying spring and fertility rather than being shown in an active or leadership role. She is implicitly being tied to the bountiful crops, but her presence seems largely ornamental. In complete reverse, V. Govorkov's 1955 poster celebrates one young man's mastery of various machinery as the title declares "I conquered." His authority is further accentuated by the fact that he towers over the equipment he now operates, personifying the "man over machine" trope (Figure 3.15).

Figure 3.15. "I conquered." (1955)

The Virgin Lands campaign was primarily a test for the "sons" to carry on the proud legacy of the "fathers and grandfathers." Plays and films about the Virgin Lands campaign – and reviews of these productions – also focused on men and relationships between men, particularly between "fathers and sons."[55] N. Pogodin's play *The Three Who Went to the Virgin Lands* (My vtroem poekhali na tselinu), which premiered in November 1955, was one of the earliest attempts to memorialize the postwar generation's experiences in the forbidding expanse of the steppe. This story about three teenagers embarking on an adventure to take part in a national project received positive coverage in the press – until *Pravda* pronounced it fatally flawed. Pogodin, according to *Pravda*, had failed to show the guiding hand of adults and Party officials in the evolution of the volunteers: "The play shows those who are being bettered but not those who are educating them, i.e. the play does not showcase the edifying and active role of the Soviet collective." This critique was also raised at the Writers' Union meeting, which charged that "the organizing and educational role of the Party must be felt more strongly, more effectively."[56] The crux of this criticism transferred onto the film *The First Echelon*, for which Pogodin wrote the script, based partly on his play. The basic problem reviewer identified was Pogodin's treatment – or rather, non-treatment – of older figures; he argued that by the middle of the film the grown-ups had become invisible in a microcosm dominated by the Komsomol youth. The film reviewer felt that dwelling on the images of the elders in a movie about the Komsomol was not paradoxical since "without adults the trip of young people to the Virgin Land would lose the scale of a large, nationwide business."[57] At the crux of the *Pravda* critique was the implication that Soviet youth could not evolve independently and required the guiding hand of the Party and other responsible adults.

Pravda not only damned Pogodin but also took a direct shot at the liberal journal *Novyi mir*, which had published the script. In particular, *Pravda's* editorial board derided the positive review penned by V.E. Kardin, a decorated Second World War veteran and literary critic who had begun his publishing career just a year prior to the play's release in 1955. Kardin's sin consisted in praising Pogodin for not only populating his microcosm with a kaleidoscope of individualized and contrasting personalities but also uniting them in a shared endeavour. Kardin wrote: "The collectives that emerge in the steppe are impressive by their sheer variety, populated as they are with contrasting personalities: idealists and gold-diggers, hard workers and bums, paupers and careerists, noted individuals and misfits, couch potatoes and drifters." *Pravda* rejected outright Kardin's assertion that it was appropriate to see these different characters labouring under the same sky, eating at the same makeshift table, and sharing similar experiences. According to *Pravda*, to equate such different types of people was to lose the sense of who was leading whom in the Virgin Lands. Thus what Pogodin successfully created – and what *Pravda* objected to – was a model of an alternative, makeshift, organic community of young people without clearly delineated hierarchies and adult supervision. Indirectly and implicitly, the debate revolved around the extent to which youth could be trusted to be left to their own (imperfect) devices – in the Virgin Lands or elsewhere.

Similar critiques emerged after the release of Iosif Kheifits's film *Horizon* (Gorizont, 1962). Like *First Echelon*, Kheifits had failed, according to film critic N. Klado, to fully develop and then resolve the central issue: generational differences and the resulting conflict. In Klado's mind, the film's title alluded to the fact that older and younger protagonists perceived different horizons. At the same time, the two generations in *Horizon*, in Klado's telling, rarely came in contact with each other, and when they did, neither side was perceptibly altered by the encounter. Klado believed that Kheifits had wasted an opportunity to address a meaningful concern of the day – generational conflict – and had chosen instead to cover a well-trodden path: a youthful individualist (errant son) leaves his collective only to return to the fold of his own accord.[58] Pogodin's play as well as *First Echelon* and *Horizon* received a great deal of attention not only because they dealt with the pressing issue of the Virgin Lands campaign but also because they were intimately linked to another divisive issue of the day: the possibility of generations coming together and making sense of one another.

If productions that neglected to emphasize the supervisory role of the Party raised eyebrows and resulted in well-meaning public critiques, then films about the deficiencies of adults led to even more vociferous debates. A range of genres reflected on the ways in which elders had failed their charges; some of the most popular 1950s and '60s films reflected on the various ways the Stalin generation seemed out of place in the postwar environment. Very much part and parcel of the de-Stalinization effort, these features were an attempt to deal, sometimes abstractly and allegorically, with the difficult legacy of the Stalin era. A whole range of genres – social drama, Second World War films, and comedies – reflected on the ways in which individuals in positions of authority abused their power against their (often defenceless) charges. Comedies gently mocked the Stalinist generation for their stuffiness and "square-ness"; Second World War films demonstrated the inability of the fathers to save their sons from mortal peril; and dramas focused on the tragic fates of young protagonists as they tried to defend themselves against a cruel and indifferent society. Although taking a broad swipe at the most obviously negative elements of Stalinist culture – rigid morality, uniformity, and knee-jerk obedience – and directed at the Stalinist generation more generally, most of these features embodied the conflict as a clash between male representatives of the two generations.

In the realm of drama, Iu. Ozerov's 1955 film *Son* became a box office hit, selling around 28.3 million tickets. The movie's dramatic tensions centred on a problem youth who commits an act of hooliganism and is consequently rejected by his surroundings: his schoolmates, friends, friends' parents, family members, and school administrators. He stumbles onto a construction site, where he is integrated into the labouring collective and mends his ways. The reviewer, Valentina Liubimova, who had written more than twenty plays focusing on children and childhood and had won a Stalin Prize in 1949, found no fault in the idea that physical labour can save a man. At the same time, she asked: "But what is labour without people? Why didn't his family or his peers help him instead of insisting on their puritanical principles?" She concluded that "among all the cold and 'righteous' characters, the 'errant' young man appears animated and curious by comparison; it's no surprise that that viewer will sympathize with him."[59] In retrospect, this film served as a bellwether for other productions that explored the notion that Soviet society, although based on notions of collective good, was contributing to the demise of its younger citizens.

In similar fashion, Iulii Raizman's *And What If It's Love?* (1961) portrays a culture that is needlessly suspicious and cruel toward its youth. Not pulling any punches, Raizman's script reflects on the extent to which adults – teachers, neighbours, and family members – are not just indifferent to their charges but downright prosecutorial and punitive. Adults pervert and twist a budding love between two teenagers, depicting it as a sexual and immoral affair in the making. Inquisitorial suspiciousness and aggressive shaming finally lead the heroine of the movie to poison herself. Although she survives the suicide attempt, the closing frames of the film make it clear that she is a shell of her former self, more interested in getting on with life than in living it to the fullest. The adult most responsible for the couple's undoing is the German-language teacher, Mar'ia Pavlovna, who not only aims to "unmask" the couple but also organizes a witch-hunt and drags the entire school community with her. Her sombre suit, her hair pulled back tightly in a meagre bun, and her mechanical body movements all turn her into a relic of the Stalinist era (Figure 3.16). She manipulates, intimidates, polemicizes, and cajoles other adults until her notions of justice and propriety are satisfied and the youth is adequately disciplined and brought to heel. Raizman's production, which critics often dubbed "the Soviet Romeo and Juliet," cast serious doubt on the ability of the adult collective to rear their charges. In *And If It's Love?*, the young barely escape the rigid moralizing of the Stalinist generation with their lives. It was this particular takeaway that brought the film so much attention from the press. The tragic fate of the hero and heroine led to ticket sales totalling 22.6 million.

Even more than dramas, films about the Second World War served as straightforward vehicles for reimagining bonds between "fathers and sons." Although filmmakers naturally gravitated toward depicting the heroism inherent in the Soviet victory, they also accentuated the relative impotence of fathers to save their sons from mortal danger. The most famous Second World War productions end in the death of the son, highlighting the idea that fathers are unable to protect their sons from the war they were (partly) responsible for starting. Andrei

Figure 3.16. Mar'ia Pavlovna's witch-hunt destroys a budding romance in
And If It's Love?

Tarkovskii's *Ivan's Childhood* (Ivanovo detstvo, 1962) features a young
Second World War partisan scout who risks his life to report the latest
Nazi troop movements to the Red Army. As an orphan, Ivan is wholly
dedicated to his unit, especially his superiors; he lives for nothing but
to avenge the death of his mother and to support his comrades. It is
clear that he is a victim of German aggression. At the same time, he dies
in his final reconnaissance mission, having been urged on by his older
mentors. As the Germans begin a deadly advance, the unit leaders, his
surrogate fathers, sense that they should send him to a military academy rather than risk his life. Nonetheless, they gamble with his life,
promising one another this will be the boy's final mission. Ivan pays
the ultimate price for his guardians' risk-taking, proving that he is but
a pawn in the deadly games adults play. In the final count, the boy is
robbed twice of his childhood: once by the Germans and then by the
men who were supposed to be his protectors.

   In a less dark but no less tragic tone, the war-themed Georgian film
A Soldier's Father (Otets soldata, 1964) tells the tale of a father searching
for his son across the war-ravaged landscape. A simple wine grower,
the father ends up traversing the length of the Soviet Union and half

Figure 3.17. Father impotently gazes upon his dying son in *A Soldier's Father*.

of Europe, ending up in Berlin. But just as he is about to reach his son, a bullet pierces the young soldier's chest in the final hour of the war. The father and son only exchange a parting glance as the son, gasping for air, exhales "father" (Figure 3.17). Echoing the tragic pathos of the Pietà, the scene of a parent embracing his dead child expressed the essence of a loss that could not be recuperated even with the glory of wartime victory. This scene signalled a complete reversal of the Stalinist epic *The Fall of Berlin* (Padenie Berlina, 1950). In its culminating scene, Stalin descends, deity-like, into liberated Berlin and gives a speech in which he promises world peace and happiness; he is greeted by enthusiastic crowds holding posters with his image and waving various nations' flags. Rejecting the Stalinist triumphant narrative, *A Soldier's Father* underscores both the senselessness of war and the impotence of fathers to change the course of their children's lives. No longer a site of the country's glorious victory, Berlin is a site of deeply personal loss, incalculable in geopolitical terms. The powerlessness of the father to change the course of his son's life is no less certain than Germany's defeat.

Comedies also took on the problem of generational issues, often portraying grown-ups – particularly fathers – as rigid, moralistic, and

Figure 3.18. Ogurtsov in *Carnival Night*.

overbearing. In an unequal battle of wits, the young protagonists easily outmanoeuvre male authority figures, who are as self-righteous as they are dull. The most popular comedy of the 1950s was El'dar Riazanov's musical *Carnival Night* (Karnaval'naia Noch', 1956), which sold 45.6 million tickets and became a yearly tradition for the entire nation. The film's protagonist is a humourless middle-aged man and a quintessential bureaucrat in charge of organizing a New Year's party at the local social club (*dom kul'tury*): Serafim Ivanovich Ogurtsov. Promotional photographs and film posters depicted Ogurtsov as a Stalin-era holdover. His lack of fashion sense – evident in his baggy, double-breasted suit and dull tie – match his dim view of his charges. His signature wide-eyed and panicked facial expression betrays an innate and unremitting vigilance against anything that could be perceived as an ideological misstep. His tousled hair comes from him jumping from one location to another, always angling to preserve his bureaucratic post (Figure 3.18). Although only middle-aged, he seems hopelessly behind the times; young people eclipse him in terms of ingenuity, skills, and attractiveness. Rather than being their wise mentor, he is an obstacle.

In terms of personality, one contemporary film review described Ogurtsov in the following manner: "Ogurtsov 'won't permit,' 'won't allow,' and' 'forbids' everything that's clever, funny, original, and novel."[60] Indeed, he rejects the idea of the masquerade ball by saying: "Why should our Soviet people hide their faces? This is very untypical." Another reviewer described Ogurtsov as a dictatorial bureaucrat: "In every act he sees something suspicious. He should be directing traffic, not artistic activities. But even if he were directing traffic, he would likely put a red light on all four sides of the intersection and then brag that not a single accident happened under his watch."[61] Every act he approves is supposed to edify but is actually deathly boring; his idea of entertainment includes classical music, a folklore troupe, and, as the star act, an academic lecture about the possibility of life on Mars. His plans are ultimately foiled by a group of young people who operate behind the scenes and manage to put on a genuinely fun spectacle for the New Year that includes a masquerade ball, clowns, a magician, and a jazz band.

Mocking a bureaucrat was clearly a holdover from the Stalinist era, when bureaucratism was a staple of comedies, as it was in *Volga, Volga*. New, however, is that the young people, rather than a Soviet superhero, best the man in the grey flannel suit. In another departure from Stalinism, this comedy is not related to a production competition or to meeting quotas but is rather about truly enjoying one's free time without supervision. Of course, the symbolism of celebrating the coming of a new year alludes to the commencement of the Thaw and the end of the Stalinist "freeze." Film director Aleksandr Orlov recalled:

> I remember the stream of light, joy and humour that this picture brought to our lives. The film was a unique event, especially for those living in the provinces. The comedy was connected with the end of the Stalin era, with the onset of the Thaw, and brought hope that now our life will surely change for the better. No wonder the heroes sing in the film's finale: "Will there be happiness? Of course there will!"[62]

Significantly, the agents of this much wished-for change were the youth. *Sovetskaia kul'tura* reported that many viewers took this film as an inspiration to switch up their own lives. For instance, a police major observed how poignantly and justifiably *Carnival Night* ridiculed all supervisors who inhibited the creativity (*tvorcheskie sposobnosty*) of Soviet youth. In the same article, M. Litvina and M. Litvin, a senior engineer and a mechanic, noted that they had begun reorganizing their New

Figure 3.19. Still from *Carnival Night* (1956). The embodiment of the sixties: youthfulness, dynamism, and spontaneity.

Year's celebration right after seeing the movie: "We would like our celebration to be as merry, beautiful and youthful [*molodo*] and fresh [*svezho*] as it was in *Carnival Night*" (Figure 3.19).[63]

The good-natured humour and the lively music certainly helped *Carnival Night* sit well with the authorities, although they were initially very sceptical about its success.[64] The situational humour, buffoonery, and jolly atmosphere of the film helped make the critique of the Stalinist past more palatable.

A slightly cheekier take on the remnants of the Stalinist mindset came in the form of Elem Klimov's production *Welcome, or No Trespassing* (Dobro pozhalovat', ili postoronnim vkhod vospreshchen, 1964). Released a few months before Khrushchev's ouster, the film faced an uphill battle, for the censors deemed it to be anti-Soviet and anti-Khrushchevian; luckily for Klimov's debut feature, the country's top filmmakers defended the young director to the very last. *Welcome* was shown to Khrushchev himself, who was thoroughly entertained

Figure 3.20. *Welcome, or No Trespassing* (1964). Comrade Dynin as "big brother."

and did not feel at all slighted. Even though A.N. Groshev, the rector of VGIK, remained opposed to the production and the Goskino censors sharply restricted the movie's circulation, the film sold 13.5 million tickets and received glowing reviews in the press, demonstrating yet again the cinema industry's capacity to defend its interests despite political headwinds. In fact, Klimov's first film, like *Carnival Night*, remains a Soviet cinema classic and is fondly remembered to this day, among film professionals and audiences alike.

The action takes place in a pioneer camp, and the antogonist is a middle-aged camp leader, Comrade Dynin, who strictly regulates the lives of the pioneers. Iu. Tsarev's iconic poster gives an accurate representation of Dynin's attitude; he is the watchful "big brother" who supervises his charges closely to ensure that rules are followed to a T. Dynin's stare unsettles, because the line between a disciplinary gaze and a threat of violence appears murky (Figure 3.20). Given the visible

power differential the image suggests, can the hand that vigilantly "protects" also smother those it is meant to guard? As one reviewer noted,
the pioneer camp re-creates greenhouse conditions: the pioneers are
simultaneously coddled and disciplined, cocooned and regimented.[65]
The uniform repetitiveness makes the summer camp deathly boring to
the pioneers, who have no way to express their individuality and creativity, except haphazardly and covertly.

One pioneer, by the name of Kostia Inochkin, breaks Comrade
Dynin's strict rules by deciding to breaststroke his way beyond the de-
marcated swimming area. For this infraction, Dynin expels him and
orders him to return home. Inochkin, however, afraid that his grandmother will suffer a heart attack upon hearing of this indignity, diso-
beys (again) and stealthily finds his way back into the camp. With the
help of other children, as well as some of the camp personnel, Inochkin
lives under the podium, under Dynin's very nose. Dynin is undone at
the event that is supposed to showcase his administrative skills. On
the day that all parents descend upon the camp to witness a carefully
choreographed demonstration of their children's talents, his staff and
pioneers stage a mini-insurrection. The event's crowning moment is
supposed to be (in a gentle mocking of Khrushchev's corn campaign)
the entrance of an oversized float featuring a corn stalk, "the queen of
the field." Hidden inside the corn stalk ought to have been the niece
of a party bigwig, Comrade Mitrofanov, with whom Dynin wants to
curry favour. The "big reveal" falls apart as Kostia Inochkin emerges
triumphant from the costume. At that moment the meticulously staged
performance disintegrates; the managed procession of acts give way to
a spontaneous act of disobedience as both children and parents storm
past Dynin to the riverbank to enjoy the summer day. Inochkin's instinctive dislike for artifice and bombast wins the day; it appears that
the "son" is more in touch with the needs of both adults and peers as he
leads them, by example rather than speechifying, to follow their hearts.

Viewers were clearly supposed to sympathize with Inochkin and
cheer on his rule-breaking accomplices. In contrast to Inochkin, Dynin,
much like Ogurtsev before him, cannot see beyond the regulations set
for him by his superiors. As one reviewer points out: "Dynin's fundamental mistake is that he believes that life is supposed to be lived
according to a manual [*zhit' po instruktsii*]."[66] Recollecting the making
of his film, Klimov commented: "What did the film oppose? It discredited two phenomena. First, pervasive idiotism that negated individuality. Second, nonsensical demagoguery which penetrated all levels
of society."[67] Both Dynin and Ogurtsev are tragic father figures in that
they overregulate not out of maliciousness, but because they know

no other way. Reviewers also recognized that although the pioneer camp Klimov outlined and the house of culture Riazanov depict may not exist, Dynin- and Ogurtsev-like types certainly abound. And it is "Dynin-ism" and "Ogurtsov-ism" that Klimov and Riazanov aimed to combat in their debut features. They made it clear that occupying a position of authority ought not automatically translate to uncritical loyalty and deference. Respect was to be earned rather than automatically assumed.

Many of the most significant films of the period discussed above suggested that relationships – both personal and civic – ought to be built horizontally rather than vertically and based on meritocratic principles rather than age. A whole slew of films of varied genres argued that perhaps the postwar generation was better suited to lead because the interwar and wartime generations had been too compromised by Stalin's dictatorship. The debate continued because it desacralized the beliefs and norms that validated the identities of men who had come of age under Stalin. To transfer the leadership of the relay to the sons also meant to implicitly tarnish the fathers' formative years, which had been written into the national narrative under Stalin. Perhaps no other movie problematized the older generation's background more than Grigorii Chukhrai's *Clear Skies* (1961). The storyline makes it clear that the Stalin-era generation had been victimized by the Great Leader but also that it had submitted to his will in persecuting innocent compatriots.

The Unmaking of the "Fathers and Sons" Myth and Stalin's Personality Cult

While post-Stalinist directors were none too shy about critiquing and gently mocking the Stalinist generation, it was still uncommon to question the sanctity of Stalin himself. In this regard, *Clear Skies* not only renounced Stalin's own criminality but also delegitimized the myth of the "great Soviet family" that underpinned the entire notion of an unbreakable union between "fathers and sons." Initially conceived as a story about a test pilot, this film struck at the very core of patriarchal authority: the trope of Stalin as the "Father of the Peoples" (*otets narodov*).[68] Chukhrai accomplished this by demystifying and dethroning aviators – Stalin's "model sons" – as the embodiment of Soviet masculinity. By demonstrating how Stalin's paranoia had cold-heartedly ruined the life of the system's most hallowed figure – a decorated pilot and war hero – Chukhrai effectively both undermined Stalin's fatherly aura and exposed the hollowness of the Stalin-era aviator cult. In the process, both the Great Leader and his "model sons" lost their ethereal quality. Like Toto in *The Wizard of Oz*, Chukhrai pulled back the curtain on Stalinist mythology to reveal the Wizard to be a mere mortal propped up by an artificial (ideological) edifice. Soviet audiences and officials revelled in Chukhrai's audacious "outing" of the so-called Gardener of Human Happiness. The readers of the movie magazine *Sovetskii ekran* voted *Clear Skies* "Best Film of the Year" in 1961; besides that, it won international recognition and official blessings from Soviet authorities when it received the Golden Star award during the Moscow Film Festival. It also sold around 42 million tickets at home and received wide distribution abroad.

More than a denunciation of Stalin's terror, the film raised questions about how power functions in a socialist context and how men relate to the authority of the collective. Whereas the Stalin-era aviators readily internalized the supremacy of the collective and the patriarch, Chukhrai's protagonist becomes a man only after shaking off his subservient position. This shift comes into sharper focus when Chukhrai's film is considered alongside another officially and popularly acclaimed production that premiered in 1948: Aleksandr Stolper's *A Story of a Real Man* (Povest' o nastoiashchem cheloveke). The movie is based on the actual exploits of Aleksei Petrovich Mares'ev, who became famous throughout the Soviet Union after Boris Polevoi penned an account of the pilot's fate in the journal *Oktiabr'* in 1946. Polevoi's story won the Stalin Prize, and Stolper subsequently turned the award-winning narrative into a movie in 1948. The film, which also won a Stalin Prize, was the second most popular movie of 1948, selling nearly 35 million tickets.

Both *Clear Skies* and *A Story of a Real Man* focus on pilots as privileged gendered tropes to relate specific expectations for Soviet masculinity in a socialist society. Jay Bergman and Katerina Clark identify Stalinist pilots in general, and Valerii Chkalov in particular, as archetypes of Stalinist masculinity who could always count on their (largely symbolic but very much unavoidable) "conscious fathers" for help and guidance. Chkalov, in his many heroic incarnations – conqueror of Nature, defender of Soviet borders from foreign foes, and military explorer extraordinaire – was ultimately but a son to the Father of the Peoples. Whatever their Herculean achievements, the nation's flying aces were first and foremost obedient sons. As such, they modelled a type of masculinity that was tempered not by steel but by fatherly attention. Stalin was more than their symbolical caretaker – he was also central to the lives of these pilots, for his mature, paternal consciousness steadied their youthful spontaneity and allowed them to achieve their potential.[69] Although both Chukhrai and Stolper drew on the cult surrounding Stalin's "hawks," they utilized the Soviet Union's "airborne heroes" to very different ends: Stolper was affirming the sanctity of the great Soviet family myth, while Chukhrai was dismantling the structure supporting the very same patriarchal system. Made at the height of Stalin's personality cult, Stolper's film expressed the organic connection men shared in the extended national family through an ever-wise, all-knowing father. Chukhrai would subvert this logic only thirteen years later, positing that individual will, guided by correct intentions, overrides allegiance to the group.

The narrative arcs of both movies feature air force pilots who overcome seemingly insurmountable obstacles in order to return to flying planes. The two men, however, attain their goals in starkly different ways. While Stolper's hero succeeds because his older brethren-in-arms give him unconditional assistance, Chukhrai's protagonist triumphs because he courageously stands up to the revered wisdom of his elders without the support of a senior male mentor. In fact, the postwar version of the pilot is saved from his abusive "father" by two figures who do not fit neatly in the hierarchical universe of the Stalin era; he receives unconditional support from his wife and his nephew, who ultimately provide him with life-saving advice. Thus while *A Story of a Real Man* celebrates authority figures and collective wisdom, *Clear Skies* privileges individual autonomy and calls into question a social order that privileges seniors' masculinity over other forms of identity.

Mares'ev's story begins with his plane being shot down behind enemy lines in March 1942. The crash badly injures his legs, and he spends the following eighteen (!) days crawling back toward Soviet-held territory, fighting off the elements, hunger, predatory animals, and the Fascists. Eventually saved by Soviet partisans, he is taken to a hospital, where surgeons amputate both his gangrenous legs. In Polevoi's description, Mares'ev becomes so entirely demoralized that he begins to feel he cannot continue living since he cannot imagine his life without flying. As Polevoi states: "All his life's goals, all his worries and joys, all his plans for the future, and all his present life's achievements – all of it was tied to aviation."[70] Polevoi comments that after the surgery, "even though his iron-clad organism easily adapted after a masterfully performed amputation and though the wounds were quickly healing, he was noticeably weakening; despite all the measures taken, he was wasting away from day to day for all to see."[71] Central to Mares'ev's mental and physical recovery is his bedside neighbour Semen Petrovich Vorob'ev – affectionately but appropriately nicknamed "Commissar" – whom a *Pravda* review described as "an old Bolshevik, an old propagandist, an architect of human souls."[72] The Commissar leaves a deep impression not just on Mares'ev but on all the men with whom he comes in contact. The experienced Civil War veteran moves into Room 42 and quickly becomes popular with everyone there. His seemingly endless dynamism and positive energy prove contagious. Polevoi's account avers that "the pilot could not understand how this man could ignore such staggering pain, and where all his energy, vivacity, and vitality came from."[73] After Mares'ev's surgery, the Commissar proves central to the recovery of his younger "brother-in-arms," taking up the role of the wise and benevolent father.

The relationship between Semen Petrovich and Aleksei exemplifies the archeypical relationship between father and son. Aleksei is virile and enthusiastic but also emotionally immature. His emotiveness and lack of ideological consciousness are tamed through the guidance of an affectionate father figure, who, having seen and experienced more, is more ideologically aware. The son does not even need to ask for guidance from his father; instead, the father intuits the son's needs and provides timely direction and guidance. The *Pravda* review praises actor N. Okhlopkov as having succeeded in portraying "a powerful, inspiring image of a Communist, for whom living means to teach, to motivate, and to lead forward."[74]

As Semen Petrovich grows weaker, having brought a sense of meaning and purpose to the young man's life, his charge became stronger and healthier, exercising and training daily in his bed. Soon after the former flying ace almost fully recuperates, the Commissar dies and leaves Aleksei to fend for himself, but arms him with sage advice: those who cower during difficult times will perish, while those who fight the odds will always prevail. Before dying, Mares'ev's mentor orders a pair of prosthetic legs to help his charge realize his Soviet greatness. As Vorob'ev's funeral cortege passes below the hospital windows, a new patient, amazed by the long lines of people following the Commissar's casket, asks: "Who died? A general or another notable?" By way of reply, Mares'ev turns to the camera and with great pathos pronounces: "A Bolshevik. A real man."

The narrative makes clear that the title of both B. Polevoi's account and Stolper's movie is not just about a single "real man," one hero. It is about the symbolic genealogical lineage of Soviet men, who encourage and inspire one another to great feats in the name of the communal good. This point is underscored at the end of the movie when Mares'ev, having saved a young pilot from certain death, offers the soldier the same advice he was once given by the Commissar: only those who fight the odds will prevail. The *Pravda* analysis of the movie underscored this point:

> A new kind of people has been created. Thousands and thousands have grown up and matured; they're the kind of people compared to whose spiritual goodness and power the most exemplary heroes of the past cannot compare. Mares'ev is not a solitary figure. Right beside him other Soviet people discharge their duties because, like Mares'ev, they carry within them traits of real Soviet people and represent worthy sons of the Soviet nation. The movie *A Story of a Real Man* correctly demonstrates how the character of such people is constructed and shaped; this is its main merit.[75]

The review praised the movie for having constructed a society in which earnest and ceaseless effort will always be rewarded. More importantly, it extolled a society in which an individual's strength – and even survival – will always be based on complying with the wisdom of those with greater authority.

But however reassuring this representation might have seemed in 1948, its success could not survive the Twentieth Party Congress, where Khrushchev excoriated Stalin, whose authority and person these kinds of movies were supposed to celebrate. In 1961, Soviet film director Grigorii N. Chukhrai decided to explore the contemporary issue of de-Stalinization through the life of a pilot. Even after the Twentieth Party Congress, Stalin's legacy remained a fraught topic. Instead of filming what would have essentially been a continuation of the Stalinist myth of the pilot as an intrepid yet humble servant of his fatherland, Chukhrai made a motion picture about a man who, *despite* the inequities of Stalin and other male authority figures, continued to believe in the virtues of communism.

Aleksei Astakhov, the protagonist of Chukhrai's *Clear Skies*, succeeds not *because of* a father figure or even Stalin himself but, to the contrary, *despite* Stalin and other party leaders. Chukhrai recalled the central idea behind the making of this film:

> The new story line embodied all those things that we thought about intensely during those years. My generation's faith in Stalin was limitless. All the best things were tied to our Communist ideals and our fight for Communism. We imagined Stalin, who was at the forefront of this struggle, to be absolutely honest and fair. Our disappointment in him was a terrible blow to us. But even this shock did not weaken our faith. Much like before, we remained true to our ideals and were ready to continue fighting for them.[76]

However transparent Chukhrai's faith in communism was, the movie raised more questions than it answered, and most of those questions raised doubts about the state's capacity to treat its citizens fairly.

While on one of his missions, Astakhov's plane is shot down, and he is captured by the Germans while unconscious. He survives the horrors of German prison camps and returns to his wife and child. His happiness, however, does not last long. Because he was captured by the Germans, no one trusts him; he is suspected of having collaborated with his captors as a POW. Since it was an accepted fact at the time that enemy forces shot Soviet soldiers, especially communists, upon capture, it followed that those who came back alive had survived only by collaborating. Slowly but surely, suspicions on the part of the collective cost Astakhov his job and his Party membership. It is surprising that Astakhov, like so many others of his background, does not end his days in the Gulag under suspicion of espionage. Astakhov, much like Mares'ev, loses his sense of purpose since he can no longer fly; though he, unlike Mares'ev, can stand on his own two feet, his comrades' suspicions cripple him psychologically. He begins to drink and submissively accepts his fate. He is the victim of a paranoid system headed by a tyrant, and his fellow communists offer him no support.

The legend of the "real Soviet man" and the myth of the "great Soviet family" run afoul in Chukhrai's version. The person who supports him is his wife Sasha rather than an ideologically conscious male father figure. In fact, Chukhrai visually establishes Stalin as the source of the pilot's misery. In the shot where a Party functionary explains to Sasha that the Party committee has excommunicated her husband, her evident loyalty and pain stand in stark contrast to Stalin's graven image looming ominously in the background (Figure 3.21). Notwithstanding Stalin's stone-cold detachment, Sasha continues to encourage Astakhov, sincerely believing in his innocence. Astakhov, however, accepts the judgment of his fraternal collective and, in a self-critical manner typical of the best of communists, even judges himself partly accountable. The alienated pilot explains: "'When trees are cut down, woodchips fly'" (Kogda les rubiat shchepki letiat).[77] "A great struggle is under way. It does not matter if one, two, ten, or hundreds of innocent people become victims. We should not feel sorry for anyone, not even ourselves, for the sake of this lofty goal." In classic Stalin-era fashion, the hero renounces his own happiness for the good of the collective, firmly believing that the Party, Stalin, and the Soviet collective would not ask for this sacrifice were it not completely necessary. Astakhov takes self-criticism to its logical extreme.

Astakhov has a change of heart after he has a falling out with his fellow factory worker and nephew, Sergei. Astakhov encourages Sergei to aspire to loftier goals, to not only fulfil his production quota but also consider the broader ideological picture. Sergei angrily replies: "I

Figure 3.21. Still from *Clear Skies* (1961). Stalin looks on as Astakhov is being excluded from the Party.

have thought about these things! But where is the justice you speak of? You keep lecturing me about heroism and morality while you yourself are a coward ... I was only a toddler when you were testing planes. I was proud of you – wanted to be just like Astakhov. And what happened? You're an apprentice, just like me. Even our salaries are nearly the same. So, please tell me where is this justice of yours?" Astakhov responds that, if he had to do things over, he would do it all the same way. He reminds his nephew that for him communism is not just a pretty word but an ideal he continues to live by. Sergei, however, persists, unconvinced by the ex-pilot's rehearsed platitudes: "I know you're a true Communist. But why aren't you a member of the Party then?" As if on auto-pilot, the uncle responds: "If it's so, then it means it needs to be this way." Finally, the nephew angrily demands: "Who needs it? Your wife? Me? Your son? The Party? Or maybe the government for which you fought?" As Sergei points out the pointlessness of his uncle's suffering, Astakhov grabs him violently by the collar and screams: "Shut up!" Having heard the unspeakable truth, having absorbed that his anguish is for naught, Astakhov reconsiders his position in the very next scene.

Following this bitter altercation, Astakhov is beyond himself, having experienced a revelation. Sasha tells him to pay no heed to the young man's brash words. Astakhov, however, is convinced that the boy is

Figure 3.22. Still from *Clear Skies* (1961). Astakhov in a moment of rebellion against Stalin.

right; he avers that Sergei is "cleaner" than they are. Astakhov cries out in a dramatic tour de force: "Why are we lying to ourselves? What are we afraid to admit to ourselves?" Agitatedly, he demands to know: "This 'When trees are cut down, woodchips fly!' Who? I ask you, who thought of this? Since when is human life disposable? Since when is vigilance equal to paranoia? I am a soldier, not a victim! I am a human being, damn it, and I deserve to know the truth." As he bellows these words, his face contorts, not only with pain, but also with the realization that he has been living a lie. As his entire frame shakes with anger, his eyes dart back and forth, his mind processing the implications of his revelation (Figure 3.22). In this context the scarring on his face is as much a testament to his wartime sacrifice as it is a reflection of the open wounds he has nursed since the war ended. His clenched fists held up high mark his transition from Stalin's meek follower to an architect of his own destiny.

Armed with a newfound righteous anger and convinced of his own dignity, Astakhov immediately travels to Moscow, intending to stay there for as long as it takes until his case, and others like his, are resolved.

He realizes that he need not sacrifice his masculinity to the state, that he need not suffer endlessly to serve his country's great cause. By then, Stalin has died. Astakhov is not only reinstated in the Party's ranks but also awarded a military award. Most importantly for him, he is allowed to fly again. His spiritual resurrection follows the death of the Father. In a Freudian twist, Astakhov, the pilot, the favoured son of the Stalinist period, can come to life in the post-Stalinist period only after the Father has passed on.

In a Houdiniesque manoeuvre, Chukhrai in this film overturned the Stalinist myth of the "Great Family." The father figure was absent during Astakhov's worst tribulations; and more than that, it is the son figure, an mere adolescent, who spurs Astakhov to see past his "defect" and travel to Moscow to reclaim his ideological credibility – and with it, his right to fly. By emphasizing his hero's unshakeable faith, Chukhrai propagated a new kind of hero: one who fights for truth rather than for the Party. Having denounced Stalin and exposed his crimes, the Party effectively surrendered its monopoly on truth and justice, if not ideologically then certainly in practice. The post-Stalinist protagonists are thus committed to the ideal of justice defined by their own contexts and ideals rather than ones prescribed by Party authorities.

The implications of this film were not lost on some in its crew. Even before filming was completed, one of them wrote a damning letter to the Ministry of Culture, claiming that it "spat in the face of our party."[78] The culture minister, E.A. Furtseva, herself came to investigate, and concluded: "Well, all of this is true, isn't it?" At the same time, she cautioned Chukhrai to make sure the mistakes of the past did not appear to carry over into the present. The minister wanted to strategically sequester the sins of the past, the sins of the fathers, and forever quarantine them. Despite Furtseva's tepid blessing, the movie continued to evoke strong responses on both sides of the issue. On 19 April 1961, after a public showing of the movie, during the discussion of it that followed, a polarity of views was evident in the charged atmosphere of the Central Cinema Hall. The internationally acclaimed movie scholar and critic R.N. Iurenev unambiguously stated that "it was important to seriously and honestly discuss all that made my generation suffer, that hindered us from looking straight into our comrades' eyes, that made us not speak openly in both life and art."[79] A self-described "ordinary" viewer in the hall, Comrade Kushchev, on the other hand, could not accept Chukhrai's version of events. He objected: "I know what it was like in the past, but you could always find honest communists who helped out. And here we have one man who receives no help from anyone for the duration of the entire movie! ... We need to show the truth on the screen and show the other side of the coin as well: the times when people were helped, the times when people went the extra mile to exonerate an innocent man. What we saw in this movie does not fully reflect the fullness of our lived reality."[80] And the acrimony did not end there, for the disagreement was larger than the movie itself.

How this movie represented the Stalinist past, and how it depicted the history of the Stalinist generation, was going to determine whether the fathers' legacy was venerated or debased. If the world the fathers had created under Stalin featured a collective that not only produced conditions for arbitrary suffering but was also indifferent to the ensuing plight of innocent people, then the postwar generation had earned the right to act somewhat independently of the fathers. And the fathers, with their transgressions in public view, would be hesitant to respond to their sons' questions about how to live life correctly. Comrade Salakhian, a viewer at the same forum, commented on the central task of this new era: "The movie demonstrates how a man ought to behave, how he should love." Most importantly, according to Salakhian, was that Chukhrai's film had posed a universal question about faith and about trust: "What do you believe in?" This was, indeed, to be the central question of the postwar generation – and for the sons it seemed risky to rely unconditionally on the fathers. Chukhrai supported this line of reasoning. Although *Clear Skies* indisputably promoted faith in the communist system, it did not offer an answer as to who was at the centre of the post-Stalinist faith. Stalin, the supreme deity, had been deposed, and those sons who blithely and mechanically followed the Father of the Peoples had been branded either "little Stalins" or cowardly collaborators. This kind of questioning alarmed the conservative forces in the Communist Party, most clearly represented by the Central Committee secretary in charge of ideology, Leonid Il'ichev, who brought the full force of the Soviet propaganda machine down upon Khutsiev's offending scene.

Thus the postwar generation – symbolized by the father–son relationship trope – began to seek new meaning and turned inward to find the answers for *themselves*, distancing themselves from the ways of their fathers. Much as in Astakhov's case, freedom for the imprisoned sons came only at the price of the father's death. In *Clear Skies*, once Astakhov's nephew announces Stalin's death, the scene cuts to a monumental visual – an actual thaw. As the sun weakens the ice holding the river back, the power of the water surges forward to a classical music crescendo that announces nature's awakening and the defeat of the Stalinist freeze. During a public discussion of the movie, Chukhrai himself commented on the symbol: "When we thought about it [Stalin's death], it seemed that everything will vanish, it seemed that night will reign eternal ... But life takes its course, and winter turns into spring and the world does not wither when one man dies."[81] Through his hero, Chukhrai shows that life after Stalin does not just continue – it flourishes.

Clear Skies legitimized individuals' autonomy, but it did so by sequestering it in the context of the Stalinist injustice that Khrushchev himself condemned. Although the scene in *Lenin's Guard* between the ghost father and the son represents a natural evolution of legitimizing "the son's" autonomy, it does so outside the Stalinist context. The conservative forces headed by Il'ichev began a campaign against Khutsiev because the film seemed to validate the postwar generation's search for meaning without the guidance of their elders. Orthodox groups, headed by Il'ichev, successfully played on Khrushchev's fear of public disorder by invoking increasing trends toward "anarchism" and "nihilism" among Soviet youth. It was one thing to resist Stalin's cult, but another to question the right of the wartime veterans to hold on to the reins of power.

Hamletism: Screening the Reflexive Masculinity of the Postwar Generation

Khutsiev's *Lenin's Guard*, a documentary-style portrayal of contemporary Soviet youth, came too close to capturing the mood of young Muscovites and became the victim of a campaign for ideological purity. The movie follows the maturation of three male friends in their early twenties who are attempting to make sense of their lives. In portraying Sergei, Kolia, and Slava's quest for larger meaning, the director structures the movie as a series of unrelated episodes. But it was not the apparent departure from socialist realist narrative practices that drew Khrushchev's ire.

Rather, the First Party Secretary was beside himself for two reasons. First, he refused to believe that a Soviet youth like Sergei could be so confused about life's purpose. Most importantly, Khrushchev vehemently objected that the script did not provide a scene in which an authority figure could help Sergei find his (socialist) way. Khrushchev especially fumed that the apparition of Sergei's father left the son in the dark about life's meaning. He bristled at this notion: "Do you really want us to believe that such a thing could be true? No one will ever believe that! It is common knowledge that even animals don't abandon their offspring."[82] Although Khutsiev's heroes were far from an exception, *Lenin's Guard* was too explicit in portraying the independence of

Soviet youth. This general trend is not at all surprising if we take into account that Hamlet – the symbol of independent-mindedness and scepticism – was one of the most celebrated icons of the sixties.

Ever since the death of Stalin the intelligentsia had extolled a man they had been forbidden to celebrate under the iron rule of the Great Leader: the young Danish prince Hamlet. Soviet literature specialists explained the absence of Hamlet on Soviet stages and classroom syllabi in the following way: "In contrast with heroes of other great Shakespearean tragedies, Hamlet ... with his tragic doubts and indecisiveness, his inability to see concrete ways of eradicating evil, was distant from contemporary Soviet audiences that were filled with active courage, optimism, a sense of clear purpose in life. Soviet audiences looked to Shakespeare for a 'real hero,' not 'Hamletism,' for them synonymous with vacillation and passive reflection."[83] But after the tyrant's death the Soviet cultural scene came to be possessed with a virtual Hamlet fever; from the mid-1950s onward, theatres built their repertoires around Hamlet, the period's "real hero," and he became a symbol of the post-Stalin era in much the same way Ernest Hemingway and Jack London had. I. Vertzman, a contemporary leading figure in the field of Shakespeare studies, explained this phenomenon: "Hamlet is nearer to us than any other Shakespeare hero, both in his strengths and his weaknesses. If it is so easy to come to love Hamlet, it is because we sense in him something of ourselves; and if at times he is so difficult to understand, it is similarly, because we do not, as yet, know ourselves too well, or rather, like the ostrich, fear such knowledge."[84]

Khutsiev's young celluloid heroes were modelled after Hamlet, whom Shakespeare specialists described as knowing "no dogmas, doctrines, pre-constructed systems of thought." The Danish prince was furthermore described as "endlessly discontent and searching, with no group, camp or party behind him, no preacher, teacher or mentor beside him, bearing him a catechism or manual of regulations in one hand and pointing upward with the other." Many in the film community praised Khutsiev's Sergei precisely for his apparent Hamlet-like imperviousness to external influences. In 1962, Viktor Nekrasov was one of many who defended *Lenin's Guard's* main hero: "I am eternally grateful to Khutsiev for not having dragged out onto the movie screen a grey-mustached and all-knowing worker who had ready-made answers for everything. Had the omniscient older worker appeared with his inspiring words, the film would have been spoiled."[85] And Grigorii Koznintsev, who directed the world-renowned Soviet screen adaptation of Hamlet in 1964, defined the term heroism both for Sergei and

Figure 3.23. Still from *I Am Twenty* (1965). The three Hamlets of
Lenin's Guard: Sergei, Kolia, and Slava.

for those celluloid heroes who followed his mould thusly: "Hamlet –
thinks. This is the greatest threat of all."[86]

The three pals in Khutsiev's film do not seem threatening, and it was
precisely their ordinariness that set off alarm bells. These were not the
garishly attired hipsters *Krokodil* ridiculed, or the spiritual drifters Komsomol leaders shamed, or even the hooligans sought by neighbourhood
patrols. Between them, Kolia, Slava, and Sergei check off all the right
boxes for realizing masculine adulthood: they hold steady jobs, engage
with civic programs, and start their own families. Even in appearance,
they cannot be distinguished from other postwar youth, either abroad
or at home. They wear fashionable clothes but do not stand out; they
smoke as if imitating Jean Paul Belmondo's mannerisms; and their
relaxed postures suggest non-threatening casualness and openness
(Figure 3.23). Rather, as their faraway looks and contemplative gazes
suggest, their sin consists of self-conscious reflection. Whenever they
come together, the three mates articulate the uncertainties they feel
about the choices they are making. Even the playboy Kolia, who generally disdains philosophizing and adopts an optimistic attitude, is defined by quiet but perceptible restlessness.

The day's conservative critics perceived Khutsiev's heroes as gratui-
tously brooding and publicly shamed them for passivity, inaction, and
pathologic introversion. A. Andrievskii, for example, chided the three
protagonists: "We see them going to work not as active participants of

the collective but as reflex-driven Hamlet figures, bent on answering the questions of how to live their lives."[87] Scriptwriter S.I. Rostotskii extended Andrievski's criticism: "I cannot see why this hero in particular is asking the question of how to live. I mean, I can't see any tragedies in his life. ... How many times would we have to repeat to him 'others died so you might live' in order for him to understand his life's goal?"[88] These comments lay bare the return to Stalinist value judgments – judgments that testified that Stalin's famous 1945 dictum pronouncing Soviet citizens "cogs of the great state machine" was anything but dead. The sons, then, were indebted to the fathers for the blood they had shed to defend the fatherland against the Nazi invaders. The sons' existentialist self-examination was proclaimed to be pure selfishness – an insult to those who had sacrificed their lives for the Soviet system. Khrushchev's comments at the Komsomol Congress perfectly encapsulated this attitude: "You young people should not become conceited. I am proud of my generation. People of the older generation lived through hunger and devastation; they restored the economy by heroic effort. They served as soldiers in the Second World War and defeated the most terrible enemy of mankind: fascism! Yes, we are proud of our times. You should take pride in our times because we are your fathers, your grandfathers, older brothers, and sisters."[89] Khutsiev's scene represented a stark contrast to these sentiments, suggesting as it did that the son had literally and metaphorically "outgrown" his father. War, with its explicit symbolism and rhetoric, could not serve as a reference point to the young men who were growing up in a much more complex postwar environment. The world that Sergei's father once knew had ceased to exist, and the lessons that defined his generation had lost their applicability in the post-Stalinist milieu. The universal truths of Stalin's time, proclaimed by the ever-wise elders, could no longer be grasped. The notion that the fathers who had been the ultimate martyrs for the cause could not serve as examples beyond the grave rubbed salt in the open wounds of the Khrushchev generation.

In literature, the generational rift was apparent in that the sixties generation had produced an argot of their own, making constructive intergenerational dialogue exceedingly difficult. In 1964, Russian literature scholar George Gibian observed that "to define differences between the generations in experience, outlook, and ways of talking and behaving is almost an obsession with some Soviet authors."[90] Three years later, Soviet critics A. Chudakov and M. Chudakova echoed Gibian's sentiments about what had become known as "youth prose": "In its negation of the verbal clichés of the literature of the past, language became the first vehicle of subversion within permissible limits."[91] Indeed, "references to the more esoteric forms of high culture, such as icon painting, abstract art, difficult classical music, and religion became frequent" and were paired with "expressions of 'unofficial' popular culture, ranging from school folklore, to underground songs, slang, parodies of folklore, foreign pop songs, and jazz."[92] In recalling her coming-of-age story during the sixties, Russian literary critic Anna Latynina reserves a prominent place for works of so-called youth prose. She remembers that even straitlaced university students like her admired the rebellious youth prose characters, who, over their parents' protestations, absconded to Estonia (the Soviet Union's ersatz Europe) to lounge on beaches during the day and relax in cafes at night – much like Hemingway's heroes.

Significantly, according to Latynina's recollection, youth prose did not always imitate how young people spoke; rather, it invented its own slang.[93] In this sense youth prose authors, such as Vasilii Aksenov, Iurii Kazakov, Evgenii Evtushenko, and Andrei Voznesenskii, did more than simply report the situation on the ground; they gave the postwar generation a readymade separate language, identity, and set of core values.[94] Films such as *Carnival Night, And If It's Love?, Welcome*, and *Lenin's Guard* were cinematic versions of youth prose and demonstrated that the theme of generational difference defined sixties artistic production.

Khrushchev clearly sensed danger in this dynamic, and in a series of public meetings with the cultural intelligentsia made clear that he expected artists to hew closely to the party line. When he assembled three hundred artists at the villa for official receptions at Lenin Hills in 1962, he lectured them about "real art" and concluded with this analogy: "And I'll tell you another thing. It can happen like this: a colonel starts up an argument with a general and the colonel is persuasive, very persuasive. And the general listens and in principle he cannot object. But he will tire of the colonel, he will stand and say: 'Listen here, you're a colonel and I'm a general. About face and forward march!' – and the colonel will turn to go fulfil his orders. So, there you go, you are the colonel and I, if you will, a general. So. About face! Forward march!" Only three months later, at Sverdlov Hall in the Kremlin, on 7 and 8 March, Khrushchev reiterated the state's authority over the arts. This time there were around four hundred invitees.[95] While interrogating the popular poet A. Voznesenskii, Khrushchev condemned him: "Comrade Voznesenskii, until you understand that you are nothing, that you are but one of the 3.5 million that are born each year in the USSR, nothing good will come of you. Stamp that on your nose: you are nothing!"

Figure 3.24. "You are nothing!" Nikita Khrushchev shouting over Andrei
Voznesenskii in Sverdlov Hall.

Director M. Romm contended that the allusion to the Nazi slogan "You
are nothing; your nation is everything" was not lost on those in the
room. Moreover, the photo of the Party Secretary publicly yelling over
the fashionably clad artist made it clear that the older generation remained in charge. Caught mid-sentence, Voznesenskii, the voice of
the postwar generation, was being upstaged, silenced, and threatened
(Figure 3.24). Khrushchev's unannounced assault rendered the young
poet defenceless. The faces of the fathers on the podium displayed a
mix of disinterest, disapproval, and menace, unambiguously exposing
the generational chasm.

The altercation in Sverdlov Hall made it clear that promoting alternative visions of man's position in society was a risky undertaking. At the
same meeting, Khrushchev also directly threatened the ideological misfits: "What, you think we forgot how to arrest people?"[96] It was also no
coincidence that he reminded the intellectuals yet again about the tragic
fate of the Hungarian Petöfi Circle, organized by the Hungarian Young
Communists during the disastrous Hungarian Uprising in 1956, which
had been crushed by Soviet tanks. Khrushchev and his conservative
supporters maintained that unguided, unsupervised youth, spurred by
the examples of Hamlet-like figures projected onto the screen, threatened to undermine the party's authority. The state ideologues had come

to fear the new intellectual currents, which were promoting a new way of understanding how to practise one's masculinity through the prism of autonomous thought. As Khrushchev unambiguously declared: "We believe that our young creative workers will carry on the cause of their fathers."[97]

Arguably, the campaign against *Lenin's Guard* succeeded in suppressing the offending scene and stymieing the work on this production. A re-edited version of the film was released in 1965 under the title *I Am Twenty* (Mne Dvadtsat' Let), purged of any references to the great Lenin and the question of generations. Most of the movie was untouched, but by the time the new version was released years later, it had lost some of its freshness and appeal. The 1965 version had a very limited release, although it became a cult classic among the urban and professional class.

Il'ichev had succeeded in blackballing *Lenin's Guard*, but it seems that his victory was a pyrrhic one, because many other Soviet films continued to treat the desire for autonomy as laudable. The 1965 film *Lebedev against Lebedev* expresses the idea of a conflicted young generation explicitly: its hero is torn between his two sides – the more noble and upright one and the selfish and amoral one. What is significant about this film's concept is the notion that the two opposing sides are found in one person and that the internal conflict is not externalized as a conflict between a protagonist and an antagonist – the two are part of the same person. Although the film was not a commercial success, it received plenty of reviews and critiques, and film professionals considered it an important expression of the era's zeitgeist.[98] In other words, Hamletism was alive and well even after Khrushchev's threats. Those who defended the film as an important expression of a process young people undergo accentuated the importance of struggling with "how to be" in this world. Others, however, insisted that this version of masculinity has no place in the Soviet order. It was perhaps actor Nikolai Cherkasov, a five-time Stalin Prize winner, who most directly denounced *Lebedev against Lebedev* in the run-up to the Twenty-Third Party Congress. On the front page of *Literaturnaia gazeta*, he attacked the film by noting that Lebedev was incapable of opposing anyone – including himself. Adding insult to injury, he insisted that compared to Lebedev, Hamlet, with his "to be, or not to be" equivocations, was an action hero extraordinaire. Indignant, Cherkasov refuses to be moved by "those weak, barely visible manifestations of will and perseverance, which in the end the filmmaker manages to squeeze out of the hero." Cherkasov ended his critique by outlining the ideal hero artists should be dedicated to creating: "an active, passionate individual, not only deeply cognizant of his life goals, but committed to implementing and protecting them in battle."[99] In short, the contrasting reviews of *Lebedev against Lebedev* encapsulated a debate that had been evolving since Stalin's death: whether to resurrect the Stalinist model of masculinity defined by action and obedience, or to advance a postwar masculine model dedicated to critical thought and independence. It was this rift in attitudes that defined the postwar generational conflict.

Conclusion

Stalin's "cult of personality" created celluloid heroes of mythic proportions. Once the Stalinist myth began to ring hollow, it was only natural that the movie heroes who gave life to this world view morphed into more palatable incarnations of contemporary realities. Because de-Stalinization had made it possible to question authority, directors began investigating issues of power, conformity, and hierarchy throughout this period – particularly when portraying the lives of the Soviet "fathers and sons." Filmmakers most frequently employed the culturally charged father–son relationship to give concrete, individualized shape to broader generational dynamics – sometimes literally and sometimes figuratively. Communist officials rarely approved of movies containing conflictual relations between fathers and sons since examinations of the "generational problem" complicated a myth central to Soviet ideology: that sons willingly and obediently assume the historic mission of their fathers to construct a communist society.[100]

Owing to Khrushchev's liberalization of the arts, however, moviemakers succeeded in complicating the formerly incontestable ideological myth. The growth of this artistic trend forced Party officials on the defensive; the only alternative the more conservative representatives could offer was more of the old Stalinist fare. In 1961, for example, the veteran film critic R.N. Iurenev critically reflected on the portrayal of young heroes in Soviet film, complaining: "When my generation was young, our highest ambition was the Arctic, the conquering of new lands. Those fantasies were tied to our desire to fly higher and further than anyone else. And this romanticism was captured by Sergei Gerasimov in his (1936) movie *The Fearless Seven*."[101] Khrushchev also waxed nostalgic about Stalin-era heroes who dutifully obeyed the Party. The same man who had denounced Stalinist art for its artificiality now criticized M. Khutsiev's *Lenin's Guard* by extolling the Stalinist youth portrayed in movies of the late 1940s, in which "our Soviet youth carry on and multiply the heroic traditions of the generations who went before, the generations that demonstrated their loyalty to the ideals of Marxism-Leninism both in peacetime constructions and at the front of the Great Patriotic War."[102]

Few of the heroes in post-Stalinist movies could match the heroics of *The Fearless Seven*. Not only were their challenges tied to the mundane problems of the everyday, but they also had an ideologically problematic relationship with authority. Protagonists featured in epic films could achieve Herculean feats since their goal was clear and their allegiances uncomplicated. As Sergei in *Lenin's Guard* and Astakhov in *Clear Skies* demonstrate, the post-Stalinist celluloid hero's goal was to find meaning after the collapse of faith in Stalin. Without such as quest, marching into the Arctic like the characters of *The Fearless Seven*, even under the guidance of wise communists, would have been disingenuous. Yet the Party authorities could not realistically object, since Khrushchev himself had banned the gratuitous idealization of Soviet reality. The frustrating notion that contemporary heroes were not heroic enough pervaded Soviet life. After all, it was this, the postwar, generation that was slated to achieve communism by 1980.

As films ceased being the didactic spectacles they once were and began focusing on the inner lives of their heroes, the men appearing on screens in the Khrushchev era defined themselves through personal relationships rather than by solving the intricacies of steel production with other like-minded men. Celluloid masculinity was no longer exclusively forged in the public realm as a sacrifice to communal interests, perpetually subject to the patriarch's judgment. Instead, directors depicted their heroes forming their identity through a process that either involved intimate relations or transpired in solitude. This is not to say that post-Stalinist heroes renounced a collectivist outlook, but that the manner in which they became aware of how to "perform" their masculinity transpired in a markedly different fashion.

In other words, the myth of the "great Soviet family," with its attendant collectivistic and homosocial character, had lost its cultural supremacy. Prompted by Khrushchev's denunciation of Stalin's personality cult, reformist directors began depicting more democratic relationships among men and sometimes inverted the hierarchical dynamics, making the progeny as wise as (if not wiser than) the elders. No longer did celluloid heroes attain membership in the Soviet collective by dutifully following the lead of a politically conscious mentor. Rather, the relationship between generations became more egalitarian.

While young men's individualism was marked by doubt and reflection, women's gender identity in Soviet film and popular culture more broadly was marked by indulgence and materialism. As the next chapter demonstrates, this divergence had a particular effect on men's romantic relationships, since the crux of the conflict had to do with how couples navigated and resisted the siren call of consumerism – a defining characteristic of the sixties.

Chapter Four

The Trouble with Women: Consumerism and the Death of Rugged Masculinity

The 1967 feature *Four Pages of a Young Man's Life* tells the story of Alesha, who at twenty-two years old is on the verge of independent adulthood. He leaves his mother and his Russian village in search of adventures and himself, making his way as a lorry driver to as far as the red-sand deserts of Uzbekistan and the frozen expanses of Murmansk. Although the film features several exotic locales, at its core, *Four Pages* deals with Alesha's inward journey. On the long, winding road, the hero discovers that love is treacherous territory. His main obstacles are women bent on achieving social mobility at the expense of spiritual and emotional fulfilment. In Alesha's coming-of-age story, women hungry for social status and financial security undermine his optimism and faith in others. In his first amorous adventure, Alesha agrees to a fictive marriage so that a fellow rural migrant can work in the city and obtain legal residence there. She repays Alesha's unconditional kindness by displacing him from his own quarters; declaring that she has found true love, she moves a Cary Grant lookalike into their cramped room.

Without so much as a complaint, Alesha steps aside, heartbroken, and continues his travels. In Murmansk, he entangles himself with a married and childless woman who strings him along until she realizes that she prefers a loveless marriage that guarantees a comfortable life over genuine affection in modest quarters. She readily abandons Alesha and runs back to her prosperous husband. These two outwardly attractive but callous women fill two important pages in his life and turn Alesha into a mistrustful and forlorn adult.

Four Pages encapsulates a point of view that sixties filmmakers generally advanced: women who strive to be urban, cosmopolitan, ambitious, fashionable, and, in a word, "modern" spell doom for romance, marital bliss, and men's independence. Alesha's experience sends a clear message about romance and marriage: they can succeed only if

Figure 4.1. "To each her own." *Krokodil* 16 (1960): 13.

women reject being modern in favour of a more traditional version of femininity. Sixties films about romance generally pin "the impossibility of connecting" on women's heightened focus on financial independence and upward social mobility. Directors did not problematize men as romantic partners and husbands in the way they critically examined them as fathers. Instead, they faulted women's desire for independence, which they defined in terms of self-serving materialism, for the death of romance and marriage.[1]

The period's cultural narratives juxtaposed the independent postwar woman against the idealized femininity embodied by the figure of the long-suffering Russian (peasant) matron. If the modern woman focused on her appearance and societal status, the asexual matriarch prioritized her husband and children. While the modern woman decorated the apartment to advertise her disposable income and trendiness, the matriarch sought only to create an oasis for her family members. For the modern woman, men represented a gateway to a charmed existence, while the matronly *mamasha* served as her partner's main champion. In sixties cinema the modern woman's desire for emancipation was coded as unambiguously selfish and thus detrimental to marital bliss. The 1960 *Krokodil* cartoon titled "To each her own" visually codifies this

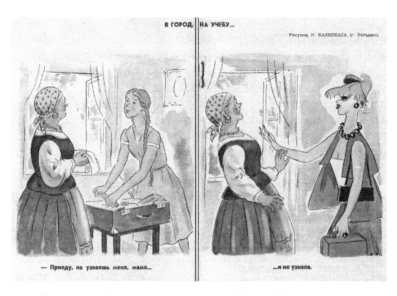

Figure 4.2. "You won't recognize me." *Krokodil* 20 (1956): 8–9.

dichotomy: the modestly clad and smiling mother of four is represented as Russian with her headscarf, indicating, perhaps, her village roots. She is unfavourably contrasted with "Westernized" femininity – here, with a woman who is so consumed by appearances that her maternal instincts are restricted to her four pets, extravagant make-up, and over-the-top fashion choices (Figure 4.1).[2]

Marriage to this kind of woman was perilous to men in two interrelated ways. First, satisfying her endless status-driven demands ruined a man's moral and professional standing. Second, by trapping men within the confines of marriage and the domestic sphere, modern women effectively prevented their husbands from establishing all-male communities that could serve as a vehicle of resistance to their dominance. Most often this middle-class, Westernized existence translated into a critique of urban life more generally. Cities corrupted all who migrated to them, as was the case with a female student in a 1956 *Krokodil* cartoon. The before-and-after frame shows that the daughter's prophetic "You won't recognize me when I return" comment has, in an unexpected and unwelcome way, come true.[3] Urban life has transformed the innocent and naive maiden into an unrecognizable stranger. The matriarch's aghast expression indicates that forsaking rural customs has perhaps corrupted more than her daughter's fashion sense

(Figure 4.2). It appears that the demands of urban modernity have erased an upbringing that championed modesty and common sense.

Sixties popular culture defined the city both as the modern woman's playground and as the crucible for postwar masculinity; the trappings of middle-class existence the city offered went a long way toward emasculating male protagonists. Sixties celluloid heroes faced an uphill battle to inspire their spoiled wives and mollycoddled children to action. Male protagonists frequently succumbed to the charms of the postwar *femme fatale*, and the only defence against her that sixties films suggested was for the man to engage in manual labour in extreme conditions. The frozen tundra, nuclear facilities, and fiery furnaces became sites for facilitating men's authentic realization; these were the places that drew men (and women) who spurned an easy life. This, of course, was not a new cultural fantasy in the Soviet context. Throughout the 1920s, Soviet writers had elevated homosocial utopias that excluded women.[4] What *had* changed was the rising menace to this all-male utopia: the modern urban woman with her insatiable desire for consumer goods. Of course, Russian directors were not inventing a new stock character; Soviet vixens were as lethal as the ones populating American *film noir* – and as common.

In sixties films, and in the sixties press, the figure of the sophisticated urban woman signalled the era's fear that consumer culture was having a negative impact on individual women and the institution of marriage. In postwar cinema, striving for at least the appearance of affluence amounted to a full-time occupation. The modern woman set out to attain material objects (furniture, household appliances, art) and to secure access to opportunities and services: vacations, job prospects for offspring, and the most sought-after cultural events. Sixties urban femininity threatened male autonomy and power because it demanded complete and utter dedication to attaining *her* perfect vision of postwar affluence. Popular culture and film aimed to discredit consumer-driven mass culture and to extol the moral superiority of a distinctly working-class or rural ethos. Soviet filmmakers in particular, and cultural elites more generally, set out to popularize the idea that a disposable income and access to consumer goods created only false empowerment and illusory emancipation. Ultimately, the desire for upward social mobility led to a profound sense of sociocultural dislocation.

These same concerns could be heard in the 1940s and '50s United States, as most famously captured in Philip Wylie's bestseller, *Generation of Vipers*. In that polemic, Wylie railed against the power and status of American women, especially in the chapter titled "Common Woman." He confidently declared: "The male is an attachment to the female in our civilization ... He does most of what he does – eighty per cent, statistically – to supply whatever women have defined as their necessities, comforts, and luxuries."[5] He warned against "Cinderellas who only want to marry a good-looking man with dough" and who expected to be rewarded "for nothing more than being female."[6] Not only did the stay-at-home mom entrap her husband, she also infantilized her son by making him prize security and certainty over freedom and risk-taking. This, of course, was not merely a personal issue; in the context of the Cold War, Wylie tied this mother–son dynamic to questions of national security. While the young would-be patriot hid behind his mother's skirt, Wylie imagined the enemy detonating "uranium, plutonium, hydrogen."[7] In Wylie's apocalyptic vision, "good-looking men and boys are rounded up and beaten or sucked into pliability" to produce "a new slave population."[8] Ultimately, Wylie saw America as a matriarchy in which "the women of America raped the men, not sexually, unfortunately, but morally, since neuters come hard by morals."[9]

Soviet chauvinism was never so overt or alarmist, but as Christine Varga-Harris points out, Soviet fiction regularly cautioned against women's undue influence by unfavourably contrasting materialistic and petty female characters with "sympathetic male protagonists emasculated by senseless feminine flourishes of taste."[10] Thus both Cold War superpowers staked their reputation on securing a comfortable life for their citizens; and each deployed misogyny to reject the consumerism that, paradoxically, formed the centre of its propaganda strategy.

Man-Eating, Gold-Digging, and Momism: The Gender Politics of Postwar Affluence

A decade after the end of the Second World War, the Soviet economy had begun to rebound. The age of postwar austerity and rationing was drawing to a close. The sacrifices endured during the war engendered a sense that material abundance had become a universal right rather than the preserve of the Party officialdom. Mimicking the optimism of other European leaders, Soviet premier Nikita Khrushchev confidently proclaimed in 1958: "A few years will pass and we shall see which country will produce more consumer goods. We believe that our country will take first place."[11] In step with other leaders of industrialized and industrializing economies, Khrushchev promised his compatriots a robust recovery and encouraged the citizenry to expect a prosperous future for themselves and their progeny.[12] This was no empty rhetoric. Not only did various consumer goods flood stores and supermarkets, but the rise in expendable incomes made previously unattainable objects – washing machines, television sets, cars – accessible to working-class families for the first time. According to one report, incomes of Soviet wage earners and white-collar workers increased by 87 per cent between 1953 and 1961; according to another, by 62 per cent between 1955 and 1962. These increases were all the more impressive when compared to past statistics: by 1952, real Soviet wage income, although slightly higher than prewar, was still below what it had been in 1928, the year before collectivization.[13]

Salaries had increased, and the state had dedicated itself to boosting the output of "light industry." It had also promised its citizens private apartments. A 1964 *Krokodil* cartoon titled "The great migration of people" both celebrated and mocked the building boom that had begun in the Soviet Union in the mid-1950s.[14] The cartoonist's admiration for this massive undertaking is evident in the scale of the image, which takes up two full pages. In the upper left corner, the explanatory note states: "In the past ten years, 107 million people have moved into new dwellings." The same cartoon makes clear that the "great resettlement" shows no signs of abating: even while multitudes are busy moving in, new buildings are being readied for yet more multitudes (Figure 4.3). But this national suburbanization drive is epic only in size – its substance has become mired in materialistic trivialities. The postwar suburban nomads are so burdened by the comforts of daily life – TV sets, colourful furniture, pets, house plants, books, radio sets, all manner of pots and pans – that moving has become an end in itself and serves no greater, loftier purpose.

These new apartment buildings figured prominently in the sixties cultural landscape as the new battleground for post-Stalinist norms. Party cadres, educators, intellectuals, and social commentators worried about what would happen to Soviet citizens when the doors to private flats were closed to the outside world. Soviet writer Vladimir Pomerantsev maintained that while it was necessary to eradicate the so-called consumer deficit and provide all workers with homes and refrigerators, there ought to be a level of restraint: "While working for a prosperous material life, we must remain above material life."[15] He recounted that before Khrushchev's emphasis on light industry, his apartment faced a building with a Spartan and utilitarian balcony. Now, however, there were "pretty curtains, fat cats, and foxtrots from morning till evening." Khrushchev himself wished to curb the rise of a materialistic way of life: "It is necessary not only to provide people with good homes, but also to teach them ... to live correctly, and to observe the rules of socialist communality."[16] As historian Elena Bogdanova put it bluntly: "The ideology encouraged consumption, but only [within] limits."[17] One answer to the apparent slippery slope of consumerist indulgence was to be found in Khrushchev's concept of communist morality.

Figure 4.3. "The great migration." *Krokodil* 22 (1964): 8–9.

As Deborah Field's incisive research reveals, communist morality became a priority for the Khrushchev regime as personal choices came to reflect political and ideological reliability. Field points out that in this moral order "every personal decision, from sexual and reproductive choices to taste in home decorations had ramifications for society as a whole."[18] One expert advised that "the ensemble of the interior" can affect "the entire internal, spiritual image [*oblik*] of a person."[19] In this schema, the personal could not be disentangled from the public, and often the individual played second fiddle to the communal. The neatness of official prescriptions received plenty of pushback from ordinary citizens as well as from judges, experts, and professionals, who were expected to enforce the moral principles Khrushchev championed.[20]

Debates about the impact of affluence and consumerism on Soviet citizens were conducted in gendered and often misogynistic terms. As Susan Reid so ably demonstrates, postwar consumerism was gendered female and proved to be a double-edged sword for the country's women. On the one hand, they were expected to embrace Khrushchev's consumerist initiative and furnish the new, prefabricated apartments in mid-century modern ways, thus signalling that the country was distancing itself from Stalinist aesthetics and the nation's recent brutal past. On the other hand, architecture and interior design played a key role in the Cold War standoff, which gave women strong influence in the superpower conflict.[21] As Reid observes, the Party-state ascribed to women, "in their capacity as consumers and retailers, a particular kind of power and expertise as the state's agents in reforming the material culture of everyday life."[22] This, of course, turned out to be a Faustian bargain. Christine Varga-Harris eloquently outlines the tough balancing act women were expected to manage: "It was she who was ultimately responsible for household consumption and for cultivating a certain kind of cultural propriety, while simultaneously 'containing' values and behaviours associated with Capitalism like individualism and materialism."[23] Reid relates a telling anecdote from the 1959 American Exhibition in Moscow: the Soviet authorities banned the distribution of free samples of consumer products "specifically designed to appeal to, and inflate, the desires and expectations of Soviet women" on the grounds that it would cause a life-threatening stampede on the pavilion.[24] The Soviet system, then, openly doubted whether female citizens would be able to control their urges; nonetheless, it made them responsible for "rationalizing domestic labor, organizing domestic space, and championing the anti-Stalinist mid-century modern aesthetic."[25]

Soviet sixties popular culture depicted both men and women as forming a human chain of greed; that said, the sexes were distinguished in their motivations: men came across as stingy, women as rapacious. Men's materialism was mocked, but it was also frequently coded differently: their covetousness seemed more "rational," if still risible. Men placed an equals sign between amorous and financial relations, aiming to quantify the realm of emotions.[26] Women, by contrast, used marriage as a bargaining tool through which to achieve excessive abundance and wealth. Although both sexes could be accused of having developed a perverse relationship to wealth, women came to be seen as the greater threat because their greed appeared uncontainable and destructive. Men could be seen as the equivalent of Ebenezer Scrooge, whose misanthropy hurt no one directly but themselves. Women were cast as Lady Macbeths who applied persuasion and seduction in order to manipulate their husbands to violate their conscience. The *femme fatale* with her insatiable appetites could break her partner's will and ruin his life. Misanthropy and avariciousness are clearly two sides of the same coin, but it is evident from the era's film and media coverage that the latter posed a much more serious threat.

Single women, as gold-diggers on the prowl, were shown to be a mortal threat to men in general and to men with means in particular. For instance, in a 1955 cartoon titled "A groom with a dowry," a senior citizen proposes to an elegantly clad and much younger woman: "Lenochka, would you like to become my widow?"[27] The cartoon turns

Figure 4.4. "Love at first sight." *Krokodil* 36 (1963): 11.

on its head the common trope of an older man targeting a young, defenceless maiden; it is clear from her put-together appearance and controlled smile that she is no innocent victim but, rather, an experienced bird of prey. For social-climbing maidens like Lenochka, material status symbols were the most potent aphrodisiac, with cars ranking at the top of the list of desirable traits for potential bachelors. The car ensured a safe distance from the discomforts of public transportation, conveyed financial security, and reflected elevated social status. A 1960 cartoon shows a man and a woman dancing on a date as she casually inquires: "George, tell me more about yourself. Do you drive a Moskvich or a Volga?"[28] In similar fashion, a 1963 cartoon titled "Love at first sight" derides women's desire for status symbols. It depicts a decadently rouged and eccentrically attired woman repeatedly and adoringly kissing the windshield of a shiny sedan belonging to a bemused middle-age *apparatchik* (Figure 4.4).[29] His good looks and personality are clearly not what she is after. By the mid-1960s, the man-eater had joined the cast of popular culture villainesses. The 1963 cartoon "Ella's trophies" imagines women posing an even greater existential threat to middle-aged

ЭЛЛОЧКИНЫ ТРОФЕИ   Рисунок Ю. ГАНФА

Figure 4.5. "Ella's trophies." *Krokodil* 2 (1963): 10.

men. Unlike the gold-digging seductresses from the late 1950s and
early 1960s, the young and attractive Ella seems concerned less with
gaining material wealth than with enjoying the thrill of the hunt for its
own sake. The "pelts" of middle-aged men remind her of the gullibility
of men who were supposed to be seasoned hunters themselves.[30] Reclining regally on her chaise longue, the Cleopatra-like Ella knows she
will have many more conquests to celebrate (Figure 4.5).

In sixties visual culture, married women were as much of a threat
to male autonomy as unattached *femmes fatales*. *Krokodil* cartoonists often worried that bossy wives played the role of the master puppeteer,
pulling the strings at home as well as at the husband's workplace. A
1956 sketch shows a certain Mar'ia Ivanovna managing an institution
whose manager is (only ostensibly) her husband.[31] While the wife issues orders, her spouse hides behind her skirt. The cartoonist makes
clear that Mar'ia Ivanovna's bossiness is second only to her incompetence and avariciousness. She uses communal resources to benefit her
and husband. Eight years later, the cover of *Krokodil* displayed a similar
marital dynamic, with the husband pleading with his mean-looking

Figure 4.6. "Mom and dad consulting." *Krokodil* 19 (1960): 16

Figure 4.7. "Explaining matriarchy." *Krokodil* 5 (1967): 4.

and sharp-nailed wife: "Would you please let me employ at least one competent worker instead of a relative?"[32] It is clear from her expression that he will lose this fight too. Both these illustrations establish a dominant view of the sixties marriage dynamic: a cowed husband and his domineering wife. This trope appeared in several *Krokodil* short stories in which wives pushed their husbands to gain access to raises, new apartments, and promotions.[33]

Artists portrayed women as engaging in a two-front war: the wife emasculated her spouse by browbeating him while emasculating her sons by mommying them. These two processes were linked: the matriarch had first to exert dominance over her husband and then take full control of her male offspring. *Krokodil* exemplified this dynamic in a 1960 cartoon that showed a wife manhandling her spouse as the son explained to her sister: "See? Mom and dad are consulting on how to best raise us."[34] In the eyes of these children, there is no confusion as to who heads the household (Figure 4.6). Similarly, in a 1967 cartoon, a wife literally roughs up her husband, demanding that he explain the concept of matriarchy to his son, whom she is protectively embracing (Figure 4.7).[35] In both images, the physically and psychologically dominant female is cast as a harpy who is as bent on dominating her husband as she is on mollycoddling her son. These approaches, though contrasting, were calculated to ensure men's submission, thus guaranteeing her authoritarian control.

Krokodil presented momism as a both a gateway and a key cause to problems plaguing postwar men. Cartoonists portrayed mothers as enabling a "soft" masculinity. The reluctance of males to complete their university studies and their refusal to engage in socially useful work outside of Moscow and Leningrad was pinned on overprotective moms. The helicopter matriarchs who embodied this kind of threat clearly occupied a middle- and upper-middle-class status. Momism in the Soviet context had distinct class overtones: privileged moms went to humorous lengths to spare their sons the indignities of manual labour. To protect their sons from the vagaries of the real world, Soviet matrons fought battles against male authority figures – husbands, university deans, foremen, and police officers – and most often won the battle. A 1958 cartoon shows a gaggle of middle-aged matrons roughing up a university dean to ensure that their sons secure spots in the entering class. The dean is clearly outnumbered, outgunned, and outflanked; he must submit (Figure 4.8).[36] These efforts all led to arrested development, that is, to men who remained boys and who depended directly on their mothers. A prime example of this dynamic was a 1961

Figure 4.8. "Entrance exam season." *Krokodil* 18 (1958): 4.

Figure 4.9. "Security shield." *Krokodil* 17 (1961): 8–9.

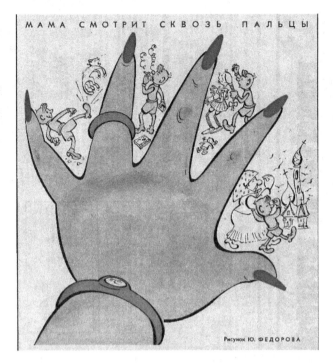

Figure 4.10. "Mom looks the other way." *Krokodil* 5 (1964): 7.

cartoon that shows a mother shielding – both literally and figuratively – her man-child with documents and certificates that exempt him from assuming any kind of adult responsibility (Figure 4.9). From cradle to grave, this mother's misguided mission comes down to infantilizing her son.

This arrested development resulted in the creation of either a hypocrite or a youth who could not fulfil his masculine duties. Fretting about the growing incidence of hooliganism, the press pinned the blame on the middle-class mother. For instance, an episode of a popular animated short named for its title character, *Murzlika*, features a certain Petia, who knows how to behave in front of adults but whose polished veneer hides a rotten core. He lies, steals, and misbehaves only when he is out of sight, then turns on the charm when in the presence of adults. A reviewer argues that without doubt, "the grown-up viewer clearly sees where Petia acquired his obnoxiousness: he reeks of 'mommy dearest' and her self-satisfied attitude."[37] This dynamic is evident in a *Krokodil*

Figure 4.11. "A protective mother hen." *Krokodil* 1 (1964): 3.

cartoon that shames mothers who turn a blind eye to their sons' mis-behaviour.[38] A litany of sins, from animal cruelty to smoking to church attendance, are linked directly to the heavily manicured, bejewelled, and plump woman's hand. Here, the sins of the son are passed back to the mother. Although the image represents a literal translation of the Russian idiom "to look through one's fingers," the cartoon also suggests that the mother's imposing hand is ready to protect her offspring from any possible consequences (Figure 4.10). Besides raising hypocrit-ical hooligans, helicopter moms prevented sons from expressing their masculine nature. In a 1964 cartoon, *Krokodil* mocks an overly protec-tive mother hen, who, so that her rooster son can sleep in, takes on the responsibility for crowing at dawn (Figure 4.11).[39] Aside the situation's improbability, the gender role reversal at the centre of the joke hints at the danger that a mother will emasculate her son.

If Soviet fathers were often portrayed as absent or uncaring, mothers erred in the opposite direction by being overprotective of their sons. In much the same way that they stunted their sons' emotional and

gender development through meddlesome interventions, women prevented their husbands from realizing themselves either as suitors or
as breadwinners. The modern woman was preoccupied mainly with
emasculating both her spouse and her male offspring; like a parasite,
her powers relied on her ability to drain the productive energies of the
males around her so as to secure a comfortable existence for herself. Despite the generally liberal atmosphere of the sixties, the cultural realm
channelled the anxieties about the era's monumental changes in plainly
misogynistic directions.

The Soviet critique of overbearing maternalism resembled the US
"momism panic" that emerged after Philip Wylie's *Generation of Vipers*
was published in 1942. The litany of sins Wylie ascribed to American
stay-at-home matriarchs bore a striking resemblance to fears the Soviet
public expressed. Historian Rebecca Jo Plant delineated this dynamic:
"Rather than venting hostility toward working women, the momism
critique expressed antagonism toward women who pursued a life of
ease by capitalizing on their relationships with men."[40] Thus the excesses of momism were tied to the excesses of consumerism. And Wylie
was hardly a fringe eccentric: his critique of "pathological mother love"
was an extension, albeit an extreme one, of arguments then being advanced by psychoanalysts, psychiatrists, and other psychological experts during the 1940s and '50s.[41] Edward A. Strecker's 1946 book *Their
Mother's Sons: The Psychiatrist Examines an American Problem* remade
"momism into both a theoretical model and a root cause for everything
that he finds reprehensible in this world," including psychoneurosis,
schizophrenia, religious fanaticism, alcoholism, homosexuality, and
even Nazi Germany and Imperial Japan.[42] In a 1951 postscript, Strecker
went so far as to claim that "Hitler, Mussolini and Stalin ... probably
became too deeply attached to their mothers."[43] These sentiments were
granted further respectability by professional organizations, such as the
Boston Psychoanalytic Society and Institute, which linked bad mother-
ing to nine psychosomatic diseases, including ulcerative colitis, celiac
disease, asthma, and eczema.[44]

Wylie's and Stecker's ideas readily translated into popular culture,
perhaps most notably in James Dean's performance in the 1955 cult
classic *Rebel Without a Cause*. Jim Stark, a seventeen-year-old on the
cusp of adulthood, defines himself in opposition to his domineering
mother and submissive father. Early in the film, Jim looks at his father Frank and tells the juvenile officer: "If he had guts to knock Mom
cold once, then maybe she'd be happy, and she'd stop picking on him."
He frequently complains that his mother and grandmother "make
mush" of his father. Although Carol Stark and Mr Stark's mother do

Figure 4.12. *Rebel Without a Cause* (1955). Jim Stark begs his father to "Stand up!"

not receive significant on-screen time, the ill effects of their momism appear self-evident. Even without being physically present, Mrs Stark rules the roost, proving Jim's diagnosis: "She eats him alive, and he takes it." The accuracy of Jim's observation is most evident in a scene where Jim comes home to see Frank on his knees cleaning up a fallen tray of food he has prepared for his wife as she lounges in bed, nursing a headache. To manifest Frank's total transgression of normative gender roles, he wears a frilly apron over his suit, all the while fearing he might make too much noise and disturb the slumbering missus. Even when Jim implores and demands that Frank stand up for himself literally and figuratively (Figure 4.12), the dad seems incapable of breaking the passivity he has chosen for himself. This scene is a clear echo of the *Krokodil* cartoons that cast mothers as household bullies who dominate their husbands. Jim rejects his father as a masculine role model and ridicules the perversion of gender roles when he exclaims: "I'll tell you one thing, I don't ever want to be like him. How can a guy grow up in a circus like that?" Thus the rebellion advertised in the film's title comes down to Jim's rejecting his father's submissiveness as a precondition for achieving adult masculinity.

As the remainder of this chapter will demonstrate, Soviet directors were no less concerned about the perceived gender imbalance caused by outsized female influence over the country's men in the "age of affluence." As they diagnosed the particularities and problems of the sixties gender order, they ultimately offered moviegoers a narrow range of acceptable female behaviour, even as they moved away from the orthodoxy of Stalinist tropes.

Behind Every Great Man ...: The Feminine Ideal in Sixties Films

While *Krokodil*, and the Soviet press more broadly, expressed vexation about the mannerisms of postwar femininity, the film industry busily promoted aspirational models for Soviet womanhood. In promoting sacrificial femininity as a gendered ideal, sixties directors were following a long-standing tradition in Soviet arts and culture. Stoic selflessness had defined proscriptive narratives about Soviet womanhood since the revolutionary era. The pantheon of socialist martyrdom was chock-full of heroines who willingly paid the ultimate price, starting with the titular heroine in Maxim Gorky's *Mother* and including Second World War heroines such as Zoia Kosmodem'ianskaia.[45] Indeed, the heroines of the 1930s and '40s "were politically active women willing to sacrifice their own well-being for the sake of the public welfare."[46] In the postwar period this gender model remained fertile soil for scriptwriters, proved popular with moviegoers, and was readily approved by the authorities.[47] Besides following an established trend, depictions of idealized feminine models reflected the perceived dangers associated with women who achieved self-realization and independence at the expense of their male counterparts. What distinguished sixties idealized femininity from earlier incarnations is that postwar heroines sacrificed themselves so as to help their fathers, husbands, sons, or brothers achieve their full potential. Thus while prewar heroines died for the cause, their postwar counterparts sacrificed their interests on behalf of their faltering male counterparts.

Three films of the "woman as angel" genre are worth discussing so as to appreciate the variations in this gender trope over time. The relationships shown in these three films clearly resonated with audiences and critics alike; the popular and official excitement over them illustrates that they tapped into genuine support for a more traditional femininity. *An Unfinished Story*, a 1955 feature, sold nearly 30 million tickets. Soviet officialdom proclaimed it a masterpiece and proudly debuted it at the inaugural week of Soviet film in Belgium, besides showcasing it for Elisabeth of Bavaria, Queen of the Belgians.[48] Because it was a blockbuster, local party administrators desperate to boost attendance at agitational lectures used tickets to this movie as bait.[49] *When the Trees Were Tall* (Kogda derev'ia byli bol'shimi) received domestic critical acclaim, attracted a sizeable audience of 21 million viewers, and was nominated for the Palme d'Or at the 1962 Cannes Film Festival. More than 40 million Soviet viewers thronged to see *Trust Me, Folks!* (Ver'te mne, liudi!), making it the second most attended movie of 1965.

When *An Unfinished Story* premiered 1955, it was strongly praised, particularly for its protagonist, Elizaveta Maksimovna, a Leningrad district doctor who makes house calls day and night. Although veteran director Fridrikh Ermler took pains to show her as a professional, her talents obviously lay in her flawless bedside manner. Her recommendations to her (predominantly male) patients have as much to do with her understanding them as individuals as they do with her medical prowess. With many patients, she insists that their physical well-being depends on maintaining a positive, can-do attitude.

Elizaveta's humble but uncompromising perseverance earns her the admiration – and, eventually, the love – of a hotheaded world-renowned shipbuilding engineer Iurii Ershov, who is bedridden after a shipyard accident. Her faith in him and her ceaseless encouragement allow him to walk again – an outcome that all other (male) medical professionals pronounced impossible. As N.N. Klado points out in his review: "Elizaveta Maksimovna's real power resides in her faith in man's limitless potential and his right to achieve happiness. The striving towards happiness ... ultimately results in victory."[50] In the final scene we see Ershov, cheered on by her piano playing, stand on his own two feet again, ready to begin their love story in earnest.

Of course, this scenario resembles the one featured in *A Story of a Real Man* (1948), where a pilot learns to walk again after being inspired by an older comrade. In *Unfinished Story*, however, there is no older comrade to offer inspiration, and even the handicapped hero himself is in the background. The true star of the movie is the uncannily kind doctor, who has a Lazarus-like effect on all her patients. However hyperbolic, this script played very well with audiences and critics alike; they were mesmerized by the striking Elina Bystritskaia. One moviegoer, a professor of history from Moscow, spared no praise: "It is no exaggeration to say that in terms of directing and acting ... *An Unfinished Story* is perhaps the best movie Soviet cinema has created to date."[51] Noted Soviet art historian I.M. Iof'ev was so enthralled by the heroine that he rhapsodized how the viewer could effortlessly imagine her – even when at her most silent and agitated – leaping into action, ready to commit heroic deeds, face danger head on, and endure deprivation. In Iof'ev's estimation, Elizaveta's character alone salvaged the film because her spiritual wealth compensated for the meagre storyline.[52] Commentators consistently praised the actress for bringing to life an authentic woman who did not hide behind the artifice of the acting craft.[53] N.N. Klado went so far as to say that it was impossible to look away from the protagonist: "You admire her exterior; her mind that shines through her eyes, her close attention to people, her kindness, her directness, her doubts, and principledness; we grieve with her and rejoice in her happiness."[54] Film critic L. Pogozheva observed that the director displayed his affection so unrestrainedly that occasionally the heroine seemed a bit too perfect – but even Pogozheva qualified that this happened in "only a few places."[55] By acclamation, the Soviet press and audiences judged Elizaveta to be the new model of Soviet femininity.

The fact that Ermler made his heroine a working professional engaged in the noblest of pursuits made his job of creating a role model easy. She combined Soviet scientific progress with a woman's gentle touch. Elizaveta cured the sick by encouraging them to be brave because "happy people recover twice as quickly." In later-sixties cinema, however, aspirational femininity only required that the heroine be the embodiment of unwavering hope and showcase unconditional faith in the human ability to improve. Not even a pretence of medical expertise was needed. This trend became most apparent in L. Kulidzhanov's 1962 film *When the Trees Were Tall*, whose protagonist Natasha is defined by charity. Movie critic N. Lordkipanidze described Natasha: "At no point does the director attempt to film her from an angle that would make her unique and turn her into a beauty. Even though making her more attractive would prove easy, he is not tempted to; the actress's face is expressive, her smile charming, and her eyes simply delightful." Natasha's modest countenance matches her humble life. The reviewer opines on how unremarkable she is: "It is difficult to explain the source of Natasha's likeability. She does not commit any particular feats and her observations and comments are rather ordinary. She works conscientiously and that's pretty much it."[56] For Lordkipanidze, Natasha's spiritual tact, honesty, and grace redeemed her lack of superheroic qualities so evident in Elizaveta Maksimovna. Despite her average appearance and unremarkable personality, Natasha acts as an agent of change: her "ordinary" patience and compassion transform the life of a man who unexpectedly bursts into her life.

Natasha grew up as an orphan after the war, having been separated from her parents at an early age. She wanted nothing more than to belong to someone, to experience the joys of being someone's child, someone's daughter. Suddenly, a man appears in Natasha's village, claiming to be her father. The young woman is so overjoyed that she welcomes this stranger, Kuz'ma Iordanov, into her life without reservation. Kuz'ma, however, is neither her father nor an honest man. He serendipitously heard about Natasha and her story from an old woman who had left the village. Fearing the police because of his conman profile, and seeking free shelter and sustenance until he can safely return to Moscow, he pretends to be Natasha's father.

Humorous mistaken-identity situations abound, but the dramatic tension of Kuz'ma's transformation looms even larger. Can he turn the corner? Can Natasha change her "father" from a dishonest loafer into an upright citizen? Natasha not only influences Kuz'ma's conversion but does so without doing much of anything. G. Medvedev, in his review titled "What happened to Kuz'ma Iordanov?," answers his own rhetorical question: "His adoptive daughter Natasha is such a pure and honest person that Kuz'ma is not able to take advantage of her thoughtfulness and her tenderness while remaining a parasite, a good-for-nothing liar."[57] Film critic G. Kapralov also notes that Natasha rarely or directly reprimands Kuz'ma. Nonetheless, her every gesture indicates her fervent hope that her father is the best father, that he will, ultimately, not disappoint her.[58] Lordkipanidze takes it so far as to say that Natasha, "the simplest of girls," possesses the kind of untainted conviction that commands respect and requires utter surrender. All three reviewers interpret Natasha in nearly spiritual language; she appears as an angelic personality in Kuz'ma's life, making his moral makeover only a matter of time. Even when the errant father admits to Natasha that he is neither her father nor an honest man, she refuses to believe him. Having confessed, Kuz'ma can return to being a parent, but this time acts in such a way that his "daughter" can be proud of him.

It is no coincidence that Kuz'ma's "conversion" takes place once he abandons the city and that a village girl guides him to righteousness. Rural settings and residents had by then become synonymous with simplicity and morality, while the opposite was true of cities and urban life. I. Gurin and V. Berenshtein's 1965 film *Trust Me, Folks!* advances this trend by featuring a heroine whose appearance, language, and conduct mark her clearly as an oasis of rural life in the midst of Leningrad. Her traditional womanhood is clearly the tonic required to salvage the reputation and life of an escaped convict. The action takes place in 1956, immediately after the Twentieth Party Congress, which marked the start of the first wave of Gulag rehabilitations. The protagonist of the film is Aleksei Lapin, one of the first benefactors of de-Stalinization.

Lapin was fated to endure two stints in the Gulag. He spent much of his youth in a camp because after his parents were sentenced as "enemies of the people." After his initial release, he landed back in prison because of criminal activities. In 1956, with only several months left in his sentence, he looks forward to becoming a person with a passport and a real name. His plans go awry, however, when he becomes implicated in an escape plan in which he has played no part. Rather than attempting to clear his name with the authorities, he flees across the frozen tundra, hoping to emerge alive and attain his dreamed-of freedom. Once in Leningrad, he has no choice but to return to the criminal life he had tried so hard to escape. Looking for a safe house, he stumbles across a household consisting of a single mother, Nina, her father, and her daughter. Nina and Lapin eventually develop feelings for each other and begin living like man and wife.

Nina's kindness and affection come unexpectedly for Lapin, who had, up till then, rarely experienced such unconditional support. Reviewer V. Pogostina notes that Nina is special in that she possesses the innate capacity to believe in her man and see him for who he really is.[59] A number of police officers observed Nina's civilizing influence on the former Gulag inmate in their review of the film: "But he was not expecting to encounter the serene, modest, and loving Nina on his path. Aleksei unexpectedly acquires a home, a family, and everything else that he previously was afraid to even dream he could attain."[60] Lapin, however, fears that his secret will endanger the idyllic life he has begun. His worst fears are realized when a special night out on the town leads him straight to law enforcement. Wanting to treat his beloved to a romantic outing, he procures tickets to a theatre that has been reserved for the police that evening.

Although his instincts tell him to flee once he enters the hall full of police officers, he stays next to Nina, hoping to go unnoticed in the sea of faces, praying that his new relationship will outlast the ordeal. However, the inspector in charge of Lapin's case, Comrade Anokhin, recognizes the most wanted fugitive and approaches him in the lobby during intermission, suggesting he give himself up peacefully. Pleading his case and promising Anokhin he will turn himself in on Monday, Lapin begs that he be given the weekend to say goodbye to Nina. Noted film critic Pogostina interpreted the policeman's clemency as a sign of the officer's insightfulness: "Anokhin's conversation with Lapin in the foyer conclusively persuades him that Lapin was indeed saved by his loving relationship [spasen liubov'iu svoei]."[61] Although the detective's mercy is key to the plot, it is Nina's hold over Lapin that has definitively "tamed" the runaway criminal.

Lapin returns to his seat and rejoins Nina, entirely unsure how to confess his past without spoiling what they have built together. Like Kuz'ma, he cannot bring himself to hurt the woman who has delivered him from a life of crime and given him a second lease on life. Unable to face her and confess his sins, he first tries to run away, but Nina chases after him, wanting to stay by him despite his past. After a heart-wrenching parting, Lapin turns himself in and is sentenced to prison. Although it may be incarcerated indefinitely, the final scene suggests that Nina has resolved to wait for Lhimapin and to support him in the meantime. Nina, like Natasha, is a simple and in many ways average woman in both conduct and appearance, but one whose inner goodness outweighs her ordinariness. Reviewers lauded her for unwaveringly supporting her man and for being an example of how people in general ought to be treated: with trust, dignity, and respect.

In the final count, some of the most talked-about heroines in sixties cinema performed wonders by restoring the handicapped back to their feet, renewing recidivist vagabonds' sense of purpose, and turning hardened criminals into upstanding citizens. These women succeeded where friends, family members, and social institutions had failed. Although at the centre of the narrative as miracle workers, these heroines end up as secondary and static characters in the sense that their role consists solely of supporting the maturation of the male character. As props and catalysts, Elizaveta, Natasha, and Nina advance the plot but are themselves unaltered by it because they are not flesh-and-blood protagonists but walking-and-talking morality lessons. The ultimate reward for these angels in human form is male companionship: paternal affection for Natasha, a wedding for Elizaveta and Nina. Ironically, the centrality of the male figures only emphasizes the extent to which men need to be helped and the extent to which they rely on women to lift them up – sometimes literally. While sixties cinema showed men being vulnerable and dependent on the kindness of their female partners, it simultaneously also cautioned that men could just as easily fall into the clutches of more sinister women.

The Sixties Vixen, Or, The Discreet Charms of the Anti-Heroine

Although the traditional feminine ideal remained both culturally relevant and financially profitable, depictions of femininity that were a far cry from the ideal proved equally as alluring for scriptwriters and moviegoers. In fact, Soviet filmmakers of the era were faulted for making anti-heroines too attractive. For instance, I. Kokoreva, who would go on to become the editor-in-chief of the Script Editorial Board of

Goskino, complained that though the appearance of a petty philistine ought to evoke only laughter or anger, Soviet filmmakers accomplished the opposite. Kokoreva contended that "all means of cinematic expressiveness are used exclusively to sympathetically and melodramatically reflect the minor events and petty feelings of people who neither commit feats nor enrich their life or the lives of others." From this perspective, it appeared that anti-heroines tantalized rather than repelled.[62] In a similar vein, director G. Mdivani complained that the movie industry ought to make more films about young women like Nina Davydova, who voluntarily gave up the glamourous city life, deciding to work at an Irkutsk hydroelectric dam. Mdivani notes that Nina avoided the fate of most female protagonists featured in Soviet film: "She could have, like thousands of her female peers, finished university studies and remained in Moscow in the comfort of her family and friends; she could have become an economist or a secretary; she could have paid her union dues and attended Komsomol meetings; she could have spent her nights going to the movies or the theater; she could have, in short, lived as most of our film heroines live."[63] Although disingenuous in their assessment that morally upright female characters got no screen time, critics accurately observed that "villainesses" often found favour with movie audiences despite their obvious flaws and that directors made them entrancing on purpose.

The most talked-about film of 1956 was *Different Fates* (Raznye Sud'by), which sold around 30 million tickets. Although the film bills itself as a story about the roads (not) taken by four average (urban) Soviet youth, the narrative is most properly viewed as the story of Tania: a quintessential *femme fatale* who over the course of the film ensnares and then upends the lives of two upstanding men. Tania's exterior signals her complete preoccupation with her own interests: she abandons two men – her husband and her subsequent suitor – because they cannot provide for her in the way she expects.

Unsurprisingly, she is well-dressed, impeccably groomed, and polished to a mirror sheen. Tania communicates her vanity clearly in that she is incapable of passing by a reflective surface without inspecting her appearance (Figure 4.13). The movie makes Tania shine even though her story is that of a "fallen woman." Although the apartment she shares with her parents is commodious enough to accommodate her and her first husband, Fedia, she nonetheless insists that he simultaneously work and attend university so that they can secure separate lodgings. One reviewer notes that Tania's credo is that husbands and suitors are supposed to provide for their wives in all areas of life. Once her first husband is no longer able or willing to perform this function,

Figure 4.13. *Different Fates* (1956). Tania as vanity personified.

Tania leaves him for a much older and already established music professor. However, once he, too, is unable to advance her social-climbing agenda, she walks away. In a very direct sense, Tania is an unrepentant gold-digging con artist who uses her looks to entrap men in pursuit of her goals.

In reporting on the voluminous mail the newspaper received about the film, *Sovetskaia kul'tura* showcased the varied terms applied to Tania: *femme fatale* (*rokovaia zhenshchina*), beautiful trash, and predator. Although much of the attention Tania received proved negative, it reinforced fans' claims that she was the film's central and most complex character – to the point that she served as "the basis of its narrative line."[64] Published notes from moviegoers expressed equal doses of disapproval for, and fascination with, Tania. Most importantly, her fate raised myriad questions for viewers: How did she come to be the way she is? Could she be redeemed? Was she a caricature or a complex individual? Shouldn't the authors have focused on more positive characters?[65] Questions about whether she was reformable were key to how the modern postwar woman was discussed. Although moviegoers commented that they appreciated that the filmmakers did not try to "fix" Tania, discussions about the possibility of Tania's salvation lingered. One moviegoer characterized Tania's character as fixed, making her redemption improbable. The *Sovetskaia kul'tura* editor was compelled to retort: "Yes, difficult. But possible."[66]

Veronika, the protagonist of Mikhail Kalatozov's 1957 feature *The Cranes Are Flying*, can be seen as Tania's successor since her story raised similar discussions about a heroine's right to be guided by self-interest rather than self-sacrifice. Veronika's chief crime was her infidelity to her fiancé Boris, who, on the very first day of the German invasion, left Moscow to fight for his country on the front lines. Shaken by the loss of both her parents and demoralized by Boris's uncertain fate, Veronika succumbs to the aggressive advances of Boris's immoral cousin Mark and marries him shortly thereafter. The movie traces Veronika's fall from grace as she struggles to come to terms with her infidelity. In the end, however, she is symbolically reintegrated into the Soviet collective as she adopts an orphan, whom she names Boris. She is shown in the final scene handing out flowers to the returning soldiers when armistice is announced.

Veronika evoked strong emotions among both party officials and moviemakers because Kalatozov portrayed his heroine in a way that made it difficult not to empathize with her plight. Judging by contemporary reactions to the film, Kalatozov succeeded in forcing audiences to contemplate Veronika's betrayal of Boris rather than condemn her. Film critic M. Turovskaia noted in her review that during war a woman's faithfulness to her partner symbolized a victory of the human spirit over the forces of death and destruction. She accused the scriptwriter V. Rozov of shying away from tackling a problem of this magnitude, focusing instead "on the pettiness of psychological breakdowns" (*meloch' dushevnykh izlomov*).[67] As Turovskaia points out, there was no place in socialist realism for heroines who suffered stress, depression, and anxiety during the nation's historical turning points. Put simply, Turovskaia saw Veronika's reaction as appallingly self-indulgent and thus anti-Soviet.

Chinese Communist Party officials shared Turovskaia's sentiment: they refused to screen *Cranes* in the People's Republic of China. In November 1958, Chinese Deputy Minister of Culture Comrade San Yan interpreted the story in strictly ideological terms: "The plot is not only uniquely un-Soviet, but it also fails to demonstrate the typical character traits of a true Soviet individual. Why is Veronika talking about losing her purpose in life ...? Why? On what grounds did she lose sight of the meaning of life?" The Chinese representative judged the movie according to standards Soviet critics would have themselves used only four years earlier while Stalin was still alive. In the Stalinist world view, Veronika could not have acted the way she did: she was, after all, "a person born under Soviet rule and as such could not be as hopeless."[68] In addition, San Yan was appalled that the scriptwriter never condemned the female protagonist, but sympathized with her and expected viewers to do the same. Veronika had to be censured and her choices repudiated in order to provide audiences with a clear lesson in acceptable communist behaviour.

The question of motive behind Veronika's "treason" drove discussions, which focused on the film's moral lesson. Critics wondered whether the heroine of *Cranes* should be forgiven for her indiscretion and protested that Veronika had done nothing, especially considering she was in midst of a national tragedy. She had not saved lives or sacrificed her own in the name of the motherland; instead, she had betrayed her fiancée who was fighting on the front, only to then languish and brood about the difficult fate that had befallen *her*. The cynics thus accused Veronika of committing a double sin: infidelity and patriotic passivity. The fact that the causes of Veronika's betrayal remained ambiguous exasperated critics. Leading Soviet film critic R.N. Iurenev wondered aloud: "Veronika's love was pure, her pain deep, her memory fresh, and her faithfulness seemingly undisputable. Why did Veronika commit the act of betrayal?" While admitting that the trauma of war and the loss of both parents partly explained Veronika's irrational infidelity, he criticized Kalatozov for not elucidating the more private, psychological reasons behind her betrayal. Despite Mark's brutish advances (Kalatozov intimates rape)[69] and Veronika's inability to defend herself, Iurenev argued that the question remained, "Why did she do it?"[70] Lev Anninskii commented that it was precisely the scene in which Veronika surrendered to Mark, betraying Boris, that had contemporary critics crying foul. He averred, however, that Soviet film critics had the right to be rattled considering that no logic could satisfactorily explain her action.[71]

The apprehension regarding the movie's heroine went beyond the movie industry and ministry offices. Veronika so dominated daily conversations that film expert I. Shilova marks the beginning of the sixties with the release of *Cranes* in 1957. Shilova recalls: "After the viewing of the movie at the State Institute of Cinematography, the student body was divided in two opposing factions. The disbelief and shock was mutual, but the 'moralists' could not, under any circumstance, accept the movie's ending and accept the author's pardon and elevation of Veronika. I, too, was among the moralists."[72] Ultimately, however, the very emotions that Veronika's critics saw as unfitting for a Soviet woman – despair, anxiousness, apathy – made her a popular figure to whom the viewers related. Veronika would turn out to be instrumental in shaping later movies in terms of allowing for more complicated, multi-dimensional celluloid characters. It was not only Soviet audiences that accepted and sympathized with Veronika's story. The lead actress of *Cranes*, the beautiful Tat'iana Samoilova, who was frequently identified with her role, took Europe by storm. Following its triumph at the 1958 Cannes Film Festival, where it earned the Grand Prize, the world celebrated the film's main protagonist. France's *Liberation* "approvingly contrasted Samoilova's purity and authenticity with that Western female icon, Brigitte Bardot."[73] Samoilova even remembered receiving a watch from her East German fans during a festival there; the gift featured the inscription: "Finally we see on the Soviet screen a face, not a mask."[74] Retrospectively, film critic Irina Shilova described Veronika's ultimate impact in the following way: "The actress's face, her figure, her black sweater – all of it testified to the emergence of new models, the bourgeoning of new ideals of this new time."[75]

This new feminine model generated numerous debates because it so directly unsettled the existing aspirational model for Soviet women – either openly, like Tania in *Different Fates*, or straddling the line, like Veronika in *Cranes*. Placed in the context of romantic relationships, these anti-heroines showed that men could become dispensable and replaceable. The notion that men did not necessarily have the upper hand in matters of the heart was made clear in the period's most popular family dramas and comedies.

Soviet Battle of the Sexes: Domesticating the Male Hero

Sixties filmmakers extolled the stabilizing effect of marriage and family life on Soviet men – but only in cases where those men could find their own "angel in human form." However, for Soviet men who were unlucky enough to fall for a real-life Veronika or Tania, Soviet films predicted a much more dire fate. In the main, the most popular motion pictures took a decidedly dim view of courtship, romance, and marriage, painting these as a minefield for male protagonists, who either lost their way or perished. Sixties features established postwar heroes as imperfect and ineffective patriarchs who often got bamboozled by their love interests. But even when women did not actively and knowingly manipulate their partners, sixties cinema shied away from happy endings, showing that affairs of the heart remained just out of men's reach. Two dramas – *Alien Kin* (1955) and *Noisy Day* (1960) – brought into sharp relief the dangers that materialism and consumerist femininity posed not only to marriage but also to men's moral compass. *Three Plus Two* and *Easy Life* were two mid-1960s comedies that extended the commentary on men as both corruptible by material comforts and defenceless against women's well-laid plans to "civilize" them through marriage.[76]

At first glance, M. Shveitser's *Alien Kin* (1955) serves as a straightforward condemnation of anti-communal attitudes. Upon closer inspection, however, the film distinguishes itself from typical socialist realist narratives in that the hero's quest to convert his materialistic wife is far from certain to succeed. Even the movie's finale only ambiguously portends the heroine's transformation. Collective farm films of the Stalin era ended with a wedding; Shveitser's *kolkhoz* story begins with one. Breaking with the Stalinist tradition of signifying a happy-ever-after finale with a Hollywoodesque wedding celebration, Shveitser's marriage ceremony foreshadows a rocky start for the *kolkhoz*'s latest newlyweds, Fedor and Stesha. The pair's marital problems begin soon after the groom moves in with his in-laws.

The household members start off on a cordial note, but it soon becomes apparent that the Riashkins harbour problematically self-serving attitudes. The father-in-law casually confesses his opposition to the *kolkhoz*: "If you refuse to participate – you're no good. If you agree – you end up cheating yourself." As time goes on, it becomes clearer and clearer to Fedor that his in-laws' insatiable greed motivates their every move and inevitably hurts the collective farm. As one of the *kolkhoz* brigade leaders, Fedor has to fight the impulse to publicly rebuke his wife's parents for their mercenary attitude.

The conflict comes to a head when Stesha's father refuses to give up one of his horses for a village-wide effort to fulfil the plan in record time. As soon as Fedor learns about his in-laws' self-centredness, he marches to the house to take the horse. There, he encounters a hostile reception. Furious, Stesha accuses him of betraying his own kin, placing the benefit of strangers above his own family's interests. The argument becomes so heated that Fedor storms out of the house, not sure what to do. He does not want to leave his bride, but knows he cannot continue living under her parents' roof. He knows he has a chance to "re-educate" Stesha, but he feels that he can only do it by separating her from her family. Stesha eventually persuades her husband to return by telling him she is pregnant. For the sake of the child, Fedor goes back, but the troubles do not end – he becomes more and more alienated from his "kin." After several similar altercations, the hero moves into a dorm because he feels he is compromising his conscience by staying under his in-laws' roof.

Stesha, egged on by her parents, decides to shame Fedor publicly, hoping the collective will defend the interests of a pregnant woman. She uses pregnancy as a bargaining chip, employing her knowledge of Soviet society's intolerance of runaway fathers. Despite their sympathies, the members of the collective do not trust Stesha's accusations since she never integrated into *kolkhoz* life. Unsatisfied with the weak response, Stesha turns to the Komsomol authorities, weeping to the officer in charge. Sympathetic to the plea of the deserted pregnant woman, Comrade Glazycheva convenes a meeting with the aim of shaming the husband into returning to his wife. At the meeting Fedor calmly defends himself, explaining: "They live in the *kolkhoz* but dislike it. Had I stayed any longer, tolerating their avarice for the sake of marital bliss, I would have acquired their miserliness." Glazycheva quickly retorts, as if speaking from a manual: "The most shameful thing about this whole situation is the fact that you have resigned yourself to failure. Have you tried to re-educate them? Probably not. The fact that your wife is not an active Komsomol member speaks volumes about your indifference to her. You were supposed to re-educate your wife, your in-laws, everybody!" Another Komsomol member, Lev Zakharych, however, comes to Fedor's defence, chastising Glazycheva for ignoring the delicacy of the case: "One size does not fit all, Comrade Glazycheva. Relationships are such complicated affairs. We should focus on helping rather than determining whom to punish and how to discipline." Although the movie establishes two contrasting approaches to reforming an errant citizen, it ultimately recognizes that Fedor cannot really transform his wife. In the final scene, Stesha relocates to Fedor's dorm room. The barren space – a clear departure from the clutter of her parent's home – marks the true beginning of their marriage. This collectivist environment becomes a place where Stesha can learn how to become a nurturing and giving parent. Stesha's sullen expression, however, casts doubt on the durability of the couple's reunion and leaves the viewer wondering whether the young couple will bridge their differences so as to make their union a lasting one.

Although the film openly condemns self-interest, critics debated whether Fedor had done enough to re-educate his wife. One reviewer contended that members of the collective had not taken a firm enough stand against the Riashkins and that even Fedor was incapable of defeating them.[77] Another critic pronounced a harsh sentence on the hero: "Fedor Soloveikov is not a proactive, dynamic hero. He is a good worker and an honest man, but he is far from being a master of his own fate [*khoziain zhizni*] and this is why he emerges from this fight with wickedness as a purely passive character." Fedor's unwillingness to convert his wife and in-laws to the communist path marked him as unsuitable for younger audiences, according to the same critic. "What kind of a positive hero does our youth expect? A popular hero, a wholesome man, who would see every day as an opportunity to wage another battle!"[78] Even the generally positive reviews maintained that Fedor, although innately virtuous, lacked the tested virility of men who had undergone the trials of tribulations of the Second World War.[79]

A lone dissenting voice, critic A. Petrosian accused the negative critics of expecting unreasonable things. He asserted that Fedor would cease to be believable as soon as he turned into a moralizer and propaganda agitator. "The positive hero," argued Petrosian, "is a living individual rather than a treatise on positive heroism or a scheme that exists only in our imagination." Petrosian also argued that, though the hero propagandized little, his actions spoke volumes. He reasoned that Stesha displayed a fundamental lack of interest in bettering herself and as such would hardly have been won over by any amount of effort on Fedor's part. He concluded that those who saw Fedor as a weak hero still saw the world in Stalinist black and white. Petrosian's generous assessment aside, commentators asserted that Fedor's passivity made Stesha's "conversion" at the end of the film disingenuous and not very believable. The reviewers complained that the director had artificially tagged on Fedor's and Stesha's happy reunion, thus spoiling the film's literary inspiration, V. Tendriakov's 1954 novella *Like a Fish Out of Water* (Ne ko dvoru). Movie critics by and large denounced the "add-on" finale as contrived and false. A. Dement'ev, for example, opined that the movie should have ended like the original story: with the Riashkins remaining completely isolated from their neighbours. "The daughter's rebellion [against her parents] and Riashkins' bitter loneliness – this is where the movie ends and this is where its main conflict is resolved ... The sentence has been passed and the score was settled."[80] Film critic R. Iurenev also remained unconvinced that Stesha had truly changed, noting that she had abused her husband too eagerly and too convincingly.[81] The same was said of Stesha in the novella; Petrosian noted that the wife treated her groom like a commodity (*zakonnoi sobstvenn'ost'iu*): "Fedor now belongs to Stesha, like everything else in her father's home."[82]

Georgii Natanson's *Noisy Day* (Shumnyi den', 1960) went a step further than *Alien Kin* in depicting a broken home by ending the film on a sombre note. This film's protagonist, Fedor, finds himself unable to resolve the tension between marital concord and moral standards, and ultimately succumbs to his wife's manipulations. Although set on Moscow's Arbat, the set-up is similar to that of *Alien Kin* in that the two central characters – Fedor and his wife Lena – are living with his mother,

Klavdiia Vasil'evna, and his three high school–aged siblings. This time, however, it is the sister-in-law who breaks up the family unit through her gluttony. Despite ample space, furniture crowds every square metre of the apartment, much of it covered with blankets and sheets. The setting is eerie, as if the occupants have either never completely settled in or are ready to flee at a moment's notice. Lena, who spends her days obsessively buying new furniture, ironically dares not use it out of fear of damaging it. The graceful, well-spoken, and attractive twenty-eight-year-old beauty strategically bullies Fedor to secure them an apartment and provide the money necessary to fill their nest with the latest word in interior design. To meet his wife's demands, Fedor abandons his promising but unprofitable scientific research at the lab and begins writing lucrative fluff pieces for magazines and delivering well-paid but meaningless public lectures. For her part, Lena defends her avarice by disingenuously appropriating the government's populist rhetoric: "Why are they constructing so many beautiful, spacious buildings? Why are they offering so many wonderful apartments? Why are they selling carpets, crystal, expensive furniture, dining sets, and paintings?" For Lena, to consume is to exist. This point is not lost on Fedor's younger brother Oleg, who warns the eldest sibling: "She will devour you."

Natanson further blemishes Lena's character by contrasting her unfavourably to Oleg and Fedor's mother Klavdia Vasilevna, who personifies the matriarch of old: long-suffering, selfless, and interested only in her family's well-being. It is no coincidence that Klavdia Vasilevna inhabits the two spaces Lena never enters: the kitchen and dining room. The widowed matron serves as Lena's foil, reminding the audience of the alternative to contemporary gender norms. The fact that at twenty-eight Lena has not borne children underscores her distance from the feminine ideal that Natanson projects onto Klavdia Vasilevna, who has raised four children. Lena's eventual insistence that Fedor choose between her and his mother represents more than a domestic ultimatum. It signifies the choice between a domestic community and shallow individualism.

One unexpected turn of events exposes how far the beautiful and immaculately dressed Lena will go to defend her treasured possessions. The conflict in the film begins when the family's youngest member, the high schooler Oleg, accidentally spills ink on his sister-in-law's table. Lena shrieks upon seeing her table ruined and proceeds to throw Oleg's pet goldfish out the apartment window. Just before she hysterically tosses his pet from the window, he screams out in despair: "But they are living creatures!" In a fit of rage, Oleg reaches for his deceased father's sabre that hangs beneath his military portrait and hacks into the furniture in front of the assembled household. A weapon that had

Figure 4.14. Evgenii Grebenshchikov, poster for *Noisy Day* (1961).

once defended the Soviet Union's borders now symbolically and literally strikes against Lena's insatiable acquisitiveness. The centrality of both Oleg's action and the instrument of his vengeance is clear from the film poster (Figure 4.14).[83] The violent act breaks the stalemate that is suffocating the household and brings its simmering tensions to the fore. The poster's upper left corner features Lena's shock; in the lower right, Klavdiia Vasil'evna steels herself for a chance to win back her son. However, the jagged shards on the poster foreshadow that the disparate fragments are unlikely to reassemble themselves and that a return to the *status quo ante* is unlikely.

The incident exposes the pressures that have built up within the apartment. Klavdiia Vasil'evna confronts Fedor and tells him that Lena has turned him into a petty philistine. Fedor defends himself, telling her that the love he feels for his spouse inspires him: how could doing something in the name of love – the most exalted feeling man is capable of – turn him into a philistine? His mother reflects critically on the notion that love inspires to do only good: "Love debases man as often as it betters him." Klavdiia Vasil'evna thus problematizes Fedor's romanticized view of love, telling him that the worst crime is not to abandon one's spouse but to betray one's humanity and dignity (*izmena chelovecheskomu dostoinstvu*). Deeply moved by his mother's words and by her obvious distress, Fedor promises to change. Ultimately, however, Fedor proves powerless against his wife's machinations and moves out. As he leaves the apartment and his family, he turns around in the street and looks up at the building's windows in the hope of seeing his mother, but he sees only the solemn gaze of his father's photo-portrait and the sabre that dominates the dining room wall. Ultimately, Fedor finds himself unable to resolve the tension between marital concord and moral standards.

The cultural authorities initially conveyed a mixed response to Natanson's film. Both the Minister of Culture E.A. Furtseva and the secretary of the Komsomol organization condemned the film by comparing it to Italian neorealism.[84] In referring to the postwar Italian film movement, Furtseva was implicitly objecting to the unhealthy focus on the sordid aspects of Soviet life. *Noisy Day* did not represent life in its revolutionary development but instead unflatteringly showed the everyday. The minister found the cast of characters – wives who care more about credenzas than their husbands, teenagers who vent their anger by swinging sabres at furniture, and weak-willed heads of households corrupted by hoarding spouses – to be more typical of capitalist Rome than of socialist Moscow. Natanson kept insisting that the movie would enlighten youth by highlighting the struggle against middlebrow, materialistic values. The final decision lay with the Secretary of the Moscow Communist Party Committee, P.N. Demichev, who concluded that the movie presented ideas that would benefit all generations. The movie was, in a sense, ideologically edifying, for it condemned bourgeois, middlebrow sensibility and showed its destructive influence. This was, of course, a generous but misleading interpretation based on how the filmscript ended. Natanson was essentially presenting the triumph of materialism over communist morality. In the end, Lena wins Fedor, and Klavdiia and the rest of the family are unable to convince him to return to the right path. A husband who knows better has succumbed to his wife's baser instincts, betraying his own conscience in the process. The father's sabre had meted out the first blow to Lena's corrupting influence, but the mother proved incapable of completing the task. Fedor's inability to defend himself against his wife's material gluttony defines his masculinity. He himself has no need for furniture, but his failure to combat Lena's consumerism makes him an unredeemable accomplice. A *Sovetskii ekran* review accentuated the positive implications of the open-ended finale by commenting that the mother would certainly fight for her son. The reviewer hypothesized that she was not alone in the belief that Fedor would return: "our entire family, the residents of our building, our extraordinary city," would all struggle to win him back.[85] Despite the optimistic take on the film's ending, the fact remains that Natanson provided Soviet audiences with a male hero who, like Fedor in *Alien Kin*, proved defenceless when confronted with his wife's unrelenting attachment to material goods. Incapable of discouraging Lena's philistinism, Fedor has succumbed to it.

Fedor in *Alien Kin* and Fedor in *Noisy Day* do not belong in the pantheon of socialist realist supermen. That said, both directors took great pains to illustrate that their wives were formidable challengers. The two Fedors demonstrated how central domestic life – and the consumerism that attended it – had become to defining postwar Soviet masculinity. Domesticity and humdrum spousal matters had become more critical to a man's identity than anything else. This would prove to be the one test the sixties movie hero often failed. By the mid-1960s, it had become evident that men were not immune to the pressures of the sixties "consumer revolution" and that their morals often fell victim to it. *An Easy Life*, a comedy that sold around 25 million tickets and became one of the most lucrative films of 1964, dealt with consumerism's impact on men themselves but offered hope that some men could be redeemed. A humorous moral tale, the film features a protagonist – Aleksandr Petrovich Bochkin – who sells out his scientific expertise and his morals when he becomes a black marketeer. Upon completing his university studies as the valedictorian of his class, Bochkin ought to have abandoned Moscow for the Far East and become a manager at a heavy industry production site. Instead, he opts to supervise a dry-cleaners. Not only does he get involved in a service profession dominated by women, but he also entangles himself in an illegal side business with a black marketeer by the name of "Queen Margot." He sells out his masculine dignity in return for an "easy life" featuring tailored suits, reservations at exclusive Moscow restaurants, and a swanky sedan. Eventually, Bochkin's sister and college friend persuade him to abandon his profiteering and move to Dal'nogorsk to begin earning an honest wage.

Although the film makes clear that both sexes are susceptible to the vagaries of materialism, *An Easy Life* casts modern and Westernized women as incorrigible connivers and plotters, while the menfolk are presented as eminently redeemable. But up until his friend and sister stage an intervention, the director feminizes Bochkin in ways big and small. He has become a fussy Muscovite dandy who dines in the trendiest restaurants and attends the most popular theatre and music performances, and in numerous scenes we find him attending to his

Figure 4.15. Bochkin in *An Easy Life* (1964) as a domestic(ated) criminal.

underground "side-business" in the kitchen, wearing a neatly pressed apron (Figure 4.15). One scene in the film communicates in the most direct way possible that this is not Boris's true nature. As he adjusts his tie in the mirror and aims to convince himself that he is proud of his life choices, his reflection speaks back. His superego pronounces a diagnosis: "You are ashamed of yourself and would truly want to live like real people do. But in order to do this, you'll have to give up your comforts and money." When the aggrieved profiteer retorts that he is ashamed of nothing as he has not cheated anyone, his conscience fights back: "But haven't you cheated yourself? At first you allowed yourself to forget that you are an engineer and then got yourself involved with that shady Queen Margot character. You have to wonder – where will all of this end?" The slippery-slope argument has an effect on the protagonist once he realizes that his college buddy is willing to give him a new lease on life in Russia's Far East. So Boris moves back to Dal'nogorsk to cure himself of easy Moscow living and restore his masculinity. His accomplice, "Queen Margot," is not so lucky: we see her in the final scene being escorted in handcuffs by two police officers. Thus, redemption for male profiteers is possible, but their female equivalents are not worthy of the same opportunity.

But a happy ending does not come to *all* the men in the movie who have traded in their values for *la dolce vita*. The husband of one of Bochkin's wealthiest customers – academic Vladimir Gavrilovich Muromtsev – had similarly sold out a respectable professional career by publishing

Figure 4.16. Muromtsev in *An Easy Life* as a vision of a masculinity wasted.

his work strictly for profit in order to cater to his domineering wife's whims. The viewer sees him at a point where he has already appropriated Vasilisa Sergeevna's own habits. One visual in particular encapsulates a masculinity betrayed: Vladimir Gavrilovich is reclining on a chaise longue, wearing a smoking jacket and petting a frou-frou dog (Figure 4.16). Although engaged in the act of reading, he is no longer committed to serious intellectual work, nor does it seem that he has ever performed a hard day's labour in his entire life. The abstract painting in the background emphasizes that his life has become form over substance. He has become his wife's creation.

Muromtsev's moment of reckoning comes when he realizes that Vasilisa has been dealing with Queen Margot behind his back and participating in the black market. It is at this point that he cannot escape the realization that he has made terrible life choices: his household exists only to feed his wife's insatiable appetites for the latest trends; his hard-earned money supports the black market; and he has failed to assert himself in his own home despite being the sole breadwinner. Instead of being respected by his fellow academics, he has become Vasilisa's lackey. As he storms through their childless home, he violently destroys every emblem of an "easy life" he can get his hands on: furniture, decorative glassware, abstract art, and vintage tchotchkes. During this moment of catharsis, he shouts at the top of his lungs: "A normal man would have gone crazy a long time ago from this barren wasteland of a life! I guard my very own junkyard! Do you know who I could have been and for what I sold myself out? For furniture! For antiques! For crystal!" Much like Oleg in *Noisy Day*, he smashes all the objects that have made him compromise his conscience and that have led him to give in to his shrewish wife. Despite the emotional and principled outburst, by the end of the film it appears that he will revert to old habits and once again follow the lead of the mistress of the house. Unlike Bochkin, who was young enough to reverse course, Muromtsev's slippery slope has taken him to a point of no return: Vasilisa remains firmly behind the wheel. Overall, *Easy Life* seems to offer two solutions to men: move to a remote area – which is inhospitable to women like Vasilisa – or chase luxury and pleasure.

The notion that men were no match for modern postwar women proved to be a winning formula for another romantic comedy titled *Three Plus Two* (Tri plius' dva, 1963). This production, based on the 1958 play *Savages* (Dikari), sold an impressive 35 million tickets and would remain a summer holiday cult classic in the coming years, as well as a staple on sixties television for the rest of the decade. With or without the punch lines, its end message was clear: in the battle of the sexes, men were very unevenly matched with women. The action centres on three pals who yearn to escape their "civilized" existence. All three belong to the professional upper middle class: Roman is a veterinarian, Stepan is a physicist, and Vadim is an aspiring diplomat. Together they decide to pack up Stepan's Moskvich and set out for the Black Sea coast to find a campground where they can live like Robinson Crusoe and get reacquainted with their "primitive" selves. They measure their distance from civilized life by how long they can go without indulging in the excesses of modern life: smoking, fancy clothes, shaving, restaurant food, and, of course, women. The review of the 1958 play observed that this was an entirely natural and understandable urge: "Who among us has not wanted to turn off from the usual rhythm of life for one month in a year and spend our vacation 'wildly' [*dikim obrazom*] without having to acquire special sanatorium vouchers?"[86] Nearly five years later, an *Iskusstvo kino* reviewer would begin his piece in the same vein, acknowledging that he himself intended to spend his summer with his male friends in exactly the same "barbaric" fashion: "For a month we quit smoking and forget about other markers of civilization such as razors and ties. Put simply, we turn into the most natural 'savages.'"[87] The play and the movie tapped into a quite recognizable, if uncommon, experience for

Figure 4.17. The uneven battle of the sexes in *Three Plus Two* (1963).

professional middle-class urban men as they sought to escape what they light-heartedly called the trappings of civilization. But in both productions, it is clear that escaping civilization means escaping women and modern courtship, given that the men have no qualms about embracing the comforts of modern life: they sleep in the cavernous Moskvich, listen to the radio, live on canned food, and catch fish with a metal harpoon and a diving tank. The modern-day Robinson Crusoes are anything but. Even their commitment to one another, for this one month of the year, disintegrates rather quickly with the arrival of two intruders.

Two attractive but demanding female strangers unceremoniously invade the makeshift campground of male solidarity. The assertive blonde and brunette newcomers insist they had claimed the spot years earlier and now demand that the men pack up and leave. When the three amigos refuse, Zoia and Natasha set up camp right next to them. When Natasha asks Zoia why they haven't simply pitched their tents on the neighbouring beach, Zoia explains: "We need to create all the conditions necessary to make their lives unbearable." Natasha jokes, "Oh, we can definitely do that." Zoia trains circus lions and Natasha is a film actress, so the two are already equipped with a skill set calculated to drive the men away. Zoia declares that "if I train real lions for a living, I can certainly handle a few porcupines." She explains to Natasha: "In training animals, it is essential to make them realize that you are more powerful than they are." To this, Natasha responds that "in our situation, we have to make the men understand that women are mightier." As the pair combine their forces and talents, they put the kibosh on the men's efforts to create a space free of "civilization." A promotional image demonstrates that the two women are the true focus of the film (Figure 4.17). Their confident poses and self-assured gazes are contrasted to the three men who hover uncertainly in the background. That the men appear out of focus symbolizes their inability to see clearly the women's successful machinations. Moreover, the men's idleness suggests a lack of readiness, while the female pair is merely suspended in action, ready to advance their interests at a moment's notice.

What ensues is a battle of wills as the two groups battle for coveted territory. This dynamic is made obvious as characters keep referring to their relations in militant terms. At one point, Stepan characterizes the relationship between men and women by resorting to Khrushchev's foreign policy terminology: "A peaceful coexistence of two opposing systems." At the beginning of the film the two camps establish a kind of détente, demarcating their territory with a string of empty tin cans. In this war, however, the men are the raw recruits, while the women are five-star generals, always three steps ahead of their opposition. Relying on Zoia's experience in training wild cats, the women at first play hard to get and then reverse course by making their targets fall in love with them. In this romantic comedy, falling in love is equated with being trained, and men are prey for female hunters. Roman sings a song that encapsulates their situation: "He who is in love, is forever subdued" (*Tot, kto vliublen, na vek pokoren*).

The film normalizes heterosexual pairings but also implies that courting and marriage do not benefit men in the long run. To participate in romance, men must relinquish any notion of independence – the war will be fought entirely on women's terms. Once they get to know the women, two of the men shave off their beards and, eventually, begin to dress up. They conclude their civilizational process by committing to their partners. The women fall into a trap of their own making by falling in love, but they do so with more awareness, for it is they who set the trap. Moreover, they change nothing about their appearance or behaviour, since they were calling the shots from the very beginning. The *Iskusstvo kino* reviewer observed that the romantic outcome was predictable but that it was less clear why the director chose to include the misogynist (*zhenonenavestnik*), Stepan the physicist, in the narrative.

It is curious that both the play and the movie include a third man, only to leave him out of the romantic triangle. The physicist remains steadfast throughout as the only one committed to an all-male community, and he falls for neither of the women, partly because he had already been married. At one point, when the two other men are worried that Natasha and Zoia are drowning, Stepan recognizes the women's ploy for what it is: "Smoke and mirrors! Manipulation! Personally, I do not worry. I've been married once already. All this is familiar to me." The closing shots do not make it exactly clear who wins out in the end: the single man or the two men who have coupled up. It appears that, Stepan, as the sole surviving "savage" exists in order to console the male audience and assure them that independence from women's civilizing influence is still possible.

Conclusion

Affairs of the heart proved to be treacherous territory for the male protagonists of sixties cinema. Heroes either required the semi-divine intervention of an angelic heroine or became pawns for a vixen's upward socio-economic climb. The movie industry as well as the Soviet press and the satirists at *Krokodil* advanced the notion that gender relations boiled down to two scenarios: women either busied themselves saving men from themselves or acted as dictators at home and as grey cardinals in men's professions. Although oppositional, both traditional and modern womanhood conveyed the idea that men could not take care of themselves. It was apparent that in the battle of the sexes, women came out on top, for they were both the source of men's troubles and their saviours.

Inseparable from the directors' concern about men losing their autonomy vis-à-vis women was the films' critique of the postwar consumerist ethos. Sixties films deployed misogynistic tropes to register their protest against consumerism. Perceived as principal agents of mass consumerism, women played a central role in entrapping men into a lifestyle that robbed them of their virility. Sixties directors cast the modern woman as the enemy of postwar masculinity while also making it clear that this enemy could not be directly defeated. The hero's only option for salvation was to escape civilization and elope to places and professions without women. On the barren tundra or in highly specialized scientific institutes, men could hope to regain some semblance of authentic masculinity. Postwar modernity – defined as it was by (sub)urbanism, comfort, convenience, and internationalism – bore the mark of feminine design and was therefore antithetical to the cultivation of rugged masculinity.

The masculine ideal in this period turned reactionary, extolling the moral superiority of backbreaking manual labour or intellectual activities marked by mortal threats (as in the case of nuclear scientists). Soviet directors essentially wished to turn back the clock and reverse the postwar era of affluence that had knocked the gender order out of whack. The reactionary conservatism in cinema mirrored what was already apparent in Soviet literature. The proponents of the so-called village prose advocated a return to a bifurcated gender order in which Russianness was represented by rural folk culture, which supposedly remained pristine and unaffected by the secular communist ideology and/or urban Western culture. Mirroring trends among Soviet literati, a segment of the film industry rejected the idea that modernization, industrialization, and urbanization changed society for the better, unfavourably comparing the social alienation of urban life with the social harmony of the village. The bucolic idyll evident in sixties literature and film featured heroines who were domesticated, desexualized, and idealized, rejecting any other form of feminine identity. This romanticized version of rural life became the only context in which men could find true love.[88]

The final page of Alesha's cinematic journey in *Four Pages of a Young Man's Life* celebrates the rural and old-fashioned as authentically Russian. The last few minutes of the film feature a romanticized view of the rural landscape. Looping the protagonist back to the geographic beginning of his journey, the concluding scene establishes that a good life is a simple one, defined by modesty and physical labour. Alesha's world-weariness seems to lift as he talks with a young lad – essentially his younger, idealistic self – who argues that life ought to be centred on communal work (harvesting, transporting goods, building cities) and on believing in a better tomorrow. The film ends with the two smiling to each other in silent agreement that, at its core, life is a happy affair. But as unambiguously as the film's finale extols the hard-working, anti-consumerist ethos, sixties cinema overall told a different story. The silver screen depicted postwar masculinity as unmistakably weak, defined as it was by either the kindness of angelic heroines or the manipulations of harridans. As the next chapter demonstrates, even in the realm of science, a field dominated by male protagonists, Soviet men could not eke out a definitive victory against the physical world, bureaucratic machinery, or their own inventions. Whether the field of battle involved scientific discovery or amorous conquest, sixties directors found men ill-equipped to deal with postwar modernity.

Chapter Five

Our Friend the Atom?
Science as a Threat to Masculinity

The 1957 launch of Sputnik 1 marked the Soviet Union as a scientific powerhouse and shifted the Cold War space race into overdrive. For a nation that had emerged from the Second World War only twelve years prior amid incalculable human and material losses, the Sputnik moment generated immense national pride and hope for a better future. Sputnik 1 boosted the regime's prestige at home and abroad, strengthening Soviet claims that the communist system was on the winning side of history. Iurii Gagarin's space flight in 1961 sealed the deal, proving that there could no longer be any question about the scientific community's ability to solve all problems facing humankind.[1] The mind-boggling achievements of Soviet science and technology turned the scientific intelligentsia – engineers, nuclear physicists, chemists, and mathematicians – into cultural icons of the sixties.[2]

By 1960 the cosmonaut had become the face of both the space program and Soviet science more generally. Standard propaganda reflected this view: "The Soviet cosmonaut is not merely a conqueror of outer space, not merely a hero of science and technology, but first and foremost he is a real, living, flesh-and-blood new man, who externalizes all the awe-inspiring qualities of the Soviet character, which Lenin's party has been cultivating for decades."[3] The fact that the cosmonaut projected sex appeal and made science itself enticing was clearly evidenced by the April 1962 *Krokodil* cover, which imagined Gagarin as an object of desire for a global audience, personified by a feminized planet Earth. The caption unambiguously proclaimed: "It's been a year since I fell in love with you" (Figure 5.1).

Cosmonauts assumed a leading position in popular consciousness as the era's sexy supermen. Historian Richard Stites described the space heroes – or, more specifically, the mass-produced images of them – as the "new social cement."[4] Ordinary people became genuinely fascinated

Figure 5.1. "It's been a year since I fell in love with you!" *Krokodil* 10 (1962), cover.

with Soviet triumphs in space. "Gagarin's achievement was our greatest pride," recalled one member of the so-called Sputnik generation.[5]
According to a 1963 survey conducted by a popular youth-oriented
Soviet newspaper, Gagarin's flight constituted the twentieth century's
greatest achievement and Sputnik represented humanity's greatest
technological feat.[6] The first manned space flight commanded such
broad public admiration that Soviet propagandists regularly exploited
its popularity to bolster the drive for atheism; for instance, *Science and
Religion* reported the remarks of a once God-fearing man: "Now I am
convinced that god is science, is man! Iurii Gagarin overcame all the
faith in heavenly power that I had in my soul."[7] Soviet science had symbolically cleansed outer space of God, saints, and angels and filled it
with new tenants: spaceships, satellites, and lunar probes. In both popular imagination and official discourse, scientists governed the heavens
above and the earth below; they were the new masters of the universe.

Even though few lay people could relate to their complex fields of
study and even though they had become the darlings of Party officialdom, scientists came to epitomize the notion of "cool." Their bad boy

image came about partly due to their irreverent attitude toward (political) authority. Unlike social scientists, who were beholden to Marxist theorems, STEM professionals obeyed only natural and universal laws. By the late 1960s, the appearance and behaviour of these unlikely celebrities had evolved into an impossible hybrid. One commentator complained about the preposterous stereotype accompanying depictions of physicists in mass media: "he plays the guitar, dances the twist, drinks vodka, keeps a lover, agonizes over abstract problems, sacrifices his leisure for the sake of his scientific calling, and trades punches with the anti-heroic physicist."[8] There was no better time to be a physicist; their Warholian fifteen minutes of fame had arrived.

Because members of the scientific/technical intelligentsia ranked high in the popular imagination and figured prominently in official discourse, filmmakers exploited the popularity of the scientist to promote a subversive masculine model. While official propaganda idealized the scientific profession and its practitioners, elevating them to cult status, directors utilized physicists, cyberneticists, and mathematicians to challenge uniformity in regard to both science and ideology. Unlike their Stalin-era precursors – explorers, geologists, and aviators – sixties scientists questioned the existence of absolute, permanent truths regarding either political dogma or scientific knowledge. In stark contrast to the brawny heroes of the not so distant past, the brainy scientist flaunted his irreverence for authority as well as his intellectual aptitude. The Stalinist hypermasculine archetypes, with their sculpted bodies and their trust in the Party, had lost their cultural capital to men whose unquestioned loyalty was to empiricism and the scientific method. The incorruptible scientist played the role of the folkloric holy fool, who, as if oblivious to the futility of his task, demands justice and truth at any cost to himself and others. The films implied that blind subservience to either the state apparatus or the cult of science led to a loss of moral and intellectual integrity.

Ironically, the very moment that propelled the Soviet Union into the global limelight as a technological superpower also led a certain faction of Soviet scientists, artists, and lay people to cautiously question the official and popular worship of science; they pondered whether the near universal eulogization of science had obscured moral problems facing the human race.[9] In newspaper columns, cartoons, novels, plays, and films, a diverse group asserted that humanity's greatest problems were moral and ethical, not scientific and technological. In the age of the atomic bomb, it had become evident that while humans might be able to bend nature to their will, it was unclear whether they could do so responsibly. Essentially, sixties cinema explored two questions central to post-Stalinist life: how to preserve one's independence within an ideologically driven bureaucracy, and how to safeguard one's humanity in an increasingly automated/mechanized world. The most hotly debated movies considered whether technological progress was depriving Soviet citizens of their humanity and whether political interference in scientific affairs was perverting technological progress. Consequently, while sixties films often portrayed physicists, cosmonauts, and engineers as courageous defenders of universal truth and justice, they also depicted their brainy protagonists as impotent. As cool as they were, they often could not defeat a mighty bureaucratic apparatus, control the physical world they were supposed to govern, or even influence their own (robotic) creations.[10]

This chapter analyses four films that tapped into the fascination – both official and popular – with the scientific/technical intelligentsia and that showcased researchers engaged in highly specialized fields as protagonists: M.I. Romm's *Nine Days of a Year* (Deviat dnei odnogo goda, 1962), S.G. Mikaelian's *Into the Storm* (Idu na grozu, 1965), G.E. Iungval'd- Khil'kevich's *Rainbow Formula* (Formula radugi, 1966), and I.S. Ol'shvanger's *They Called Him Robert* (Ego zvali Robert, 1967). These films experienced very different fates: *Nine Days* attracted around 25 million viewers domestically and garnered multiple festival awards abroad;[11] *Storm* sold approximately 40 million tickets;[12] *Robert* received a very limited distribution; and *Rainbow* was censored and never released.

All four of these productions drew largely negative attention from the authorities. Ideological watchdogs paid close attention to these motion pictures because they problematized the positivist view of science and cast doubt on the idea that man can govern his physical environment and the invisible forces that control it.[13] Also problematic was the productions' insistence that authentic scientific pursuits be unambiguously separate from Party dictates and ideological pressures. These four movies alone cannot provide a truly generalizable picture of the day's discussions on science; even so, the heated exchanges they sparked clearly marked out the cultural fault line that separated the Stalinist and post-Stalinist views of Soviet masculinity.

The Cult of Science without the Scientist

Even before the Bolsheviks came to power, they declared that science would be a panacea for Russia's problems. The Communist Party staked its legitimacy on technological progress, aiming to revitalize the nation's infrastructure, reduce socio-economic disparity, and restore the country's international standing. Science replaced God, becoming the centrepiece of the official Soviet faith. Bolsheviks were convinced that scientific discoveries and reasoning would liberate the masses from religious superstition and foster political consciousness. Communism and technological progress became two sides of the same coin; one was unimaginable without the other. Marxism justified this positivist perspective by arguing that machines determine the course of history. Marx, after all, had contended that technology alters the political course of history as well as social attitudes, besides bringing about new socio-economic orders.[14] As historian Ethan Pollock concisely put it: "If Marxism-Leninism was scientific, and science would flourish if it was based on Marxist principles, it followed that science and Soviet Marxism should mutually reinforce each other."[15]

Considering how central science was to Soviet power from the very start, it is curious that during the Stalin era, official propaganda shied away from using the scientist to embody socialist masculinity and science. Up until 1953, films, novels, and the press portrayed researchers alternatively as Stalin's dutiful pupils or as villains who, because of megalomania and/or undeveloped class-consciousness, aimed to sabotage the workers' state. When the Soviet media praised its scientists, it focused on the broader competition between socialist and capitalist science rather than on the brilliance of specific scientists or even scientists as a profession above others. Scientific "genius" under Stalin applied to those researchers who best applied Stalinist teachings to their investigative methods rather than to those who approached scientific problems in original ways. Because science took a back seat to ideological dogma, propaganda appreciated scientists as followers of the Party line rather than as innovators. Even when the big screen featured the life of a famous Soviet scientist, the film stressed the day's ideological priorities while purposefully downplaying scientific practice and theory. Besides playing Stalin's loyal protégés, engineers and scientists often filled the role of villains, doubling as enemies of the people or inadvertent accomplices to foreign spies.[16] The main function of these productions was to create public distrust of and aversion to Western ideas rather than promote an appreciation for science and its practitioners.[17]

A.M. Room rooted the storyline of two of his films – *The Court of Honor* (Sud Chesti, 1948) and *Silver Dust* (Serebristaia pyl', 1953) – in the scientific realm and emphasized the need to protect Soviet discoveries against immoral Western scientists. *The Court of Honor*, based on an A. Shtein's award-winning play *The Law of Honor* (Zakon chesti, 1948), tells the story of two Soviet scientists who, out of both vanity and naivety, surrender their institute's hard-won research results to American spies, who have posed as legitimate scientists.[18] The secret agents convince the unsuspecting doctors Losev and Dobrotvorskii that "science knows no borders" and that their discoveries on the reduction of cancerous tumours belong to all humanity. The protests of their co-workers come to nothing as these heads of the institute indulge their pride, thinking about the international recognition awaiting them. But instead of standing ovations from the world community, they are faced with their compatriots' court of honour for betraying national interests. In *Silver Dust*, Room painted an even more hysterical portrait of Western scientists and the danger they posed to world peace. The 1953 production is a fantastical yarn about a "typical" American scientist who discovers a new weapon of mass destruction but dies of his own invention before he can use it for his own immoral purposes.

Consequently, until Stalin's death, scientists played second fiddle to men who approached science as a physical rather than mental activity. Aviators and geologists, rather than laboratory researchers, came to embody the possibilities of Stalinist science. Even as science *qua* science garnered increasingly more official press coverage during and after the First Five-Year Plan, filmmakers cast pilots and explorers as embodiments of ideal Soviet masculinity and science in action.[19] These men did what the real empirical scientist, the grandfather-next-door types, only theorized about: they conquered time and space in the name of Soviet supremacy. While scientists were postulating, explorer aviators were accomplishing the impossible and setting world records. Pilots in particular occupied a special place in the pantheon of Soviet heroes. Stalin himself built his public persona through his association with warriors of the heavens and established his father-of-the-people image by treating aviators as his favourite "sons."[20] In fact, two pilots, Otto Shmidt and Valerii Chkalov, share the dubious honour of being the only two individuals ever shown embracing Stalin on the front page of *Pravda*.[21] From 1932 to the beginning of 1939, pilots who broke records for non-stop long-distance flying, who were the first to fly transpolar routes from Eurasia to North America, and who established the world's first scientific outpost at the North Pole figured as the true representatives of Soviet science. Aviation showcased socialist modernity in that it displayed the country's technological advancement, economic development, and military might.

By the end of the Stalinist period, scientists lacked the ideological attributes that would make them archetypal heroes. On the one hand, films often depicted empirical scientists as distinguished but indistinguishable figures in lab coats, whose strict observation of Marxist/Stalinist principles led them to their "breakthroughs." On the other hand, directors marked scientists as figures so consumed with their research that they lacked a developed sense of national pride, making them a prime target for foreign spies. Because scientists played an ambiguous role in Stalinist culture, they, unlike aviators and explorers, remained on the sidelines of the popular imagination. Throughout Stalin's reign films represented science as an *activity* that happened outdoors; it was seldom represented as a purely intellectual occupation detached from the state's agenda. Science was, above all, a practical affair meant to bolster the state's Five-Year Plan targets. Correlated as it was with production quotas, science expressed the state's focus on the limitless potential of the human body. The politics of de-Stalinization, however, profoundly changed the trends established during the Stalin era. Sixties films presented science as an intellectual pursuit for only the most cerebrally gifted; it also divorced films about science and scientists from the Five-Year Plan.

This is not to say that the theme of production vanished from public discourse during the sixties; Khrushchev and Brezhnev were no less fond of gargantuan projects than their predecessors. Many sixties schemes – the Virgin Lands campaign, the amalgamation of collective farms into agro-cities, the cultivation of corn, and Siberian river reversal projects – smacked of a Stalinist approach to modernizing the national economy. Khrushchev retained the megalomaniac aspects of Stalinist projects and expanded the scope of science's reach as "the conquest of nature now extended to the micro-world and the heavens."[22] The 1961 New Party Program further accentuated the state's push to modernize the national economy and infrastructure, arguing that the strategic use of science and technology would allow the Soviet Union to overtake the United States in per capita production by 1970, achieve communism by 1980, and construct a new type of society/individual in the process. Despite the continued emphasis on productivity indicators, the liberalization that occurred in the arts and politics during the de-Stalinization drive also affected the sciences. By denouncing Stalin's spurious scientific tenets, Khrushchev helped elevate Soviet science to international standards. Once science was freed from undue ideological constraints, Khrushchev afforded the intelligentsia an opportunity to base the conflicts in science-themed films around morality rather than productivity.

After 1956, morality and conscience re-entered official rhetoric and became tied to scientific issues. By the Twenty-Second Party Congress in 1961, the Communist Party had proclaimed itself to be "the mind, honour, and conscience of our age, of the Soviet people, as it performs great revolutionary transformations."[23] At the same Party Congress the authorities issued a new party program, with the "Moral Code of the

Builder of Communism" as its centerpiece. Even a cursory glance of its twelve points – conscientious labour for the good of society, a strong sense of public duty, fraternal solidarity with the working people of all countries – reveals that post-Stalinist officialdom "interpreted morality in functional terms, as something reinforcing the power of the state."[24] As the state scaled back on coercing obedience, official propaganda insisted that obedience to the state was a matter of conscience. At the same time, by highlighting morality and conscience as two primary traits of the New Soviet Man, the authorities put into motion a process of public contestation about what these terms meant in the post-Stalinist context.

Scientists, as modern-day visionaries, not only acted as guarantors of a utopia to come but also represented the indispensability of independent, as well as moral, thought and action. These men contemplated abstract problems simply because those problems fascinated them, despite the fact that solving them would not affect industry's day-to-day operations. After the debates about modern science in general and nuclear physics in particular became more public after 1953, filmmakers utilized scientists as a group that had to wrestle daily with the possible negative uses of their discoveries. The films discussed here continually stressed the idea that critical and uncensored thought, combined with moral responsibility, were key to a truly modern masculinity and a truly modern science– an ideal that defined the celluloid scientists of the long 1960s. In these kinds of movies, the moral duty of scientists to the people was paramount, yet their guiding principle was scientific objectivity, not Party dictates.

Can Science Have a Conscience? Scientific Masculinity with a Poet's Soul

Sixties filmmakers on the whole extolled science and objective reasoning as necessary correctives to Stalinist excesses and pseudo-science; nevertheless, some directors intimated that blind faith in science would produce the same kinds of moral degradation.

The four movies examined here – *Nine Days of a Year*, *Into the Storm*, *They Called Him Robert*, and *Rainbow Formula* – appreciated the need for technical modernization but implied that without an ethical compass, man's technological evolution could only signify a pyrrhic victory. As such, these motion pictures should be seen as part of a larger conversation about technology's complex effects on human personality and relationships. The arts, from literature to theatre to satire, dove head first into addressing the impact of scientific advancement on human psychology and personal relations. In Viktor Rozov's 1962 film script

A, B, C, D, E, the protagonist expresses doubt about technology's ability to bring about true contentment: "People invented the color television and the tape recorder ... They are close to unlocking the secrets of protein synthesis and flying to the moon, but this does not make them any more honest or happy."[25] Similarly, a protagonist in D.A. Granin's popular 1961 novel *Into the Storm* – a top research scientist – asserts that qualities such as integrity and sincerity trump technological prowess. The respected physicist poses a hypothetical question to his star student: "What, in your opinion, distinguishes people from animals? Atomic energy? The telephone? I would say: morality, imagination, ideals. Men's souls won't be improved because you and I are studying the earth's electrical field."[26] Perhaps the most famous poem presaging the potential depersonalization of humanity as a result of modern technology is A.A. Voznesenskii's *Oza* (1964), a long poem set in the country's premier nuclear research facility. *Oza* summed up the feelings of those who were sceptical of the idealistic promises underpinning Promethean science: "All progress is reactionary if it breaks man down" (*Vse progressy reaktsionny, esli rushitsia chelovek*).[27] Noted Soviet philosopher E.V. Il'enkov engaged the scepticism these artists expressed in his 1968 monograph and warned Soviet philosophers and psychologists to resist cybernetic models of the mind that portrayed individuals as no more than sophisticated self-regulating machines.[28] If Stalinist science based itself on interventionist action, post-Stalinist intellectuals called for more observation and contemplation in order to fully appreciate technology's effects on humankind.

This ambivalent attitude toward science reached beyond the circles of the intelligentsia and became public during the so-called physicists' and poets' debate (*fiziki i liriki*). That debate began in 1959, when the editors of *Komsomol'skaia pravda* published an editorial by the famed Soviet writer Il'ia Ehrenburg. Ehrenburg commented that neglect of one's emotional life and an exclusive preoccupation with science "lead society to decay or catastrophe."[29] His passionate defence of emotions and the arts was prompted by a letter from "Nina V.," a Leningrad student. Nina had written to the famous author seeking relationship and life advice. She had recently broken off an engagement with "Iurii," a successful engineer who cared about little except his work. He hardly visited his elderly mother, made friends only with those who could help him achieve his professional goals, and thought that any interest in art, literature, or history was a waste of time in the Atomic Age. Ehrenburg's editorial on the much-needed respect for human emotions and creative achievements resonated with the editors and readers of *Komsomol'skaia pravda*, evoking a strong response from readers. Engineer I.

Poletaev, for example, who represented those who supported "Iurii," felt that science positively moulds human consciousness: "We live by the creativity of reason and not of feelings; we live by the poetry of experiments, theories, ideas, and construction. Our epoch demands the whole of man and we have no time to exclaim: 'Oh, Bach! Oh, Blok!'"[30] Although the debate failed to establish consensus, Boris Slutskii captured its spirit in his renowned poem "Fiziki i liriki," which appeared in *Literaturnaia gazeta* in October 1959. In it Slutskii observed that physicists were "in" and poets were "out" not because of foul play on part of the scientists but simply because of "natural laws." The poem exudes a sense of regret that artists had squandered their chance to affect popular consciousness.

It doesn't even hurt me,	*Tak chto dazhe ne obidno,*
It is rather interesting and strange	*a skoree interesno*
Seeing how our soapy poems	*nabliudat', kak, slovno pena,*
Drop away	*opadaiut nashi rifmy*
As their greatness little by little,	*i velichie stepenno*
gives way to logarithms.	*otstupaet v logarifmy*

The *fiziki* versus *liriki* debate provided plenty of fodder for the satirists at *Krokodil*, who exploited it for two main purposes: to cast a spotlight on the many potential perils of scientific research; and to mock their compatriots' misguided views on the role technology ought to play in modern life. Both these themes made themselves manifest throughout the sixties on the pages of *Krokodil*. Even when they did not depict scientific progress as dangerous in the literal sense, the cartoons in *Krokodil* pondered whether scientific progress would one day deprive humans of the qualities that make them human. One such cartoon depicts a school-aged boy, Vova Ivanovich, fantasizing about a not-too-distant future in which all daily tasks – from going to the grocery store to picking mushrooms in the woods – would be made effortless by machinery.[31] Little Vova imagines that even the most basic chores, such as taking a bath and walking about town, will one day be automated and performed by machinery. Instead of wasting time on these responsibilities, humankind could dedicate itself to what matters most in life: playing soccer. The caption reflects the young lad's understanding of the coming utopia: "When we achieve communism, humanity will be divided into teams of eleven people and we will get busy doing what matters most" (Figure 5.2). This kind of thinking represented the party's great anxiety, about which the Central Committee warned in one of its decrees: "Deeply flawed is the assertion that

Figure 5.2. "Vova Ivanov fantasizes about the future." *Krokodil* 35 (1958): 8–9.

together with the automation of production in the communist society, physical labour will also disappear."[32]

Besides being apprehensive that technology would make Soviet citizens lazy, satirists worried that robots would eventually replace human labour and make factory workers redundant. On its June 1959 cover, *Krokodil* juxtaposed an image of a high-tech factory with a remotely controlled robot engaged in a low-skilled, manual task. The former image met with the approval of the magazine while the latter was ridiculed as preposterous and regressive (Figure 5.3). There evidently existed a correct way to approach technological innovation: technology was supposed to make physical activity more efficient rather than redundant and should not distance the worker from the labour.

The fear that inventors might buy into their own hubris and believe themselves to be masters of their own creations was mocked in a cartoon illustrating two men running from a robotic dog they have brought to life. As they flee from their Frankenstein, one yells to the other: "I told you it would have been better to invent a turtle" (Figure 5.4).[33] The sketch depicts (amateur) innovators as likely to get carried away with their ambition to create things they cannot realistically command. Discernible also is the idea that technology cannot be seen as exclusively benevolent. Much like any other human activity, technological advancement, however impressive it may seem at first, carries unforeseen consequences, which must be vigilantly guarded against.

Nine Days, Storm, Rainbow, and *Robert* extended the *fiziki* versus *liriki* debate by presenting the scientist as the guardian of both scientific and ethical standards. These filmmakers defined intelligence as

Figure 5.3. "For! & Against!" *Krokodil* 18 (1959), cover.

Figure 5.4. "We should have invented a turtle!" *Krokodil* 5 (1960): 15.

an expression of independence and moral rectitude: "Intelligence is a mark of a man whose opinions are entirely his own while a *mesh-chanin*, unconcerned with either fact or morals, is guided by so-called 'conventional wisdom.'"[34] Thus the celluloid scientist became a Robin Hood type; although he could not speak or act as an ordinary guy on the street, he still bravely guarded and secured the common person's interests. The scientist *cum* defender of humanity battled nature, rather

Figure 5.5. Still from *Nine Days of a Year* (1961). Menacing and ominous scientific spaces.

than the rich, to provide humanity with a better life. Courageously and nobly, he fought the odds, willing to lay down his life for the cause, but he never sacrificed his moral principles to achieve his aim.

A celebrated sixties icon was the nuclear physicist Dmitrii Alekseevich Gusev in M.I. Romm's *Nine Days of a Year* (1961).[35] In many ways, Gusev was the prototype for the celluloid scientists who followed him. On the surface, the film follows Gusev and a motley crew of fellow nuclear physicists at a distant Siberian research institute, the famed Akademgorodok, as they attempt to create a thermonuclear reaction. The film begins with a successful experiment during which both Gusev and his mentor, Sintsov, expose themselves to radiation. The amount of radiation Sintsov suffers is lethal, and Gusev, who has been exposed significantly less, takes over his mentor's project. Knowing that even the briefest additional exposure will kill Gusev, doctors insist that he dedicate himself solely to theoretical research. Gusev, however, categorically refuses to do so, returning to continue the life-threatening investigation. During another successful test, the young physicist is fatally contaminated. His only hope is a surgical procedure that has never been performed on a human and that the doctors believe is bound to fail. The evening before the surgery, Gusev learns that the final, lethal experiment was not, in fact, a thermonuclear reaction, making his story all the more tragic. He thus subjects himself to a near-pointless operation in order to continue his mission.

Figure 5.6. Still from *Nine Days of a Year* (1961). Gusev as a victim
of unrealized scientific progress.

In addition to this moving but depressing narrative, the film offers a
bleak and ominous landscape. Many scenes are replete with characters
who appear ant-like, dwarfed as they are by the size of the facilities
and equipment (Figure 5.5). Rather than a liberating force, the scientific
apparatus engulfs, entraps, stifles, and threatens. It is clear that the scientists are not controlling the physical parameters of their professional
environment, let alone natural forces. Even more importantly, Romm
provides viewers with a visual representation of Gusev's mortality and
his defeat at the hands of the very phenomenon he wanted to harness
for humanity's benefit. Suffering from radiation, the main hero cuts
a pathetic figure, unable to will his body to move. Without wounds,
scars, or visible signs of struggle, Gusev's sacrifice fails to impress visually; he comes across simply as a tired, defeated, and impotent outline
of a person in a generic mid-century modern apartment (Figure 5.6).

Gusev is the kind of self-sacrificing socialist realist hero of whom Soviet critics ought to have dreamed. A reviewer in a provincial newspaper
was more than effusive in his praise, commenting that Gusev represented the future Soviet citizen. He was not only a contemporary ideal

but also a sign of things to come, a harbinger of a communist tomorrow: "He is remarkable in all respects; he is on the cutting edge of his epoch's discoveries, he cannot imagine life without active and creative work, and he sacrifices everything in the name of a noble cause."[36] Another critic also sang Gusev's praises: "The fate of the movie's hero ought to be an example of an outstanding, noble human life, which signifies not only a scientific, but also a civic and moral victory."[37] For these reviewers, Gusev was much more than a scientist; he was the embodiment of a moral ideal.

While Gusev seems to represent a relatively straightforward example of a socialist realist hero, art critics Valentin Liukov and Iurii Panov could not forgive the protagonist (or the other characters) for their "social myopia" (*sotsial'naia blizorukost'*)."[38] These authors argued that, on the face of it, the young scientist was "noble and humane by nature" and "unconditionally committed to science, for which he is ready to sacrifice everything – even his own life." But on second glance, the hero clearly lacked ideological consciousness; his political horizons were far too narrow. Panov and Liukov accused the protagonist of spending too much time in the lab and not enough time censoring the heretical proclamations of his friend and colleague, Il'ia Kulikov. "Where is Gusev's political consciousness?," asked the two critics, when Kulikov declared that "his own convictions do not change depending on the latest newspaper headlines" and that "he is surrounded by cavemen and cretins who insist on dragging Marxian principles into science." Panov and Liukov concluded that Gusev was heroic only when it came to science: "Gusev is relentless in achieving his goal, but overly accommodating when it comes to defending his ideological beliefs." The authors claimed that Gusev would hardly have appeared heroic were it not for Kulikov's "arrogant nihilism." Ultimately, the reviewers resolved that the physicist's main fault was that he "is engaged in science for science's sake." They found his statement "One mustn't stop thinking" (*Mysl' ostanovit' nel'zia*) too indulgent, too politically naive.

This critique, however damning, was counterbalanced by glowing reviews by two other respected and influential cultural critics. I. Chicherov took issue with Liukov and Panov's review: "It is pointless to address their indictments; anyone who has seen the film will be forced to agree that everything that has been said about *Nine Days* is patently untrue."[39] Chicherov valued the film for its portrayal of Gusev and Kulikov as worthy leaders of the nation's collective efforts to make scientific progress. Even the usually fault-finding L. Pogozheva praised the film for providing moviegoers with food for thought instead of giving them ready-made answers.[40] Pogozheva also contended that the heretical Kulikov and Gusev were not different at their core: both heroes were incapable of grandstanding and unwilling to do so, and both approached contemporary issues with intelligence and tact, for both were interested in all problems affecting humanity. The critic revelled in the fact that the celluloid scientists were living in an atmosphere charged with anticipation for the discovery-to-be. Pogozheva poetically concluded that these were "the noble knights" of ideas that were transforming the world.

Whatever ideological headwinds Romm's production faced, *Nine Days* marked a watershed in Soviet film history, for it showed the *intelligent* legitimating himself as a true socialist realist hero. After the success of *Nine Days*, the scientist *intelligent* joined a motley crew of celluloid tropes – the intrepid Civil War hero, the exuberant *kolkhoz* worker, the cheery Cossack, and the brawny aviator – to provide moviegoers with an alternative vision of Soviet masculinity. As prototypes, Kulikov and Gusev manifested the tension inherent in depicting scientists as emblems of Soviet masculinity. On the one hand, scientists, as figures fixated on their research, bolstered the official rhetoric that an individual's self-fulfilment comes through self-sacrifice to the common cause. On the other, as figures dedicated to objective truth rather than ideological imperatives or careerist exigencies, scientists personified the intelligentsia's views on the limits of official power and the inviolability of individual and creative freedoms. Because Kulikov and Gusev occupied such ambivalent positions, Romm was able to produce complex protagonists who expressed a dual message. A commitment to his calling and a willingness to sacrifice the personal for the professional made the empiricist a perfect poster boy for official propaganda. At the same time, the intelligentsia promoted the new hero because his impartiality and dedication to truth rendered him an ideal guardian of humanistic ideals. Although the hero-*intelligent* seemed tantalizing on paper, authorities worried that heroes like Kulikov and Gusev were not political enough since they spent more time on-screen pursuing their research than participating in national political life.

That *Nine Days* had made "thinking for thinking's sake" acceptable was evident from the near universal warm welcome M. Mikaelian's film *Into the Storm* received in 1965.[41] Like Romm's movie, at first glance *Storm* is a narrative about scientists trying to understand the dynamics behind storms in order to control them. Just as Gusev insists on conducting research in the thermonuclear chamber, aware that he is potentially exposing himself to fatal doses of radiation, the young physicists in *Storm* fly into the epicentre of storm clouds, risking death, to get to the bottom of their research problems. Although science is inextricably linked to this plot, the conflict actually revolves around a question one of the protagonists, the young, career-minded Oleg Tulin, asks his idealistic colleague and friend, Sergei Krylov: "Do you have to silence your own voice to get anywhere in life?" (*Nado li nastupat' na gorlo sobstvennoi pesne?*) In the same way that Kulikov's cynicism is contrasted with Gusev's moral high-mindedness, Tulin's opportunism is a foil to Krylov's ethical standards. Thus the real conflict is about moral compromise; Tulin's life consists of a series of calculated concessions while Krylov's is defined by his inability to go against what he knows is morally right.

The film's narrative begins in 1952. The opening scene features the two friends sitting next to each other in a university classroom, discussing a scientific problem while the professor is lecturing on the harms of cybernetics as "a bourgeois pseudo-science." The professor interrupts the pair and acidly asks Krylov if he would rather be somewhere else since the lecture seems to be interfering with more pressing issues. Krylov responds without hesitation: "Yes, maybe that is a good suggestion. You see, cybernetics is simply mathematics and computer science and not some kind of pseudo-science." When Krylov is ordered to see the dean to discuss his heretical comments, Tulin advises his friend: "Confess, show remorse, promise improvement, and tell them you were not understood correctly." During his interview with the dean, Sergei at first takes his friend's advice, but then relapses, arguing that cybernetics is not a product of American reactionary politics but represents the way of the future. Krylov is expelled from the university, but through sheer perseverance over several years becomes a member of a lab team investigating the phenomenon of storms and storm clouds.

While a member of the research team, the talented and hard-working Sergei not only establishes his professional credentials but also affirms the need to remain true to the principles of scientific research regardless of political pressures. Sergei's formative experience occurs as he watches his mentor, academic Dankevich, try to expose the fraudulent research of an opportunistic fellow "scientist." Dankevich's nemesis, academician Denisov, has declared that he will be able to subject storms to human control in the very near future. According to the objective research Dankevich has performed, however, it is obvious to any impartial observer that human control of inclement weather is very far off. The vast majority of Dankevich's friends and colleagues attempt to reason with the celebrated physicist that there is no point in disputing research that has no scientific basis. Tulin charges Krylov to convince his mentor not to publicly discredit Denisov. He cynically proclaims that "more often than not, truth suffers defeat in an argument" and that "the personality cult might be gone but its servants still remain." To the many warnings he receives, Dankevich simply responds: "If people are being deceived, we are obligated to speak the truth ... We are still conditioned by the memories of our sinister past."

At the public presentation of Denisov's plan, most of those assembled accuse Dankevich of throwing public money to the wind. Denisov charges Dankevich with caring more about abstract theoretical subjects than about the well-being of the country's economy. Reminding Dankevich that Soviet citizens live in a planned economy, his opponents press him to reveal when his research will yield the kind of results Denisov's study projects for the immediate future. Dankevich admits that he cannot promise usable findings for the next ten to twenty years, and probably not even during his own lifetime. Denisov then further barbs his opponent by saying that the next ten years will be more of the same in that Dankevich's team will produce only unsuccessful test results. Unflustered, the old expert reminds everyone of the golden rule in scientific research: "Even failed experiments are valuable." As the chairman motions for a vote on the issue, Dankevich laconically objects that "problems in science should never be decided by majority vote. Nature has ordered the world in such a way that incompetents [*bezdary*] always form the majority." Unsurprisingly, Denisov wins the argument as a champion of the agricultural sector, securing the bulk of state funding. Dankevich, defeated but implacable, continues his own research but soon dies from a heart ailment.

Mikaelian's film demonstrates in no uncertain terms the harm that politicking and ideological bravado do to science. The principles behind scientific research are shown as fairer and more far-sighted than rules governing the political system. This dynamic makes true scientists like Dankevich, as masculine figures, stand apart from ordinary men and from demagogues like Denisov. But as Romm and Mikaelian point out, mastering theories and abstract concepts is clearly insufficient: the scientist, as a gendered and moral ideal, must protect the laws that govern scientific study like a medieval knight protects his honour. When Krylov and Tulin are juxtaposed, it is clear that Tulin is the lesser of the two men even though both are brilliant physicists. Krylov's incessant search for objective truth, regardless of the consequences, contrasts sharply with Tulin's careerist manoeuvrings. Tulin is a positive figure in the sense that he is a champion of the kind of science Dankevich practises, but he tolerates injustice and, in the process, becomes an accomplice to the wrongs being committed. Tulin lives in perpetual angst over how to make institutional and political dynamics play out in his favour. By contrast, Krylov's reasoning is straightforward: he never puts his science before his sense of right and wrong. He does not see the two as mutually exclusive. Thus the true heroes of *Storm* are Dankevich and Krylov, who, in the words of an *Iskusstvo kino* reviewer, represent "the paragons of human character and the personification of the mindset that seeks out truth relentlessly, impervious to the rule of authorities and established norms."[42]

Flawed Science, Flawed Scientists

Although moral integrity made scientists the archetypes of sixties masculinity, filmmakers nonetheless accentuated their heroes' key weakness: their seeming disinterest in the emotional, lived realities of their contemporaries. These men have dedicated themselves to cosmic problems and issues, with the result that people's feelings strike them as trivial. This perspective allows them to rise above petty political gamesmanship and conduct themselves with the bigger picture in mind; the fact that science is on their side assures them that their vision will vindicate them. But at the same time, their seeming inability to identify with the "baser" human passions and instincts renders them cruel at times. As the chapter on fatherhood demonstrates, sixties directors made empathy, selflessness, tenderness, and patience central character traits of postwar masculinity. Scientists were not immune from this standard, which meant that the challenge for them was to balance thinking broadly enough to achieve monumental results with remaining grounded enough to benefit their communities in the here and now. In both *Nine Days* and *Storm*, the heroes fail to maintain long-term romantic relationships. Gusev alienates his wife Lelia, making her feel as if she is no more than a pet, while Krylov does little to win and keep the affection of his girlfriend, Lena, despite her best efforts. For both these physicists, the more important relationships are with their alter egos: Kulikov and Tulin. Because they share the same interests, the same language, and the same lifestyle, the men develop much more substantive emotional connections with each other than with their wives/girlfriends.

Romm and Mikaelian developed the notion that men of science are strangers to the emotions that drive the rest of humanity; directors Georgii Iungval'd-Khil'kevich and Il'ia Ol'shargev treated the same phenomenon satirically. Their two motion pictures were shot almost simultaneously and featured the same basic plot. Both films, *Rainbow Formula* and *They Called Him Robert*, tell a story of physicists/cyberneticists who invent android robots that look exactly like them. Through a series of coincidences, the robotic doppelgängers end up escaping the control of their creators, causing innumerable headaches to everyone involved.

Both films are comedies-of-errors; their robots' interactions with passers-by and the trouble the inventors have in capturing their creations produce a comedic and light-hearted mood. Nonetheless, a more serious message underpins both films. Both heroes are so entirely consumed with their scientific projects that they have little time for or interest in anything else. Paradoxically, the work of these scientists is meant to benefit humanity, yet both men have long lost their human touch.

Iungval'd-Khil'kevich directly addressed the lack of emotiveness in Soviet society in his directorial debut *Rainbow Formula*. He pointed out in a *Sovetskii ekran* interview that he wanted to comment on a phenomenon he termed "robotism."[43] Asked to clarify what he meant by this term, the young director explained: "The thing is that robots are everywhere around us; they occupy important positions and walk beside us and we don't even notice it. It's even possible that robot-like characteristics exist in all of us." The movie's scriptwriter defined *robotism* as "the absence of soul, insensitive treatment of others, and a thoughtless consideration of deep problems." One of the main culprits of robotism is the scientist Vladimir Bantikov, who creates his robotic double, Iasha, as a means to avoid the institute director's annoying demands that he attend innumerable committee meetings, symposia, conferences, and seminars.

Because Bantikov has made the robot self-regulating, Iasha begins to think of himself as superior to humans. Iasha resents the fact that he is controlled by an entity he considers primitive. He berates his designer and his kind for what are, in his mind, grave weaknesses: sleeping, falling in love, getting sick. The robot declares: "I ought to be in charge. You ought to stick to cleaning potatoes" (Figure 5.7). The scientist tries to convince his creation that positions of authority are best suited for humans precisely *because* they are emotionally perceptive and multifaceted, while the robot maintains that effectiveness and productivity are the most important marks of a leader. Frightened by Iasha's megalomania, Bantikov tries to dismantle "the monster," but he can no longer control it, and the robot escapes into the world, determined to govern people.

The relatively simple task of catching the delinquent android is complicated by the fact that Iasha invented a device he calls a "plastifikator," which allows him to change his face at will. Bantikov instructs the police that, despite his ability to change his appearance, Iasha will be easily recognizable by its robot-like qualities: lack of a sense of humour, lack of natural bodily movement, lack of empathy, and lack of common sense. Unfortunately, the city is full of people, especially administrators, who do not exhibit basic human traits, which makes the search for Iasha problematic. The notion that Soviet society did not lack citizens

Figure 5.7. Still from *Rainbow Formula* (1966). Bantikov squares off
with his Frankenstein, Iasha.

and leaders suffering from robotism drew the ire of the Goskino editors,
who banned and shelved the film, accusing Iungval'd-Khil'kevich of
spreading "anti-Soviet propaganda."[44] Although the May 1966 issue of
Sovetskii ekran enthusiastically announced that Soviet audiences would
have a chance to watch Iungval'd-Khil'kevich's comedy in a couple of
months' time, the premiere never took place.

Rainbow was never released; even so, it represents a valuable historical document about attitudes toward science and the value of human
emotion. Even though the action revolves around stopping Iasha's
quest to rule the world, the cause of the unrest and panic is Bantikov.
His wish to dedicate himself solely to creating a formula that will permit him to summon the rainbow at will leads him to construct a robot
without thinking about the consequences of his actions. Even his love
interest, Liusia, is angered that he has "attempted to replace a living,
feeling human being with a robot." Thus Bantikov's message is that
sixties masculinity cannot be defined solely by intellectual aptitude – it
requires equal proportions of emotional and cerebral strength.

Filmed at the same time as *Rainbow*, Il'ia Ol'shargev's *They Called
Him Robert* features a young scientist, albeit a much more urbane one,

Figure 5.8. Still from *They Called Him Robert* (1967). The android's
attempt at romancing Tania.

who builds an android. Unlike Bantikov, however, Sergei Kukin creates
his double to prove his genius. He names the "RB-235" unit Robert and,
wishing to make his model the most advanced android, releases him
into the world. Robert's interactions with the world are not what the
scientist expects, and Robert soon runs amok, unsuspected by any of
those who surround him. As Kukin's team tries to catch him, without
much success, he becomes increasingly curious about human emotions
even though these feelings "do not compute."

Unlike in *Rainbow*, the focus of *Robert* is not on seizing all robot-like
characters and identifying the soulnessness of Soviet citizens. Instead,
it is a story of a robot discovering the depth and breadth of human emotions and interpersonal relationships (Figure 5.8). The popular theme
song for the film accentuates the unique beauty of human feelings.
Sung from the perspective of the robot, the lyrics make the case that
even the most advanced android's capabilities will fall short it attempts
to comprehend and replicate emotions.

Eventually Kukin shelters Robert behind the walls of the institute
even though Robert continues to insist that he wants to understand
what it means to experience emotion. The android understands that

smelling grass after rain is not simply a tactile sensation but involves an emotional dimension that he, as cybernetics' most perfect and exact creation, cannot acquire. The female protagonist, Tania, like Liusia in *Rainbow*, berates the scientist for making light of human feelings. In no uncertain terms, Tania blames Kukin for the fiasco with Robert. She firmly tells him that people like him – people who lack the most basic appreciation for emotional warmth – are ill-suited to working with robots. Thus, in an ironic twist of events, a robot becomes more human than his architect.

Rainbow and *Robert* illustrate the limits of science, or, rather, the limitations of science when conducted by men of limited vision. Yet Romm's and Mikaelian's films are anything but straightforward regarding the benefits of science and are not exactly optimistic about man's ability to control nature for humanity's benefit. A cynic and a pessimist who is also a brilliant mind, Kulikov continuously challenges Gusev's idealism and his well-worn slogans and maxims. In a posh restaurant in Moscow, Kulikov barbs his friend and colleague about the purpose of his work and the sacrifices he is making. The urbane sophisticate mocks the idea that Gusev's attempts to create energy from neutrons will not be used for nefarious purposes. He provides his idealistic friend with numerous examples to prove his point: with the help of modern chemistry, Germans created poison gas weapons; the invention of the internal combustion engine allowed the British to produce tanks; and the discovery of the atomic chain reaction gave the Americans the first atomic weapon. Kulikov warns Gusev that his attempts to better humanity's material conditions are simultaneously inroads to the making of a new weapon. He rhetorically asks his college friend: "Do you think man has really become smarter in the past thirty thousand years? Not by an iota!" Looking around the restaurant, Kulikov implores Gusev to also cast a glance; compared to men and women who lived four thousand years ago, citizens of the "modern world" resemble Neanderthals in appearance. Moreover, Kulikov claims that humans, whatever political system they live under, have regressed morally: "A Genghis Khan could have never thought of concentration camps and gas chambers."

A couple of other pointed scenes in *Nine Days* cast doubt on whether humanity has evolved enough to treat scientific discoveries responsibly and peacefully. At a wedding reception, two scientists are trying to explain to a well-meaning but oblivious woman the purpose and significance of Gusev's research. The plump middle-class woman bedecked in jewellery is simultaneously anxious and overconfident about scientific issues – both reactions a product of her ignorance. To illustrate the principle behind Gusev's research, the two men ask their interlocutor to imagine the energy contained in a hydrogen bomb. They tell her: "Well, Gusev wants to take this energy and put it to work." With panic in her voice, the woman asks: "Put the bomb to work?!" The experts elaborate that the particles needed for the kind of energy Gusev wants to create are present everywhere – even at their table. The woman, now amazed, exclaims: "Lord, how simple!" And though this episode aims to amuse, it confirms Kulikov's impression that the general public cares little (and understands even less) about modern science and therefore cannot be trusted with the era's most revolutionary discoveries.

Gusev's father, a simple Russian peasant, also wonders about the worth of the kind of research his son conducts, especially after he sees how damaged his son's health has become as a result of his experiments. During a rare heart-to-heart conversation, the father asks his son if his life's calling was worth the sacrifice. Although his son responds tersely that the cost was worth the price, the father insists: "Maybe it was all for nothing? Who needs it?" (*Komu eto nuzhno?*). At first, Gusev responds philosophically that man cannot stop thinking and that even if all current research was forgotten, future generations would, inevitably, cover the same tracks. In an effort to understand his son's perspective, Gusev senior simply asks: "Did you make the bomb?" The nuclear scientist answers in the affirmative and justifies himself by saying that his participation in making the bomb ensured the safety of half the world's population. To the end, Gusev believes that even destructive discoveries are a product of peaceful intentions in the Soviet context. But even members of Gusev's own lab facility are divided. Romm lingers on a conversation between two specialists, one of whom is trying to convince the other that war is responsible for all of modern science's greatest discoveries: without military conflict, there would be no modern science.

It is clear, then, that some critics and officials objected to the movie's pessimistic tone and lack of ideological rectitude. Georgii Kapralov, who worked on *Pravda's* editorial staff at the time of the film's Moscow premiere, recalled that many wanted *Pravda* to publish an unambiguously critical review. The fact that one scientist dies at the beginning of the film and that the central character is on the brink of death at the story's end, combined with Kulikov's uncensored scepticism, generated strongly negative attention for the film. According to Kapralov's recollections, the positive review he submitted sat unpublished for two weeks. On 19 March 1962 he received a call from the typographer in the middle of the night, informing him that a review of *Nine Days* had come out, but that it was not his.[45] The editor for the science section, Vladimir Orlov, had written a damning critique of the movie, condemning

Kulikov's "heretical aphorisms of clearly Western origin." Incredulous, Orlov accused the film of misrepresenting the intellectual atmosphere of the scientific institute and its community. He commented: "It is hard to believe that these scientists only recently passed their exams on historical materialism."[46]

Like *Nine Days*, *Storm* questions the future of science in a system that is heavily affected by ideology and internal politicking. The movie ends with Krylov and Tulin setting out to do research that their mentor, Dankevich, had intended to complete. And as storm clouds gather above the pair of physicists in the final scene, one wonders how long it will be before another change in the bureaucratic chain results in another series of bureaucratic battles for Krylov and other ethical scientists like him.

Conclusion

Although B. Slutskii's poem "Fiziki i liriki" declared that scientists and logarithms had won out over poets and rhymes, filmmakers of the period showcased a masculinity that sought to accommodate both ways of approaching the world. The scientists striding across the silver screen in the sixties possessed great insights into how the earth and the universe function but were also expected to showcase a developed emotional register. Post-Stalinist celluloid intellectuals thus struggled to understand their environment rather than conquer and control it. For these men, the process was as important as the product, if not more so. One reason for this dynamic is that the period's filmmakers had created an unconquerable world for their heroes. Moviemakers were not interested in depicting men during their moments of glory; what drew them was the long stretches of time when their faith remained unshakeable even though the end was nowhere in sight.[47]

Sixties filmmakers who used the scientist as a protagonist found themselves in a position to revise two central aspects of Stalinist masculinity. First, the de-Stalinization of the scientific establishment had strengthened the autonomy of scientists conducting research, which led filmmakers to apply the principles of objective and rational study to the human experience overall. In an ironic twist, the focus on science served as a pretext for promoting a deideologization of Soviet reality and morality. The masculinity of the scientist reflected a profession that was now largely outside the purview of ideologues. Unlike the aviators, soldiers, and Stakhanovites before them, scientists were not beholden to a Five-Year Plan mentality; scientific principles, rather than record-setting, governed their lives. Il'ia Kulikov, a protagonist in Romm's *Nine Days*, for instance, derides a slogan urging scientists to "discover a particle in this quarter." He scoffs at the institute's bureau-cratese: "The discovery of a particle is a remarkable occurrence. What difference does it make if it happens during this quarter or at the begin-ning of the next?" While science and its practitioners were clearly in the service of the state and the people, their ultimate loyalty lay with sci-entific standards rather than ideological dogma. The attitude that there are laws – be they natural or moral – that take precedence over party dictums profoundly affected the era's understanding and depictions of masculinity.

Second, the image of the post-Stalinist scientist offered a novel view of nature and man's role in it. Stalinist heroes had affirmed their mas-culinity by taming the elements and conquering nature; post-Stalinist scientists did so by accepting failure and continuing to fight despite endless setbacks. Although the conventions of socialist realism obliged sixties scriptwriters and directors to show the hero vanquishing the nat-ural world, the day's films nonetheless tinged the happy ending with a dose of ambiguity: the successful solution of one scientific mystery marked the beginning of the next. The open-ended conclusions in these films conveyed the unorthodox idea that man is, ultimately, relatively impotent when faced with forces of nature. *Rainbow* and *Robert* – the two films in which scientists create an android doppelgänger – show man as incapable of mastering his own emotional world, let alone his environ-ment. Thus the four unconventional and closely scrutinized films exam-ined in this chapter use members of the scientific-technical intelligentsia to demonstrate that human mastery over nature is but a chimera. How-ever brilliant the scientists and however cutting-edge their scientific approach, they have to calibrate their masculinity to correspond to the reality that their lives are, at the end of the day, at the mercy of factors beyond their control, and that their feats are at best temporary.

As Vail' and Genis point out, however, by the late 1960s the scientific community's unique social position had turned out to be a Faustian bargain.[48] Once the scientists joined the nation's socio-political elite, the party forced them to support and advocate the party's agenda. As soon as the scientific establishment became a handmaiden of the state, it traded its outsider image for official funds, security, and privilege. As a result, scientists slowly disappeared from the nation's movie screens as symbols of a deideologized and heterodox masculinity. Nonetheless, the image of the quixotic, idealistic scientist remained alive beyond the sixties: many dissident scientists, such as Andrei Sakharov, would staunchly defend universal human rights and individual freedoms in subsequent decades.

Chapter Six

De-Heroization and the Pan-European Masculinity Crisis

A key scene in Sergei Gerasimov's two-part film *Journalist* (Zhurnalist, 1967) features a polite but contentious conversation between the French actress Annie Girardot and Gerasimov himself.[1] Seated in a bistro in Brussels, Gerasimov, a giant of the socialist realist tradition, asks Girardot whether movies replete with images of graphic violence and misery serve a social purpose. He tries to convince the face of sixties Italian and French avant-garde cinema that art ought to celebrate the positive sides of human existence.[2] Girardot, however, endorses art's responsibility to depict all aspects of contemporary life: violence, alienation, suicide, and ennui. She points out that a film industry dedicated only to commemorating man's promise of greatness produces an incomplete view of the world. Gerasimov pushes back, insisting that the depiction of man's darker sides lacks any educational benefit and instead serves a purely commercial function. For her part, Girardot maintains that intense passions and emotions – however dark – can bring audience members closer to self-awareness. Their deliberation at an impasse, the two friends call a truce, and each sings a beloved national song to conclude the amicable dinner gathering.

This self-conscious exchange over *digestifs* and cigarettes encapsulates the 1950s and '60s cross-continental debate about art's purpose. The scripted dialogue outlines a now familiar story about the divergent roads European and Soviet cinema took in the postwar era. While the former experimented with film form and participated in the sixties rebellion against the social status quo, the latter failed to innovate artistically and ignored the complexities inherent in modern societies and human psychology. While one was as laissez-faire as the free market, the other was as tightly regulated as the Five-Year Plans. Characterizing postwar Soviet and European cinemas as natural opposites remains attractive because the principal parties rarely deviated from this narrative themselves. The charged Cold War atmosphere accentuated, if not mandated, that the two sides differentiate themselves from each other.

The two warring sides had so thoroughly invested themselves in these roles that even a cursory glance at archival documents, newspapers, and professional journals superficially confirms the idea that Soviet cinema, despite the post-Stalin era reforms, remained more conservative than its counterparts in Eastern and Western Europe. Indeed, the Soviet public forum loudly defended the socialist realist tradition against the "perversions of modernism." The following statement was rather typical of sentiments expressed throughout the sixties in Soviet newspapers: "Our film critics have done a bit to unmask the distortions evident in contemporary bourgeois art in order to showcase how decadence has affected Western artists' desire to portray 'life as it is.'"[3] It was in this spirit that Soviet commentators categorically rejected documentary, absurdist, and surrealist trends from the other side of the Iron Curtain; ad nauseam they repeated that Europe's obsession with existentialism proved that the flesh of capitalist culture was approaching the final stages of decomposition. Scriptwriter N. Abramov argued in 1963 that abstractionism and surrealism clearly reflected the neuroses inherent in capitalist societies and that, in the Soviet context, those artistic movements represented mere alien phenomena.[4] Even neorealism, which the Italian Communist Party saw as advancing working-class interests, was viewed by Soviet authorities as progressive in a capitalist context only. Similarly, the Soviets were not enthused by the British New Wave even though it was sharply pro-labour.[5] The reactionary Soviet attitudes played into the hands of European and American observers, who branded the Soviet film industry as orthodox, static, and repressive.

But any insistence that the European and Soviet film industries evolved in diametrically opposing directions oversimplifies, if not misrepresents, the conditions on the ground. Postwar cinemas, regardless of ideology or national tradition, actually constructed comparable heroes, narratives, and aesthetics because they shared a common set of concerns and philosophical frameworks. It was not that Soviet artists aped trends from abroad (as their critics alleged), but that they developed a mutually intelligible frame of reference with their European colleagues since both groups were of the same historical moment. Analogous social, economic, and political developments across the continent inspired a cinematic heritage that transcended Cold War borders and displayed their artificiality. This is not particularly surprising, since artists operated within a larger cultural ecosystem. Much like in

Gerasimov's *Journalist*, film professionals not only met frequently and watched one another's productions but also formed close friendships.[6] Setting aside professional interests and their love for the medium, sixties directors wanted badly to make sense of their contemporaneity. And nothing embodied the spirit of the times and of postwar cinemas more than the deheroized protagonist.

During the 1950s and '60s, the European and Soviet film industries created narratives in which protagonists were lost at sea, disoriented by personal and professional expectations and seeking life's larger purpose. This direction in postwar filmmaking – whether labelled neorealist, New Wave, or new school – could best be described collectively as the "cinema of searching." Central to this opus was a heavy reliance on a visually expressed mood rather than on dialogue. The protagonists emerging from the new cinemas of the postwar era were hardly men of (constructive) action; they were defined rather by a lack they were unable to fill or even express. Common to these wandering souls was a spiritual ennui and alienation that prevented them from connecting with others and themselves. Although national in character in terms of storylines and cultural references, these cinematic waves knew no ideological boundaries because they expressed similar reservations about postwar optimism. The "New Wavers" worried that prosperity, convenience, and comfort – the calling cards of modern postwar life – compromised individuals' humanity. Since there were no great causes to be won or meaning-of-life questions that could be answered, the protagonists in New Wave productions could hardly be called heroes. Jimmy Porter, one of the most famous "unheroes" of the British New Wave, embodied the nihilism, cynicism, and misogyny of the postwar generation: "There aren't any good, brave causes left. If the big bang does come, and we all get killed off, it won't be in aid of the old-fashioned, grand design. It'll just be for the Brave New-nothing-very-much-thank-you. About as pointless and inglorious as stepping in front of a bus. No, there's nothing left for it, me boy, but to let yourself be butchered by the women."[7] Except for the blatant sexism, Soviet filmmakers articulated comparable anxieties. In the 1962 film *Nine Days of a Year* the physicist Kulikov mocks the notion of progress: "Surely you cannot think that man has become more intelligent in the past 30,000 years? The first man to strike fire was more brilliant than the discoverer of quantum physics. Besides, a Genghis Khan could have never thought to fertilize fields with human ashes, stuff mattresses with human hair, or make lampshades from human skin." In both Europe and the Soviet Union, the positivist idea that men could remake themselves and influence the course of history had given way to a victimhood narrative. A crop of postwar directors saw their male compatriots as occupying the passenger seat, at the mercy of impersonal forces outside their control.

By 1965, so common had the Soviet film industry's preoccupation with men's disorientation become that the term deheroization (*degeroizatsiia*) entered the common argot. It was trotted out to mark any fictional hero as inauthentic and as "too small" to convey the world importance of Soviet Union's historic mission. To accuse an artist of deheroization also meant to censure him (or her) for following "Western fads."[8] Gerasimov defined deheroization as "a failure to interpret reality from a heroic position" and as the result of artists failing to stake out a clear ideological position and differentiate (for the moviegoer) bad from good, ugly from beautiful, principled from corrupt.[9] During the 1960s the very highest echelons of power considered this issue central to the Soviet Union's ideological competition with the West.[10] Officially, these unheroic characters came to be viewed as part of psychological Cold War tactics, as Trojan Horses concealing dangerous and alien ideologies. Soviet art critic V.A. Razumnyi noted in 1963 that the phenomenon of deheroization exemplified just how entrenched reactionary bourgeois art trends had become in the Soviet Union. He warned that aesthetics must never be separated from politics and that Western postmodern philosophies, with their pessimistic view of human nature, were negatively affecting the Soviet people's attitudes.[11] Even the generally moderate chairman of the Cinematographer's Union, Ivan Py'rev, pronounced: "Unlike capitalist artists who fear the end of the world, who speak of a lost generation, and who contemplate the futility of human existence, we, the Soviet artists, have to celebrate life on our planet and uphold humanistic life-affirming principles."[12] The allegation that deheroization was something alien simultaneously tapped into the authorities' Cold War paranoia and was the reason why censors repressed any depictions of masculinity that, although representative of "life on the ground," contradicted ideological slogans about Soviet life.

The four preceding chapters dealt with concrete postwar issues Soviet men were seen to struggle with; this chapter focuses on depictions of existential angst in both Soviet and European cinemas. Each of this chapter's four sections places one Soviet motion picture in dialogue with a representative example of the Polish Film School, British New Wave, Italian auteur filmmaking, and the Czechoslovak New Wave. Although the cinematic styles are varied, all four cases highlight that European and Soviet filmmakers approached their topics from an existentialist point of view, one that plucked the protagonist from the larger-than-life historical framework and drew him closer to life-size. All these cinematic features largely aimed to observe and diagnose rather than solve and cajole. Few Soviet films were as boldly experimental as their European counterparts – the times did not allow it – so examples of Soviet films that *were* are significant for two reasons. First, these films garnered much attention from the authorities, the intellectual community, and filmmakers abroad. Second, because of the immense (public) coverage these productions received, they influenced the cultural arena to a degree disproportionate to their modest numbers and thereby set the parameters for representing "authentic" Soviet heroism.

Cold War European Cinema without Borders

As the atrocities of the 1930s and '40s became a matter of public debate in the 1950s and '60s, many Soviet and European intellectuals became more doubtful about any ideology's ability to give meaning to individuals. If anything, it seemed that political ideologies had caused untold misery in the interwar and wartime years. Conversations about concentration camps, state-sponsored mass repressions, and nuclear bombings generated widespread cynicism about any governing system's capacity to tame the human propensity for evil. French playwright Eugene Ionesco's 1958 sentiment fittingly expressed the scepticism prevalent among the postwar intelligentsia more broadly: "If there is something that needs to be demystified, it is those ideologies which offer ready-made solutions."[13] Ionesco's statement echoed Soviet filmmakers' notion that ambiguous finales were more authentic. This attitude was best evidenced in 1961, when novelist Viktor Nekrasov applauded Khutsiev's *Lenin's Guard* specifically for "not having dragged onto the movie screen a grey-mustached and all-knowing worker who had ready-made answers for everything."[14] Thus both Soviet and European artists, burdened with the great moral tragedies of their time, sought new ways to conceptualize the realities of the human condition, rejecting easy solutions. Increasingly experimenting with cinematic form, Eastern and Western European filmmakers used motion pictures to express the scepticism, alienation, and ambivalence evident in literary and philosophical circles since the late 1940s.

As Europeans gradually confronted the memory and moral trauma of the Second World War, questions about the human condition and humanity's purpose proliferated regardless of ideological allegiance. The triumph of totalitarian regimes across Europe, the tragedy of the Holocaust, and the bombings of Hiroshima and Nagasaki compelled artists and thinkers across Europe to contemplate evil as a permanent feature of human existence and to identify absurdity as fundamental to the human condition. Hannah Arendt's 1945 essay "Nightmare and Flight" accurately predicted that "the problem of evil will be the fundamental question of postwar intellectual life in Europe."[15] Soviet intellectuals reflected on the widespread complicity and conformity that had bred the Stalinist Terror, conducting similar cultural autopsies. This was on full display in M. Romm's 1965 documentary *Ordinary Fascism*, which condemned not just the Nazi regime but all dictatorships, all totalitarian propaganda, all group-think, and all mass violence.

Having collapsed under the weight of their own ethical morass, the fallen idols of personality cults across Europe left behind a moral vacuum that New Wave directors felt obligated to fill. Film historian Geoffrey Nowell-Smith elucidates this pan-European process best when he observes: "If there is a feature common to all the new cinemas of the 1960s, it is that they set out to rectify something false or misleading in the way the life of their country was portrayed and in so doing came up with an alternative image which they hoped was more accurate or more relevant to modern life as they understood it."[16] Czechoslovak New Wave expert Peter Hames concisely characterized this trend when he noted: "The period of the New Wave presented a heightened aesthetic response in a society emerging from a period of enforced cultural orthodoxy."[17] Following the lead of Italian neorealists, who influenced European and Soviet cinematography long after the movement's zenith in the late 1940s, postwar directors across Europe abandoned elaborate studio sets and turned their particular attention to the daily lives of the working classes and "ordinary people." Postwar directors were motivated by a similar agenda even when they identified with different political camps or belonged to none at all. Postwar Italian directors sneered at domestic "white telephone cinema" (*cinema dei telefoni bianchi*) that imitated Hollywood films of the 1930s and that propagated fascist ideology;[18] young French filmmakers mocked the old-fashioned *cinéma de papa*, or "dad's cinema," throughout the 1950s; new Soviet talent agitated for a revival of "sincerity" in the arts; and up-and-coming British moviemakers ridiculed their nation's films for being "snobbish, anti-intelligent, emotionally inhibited, willfully blind to the conditions and problems of the present, and dedicated to an out-of-date, exhausted national ideal."[19]

This pan-European search for cinematic sincerity and authenticity began in the late 1940s, when the Italian neorealists began to chip away at the pillars of fascist society, attacking the uncritical respect for family, official authority, and class hierarchy. Postwar Italian filmmakers, whom the New Wavers of the sixties followed in spirit, if not in letter, aimed to "promote a true objectivity – one that would force viewers to abandon the limitations of a strictly personal perspective and to embrace the reality of the 'others' ... with all the ethical responsibility that such a vision entails."[20] Roberto Rossellini, a central figure in the movement, himself noted: "For me, Neorealism is, above all, a moral position. It then became an aesthetic position, but at the beginning it was moral ... Ideas, not images, are important."[21] In a reversal of the Mussolini-era hero-mongering productions, neorealists elevated previously underrepresented social classes, often (though not always) casting non-professional actors. They turned their cameras to partisan bands (Roberto Rossellini's *Roma, città aperta* [Rome, Open City, 1945], and *Paisà* [Paisan, 1946]), to the unemployed proletariat (Vittorio De Sica's *Ladri di biciclette* [Bicycle Thieves, 1947]), and Sicilian fishermen (Luchino Visconti's *La terra trema* [The Earth Trembles, 1948]). Instead of glossing over sociopolitical reality, neorealist directors critically (re) interpreted Italian history.[22] Italy's long-standing problems – such as regional disparity, political corruption, and class inequality – received attention for the first time.[23]

The most immediate and visible example of neorealism's transnational influence could be observed in the British Free Cinema movement.[24] On 5 February 1956, the National Film Theatre hosted the first of six film events featuring non-professional experimental shorts. The co-founder of the movement, film critic and director Lindsay Anderson, underscored that the Free Cinema movement had surfaced because mainstream British cinema had become politically impotent.

According to Anderson, contemporary British film was not contemporary at all; it rejected the responsibility to criticize, it privileged depictions of a metropolitan southern English culture; and it silently supported the country's class inequalities. He protested that many profound postwar social changes were receiving no attention on the big screen: "According to the testimony of our filmmakers, Britain is a country without problems, in which no essential changes have occurred in the past fifty years, and which still remains the centre of an Empire on which the sun will never have the bad manners to set."[25] In Anderson's view, domestic motion pictures remained curiously silent on a range of present-day topics: mass strikes, Teddy Boys, nuclear tests, and Hungarian refugees. In light of the willful ignorance on the part of cinema industry leaders, Anderson demanded that moviegoers consider whether they should continue to accept the wholly fictionalized images that British productions were offering.[26]

Building on the recognition the Free Cinema movement received, a core group of British directors produced a number of films between 1959 and 1963 that received critical attention because of their documentary depictions of working-class realities. These motion pictures became known collectively as the British New Wave, or, less charitably, as kitchen sink dramas.[27] These productions became notorious in Britain and abroad in part because they included obscenities, violence, and suggestions of nudity, all thanks to a relaxation of censorship standards. Under the conditions set by the British Censorship Bureau, the X certificate came to be reserved for horror films as well as dramatic productions that dealt with "mature content." The X label allowed British cinematographers to, for the first time, examine previously taboo topics. The British New Wavers capitalized on the draw the X label exercised on curious filmgoers; in doing so, they ratcheted up the domestic popularity of their productions and made visible the previously sanitized working class subculture. Besides presenting moviegoers with the more scandalous, if not salacious and exoticized, aspects of working-class reality, these films shocked with their portrayals of poverty and monotony that marked life in much of of England's industrial north.

Soviet reformist filmmakers were no less ambitious than their Italian and British counterparts in their determination to reimagine Soviet society by rejecting the excessive idealization and kitsch typical of Stalin-era socialist realism. Katerina Clark points out that "even before Stalin died (as early as 1951) critics began to complain that there was too much 'varnishing of reality' [*lakirovka deistvitel'nosti*], a charge that was heard more loudly and insistently once Stalin had died in 1953."[28] For instance, in 1962, after Khrushchev's renewed attack on Stalin's personality cult at the Twenty-Second Party Congress, noted Soviet film critic V.A. Razumnyi called for a transformation in Soviet filmmaking: "If many directors are considering elevating themes such as transferring technical equipment to the kolkhozes or the necessity of marshland reclamation, then we need to instruct them that these are not the problems we should be addressing."[29] Razumnyi advocated that filmmakers concentrate on the formation of a new kind of individual, new kinds of interpersonal relationships. Although his commentary makes it clear that the so-called production films no longer held cultural relevance, the fact that this exhortation required repeating reveals how reluctant the industry was to abandon monumentalizing Soviet life and embrace experimental cinema.

No less than British and Italian filmmakers, Czechoslovak and Polish directors played an important role in presenting more complex heroes living in an ambiguous universe. They had found ways to creatively combine socialist realist themes and aesthetics with those typical of experimental postwar filmmaking. The so-called Polish Film School during the late 1950s and early 1960s and the Czechoslovak New Wave during the mid- to late 1960s illustrated the possibilities of unique national artistic traditions within the socialist camp and expanded the limits of the permissible in the context of socialist realism. The directors of the Polish Film School developed strategies for problematizing the heretofore schematic narratives about the Second World War; in so doing, they complicated viewers' perceptions about human nature in general and masculinity in particular. By not romanticizing or simplifying war – the ultimate homosocial environment – they cracked the edifice of the monumental socialist realist hero and punctured the myth of the indissoluble homosocial fratriarchy. The Czechoslovak New Wave went even further, placing the contemporary socialist citizen in absurd and surreal situations that rendered life in the Eastern Bloc simultaneously comical and horrifying. Czech and Slovak directors mercilessly mocked both their national character and human nature, with the result that their heroes epitomized ideological defeatism and deheroization. It is no surprise that by the time Soviet tanks rolled into Prague in 1968, conservative Soviet filmmakers were accusing their Czechoslovak counterparts of actively promoting "unhealthy attitudes" and inciting reactionary activities.

The Second World War as Crucible for Soviet and Polish Masculinity

The controversial Polish director Andrzej Wajda not only transformed postwar Polish filmmaking but also laid the groundwork for overturning previous representations of the Second World War in the countries of the Warsaw Pact. Wajda's famous 1950s trilogy – *Pokolenie* (*Generation*, 1955), *Kanał* (*Kanał*, 1957), and *Popiół i diament* (*Ashes and Diamonds*, 1958) – reinvented the concept of heroism in wartime. Instead of soldiers who confidently battled a cartoon enemy, Wajda presented much more ambiguous characters who simultaneously expressed courage and doubt, acting with both determination and folly. Moreover, Wajda was one of the first Eastern Bloc filmmakers to show the Second World War as a psychological state that affected participants in distinctly different ways. Polish dissident and writer Adam Michnik commented on the ambiguity of Wajda's protagonists: "In each of them he sees Polish honesty and courage, Polish naivety and confusion, and the inevitability of Polish defeat. His characters lose as Poles and as citizens. Their redemption is resistance to fate, a fate which inevitably ends in undeserved defeat."[30] Abandoning socialist realism, which dictated that sanctified heroes emerge victorious convinced of the righteousness of their mission, Wajda gave voice to ordinary men who experienced fear as well as bravery and who died knowing that, perhaps, their death had no purpose.

With his trilogy Wajda undermined the Stalinist interpretation of the war years, minimizing the ideological dimension and accentuating the scale of human suffering through the individual fates of his complex heroes. Wajda's perspective, although specifically Polish in its tradition of romanticism, lay a foundation for Soviet directors who also wished to complicate the sanitized vision of war that Stalin had imposed after 1945. Even though Wajda's trilogy tackled traumatic and contentious events specific to Polish history and sought to intervene quite literally in the construction of public memory in his homeland, his depiction of the Second World War resonated with artists across the Eastern Bloc as they combated Stalin's artistic dogma and his historical interventionism. In a recent round table discussion, Russian directors and art critics of various generations frequently cited Wajda as an inspiration for their own work; in fact, they reflected nostalgically on the significant influence the Polish Film School had on Soviet filmmaking long after the mid-1960s.[31] Wajda's influence over Soviet filmmakers was in no small part due to a general feeling of dissatisfaction with the status quo among Eastern European and Soviet intellectuals after Stalin's death.

Of all the countries in the Soviet bloc, Poland and Hungary bucked hardest against the existing state of affairs. Mirroring and engaging Vladimir Pomerantsev's call for more sincerity in literature in 1953, Polish writers openly questioned the artistic value of socialist realism.[32] In 1954, I.I. Anisimov, the director of the Soviet Gor'kii Institute for World Literature, sent a report to the Central Committee, notifying the authorities that on his recent trip to Poland he had encountered a hostile environment, which he believed had been influenced directly by Pomerantsev's "reactionary views." He reported that one leading journal questioned "the value of achievements in the realm of the arts under the current regime" while another insisted that "socialist realism, as a creative principle, has become bankrupt."[33] Less than a year after Anisimov's visit, Polish poet and Communist Party member Adam Ważyk renewed the call for artistic self-determination and expressed disdain for socialist realism and its insistence on presenting a varnished reality.[34] His A Poem for Adults (Poemat dla dorosłych) invokes Charles Fourier, a nineteenth-century French utopian socialist thinker known for his outlandish theories, such as that the seas would one day lose their salinity and turn to lemonade and that the North Pole would some day be milder than the Mediterranean.

Fourier, the dreamer, charmingly foretold
that lemonade would flow in the seas.
Does it flow?
They drink sea water,
crying:
"lemonade!"
returning home secretly
to vomit.

Between 1955 and 1963 a group of directors, known collectively as
the Polish Film School, took advantage of the temporary cultural and
political thaw to liberate the national consciousness from the patent
fabrications that had permeated Stalinist politics. Andrzej Wajda, Andrzej Munk, Jerzy Kawalerowicz, Wojciech Has, Kazimierz Kutz, Tade-
usz Konwicki, and Stanisław Różewicz, all of whom had trained at the
Łódź Film School, contributed to the renaissance of national filmmaking and fashioned a world-renowned artistic school. Moviemakers of
the Polish Film School created works influenced by Italian neorealism
and imbued with a sense of social consciousness, that directly or implicitly addressed the (memory of) Second World War and reflected on
the concept of romantic heroism and Polish nationhood.[35]

By the late 1950s, Polish artists, especially filmmakers, had become
quite outspoken in their opposition to official interference in the arts.
Soviet authorities felt uneasy about these developments, which in Poland could not be contained. At the 1960 Karlovy Vary Film Festival in
Czechoslovakia, a spirit of defiance seeped into the proceedings. Cynthia Grenier, international film critic and "Life" editor of the *Washington Times*, observed an unusually charged atmosphere in Karlovy Vary
that year: "A young Polish scriptwriter, Aleksander Ścibor Rylski stated
calmly to some two hundred movie people and journalists in the Open
Forum that he had not seen a good Soviet movie in years, and that Soviet
concepts of human nature tended to be far too simple for his tastes."
Even more electrifying was the provocation Rylski launched later that
day at the indignant M. Romm: "I don't see why Mr. Romm wants to
put this discussion on a political basis. For me, capitalism and socialism
are not barriers separating art forms. A film is good or bad. Not socialist
or capitalist. A bad socialist film is just as bad as a bad capitalist film."[36]

Wajda created his postwar trilogy amid this rebellion against artistic
conformism, and in doing so he played a key role in promoting fresh
thinking about both the legacy of the Second World War and the human
condition. Although the revision of Stalinist narratives and artistic principles went much deeper in Poland, by 1956 Soviet war films too were

beginning to address topics that had once been anathema in the public sphere, such as the fate of the huge numbers of Soviet POWs, the early military defeats of the Red Army, treason in the ranks, and the incompetence of the top brass. Perhaps the most important change in the Stalinist master narrative was the acknowledgment that war had brought much needless suffering to both civilians and soldiers.[37] This development in the Soviet context tied in directly to Khrushchev's admission at the Twentieth Party Congress that the catastrophic human and material losses of the initial months of the war could have been avoided had Stalin heeded the numerous warnings about the attack; had he not disregarded the need to boost arms production; and had he not wiped out much of the top military leadership during the Great Terror.[38] In no uncertain terms, Khrushchev demanded: "Did we have time and the capabilities for such preparations? Yes, we had the time and the capability ... Had our industry been mobilized properly and in time to supply the army with the necessary material, our wartime losses would have been decidedly smaller."[39] His message undercut Stalin's personality cult, as he intended, but it also laid out a rather bleak view of the war as an avoidable tragedy rather than a triumph of the Communist Party leadership. The revelation simultaneously discredited Stalin's image as a brilliant military leader and sharply revised the view that the Party had done all it could to protect its citizens. By exposing Stalin's blunders before and during the German invasion of the Soviet Union, Khrushchev was essentially allowing Soviet citizens to contest the memory of the Second World War – or at least its opening months.

By picking up on the de-Stalinized interpretation of the war, Soviet artists were more able – like Wajda – to evade the socialist realist viewpoint and depict man in an environment defined by senseless carnage. Moreover, because Khrushchev had extolled the ordinary folk, rather than Stalin and his top generals, as the war's true heroes, writers and filmmakers could pay more attention to the experiences of average soldiers in their own wartime hell. Thus Khrushchev's decision to expose what had actually happened in the first months of the German invasion became the jumping-off point for a re-examination of Stalinist notions of Soviet masculinity. Because Khrushchev's report painted civilians and soldiers as lambs being led to the slaughter by the so-called Father of the Peoples, Khrushchev-era writers and filmmakers gravitated toward depicting the rank and file navigating the treacherous terrain of war by themselves – often helpless, disoriented, and abandoned by their fellow comrades.

Thus both Polish and Soviet directors, motivated by the urge to unearth a more authentic, more representative experience of the war, revised a key aspect of Stalinist masculinity: the protagonist's connection to the patriarch and the fraternity. Directors of war films in the post- Stalin era replaced the ideological pathos that tied men horizontally to the patriarch and vertically to the fratriarchy with a humanitarian pathos that symbolically linked men's fate and happiness to a feminine object of desire. In postwar Soviet movies the soldier fixes his gaze on his wife, mother, or girlfriend and fights to reunite with them. The Polish patriot instinctively serves the motherland, giving his life to protect a sovereign and independent nation. The hero therefore most often acts in solitude, for the patriarch is either absent or unable to help and the fratriarchy suffers from disorganization and disunity. In both scenarios, however, the fantasy never materializes: the hero rarely unites with his family or lives to see the nation liberated. The focus of postwar films about the Second World War thus becomes the inevitable trauma of the masculine subject.

Sergei Bondarchuk's directorial debut, *Fate of a Man* (Sud'ba cheloveka, 1959),[40] and Wajda's *Kanał*[41] together encapsulate the larger cinematic trend that revised the definition of war and undermined the principles underpinning Stalinist masculinity. At first glance, the two films have little in common. *Kanał* tells the story of the Third Platoon during the final days of the Warsaw Uprising (late September 1944), chronicling their attempts to save themselves from a Nazi onslaught by slogging through the labyrinthine sewage canals beneath the city centre. Bondarchuk's film focuses on an ordinary Soviet soldier as he relates the horrors he underwent during the war: capture at the very beginning of the war, concentration and forced-labour camps in Russia and abroad, and the death of his entire family. Despite the obvious differences in content and narrative conventions, *Kanał* and *Fate* broke new ground in that they placed previously marginalized events and groups centre stage and began restructuring the Stalinist masculine trope to more accurately reflect the trauma of war.

Both films address and build on wartime issues that had, up to that point, received scant attention in the public sphere. *Kanał* was the first film to depict the Warsaw Uprising in a historically accurate way. The very portrayal of the uprising presented an enormous ideological challenge because it reflected positively on the participation of the home-grown resistance movement, the Home Army, which the Communist authorities cast in a negative light after the war. Wajda faced an even more difficult choice regarding how to convey the Red Army's refusal to aid the anti-Nazi insurrection even though it was positioned a mere 100 metres from Polish positions across the Vistula. The uprising, which began on 1 August 1944 as part of a nationwide rebellion

(Operation Tempest), was supposed to last only a few days until Soviet forces reached the city. But because the Soviet advance halted before it entered Warsaw, the Polish resistance had no option but to continue fighting the German war machine unaided for sixty-three days until forced to surrender on 2 October 1944. As a result of the Soviet betrayal, 200,000 Poles died in the uprising.

Since this event figured as a national tragedy and could have ignited an explosive political scandal, Wajda expressed the tragedy of the treason symbolically without explicitly mentioning the presence of the Soviet army. Two members of the platoon, Stokrotka and Korab, manage to reach an exit that leads to the Vistula but soon realize that it has been sealed shut, condemning them to death. To turn back would mean certain death by asphyxiation or exhaustion. As the camera captures the couple for the last time, Stokrotka presses her face against the iron bars, impotently looking across the river, symbolically gazing at the freedom she will never reach. Before the viewer leaves the young pair condemned to death, we see Stokrotka's perspective – he looks directly at the positions where the Soviet armed forces are standing idly while innocent people, like Stokrotka and Korab, perish. As Wajda himself remarked: "I could not show that Soviet troops were waiting on the other side of the Vistula river while the Warsaw Uprising died on this side. It was enough that I led the protagonists of my film to the canal's outlet, from which they could see the other side of the river. The audience knew what I wanted to say."[42] The effect was undeniable. A survivor of the uprising reflected on the film's importance: "Until now, ordinary heroes have been, for many years, pushed into the shadows, into silence, into the mudslinging of false accusations and slander."[43]

Bondarchuk tackled a national tragedy of similar magnitude in his *Fate of a Man* in that he made a former POW, a member of a highly stigmatized group, the protagonist of his film. In the Soviet context, Private Sergei Sokolov was an unusual choice for a hero, for POWs were considered politically suspect (officially at least), and would remain so until 1956. The Stalin-era authorities believed that POWs who had survived German concentration camps must have acted disloyally in order to save their lives.[44] Stalin's policy treated these returnees as automatically guilty of treason. As Aleksandra Kollontai, the Soviet ambassador to Sweden, commented in mid-1940: "The Soviet Union does not recognize Soviet POWs. We consider Soviet soldiers who fell into German hands deserters." Around 2.8 million veterans – roughly 14 per cent of the total – had returned as POWs, sometimes through forced repatriation. A minority of returning POWs faced the firing squad or Gulag sentences, but most of them were consigned to the margins of postwar society, unable to relocate, hold a steady job, receive any state assistance, or (in many cases) reunite with their families and loved ones.

In Bondarchuk's film, Sokolov tells his life story to a stranger as they wait for a river ferry. Sokolov immediately establishes himself as a loyal servant of the state, one whose life bears the scars of the regime's campaigns and wars. Born in 1900, he fought with the Red Army during the Civil War, participated in the anti-kulak drive in Kuban, and lost his entire family to famine before finally settling down in his native Voronezh, marrying his wife and becoming a father of two. Bondarchuk takes the time to illustrate Sokolov's ordinariness, showing him labouring, witnessing the birth of his children, drinking (frequently), and enjoying marital bliss. But the domestic idyll proves short-lived – the Second World War yanks him from his natural environment: the family nest.

Besides giving voice to the experiences of people who would have otherwise gone unrecognized or been stigmatized, Bondarchuk and Wajda bring into sharp relief the war's psychological dimension. In both films, the first third of the narrative is bright, full of light and energy. Wajda begins his film twenty-four hours before the platoon enters the sewage system, when the soldiers are still fighting, still willing to defend their city and country. Once they enter the canals, however, hope, as well as light, disappears. Indeed, the sunlight that breaks up the stinging darkness of the deadly underworld signifies danger and uncertainty.

As with Stokrotka and Korab, sunshine denotes a dead end, for the sunlit openings provide the Nazis with a means to fill the labyrinth with poison gas. Wajda makes a direct reference to Dante's *Inferno* when one of the platoon members, gone mad from exhaustion and horror, quotes the poet: "I saw a people smothered in a filth that out of human privies seemed to flow."[45] As the *New York Times* reviewer noted after seeing the movie, "the monologue of the musician gives us to understand ... that Dante had been in the sewers before the Uprising fighters, that this is hell, and that all living things have been condemned to this hideous, stinking cesspool."[46]

Bondarchuk's film reflects the same sort of emotional devastation wrought by war. Once Sokolov boards the train to the front line, he enters his own underground hell. Everything he witnesses on his journey through the war breaks him down from within; little by little he dies inside as he tries to preserve his sanity under the most inhumane conditions. Like the Polish resistance fighters, he will never be able to emerge whole out of the metaphoric inferno. The only flashes of light Sokolov glimpses consist of flashbacks to his marital life and images of his family members begging him to return home. But, as in Wajda's *Kanał*,

Figure 6.1. Still from *Kanał* (1956)

these tantalizing hints of life are but a mirage in a barren landscape of war; when Sokolov returns home, he discovers a bomb crater where his house used to be and learns that his wife and daughter died three years prior. He cries: "This life of mine is nothing but a nightmare... It turns out that for two years I have been talking to the dead." Thus for both Sokolov and the Polish soldiers, war becomes history's literal and metaphorical torture chamber (Figure 6.1). Although the protagonists in both films are German captives, numerous scenes magnify their sense of entrapment – and the essential exitlessness of the human condition (Figure 6.2).

Kanał and *Fate of a Man* represent narratives not of nations coming together and becoming whole, but rather of their breaking down and disintegrating under the weight of wartime horror. Film scholar Paul Coates's assessment of the Warsaw Uprising holds true of Sokolov's experience as well: "Thus Uprising is not the Romantic rebellion cherished in popular memory but a nightmare of abandonment, one of the 'crimes and follies' of Gibbon's vision of history."[47] Bondarchuk and Wajda represent the collapse of national community through the breakdown of the fratriarchy that symbolically ties the soldiers into a unified whole; both films trace the dissolution of the fraternal order as brothers betray and abandon one another.

Figure 6.2. Still from *Fate of a Man* (1959).

Fate of a Man consists of a series of episodes showcasing that coward-ice and treachery, not valour and loyalty, defined the relations among Soviet soldiers. Right after capturing them, the Germans hold the POWs in an Orthodox church. A religious man, not wanting to commit a sacri-legious act by relieving himself in a place of worship, bangs on the doors of the church and begs his captors to let him out for a minute. His plea is met by a round of bullets from the other side of the door. The other prisoners, whose sadistic laughter has taunted the poor soul and echoed loudly off the church walls, fall silent as they watch the God-fearing man fall dead to the floor. The scene, so surreal and nightmarish, mirrors the inferno atmosphere of Warsaw's sewers, where the voices of the lost soldiers eerily echo against the surface of the underground Styx.

In the same church, a POW named Kryzhnev light-heartedly tells a fellow inmate that he will eagerly betray him as a Party member to their German captors: "If in tomorrow's line-up they start calling out for Jews, commissars, and communists, it won't do you any good to hide, Lieutenant. What did you think? That by getting rid of your uni-form you will pass for a private? Well you won't! I'll point you out right away! Besides, will you be ashamed to admit that you're a com-munist?" When the lieutenant pleads for mercy, Kryzhnev simply responds: "I have myself to think about." Having overheard the con-versation, Sokolov decides to punish the turncoat soldier and save the younger officer; he motions to the lieutenant to hold Kryzhnev's legs and then strangles the would-be traitor. Thus the only murder Sokolov commits in the film is against his compatriot; more importantly, he does not choke him because he conspired against a communist but because he cannot abide treason. Significantly, after the two men kill Kryzhnev, they do not make an example of him but move to a different corner of the church in order to avoid trouble. *Fate of a Man* further explores the theme of a degenerating masculine community by filming men in Nazi camps as they go mad from mental and physical exhaustion. In one labour camp, where the POWs have to haul rocks up a steep mountain, Sokolov attempts to prop up a weak prisoner and push him forward so that the guards will not shoot him. As they pass a Nazi officer, the worn-out POW locks eyes with his torturer in a way that betrays temporary madness from sleep and food deprivation. The German approaches the POW and cold-heartedly pushes him over the cliff. The scene displays the enemy's cruelty, but it also marks the breakdown of the monumental masculinity that exercised an absolute monopoly under Stalin and points to a damaged fratriarchal system. The soldier dies because camp life has worn him out; his apparent defiance is the result of his exhaustion rather than moral or ideological conviction. His death, moreover, does not evoke protest from his fellow inmates or serve as a mobilizing call to action. He vanishes unnoticed and unmourned by his fellow men.

Whereas Bondarchuk expresses the disintegration of the fraternal collective in episodic fashion, Wajda traces the gradual collapse of the Third Platoon as their quest to liberate Poland ends in captivity and death. Almost as soon as the platoon descends into the sewers, its members become separated through a series of circumstances; after that point, the film follows three separate storylines that come together in the protagonists' tragic finale. The platoon members' separation speaks to the disunity of the fratriarchy; the final scene references the irreparable disarray of the masculine order. Lieutenant Zadra, the platoon commander, emerges from a manhole with his Sergeant Major Kula onto deserted city streets and a pulverized city. Exhausted, and mired in excrement, Zadra is nonetheless ready to pick up arms and continue fighting. As he rejoices in his temporary reprieve, he becomes aware that his men (his metaphoric sons) are not coming up immediately behind him as he expected. When asked where rest of the company is, Kula admits having lied that they were behind them: "They're all lost. We've left them behind long ago. I lied when I said they were following." As the realization dawns on Zadra that his men are still hopelessly wandering in the infernal maze, he shoots Kula, the last remaining member of the platoon, shouting, "You coward!" Then, with a look of a man gone mad with grief, he descends back into the sewers and certain death, murmuring repeatedly: "My company! My company!" The climax of the film thus confirms that isolation and breakdown are the governing formal and thematic principles of *Kanał*. As in *Fate of a Man*, the masculine community suffers treason, disunity, and lack of discipline.

Although Wajda and Bondarchuk created these unorthodox and unheroic narratives from different motives – Wajda, to commemorate the Warsaw Uprising and reflect critically on romanticized interpretations of Polish history; Bondarchuk, to rehabilitate the memory of Soviet POWs and commemorate the suffering of rank-and-file soldiers – both directors revised the Stalinist myth of the Second World War. *Kanał* and *Fate of a Man* not only furnish a more realistic experience of war as a site of trauma for many but also undermine the core symbolism associated with war as a formative arena for masculine identity; in these films, war does not strengthen the bonds that buttress the fratriarchal community; it snaps them. Moreover, by utilizing representatives of previously marginalized groups and accentuating the trauma of war, Wajda and Bondarchuk use the modern soldier to destabilize the mythical and epic warriors of a romanticized past: *bogatyr* – Russian medieval knights – and *uhlan* – Polish cavalry officers. Ultimately, Sokolov's reflection on his front-line experience aptly illustrates that war became the embodiment of trauma for the postwar masculine subject: "Sometimes I cannot sleep at night. I just stare into the darkness and think to myself: Why has life tortured and punished me so?"

Working-Class Masculinity and the Fear of Selling Out in the United Kingdom and Soviet Union

The great majority of Soviet films focused on the lives of the working classes, yet the socialist realist insistence on optimism and didacticism largely prohibited directors from exploring the full range of working-class realities. Even during the sixties liberalization, directors had to exercise restraint in representing the less attractive sides of working-class life, for the state continued to idealize the figure of the worker. Because Soviet art professed faith in the worker and his potential, films that showed spiritually flawed working-class characters had to emphasize the certainty of their rehabilitation. To criticize the working class without demonstrating faith in its progress under a regime that billed itself as "the workers' state" was to imply that the Party was failing in its fundamental task. In this context, Mark Osep'ian's *Three Days of Viktor Chernyshev* (Tri dnia Viktora Chernysheva, 1967) was arguably the first Soviet film to refuse to romanticize the ordinary worker. In offering a portrait of an outwardly obedient but apathetic and petty-criminal working-class youth, Osep'ian sketched a profile of working-class masculinity that resembled one that had emerged during the British New Wave in the early 1960s.

Between 1959 and 1963, British cinema produced a number of films that generated critical attention at home and abroad because of their real-life depictions of working-class masculinity. For the first time in British film history, the big screen showed scenes filled with obscene language, moral depravity, and sexual violence. Besides presenting moviegoers with scandalous moments of working-class reality, directors shocked them with portrayals of the poverty and monotony that defined daily life in industrial neighbourhoods. These motion pictures, which came to be known as the British New Wave,[48] collectively presented working-class characters who defied the status quo. By carefully documenting a heretofore underrepresented group and subculture, British New Wave directors underscored the hollowness of the officially propagated values that benefited the ruling echelons of society. In their efforts to capture the ignored or idealized sociological realities of working-class and lower-middle-class individuals, these filmmakers expressed a discontent with "the Establishment" and "the phonies" who unthinkingly followed the pack.[49]

The British New Wave made the nation's rulers take a long, hard look at the crass, violent, and dull existence of most of the British working class. In doing so, filmmakers undermined the upper crust's dominant construct of the working class as less educated but noble, rowdy but malleable. These films thus represented the British intelligentsia's protest against the privileged classes' unchallenged monopoly on power. This critical stance was perhaps best expressed by playwright John Osborne, whose 1956 play *Look Back in Anger* gave voice to the anti-Establishment movement: "I can't go on laughing at the idiocies of the people who rule our lives. We have been laughing at their gay little madness, at their point-to-points, at the postural slump of the well-off and mentally under-privileged, at their stooping shoulders and strained accents, at their waffling cant, for too long." Thus the working-class heroes of the British New Wave – the so-called angry young men – served as mouthpieces for intellectuals who mocked the monarchy, the church, and the Parliament as hopelessly outdated. Britain was, they argued, "hidebound by class, struggling under the weight of its imperial history, tired, dreary and conformist."[50]

Despite claims that their films strove for documentary objectivity, neither the British New Wave directors nor Osep'ian recorded the lives of their working-class protagonists with ethnographic accuracy. This is not to say that their films did not endeavour to accurately document working-class lives. On the contrary, the motion pictures amazed audiences with their unvarnished depictions of working-class environs. Indeed, compared to the (highly) stylized films that preceded them, social realist productions seemed shockingly realistic. British directors in particular were so bent on re-creating the domestic lives of their main characters that critics dismissively referred to their productions as "kitchen sink dramas." These films deployed working-class masculinity in the form of cautionary tales about mass culture and the spiritual deadness it breeds. Their mercurial celluloid protagonists, even when exasperatingly inconsistent in their logic and actions, answered only to themselves. They did not undermine the system with any larger agenda in mind; instead, they preoccupied themselves with (relatively) petty grievances and pleasures. Thus these supposedly sociological portrayals of working-class youth functioned as symbols of how societies that expect and encourage conformism eventually produce men who, as Oscar Wilde put it, "know the price of everything and the value of nothing."

Although the concept of working-class "angry young men" figured much more prominently in British than in Soviet cinema, Osep'ian's film is nonetheless significant in that it expresses the views of an equally disgruntled intelligentsia. As mentioned above, most of the time Soviet directors could not cast working-class characters in a negative light without risking censorship and temporary restrictions on filmmaking activity. Moreover, socialist realism obliged directors to focus on positive and hopeful resolutions. To approach feature films in an objective documentary fashion à la Free Cinema meant certain official condemnation. In 1963, A.V. Romanov, chairman of the State Committee of Cinematography, criticized "certain artists" who, wanting to be fashionable, unthinkingly followed a Western trend that called for depicting "life, caught unawares" (zhizn' zastignutaia vrasplokh). Romanov publicly shamed Soviet artists for "uncritically reproducing the trivialities of daily life in a naturalistic fashion" and for "focusing specifically on dark, ugly, and sick social phenomena."[51] Considering the ideological obstacles, the mere appearance of Three Days of Viktor Chernyshev was an achievement. The film received very limited distribution; even so, its emergence merits attention since it depicts of working-class masculinity as a means to outline a broader disintegration of social values and norms.

Karel Reisz's 1960 Saturday Night, Sunday Morning, as a production representative of the British New Wave, shares many philosophical and artistic principles with Osep'ian's *Three Days*. Both movies build the narrative by filming an ordinary weekend in the lives of two typical working-class lads. *Saturday Night* is set in Nottingham and *Three Days* in Moscow, but both show working-class pastimes and neighbourhoods in an unflattering light: morally impoverished and mired in world-weary ennui, the suburban landscapes depress the senses. Moreover, days pass without anything happening to distinguish one hour from another; only trivial household dramas break the tedium.[52] The two "heroes" inhabiting this sterile spatial and temporal environment – Arthur Seaton and Viktor Chernyshev – share a similar biography and stand in for their respective cohorts. Both represent the legions of eighteen-year-olds who choose factory jobs after receiving a patchy high-school education and who look forward to spending their hard-earned money on having a good time. Arthur and Viktor labour six-day workweeks and, unburdened with the responsibilities of family life, look forward to partying on Saturday night and recovering on Sunday morning. By setting the action almost entirely over one weekend, Osep'ian and Reisz green-flag the assumption that nothing meaningful happens over the course of the workweek while the heroes inhabit their work space. To truly delve in working-class youth culture, the two directors investigate their protagonists' leisure time.

Neither Viktor nor Arthur can be described as "bad apples," but neither do they live by a set of lofty ideals. As they commit or participate in misdeeds – Arthur has an affair with a co-worker's wife, whom he impregnates, and Viktor looks on as his neighbourhood gang beats up an innocent bystander – they display a lack of any real values. Thus, in addition to having similar biographies, they share a life philosophy – or, more precisely, the lack of one. Arthur lives by the credo "All I want is a good time. The rest is propaganda!," while Viktor, who lacks Arthur's bravado, declares, "I am just like everyone else" (*Ia – kak vse.*). Arthur is more belligerent than Victor, but both characters, dissatisfied with the monotonous future they know lies ahead, want desperately to be left alone to pursue their small pleasures, to lose themselves in the moment. Even their petty rebellions lack any real meaning. They act out simply to confirm to themselves that they can still make some choices, even if those choices are illusory. This is self-destructiveness masquerading as the exercise of free will. Literary critic Nona Balakian accurately assesses the internal make-up of these angry young men: "Cowardly and suspicious in their human relations, motivated solely by self-interest, uninhibited in language and disrespectful of women, they are heroic only in their resistance to the straightjacket mold tendered to them by society."[53] The manner in which a Soviet critic described Viktor applies equally well to Arthur: "A void exists where there should be a personality and this vacuum is always ready to be filled with any random content."[54] Viktor and his crowd simply hang around their neighbourhood, waiting for something to happen to them.

They pass their time hanging around the corner, recycling jokes, bragging about their sexual conquests, and harassing passers-by. Arthur and his mates similarly spend their time off drinking themselves into a stupor, chasing potential mates, and aggravating the local middle-aged busybodies. They do not search for adventure; they do not exhibit curiosity about the world around them; they neither espouse beliefs nor seek them out. In stark contrast to the idealistic heroes of Khutsiev's *Lenin's Guard*, Viktor and his friends do not ask their elders "how to live" but simply accept life as it comes.[55]

Because they neither profess allegiance to any ideology nor search for answers, Viktor and Arthur represent the ultimate free agents and as such symbolize their respective systems' worst fear. After all, a man without convictions cannot be manipulated or mobilized to do the collective's bidding. The book on which Reisz's film was based powerfully expresses Arthur's disdain for any type of authority: "I know whose faces I've got in my sights every time the new rifle cracks off: the snot-gobbling gett that takes my income tax, the swivel-eyed swine that collects our rent, the big-headed bastard that gets my goat when he asks me to go to union meetings or sign a paper against what's happening in Kenya. As if I cared!"[56]

The heroes' passivity and egocentrism is motivated largely by their sense of entrapment. Arthur and Viktor perceive the benefits of participating in the system that provides them with material security but simultaneously feel repelled by the uniformity and conformity such an arrangement breeds. When Arthur sees his father sitting in front of the television after a full day's work, he reflects on his parents' generation with barely disguised contempt: "They've got a TV set and a packet of fags, but they're dead from the neck up." And while Arthur excoriates the "mindless masses" for their uncritical participation in the world of consumerism, he welcomes his paycheque, eagerly spending his salary on Teddy Boy suits. As literary scholar Peter Kalliney observes: "Arthur defines his political relationships through contradiction, both lauding the state for the stability and material comfort it has effected and deriding it in visions of violent revolution."[57]

The same contradictions define Viktor, who only perfunctorily engages in any sort of activity that is state-mandated. At the same time, he makes several positive references about turning eighteen and completing the two years of compulsory army service. In the factory he is

obligated to sit through a Komsomol meeting; although he has no interest in the proceedings and refuses to take an active part, he endures
the event with polite passivity. On Sunday afternoon, he is required to
join members of his factory to go to a local *kolkhoz* and "volunteer" to
harvest. As soon as he finishes the task courteously but unenthusiastically, he joins his neighbourhood gang in accosting and beating up an
innocent stranger who rightfully complained that they had jumped the
line in the store. When he returns home from the police headquarters,
he tells his bawling mother that she should not worry because he will
soon join the armed forces. Like Arthur, Viktor inhabits a liminal space;
propelled by societal pressures that have long been in place, he partic-
ipates in the system without feeling a true sense of belonging, hoping
all along that the army will succeed in integrating him into the larger
collective and diminish his sense of alienation.

If war symbolized history's torture chamber for Bondarchuk's and
Wajda's heroes, then contemporaneity feel like a makeshift prison for
the young working-class heroes in Reisz's and Osep'ian's productions.
Like Sokolov and the Warsaw insurgents, they are held captive by forces
larger than themselves and are desperately trying to make peace with a
world that seems profoundly alien to them. They observe their parents'
stagnant world and feel no connection to it. They obey because they must
but also revolt from time to time in order to remind themselves – and
others – that they still possess a modicum of autonomy.

Men as Victims of Middle-Class Angst in Italy and the Soviet Union

In many ways Marlen Khutsiev's 1966 feature *July Rain* (Iul'skii
dozhd') was condemned to failure before it was even conceived, although its subject seemed innocuous enough: the gradual dissolution
of a romance between twenty-seven-year-old Lena and thirty-year-old
Volodia. As Khutsiev himself commented: "Our industry has a habit of
making films about budding romances and we wanted to investigate a
disintegrating relationship."[58] The director's fourth feature film, which
came hard on the heels of his notorious 1962 production *Lenin's Guard*,
sparked controversy because it privileged the themes and filming techniques manifest in the work of French and Italian auteur filmmakers of
the 1960s, such as Michelangelo Antonioni, Alain Resnais, and Feder-
ico Fellini.[59] Like his Western European counterparts, Khutsiev became
intrigued with how to make the internal worlds of his protagonists
the centrepiece of the narrative, and how to express the protagonists'
psychology through visual rather than logocentric means. Film critic
N. Zorkaia praised Khutsiev in her 1968 review of the film: "On the

surface of it, the story is about a young couple that breaks up for reasons not manifest in either action or dialogue ... But the totality of the film's visual structure – apparent in the cohesion of the atmosphere, the mood, faces, imprints of daily life, and the unrushed, even sluggish, movements of the camera – reveals the outlines of an entirely different movie."[60]

In the early 1960s grumblings had begun about this (supposedly) elitist and distinctly Western European approach to moviemaking. At the 1963 meeting of the Cinematographers' Union Organizing Committee, Ivan Pyr'ev, head of the union at the time, criticized pretentiously philosophical and purposelessly gloomy motion pictures. He contended that such movies are easy to spot: "slow-moving gray clouds fill the screen, the rain falls incessantly, and the music drones on flatly. The takes are so inordinately long – as if their mere duration would allow the viewer to glean the film's affected philosophy." The supposedly typical protagonist of such productions also came under Pyr'ev's close scrutiny: "In this oppressive atmosphere, the hero is continually depressed. He skulks persistently in mock seriousness, and cannot, for some reason, verbalize his worries."[61] Such films, Pyr'ev insisted, contained nothing of artistic value but merely imitated the "modernist bourgeois West." He mocked "experts" who viewed such sham artistry as original and innovative: "'Almost like Antonioni! No worse than Resnais!' they gush." On another occasion in 1963, the Secretary of the Communist Party, L.F. Il'ichev, commented on the ideological harm these kinds of films were inflicting in the Cold War context: "Egomania, affectation, offensiveness, ideological flirtation with the bourgeois world, a perverted predilection for the dark and commonplace, willful neglect for the exalted and jubilant – all this is nothing short of a betrayal of our revolutionary tradition."[62] Thus, although *July Rain* could hardly be called politically sensitive in its theme, it too closely resembled the work of Western European auteurs, and, more importantly, it depicted the Soviet microcosm as distinctly *un*revolutionary. Because Khutsiev, like Antonioni or Fellini, filmed the world as a projection of the protagonist's inner anxiety, his movie heroes came across as decidedly unheroic: indecisive, impotent, and victims of their own imaginary psychoses.

In contrast to the working-class heroes of the British kitchen sink dramas, who define themselves through their deafening declarations and bravado, the middle/upper-class heroes in Antonioni's, Bergman's, Fellini's, and Resnais's films are barely able to express the feelings of inadequacy and purposelessness that have consumed them. Additionally, because auteur directors communicate the hero's emotional world visually, the protagonist's convictions often remain understated, elusive, and implied; the hero rarely presents his credo declaratively the way Arthur does in *Saturday Night, Sunday Morning*: "I'm out for a good time. All the rest is *propaganda!*" Unlike the heroes of auteur dramas, British working-class heroes never suffer disorientation; even when self-destructive, British New Wave heroes rarely exercise debilitating self-reflection. Moreover, unlike the heroes in Reisz's films, who believe they can – in however small a way – shape their own fates, auteur protagonists live in a world run by their phobias, which they cannot control or of which they are unaware. Despite the obvious difference between the two types of heroes, Soviet critics found both views of masculinity too dark. The protagonists of British kitchen sink drama repulsed Soviet columnists with their misogyny, parochial world view, and lack of political consciousness, but they were no more enamoured with Italian and French auteur work that presented masculinity as a psychological state framed by alienation and the inability to communicate with one's fellow man.

Since Soviet authorities viewed Viktor in *Three Days* as an unauthentic depiction of Soviet masculinity, they could hardly be expected to greet Volodia, the protagonist of *July Rain*, with any greater enthusiasm. Indeed, the pre-eminent film critic R. Iurenev derided Khutsiev's attempt to transpose themes central to Western European filmmakers onto the Soviet context. He remarked ironically that the film's preoccupation with showing social gatherings and relationships devoid of genuine emotional connections constituted a masterfully executed but ultimately dissatisfying impersonation of Western European filmmakers: "Aha! Alienation! The inability of people to communicate! *La dolce vita!* Dejection and the vexation of spirit! (*Sueta suet i tomlenie dukha!*)."[63]

Notwithstanding their acerbity, the reviewers accurately established the link between Khutsiev's work and that of Italian and French auteur filmmakers. *July Rain* clearly was a response to and expanded on themes and techniques that Antonioni offered in his now iconic sixties trilogy *L'avventura* (The Adventure, 1960), *La notte* (The Night, 1961), and *L'eclisse* (The Eclipse, 1962). Using a romantic relationship to explore modern-day alienation, Antonioni narrates the couple's fate – or, more precisely, the story of their estrangement – by representing the contours of emotion rather than action. Moreover, Antonioni's three films contain the sort of artificial dialogue that underscores the futile search for meaningful connections. The Italian director's trilogy presents the viewer with an empty landscape populated solely by two people growing apart emotionally but desperate to reconnect physically.

Figure 6.3. Volodia and Lena in *July Rain*.

Antonioni's trilogy deals exclusively with the subject of a couple drifting apart or acknowledging the unbridgeable rift between them. In this regard, *July Rain* is closest in spirit to *La notte*. Both feature a pair of intellectuals – Lena/Volodia and Lidia/Giovanni – in an urban setting (Milan and Moscow). Like Antonioni, Khutsiev tells the couple's story from the heroine's point of view.[64] Both women clearly recognize the decay that renders their relationship all but untenable. With quiet desperation they attempt to establish contact with their male partners, who are too absorbed in their own fears to act decisively or even speak directly to the existentialist problems facing them. In each film, the chasm separating the romantic pair is palpable in that they rarely hold each other's gaze. Both literally and metaphorically, they spend their time looking in different directions and with contrasting perspectives (Figures 6.3.and 6.4). Scholar Tim Harte's characterization of Lena applies equally well to Lidia; she is a modern woman who chooses to "rise above her cultural milieu and to move beyond the boundaries of time-honored culture."[65] Like their partners, the women have few answers; unlike their mates, the female protagonists make choices that are in line more with their

Figure 6.4. Giovanni and Lidia in *La Notte*.

own moral compass than with society's expectations. This difference
in perspective and approach – expressed in explicitly gendered terms
– ultimately dooms the two relationships and portrays the men as the
architects of their own demise.

Giovanni and Volodia's lack of self-confidence affects their ability to
act ethically and with conviction; both are intellectuals who lack a moral
compass and feel trapped by the societal structure that supports them
and buttresses their social privilege. As intellectuals, their hallowed station in life offers them mobility and material security but denies them
the freedom to speak their conscience; they are wholly beholden to the
system. Both Giovanni, a (moderately successful) novelist, and Volodia,
a (reasonably proficient) scientist, belong to their societies' elite; they are
conditioned to deference and lack the willpower to wean themselves from
the social cachet they have acquired. Giovanni and Volodia become so
pliant and accommodating that they lose their authenticity and, with it,
their humanity.

The alienation of both Volodia and Giovanni is absolute. They have lost all connection to their souls, cannot relate to their romantic partners, and have no real friends. They are disconnected from within and without. For instance, one of Volodia's friends pays him a backhanded compliment: "He is antimagnetic, freeze-resistant, waterproof, anticorrosive, infusible, and won't combust in the Earth's atmosphere. I am not afraid for him." Volodia's apparent imperviousness to any external stimulus speaks to his inability to feel. Lena, too, wonders who her boyfriend really is and what makes him tick. As they lie awake at night after a party, she coquettishly asks him: "You are so healthy. Have you ever been sick? If you came down with something, I could take care of you. And I've never seen you cry! Why don't you ever cry?" When they break up at the end of the film after months of courtship, Lena laments that she knows Volodia no better than she did when they started their romance. She confesses to him: "When my cousin asked me about you, I told her about your many laudable traits: kindness, sense of humor, sobriety, and devotion. If she inquires, I will not be able to explain to her why I did not get married to you." Lena decides not to tie the knot with Volodia despite all his redeeming qualities because he hasn't a distinct character. Like a chameleon, he adapts to any environment easily since he has no ideals of his own. Although outwardly different from Viktor Chernyshev, Volodia also lacks a coherent set of guiding values; however, he masks this lack with professional success, a respectable circle of friends, and a pleasant demeanour. He climbs the social ladder not because he is driven to succeed but because inertia commands his every move. Thus both Viktor and Volodia express a certain malaise of modern life that is characterized by a spiritual and moral numbness.

In *La notte* Antonioni introduces us to life in the posh industrial centre of Milan and demonstrates that the sense of alienation reigns here as it does in Moscow. Antonioni focuses on a successful but insecure novelist, Giovanni Pontano, and his wife, Lidia. The movie traces a day in the life of the couple and zeroes in on their marriage, which seems to have died long ago. Like Lena trying to forge a bond with Volodia, Lidia continuously attempts to re-establish contact with her spouse, but her efforts come to naught. Their disconnectedness is palpable from the very beginning since they do not speak to each other for the first twenty minutes of the film despite occupying the same space. To accentuate the distance between them visually, Antonioni avoids placing the couple in the same frame throughout the film. Moreover, the spouses rarely inhabit the same immediate space; they circle around each other in near vicinity, as if trying to avoid addressing the unbridgeable chasm that separates them.

Antonioni makes Giovanni's feelings of isolation and imprisonment palpable all the way through the narrative. Unlike Lidia, who is
filmed outdoors for much of the movie, enclosed spaces continually
entrap Giovanni. Even within these interiors, Antonioni frames Giovanni within lines and grids that evoke the sensation of prison bars. At
a book-signing party where Lidia clearly feels smothered, Antonioni
shows her looking at her husband's portrait in a display case, symbol-
izing both the distance between them and how boxed-in his life has
become. Although Giovanni is fully aware of his exitless state, he cannot resist or fight it. He confesses at one point: "The way I feel ... I don't
know if I'll ever write again. I know what to write, but not how to write
it. It's called a crisis; it's very common among writers today. But in my
case, it's affecting my whole life."

Like Volodia, who calmly assents to having his name omitted from a
scientific report he has written and replacing it with his boss's, Giovanni
sells out his talent to a millionaire who wants him to write about his factory. Giovanni himself, clearly unhappy and unsure about what he has
achieved as a writer, admits the industrialist's dominance: "Isn't writing an antiquated rather than irrepressible instinct? A lonely craftsman
putting one word after another. You have the advantage of constructing
your stories with real people: you create real houses, real cities – the
rhythm of life, the future, is in your hands." The entrepreneur confesses
self-importantly that, indeed, he has always regarded his many enterprises as works of art. Although it remains unclear whether Giovanni
will sell out and become the millionaire's pet intellectual, Giovanni's
refusal would suggest a disingenuous self-confidence, since he himself
divulges that his life "wouldn't be tolerable were it not for its distrac-
tions" and that he "no longer has inspiration but only memories."

Giovanni and Volodia are not isolated phenomena, but rather products
of a morally sick milieu. Like Viktor and Arthur, whose working-class
contexts determine their life's trajectory, Giovanni and Volodia cannot
extract themselves from their privileged positions, which, despite the
comfortable lifestyle they offer, bring little satisfaction. Both Antonioni
and Khutsiev take time to depict the ennui of an entire social class. Antonioni begins his film with Lidia and Giovanni visiting their friend Tommaso, who is slowly dying in the hospital. The lengthy scene featuring
a contrived interaction between "friends" suggests a decaying society
and culture that are being kept alive artificially. Antonioni focuses on
the disingenuousness of the surroundings: the ultramodern institution
houses only beautiful "nurses" who deliver champagne to patients'
rooms because of its "antidepressant properties." Tommaso himself reflects on the hypocrisy underpinning his environment: "Hospitals are

becoming more like night clubs. People want a good time to the end. Nonetheless, in my state, one craves champagne. I don't like it but have developed a passion for it." Antonioni provides a tableau of an upper class collapsing from within, choking on its postwar economic boom and its moral emptiness.

But Moscow intellectuals and socialites come off no better in Khutsiev's film. Although the Soviet upper crust cannot revel in the same kinds of wasteful displays of wealth and excessive opulence, they nonetheless resemble their Milanese counterparts in that none of their relationships have any real depth. Although Khutsiev spends the great majority of the film focusing on group activities, parties, and outings, the overall impression is one of ennui. The games, the guitar-playing, and the jokes all act as a defence against meaningful interactions; honesty and directness would slowly expose the bogus edifice propping up these social dealings. Film critic Iurenev observed: "During the two parties and one picnic Khutsiev shoots, we observe people who, despite disliking each other, insist on having fun together. They dance, flirt, and entertain one another without really listening or establishing any real emotional links."[66]

La notte and *July Rain* do not proscribe but rather diagnose. Khutsiev and Antonioni unambiguously depict the protagonists' deficiencies, but not as demonstrations of individual idiosyncrasies or as consequences of personal history. Instead, these male characters appear as products of a specific milieu, a particular historical context. These heroes do not warn about the dangers of particular life choices, but instead display the moral stupor characteristic of a shallow urban middle-class and an affected intellectual *mentalité*.

The Unfunny Business of Being a Small Man in an Absurd World

On 22 August 1968 – a day after four Warsaw Pact countries invaded Czechoslovakia – a strange meeting took place at the headquarters of the Cinematographers' Union. The expanded Executive Committee of the union met to adopt a resolution regarding "the events in Czechoslovakia" (*postanovlenie o sobytiiakh v Chekhoslovakii*). Without exception, those who spoke from the podium condemned the reactionary forces inside that country, approved of the military intervention, and accused the Czechoslovak intelligentsia of abetting capitalist propaganda. Filmmakers came under particular scrutiny. Scriptwriter A.E. Novogrudskii argued that long before the Czechoslovak intelligentsia published the Two Thousand Words manifesto, Czechoslovak directors had produced "two thousand – if not ten thousand – film frames of emphatically antisocialist motion pictures."[67] Novogrudskii pointedly observed that such anti-socialist trends were manifesting themselves in plain sight: Ivan Svitak had argued in the Czechoslovak journal *Film and TV News* (Filmové a Televizní Noviny) that socialist motion pictures need not have a Marxist focus. Film critic A.V. Karaganov also assessed the role of the filmmakers as crucial: "Objectively, Czechoslovak [cinema] became a weapon that intensified ideological disorder and boosted the position of antisocialist forces. This process began in approximately 1962–63 and continued to the present day."[68] Film critic L.P. Pogozheva joined Karaganov's assessment by identifying antihumanism and deheroization in Czechoslovak cinema as the medium through which bourgeois forces were exerting their nefarious influence and threatening the unity of the socialist camp.[69]

Those assembled told numerous stories of Czechoslovak filmmakers who looked down on the orthodox form of socialist realism and its advocates. As if conducting a post-mortem, those assembled recalled the many instances of Czechoslovak defiance and arrogance. A.B. Stolper, whose *A Story of a Real Man* earned him a Stalin Prize in 1948, recalled how frequently Czechoslovak colleagues accused their Soviet counterparts of being "old-fashioned, out-of-step with current trends, orthodox etc." Stolper encouraged his audience to draw relevant lessons from the Prague events and exhorted those present "to remain maximally principled and not permit the kind of 'art for art's sake' philosophy so snobbishly propagated by the Czechs."[70] The editor-in-chief of *Sovetskii ekran*, D.S. Pisarevskii, further stoked anti-Czechoslovak sentiment, recalling an incident at an international symposium of film critics in Yugoslavia during which Czechoslovak film critic Antonín Liehm claimed that the force of contemporaneous Czechoslovak art lay in the recognition that socialism is not humanity's ideal. Pisarevskii recalled that Liehm openly rejected the writings and principles of Julius Fučík, a Czechoslovak Communist author and functionary who died in Nazi captivity and whose book *Notes from the Gallows* became obligatory school reading after 1948. Instead, Liehm declared Czechs to be "a nation of Karel Čapek and Franz Kafka."[71] Pisarevskii interpreted Liehm's statement as denoting a rejection of socialist realism and an endorsement of absurdism, surrealism, and existentialist hopelessness as rendered in Čapek's and Kafka's writings. For all the indignation at Czechoslovak hauteur, the conservative members of the Soviet intelligentsia speaking at the August emergency meeting had correctly assessed the broad outlines of a film movement that had come to be known as the Czechoslovak New Wave.

Lasting from approximately 1962 until the Soviet invasion of Czechoslovakia in 1968, the so-called Czechoslovak film miracle became

Europe's foremost film movement because it effectively transferred the absurdity of the modern human condition onto the screen. Its focus on the relationship between the individual and authority/ideology/society within a Cold War framework made it all the more popular and relevant to audiences outside its borders. But its accomplishments did not stop there. Czechoslovak directors were able to build on neorealist cinema to reinvent the visual possibilities of cinema. Their focus on surreal or absurdist allegory allowed Czechoslovak filmmakers to blur the difference between the real and imaginary, the possible and the abnormal. Ultimately the Czechoslovak New Wave created films that, in the words of the era's most famous cameraman Jaroslav Kučera, "pose basic questions, even if they don't answer them, and may never find the answers, and ultimately advance our knowledge of ourselves, no matter how painful that knowledge may be."[72]

This monumental film movement also popularized a new type of masculinity with deep national roots: the small man, or "small Czech" (Čecháček), or Clueless Johnny (Hloupý Honza). The diminutive stature of Czechoslovak New Wave "heroes" – in terms of appearance, class background/education, and mental profile – had both cultural/historical and artistic significance. Ewa Mazierska points out that truly heroic characters had little traction among Czechs, who more readily accept irony than pathos: "Czechs celebrate their suffering rather than their victories: the true heroes of the Czech nation are its martyrs."[73] Adjectives that best describe the leading men of Czech film, according to Mazierska, include compliant, servile, docile, conformist, unambitous, and provincial. Petra Hanáková argues that the stereotype of the small Czech has persisted in literature and the arts over the last hundred years, because adaptability is his greatest asset.[74]

Irony and humour – two elements essential to Czech art and culture – have shaped the function and reception of the "small Czech" hero in specific ways. During the Czechoslovak New Wave, Hloupý Honza became a reflection of the general society but, embarrassingly, mirrored the sides the populace took great pains to hide. Like a House of Mirrors in an amusement park, the small Czech evoked laughter while at the same time showing the viewers in an unflattering light. The genius of Czech directors at the time thus lay in their ability to temper their irreverent and critical tone with humour. Daniel František suggests that irony and humour in general are the weapons of the powerless and that this connection largely explains why both these elements are so common in Czechoslovak films as well as in Czech culture at large. Devoid of political power, the inhabitants of Czechoslovak lands have used irony and humour as means to come to terms with their diminutive position. Various authors have argued that the presence of irony distinguishes Czechoslovak cinema from the cinemas of other countries in the region, most importantly those of Poland and Hungary.[75]

Indeed, unlike Wajda, who depicted his characters as (symbolically) coming in direct contact with historical forces, the protagonists of, for instance, Pavel Juráček's, Jan Němec's, and Miloš Forman's films threw their characters into an absurd or allegorical universe in which concrete historical forces were absent. Like Italian neorealists, Czechoslovak New Wave directors filmed their unassuming heroes in their natural environment performing seemingly everyday activities such as chasing an elusive paper trail through the bureaucratic maze, pursuing a love interest, or attending social functions. Juráček fittingly summarized the movement's attitude in a July 1968 interview: "One day I realized that there are moments when noble historical events can go to hell, because there are other things – human, personal, private things – that frequently are more important and essential. You can't forget them or brush them aside the way you can the others."[76] Unlike in the neorealist universe, in Czechoslovak films things are rarely what they seem, and superficially ordinary activities reveal greater and more profound meaning. Just as in the auteur films of Fellini and Antonioni, objects, dialogue, and casual glances construct an emotional atmosphere that defines and often constitutes the narrative. Moreover, like Fellini, Czech directors used the realm of the fantastical – daydreams, nightmares, and visions – to project the hero's particular perspective. Thus the Czechoslovak New Wave blended elements of neorealism and Italian auteur cinema, focusing on the mundane but through the highly subjective eyes of its protagonists.

Czechoslovak New Wave directors shied away from making pronouncements about larger historical events. Even films that focused on the Second World War – such as Alfréd Radok's *Long Road* (Daleká cesta), Jan Němec's *Diamonds of the Night* (Démanty noci), Jiří Menzel's *Closely Watched Trains* (Ostře sledované vlaky), and Ján Kadár's and Elmar Klos's *The Shop on Main Street* (Obchod na korze) – placed as much emphasis on depicting universal human foibles (cowardice, passivity, insecurity, irrationality) as they did on wartime activities. Unlike Polish films, in which the nation and Polishness loomed large, Czech directors avoided the figure of the "mad patriot" and privileged the civilian perspective; they also cast Jews in principal roles. Thus in contrast to Wajda's 1950s trilogy, which owed part of its emotional power to a moving depiction of a national tragedy, the films of the Czechoslovak New Wave captivated as universally applicable statements on human nature. As such, Czechoslovak New Wave movies not only contradicted socialist realist principles but also raised questions about the nature of power, violence, and morality.

Such trends proved difficult to stop, not only because these motion pictures played a central role in the dissident movement (as Soviet officials correctly asserted), but also because they aptly encapsulated a national tradition and tapped into finely tuned cultural sensibilities. As director Jiří Menzel bluntly put it in the spring of 1968, "everything about us, and things that represent us, display a sense of humor. It's not inherited, this humor of ours. It has been forced upon us, because if you don't have a sense of humor, you can't possibly live in Czechoslovakia."[77] Thus this humour – sometimes acerbically and sometimes compassionately ironic – openly ridiculed and undercut the serious political and educational role officials expected socialist masculinity to play. This mockery of men reared by the socialist system amounted to sacrilege, and only the historical import of the Prague Spring movement made the appearance of such irreverent heroes possible.

Celebrated director Oldřich Lipský's science fiction film *Man from the First Century* (Muz z prvního století, 1961) was a precursor to other Czechoslovak New Wave films that resorted to allegory to mock the Czechoslovak national character and to cast doubt on the human capacity for reason. The film begins in 1961, when an inane upholsterer named Joseph, who is in charge of padding the country's latest space rocket, accidently flips the take-off switch and launches himself into space without anyone else on board. He comes back home in the year 2447 with Adam, an alien companion who wants to explore the human race. Adam and Joseph witness a peaceful and bountiful planet inhabited by an enlightened and contented populace. The population's high quality of life is best reflected when one character declares: "Every now and then I like to cut up an onion to remember what it feels like to cry." The residents of Earth have evolved so much that they dub Joseph "the man from the first century." Although they find his knowledge of the world charmingly antiquated (for example, upon arriving and witnessing the material abundance, he asks: "Is this the West? Or East?), they recoil at his barely concealed greed, slothfulness, and philistinism.

Lipský's "man from the first century" demonstrates the mental and moral unpreparedness of the contemporary Czechoslovak citizen for a utopian future; it also also implicitly mocks the socialist authorities for raising and nurturing this type of personality – or for being unable to re-educate the Josephs of the world. When Joseph's hosts present him with a machine that instantly delivers anything a person requests from the "universal citizens' catalogue," the not-so-noble savage goes mad with greed. Unable to restrain his materialism, Joseph begins tearing pages from the catalogue and feeding them frantically into the futuristic contraption. Within moments the room becomes overcrowded with myriad packages containing needless products. Even a giraffe – the ultimate symbol of unbridled consumerist impulse – appears as one of Joseph's "necessities." Joseph's guide, incredulous at the spectacle, wonders aloud: "Why would anyone need this much stuff?" Joseph's avarice represents a clear condemnation of avarice and as such supports the state's enlightenment mission; at the same time, the spectacle demonstrates how miserably the socialist order has failed in producing upstanding citizens who can shoulder the responsibilities of a utopian society. Implicit here is also the typical sixties critique of the Communist Party's obsession with technological progress and of its relative negligence of man's spiritual development.

As the citizens of Earth grow weary of their unexpected visitor, Joseph – in a move typical of a small-time bureaucrat determined to hang on to his petty privileges – begins to ascribe to himself qualities and skills he does not possess in order to keep his hosts' attention. For instance, he states that his cranial capacity is equal to the most advanced computer system they possess. Once this hoax falls through, "the man from the first century" attempts to curry favour with his hosts through fear. He warns the earthlings that Adam, his alien companion, plans to destroy humankind. When the fear-mongering also fails, Joseph realizes that his cover is blown and makes a hasty retreat to his rocket. As he leaves the future society, the narrator warns the viewer: "Look out, people! He's coming back to *you*!" This rather bleak assessment of the human potential for improvement and progress represented Czechoslovakia in Cannes in 1962. While the Czech national tradition could comfortably accommodate the "small Czech" exposing the absurdity of sociopolitical systems and the human condition, the Soviet experiment had little tolerance for bizarre juxtapositions and humorous allegory.

E. Riazanov's comedy *Man from Nowhere* (Chelovek niotkuda, 1961) represented a retreat from the Stalinist musical comedy and marked an end to any experimentation with the genre. In his memoirs, Riazanov refers to his film as "comical un-scientific fiction" (*komicheskaia nenauchnaia fantastika*) and notes that this was the first motion picture in the history of Soviet filmmaking in which absurdist humour informed the entire production. As Riazanov soberly observes, however, the highly publicized ideological persecution of *Man from Nowhere* sounded the death knell for an entire trend in film comedy.[78]

The film begins with a group of Russian anthropologists in search of the legendary Tapi tribe in a distant mountain range. The protagonist, Vladimir Porazhaev, accidentally falls through a mountain crevasse and finds himself among the mythical Tapis. The cannibalistic clan wants to eat him because he speaks in prosaic "rhythms" instead of blank verse, but the idealistic scientist manages to escape certain death with one of the tribe's members, whom everyone refers to as Screwball (*Chudak*). The enthusiastic anthropologist takes "the savage" back to a Moscow of a not-too-distant future, where pandemonium ensues as Screwball runs amok, learning how to be "human." The cannibal enters a running race and easily beats the competition, attends a theatre performance where he attempts to catch and eat the actor playing the villain, and tries to win the attention of a certain Olia in outlandish ways. The humour in this gaffe-filled comedy of errors revolves not so much around Screwball's mistaken identity, but around a pastiche of situations linked solely to the caveman's eccentricities.

Over the course of Screwball's frenzied sojourn, the young scientist attempts to teach the savage cannibal how to be "human" and to impress core Soviet values on the uncivilized barbarian. For instance, while flying over Moscow in a (by then readily available) helicopter taxi, Vladimir shows the Yeti a symmetrical, highly structured, and seemingly unending cityscape as proof of his civilization's brains and brawn. In a couple of instances he pontificates on the virtue of hard labour: "It has been scientifically proven that those who do not work revert back to monkeys ... He who does not work is not a human being." But despite the obvious positive reflections on the Soviet order, the officials in the Cultural Department of the Central Committee complained that "certain episodes contain ideologically suspect undertones that imply that the savage is morally better than the people he encounters in our own time." And the rebuke did not stop there. In 1961 the Cultural Department of the CPSS Central Committee protested the release of E. Riazanov's film. The two high-ranking officials in the cultural department who wrote the report, D. Polikarpov and V. Baskakov, rather dramatically accused the film "of compromising our cinematography in the eyes of the public, for at its very core, being inimical to the principles and traditions of Soviet art, and for essentially leading to the disintegration and destruction of film as an art form."[79] As late as 1964, when the Ideological Commission of the Central Committee met with the members of the country's largest film studio to discuss how to enhance the effectiveness of the industry's propagandistic mission, *Man from Nowhere* remained Mosfil'm's *enfant terrible*. The ideological commission criticized Riazanov's film severely: "In a number of cases directors and cameramen make uncritical use of techniques characteristic of modernist bourgeois art and make allowances for formalistic gimmickry (*triukachestvo*), both of which weaken the film's educational properties. *Man from Nowhere*, more than other productions, suffers from these weaknesses."[80]

What the highest Soviet authorities found problematic about Ri-azanov's film – and what they protested against so vociferously during the Prague Spring – was the seemingly frivolous way in which alle-gorical surrealism conceptualized the historical position of the socialist realist hero. While socialist realism extols individual protagonists as symbols of history's inevitable march toward communism, surrealism turns the notion of human agency and historical progress on its head. Since the hero finds himself in worlds that do not operate according to rational laws, he no longer exerts control over his destiny and becomes a prisoner of chance. Like the alienated/angry heroes in the British New Wave and in Antonioni's films, protagonists in absurdist and sur-realist productions can hardly pretend to command their own lives, let alone shape historical progress.

Conclusion

European postwar scepticism found itself at loggerheads with Soviet humanism because it cast doubt on the notion that individuals, guided by socialist ideology, can conquer nature, establish equitable relations among men, and perfect the human personality. After the Twentieth and Twenty-Second Party Congresses in particular, the party amplified its call to artists to restore the socialist project's popular standing and re-establish truth, freedom, and reason as the governing principles of the post-Stalin era. Party authorities called upon Soviet intellectuals to challenge postmodernist cinema since it supposedly encouraged cyn-icism regarding objective reality, social morals, and accepted norms of behaviour.

This effort became most pronounced in denunciations of deheroi-zation in Soviet art. Party authorities rejected interpretations of re-ality in which protagonists were taken over by events rather than shaping them. Conservative forces consistently attacked films that lacked a positive perspective, eschewed a sequential narrative, devel-oped stories without a clear-cut optimistic conclusion, and featured a flawed anti-hero. Party ideologues saw these aesthetic choices as anti-humanistic and thus anti-Soviet. Official pressures notwithstanding, sixties directors successfully exploited the authorities' aspiration for global recognition to produce ideologically suspect films that would be tolerated for their promise to garner international renown and establish Soviet cinema as a cultural force with which to be reckoned.[81] Soviet critic L.P. Pogozheva best expressed the paradox Soviet filmmakers faced when she declared that the Soviet art establishment would have to carefully manage its own public image if it expected to sway attitudes abroad. "We must win over world opinion," argued Pogozheva, "since the eyes of the progressive world are on us."[82] The Soviet authorities thus expected the impossible: to promote socialist realism in a way that would win awards in Cannes, Venice, San Francisco, and Berlin without, however, adapting socialist realism to changing international aesthetic and philosophical trends. This paradox nonetheless created the space necessary for Soviet experimental films to see the light of day.

As the films analysed above demonstrate, the postwar intelligentsia intermittently managed to incorporate non-Soviet philosophical currents and aesthetic trends. The attitude M. Romm expressed at the All-Russian Theatrical Society (Vserossiiskoe teatral'noe obshchestvo) in 1962 explains the determination (and success) the Soviet New Wave directors had in creating films that challenged the tenets of socialist realism: "We have become accustomed to thinking that nothing of merit happens in the West. This attitude is curious considering that Russia once distinguished itself internationally by its unequaled translations of world literature. The Russian intelligentsia was once world-renowned as being unrivaled in its knowledge of world culture. This is also one of our traditions and we should celebrate it."[83] Arguably, this attitude made possible the challenges to the notion of heroism enforced by socialist realist doctrine since 1934.

Like their Eastern and Western European counterparts, Soviet directors challenged the idea of epic heroism that was so prominent in cinematic repertoires across the continent. Whether the hero stood in for the British Empire, Fascist Italy, Stalinism, or Polish nationhood, he was meant to unambiguously convey to the viewer that history was on the side of the nation/ideology he represented. As postwar New Wavers drew their cinematic heroes to scale, they also challenged other key myths of the interwar era: war ennobles men; technology is humanity's handmaiden; cities stand as sites of human evolution, the consumerist ethos unequivocally improves a society's quality of life. Rather than being a reprieve from the wartime hell, postwar modernity became a different version of hell. Rather than disfiguring their bodies, the so-called era of affluence and economic miracles scarred their humanity. The uniformity of (sub)urban dwellings, the impersonal nature of mass culture, and the ubiquity of corporate culture all called into question the ability of men to set themselves apart and live authentically.

The crisis of masculine confidence that evolved over the course of the long 1960s has, arguably, not been resolved to this day, for it is symptomatic of postwar modernity itself.

The End of the Long Sixties and the Fate of the Superfluous Man

The long Soviet sixties was an era of hopes and anxieties. Widespread optimism emerged once Nikita Khrushchev replaced Stalin-era coercion and terror with incentives and popular participation. The approval for independent thought and action generated a great deal of popular enthusiasm about the nation's future. But at the same time, the populace experienced angst because rapid modernization had rendered daily life unrecognizable. After 1956, Soviet citizens had to wrestle with changes on a tectonic scale: massive (sub)urbanization, the reopening of "the woman question," the increased assertiveness of Soviet youth, the dominance of science in everyday affairs, and growing interaction with the outside world. This radical transformation affected all segments of the Soviet population, whose expectations – and fears – were most visibly expressed in depictions of Soviet masculinity.

Over the course of the long sixties, Soviet politicians, filmmakers, and moviegoers eagerly discussed the country's silver screen heroes in their attempts to determine which masculine ideal best captured the new zeitgeist. Ordinary citizens and public figures voiced opinions on the day's feature films because they considered movies more than idle escapism. There was a clear sense that cinematic narratives were passing judgment on the spirit of the times. Celluloid protagonists channelled palpable fears that men (and the nation) would be unable to keep up with the radically new socio-economic and political trajectory that Khrushchev had charted out. Vibrant debates about the nature of post-Stalinist masculinity demonstrated both the central role gender representation played in de-Stalinization and the Communist Party's inability to set the limits of the modernization Khrushchev had launched.

As Khrushchev insisted that the Party fundamentally modernize the country after the postwar freeze, Stalinist conceptions of masculinity came under scrutiny as distinctly unmodern. Khrushchev sought to distance himself from Stalin's repressive legacy and to shape the Soviet Union into a country that could overtake the United States and achieve communism by 1980. As he did so, he dismissed masculine figures who zealously dedicated their muscled bodies to mining tons of coal in a single shift or conquering the Arctic in the dead of winter. The Civil War hero Chapaev, the miner Stakhanov, and the pilot Mares'ev had all reflected the Stalinist regime's priorities; in much the same vein, the country's modernization project would require its own distinctive masculine model. An eclectic band of Soviet filmmakers seized on Khrushchev's reformist impulses to proffer male characters who departed sharply from the epic heroes of the Stalin era. The Stalinist superhero had been an ideal type; sixties protagonists were psychologically complex individuals. This was part of an effort to reframe audiences' understanding of the world.

The four thematic chapters in this book showcase how a stratum of Soviet filmmakers exploited the era's temporary liberalization to construct masculine models fit for post-Stalinist times. Sixties film protagonists embodied the paradox of the era by expressing both confidence in their ability to act independently and fears that modernization would curb their masculine privilege. De-Stalinization had freed directors from the obligation to paint their contemporaries as nearly infallible, but it also produced heroes who were perpetually in search of a compass. The era's most popular and most controversial films showed men adrift in a range of social functions: as fathers, as role models for the youth, as husbands, as masters of science. Film protagonists could not find a solid footing in any of these roles, caught up as they were in questioning their choices. Post-Stalinist celluloid heroes now had a sense of autonomy, yet they also seemed unable to assert themselves in a world where preschoolers and pre-teens exercised a monopoly on morality, young men fulminated against their father's (Stalinist) sins, mass consumerism had made women the dominant economic actors, and science offered more questions than answers.

Although the superfluous man proved to be rather popular, he was not without detractors. Audiences, film professionals, and Party authorities unsettled by the rapid change under Khrushchev censured sixties heroes as too soft for the intensifying Cold War competition. They argued that these moody and indecisive movie characters inadequately expressed the socialist system's superiority and did not communicate the correct values to Soviet moviegoers. The more hardline forces contended that if the Soviet Union was to overtake the United States and mobilize the populace in this effort, it needed Stalin-era supermen. Egor Trubnikov, the hero of Aleksei Saltykov's 1964 blockbuster

The Chairman (Predsedatel'), seemed to reflect this desire for a return to the hypermasculine model of the *status quo ante* and to herald a renewal of the Stalinist project and subjectivity. A man in his fifties, Trubnikov was born at the turn of the century and had fought with the Bolsheviks from the first days of the revolutionary struggle. He had emerged from the bloodbath of the Great Patriotic War alive but handicapped: he had only one arm. Now, instead of retiring after the war, he has returned to work to participate in the country's reconstruction. Rather than pity his lot like Sokolov in Chukhrai's *Fate of a Man*, Trubnikov has chosen the hellish task of reviving a collective farm at a time when *kolkhozes* are enduring crippling material and manpower shortages.

In his attempt to revive the collective farm, Trubnikov employs brutal methods such as loud confrontations and relentless criticism. His unpleasant personality and his forceful ways make any interaction with him wearisome and disheartening. Despite his obvious flaws, many sixties moviegoers praised his unwavering commitment to the goal. Movie critic E. Surkov warned that Trubnikov was not an average positive hero and that his virtues should be looked for elsewhere. The critic reminded readers that the war had cost Egor much more than one arm: it had destroyed his good-natured naivety: "The war had scorched and burnt him, but it did not shake his fate and instead irreversibly fortified his character."[1] Describing the country's new favourite celluloid hero, *Sovetskii ekran* reporter A. Obraztsov waxed lyrical: "They say that Egor Trubnikov is rough around the edges, that he is a recluse, that there is not an iota of warmth in him ... Ul'ianov successfully combines in his character both tough reality and lyricism, both manliness and tenderness, both facts and inspiration."[2] In February 1965, *The Chairman* was shown to the men and women of the Kirov *kolkhoz*, located just outside Kaliningrad. A journalist and a photographer from *Sovetskii ekran* were there to document people's reactions. The reporter noted the tense atmosphere in the hall and the intensity with which the audience absorbed the action and dialogue on the screen. When discussing Trubnikov's lack of empathy for the *kolkhoz* workers, audiences members defended him, saying that strong-willed men were needed in 1964 as much as they had been needed twenty years prior.

One journalist opined that those who criticized Trubnikov for his character faults were exaggerating. "What could be worse for art," he demanded, "than the requirement to portray ideal representatives for every profession ... instead of incisively uncovering true-to-life characters, realistic circumstances, and human fates!"[3] Despite Trubnikov's tyrannical tendencies, many moviegoers supported him. "If only we had this kind of chairman!" "Egor is like a mother who sometimes has to apply tough love with her children. Had he not been as strict, he might have not achieved his goal."[4]

Some movie critics fought against the canonization of Trubnikov as a quintessential post-Stalinist hero and role model. Their comments made it clear that Trubnikov's methods were too "Stalinist" for them. The *kolkhoz* chairman was the antithesis of a self-conscious, reflective hero. The following comments speak volumes about the kinds of arguments Trubnikov's opponents advanced. B. Balter: "Delirious maniac, a fanatic ... He can do as he pleases. He grabs people by the throat. Did such men exist? They existed. But even the expression 'the goal justifies the means' existed." A.P. Vinogradov: "If our Western ideological enemies see this movie, they will surely say: 'You want communism? Well, here it is!'"[5] While some critics saw in him a modern-day Chapaev, other saw him as no better than a thug, or, as N.N. Klado called him, "a conductor without an orchestra."[6]

Attempts to update the socialist project after Stalin's death continued apace but faced increasing pressures after Khrushchev's ouster in 1964. On 14 February 1966, sixteen months after L.I. Brezhnev became General Secretary of the CPSU and sixteen months before Soviet tanks rolled into Prague, twenty-five prominent members of the scientific and artistic intelligentsia sent Brezhnev a letter protesting attempts to rehabilitate Stalin.[7] Prompted by rumours that neo-Stalinists in the Soviet leadership were pushing for Stalin's rehabilitation at the 1966 Twenty-Third Party Congress, the document rejected even a partial relegitimization of Stalin's legacy.[8] The country's leading scientists, artists, writers, and filmmakers argued that a defence of Stalin's crimes would violate the trust citizens had placed in the CPSU and damage the Soviet Union's international prestige. The signatories included directors Grigorii Chukhrai, Marlen Khutsiev, and Mikhail Romm, whose films had played a major role in overturning key aspects of Stalinist rule, besides helping define the sixties era. Brezhnev never officially restored Stalin's personality cult to its former glory, though it did repress those who spoke openly against the memory of the Great Leader, while gradually resanctifying Stalin's place in history.[9]

One did not have to look far to identify Stalin's partial restoration. Historian Mark Sandle notes that the Brezhnev leadership aimed to restore Stalin's public image as a great military leader and to that end devoted "massive amounts of energy and paper to re-falsifying the role of Stalin in the victory over Hitler." Moreover, because Khrushchev had publicly condemned Stalin's disastrous handling of the Second World War in his secret speech, "the Twentieth Party Congress was virtually written out of the annual CPSU histories produced in the 1970s."[10]

Grigorii Chukhrai's 1961 film *Clear Skies* also fell victim to this campaign, for it portrayed postwar Stalinism in unambiguously unflattering colours and depicted "the Gardener of Human Happiness" as a tyrant. Even though Chukhrai was a Party member, and even though the motion picture won the Grand Prix at the 1961 International Moscow Film Festival, it disappeared from movie screens and television programs virtually overnight.[11] The authorities applied the same kind of pressure on Soviet literary life in 1970 when they removed Aleksandr Tvardovskii from his position as editor of *Novyi Mir* and replaced him with the neo-Stalinist party hack Mikhail Suslov. In repressing the journal that had secured the publication of A. Solzhenitsyn's *One Day in the Life of Ivan Denisovich* and I. Ehrenburg's *The Thaw*, the regime had struck at an important symbol of de-Stalinization and post-Stalinist modernization. Lacking a public outlet for alternative ideas, the intelligentsia increasingly turned to dissident self-publishing (*samizdat*) to air views incompatible with official doctrine.[12]

The movie industry fared no better than the literary establishment. Although the Stalin-era "film famine" did not recur and the studios continued to produce around 130 films per year, filmmakers' autonomy was now a shadow of its former self. Valerii Golovskoi, who worked as an editor in the journals *Iskusstvo kino* and *Sovetskii ekran* between 1965 and 1980, reflected unenthusiastically on the state of cinema between 1968 and 1985: "The regime determinedly and ruthlessly stifled any sign of non-conformism [*inakomyslie*] ... Even when the big screen featured contentious, unorthodox films, it was, more often than not, a result of bureaucratic oversight, clever manipulation of antagonisms between party and governmental apparatuses, or simply the artist's intractability."[13] Echoing Golovskoi's sentiments, historian George Faraday notes that the Brezhnev regime renewed the emphasis on ideological and aesthetic orthodoxy, actively promoting compliant directors and marginalizing dissenting ones, and placing approximately sixty "unacceptable" films "on the shelf" between 1967 and 1985.[14]

The weakening of the industry's independence began in 1969 with a party resolution making film studio editors directly responsible for the films they produced. Realizing that the central organs of the Party and the government lacked the raw manpower to oversee the production of more than one hundred films a year, the CPSU Central Committee shifted the burden onto the more numerous and eager cadres of studio executives. Assailed by the government's coercive methods, the Cinematographers' Union, itself the product of sixties liberalization, became moribund. The association that had vigorously defended scriptwriters against the censors' red pencil and negotiated qualified independence for filmmakers in the late 1950s and '60s turned into yet another listless administrative link in the bureaucratic chain after 1968.

Official efforts to restore the myths of the Stalinist past and to tighten control over the film industry seemed to all but erase the figure of the superfluous man; but key elements of superfluous masculinity remained prominent in Brezhnev-era masculine tropes, even when hidden in plain sight. But individual experiences, private emotions, and interpersonal non-homosocial relationships typical of sixties heroes were no longer front and centre on the cultural landscape. The Brezhnev leadership used both films and television miniseries to relegitimize Stalinist masculinity with its stress on patriarchy, ideological consciousness, and allegiance to the state's historical mission. I agree with Elena Prokhorova that after 1968 the state privileged spy thrillers, police procedurals, murder mysteries, and historical melodramas because it wished to reimpose a clear narrative arc and structure that the sixties cinema had undermined.[15] The favoured genres of the Brezhnev period endeavoured to replace sixties emotive intellectuals with tougher and more dynamic protagonists – although this effort did not always bear fruit. The regime glamorized Civil War and Second World War film heroes in order to rearticulate a masculinist, patriarchal paradigm within a grand historical schema and thereby project the virility and grandeur of bygone eras onto a lacklustre contemporaneity. Soldiers, detectives, and police officers – embodiments of state power – employed a detached rationality and a highly developed sense of patriotic duty to conduct their lives and better their communities. In the context of this cultural re-Stalinization even Lenin's image required "butching up" in order to counter the benign and gentle aura that sixties artists had ascribed to the occupant of the mausoleum in Red Square. According to Golovskoi, a secretary of the Communist Party Central Committee, L.F. Il'ichev, declined to widely distribute M.I. Romm's 1970 documentary on Lenin because the leader of the October Revolution came off as insufficiently stern.[16]

The (re)turn to grand historical narratives and monumental masculinity reflected the authorities' preoccupation with projecting its authority; it also mirrored more general concerns about the state of Soviet masculinity. Widespread disillusionment emerged during the early to mid-1970s and brought about a retreat into the country's more glorious (and certain) past. Historian John Bushnell noted a pervasive and deep-rooted pessimism among the Soviet middle class under Brezhnev, contending that that the middle class's perception of, and anxiety about, the country's economic underperformance had coloured other (non-economic) spheres of activity: "Skepticism about official economic policy is but one manifestation of middle-class disengagement from the regime's goals. Civic cynicism and alienation are so pervasive that by comparison post-Watergate America seems a hotbed of utopian optimism: few members of the Soviet middle class will admit that they do more than go through the motions of their professional and civic duties."[17]

The pessimism Bushnell outlines fed into the populace's need for a more stable and clearly delineated universe. Widespread optimism about the country's future under Khrushchev had allowed directors to present more ambiguous representations of masculinity; now, the popular perception that the domestic situation under Brezhnev had started on a downward trajectory was stimulating a demand for more clear-cut masculine models.[18] Elena Prokhorova is exactly right in pointing out that Brezhnev-era cultural production was obsessed with the past – as long as it was repackaged as "the era of true heroes, clear goals, and resolved (and resolvable) conflicts."[19] At a time when the Soviet Union was plagued by alcoholism, an astronomical divorce rate, and a consensus that "society made it very hard to do 'man's work,'" heroes who asserted themselves confidently in the public and private spheres proliferated on the silver and TV screens. Prokhorova eloquently captures the gender dynamics of the period: "The return to more heroic times allowed the Soviet male a ready-made and sanctified space for fantasizing about a regained space of mission, resolution, and action – in short, the standard masculinity set."[20]

Perhaps no other phenomenon signified the conclusion of the sixties cultural project more irrefutably than the blockbuster television miniseries *Seventeen Moments of Spring* (Semnadtsat' mgnovenii vesny). The show's depictions of gender roles, its narrative techniques, and its glorification of the past all pointed to a reversion to Stalinist tropes. T.M. Lioznova's 1973 serial, consisting of twelve seventy-minute episodes, took its inspiration from Iu.S. Semenov's equally popular novel of the same title. The protagonist of both the novel and the television series is a Soviet intelligence agent, Maksim Maksimovich Isaev, who infiltrates the very top of *Sicherheitsdienst* – the SS's own intelligence agency – in the early 1930s. Once there, he assumes the identity of Standartenführer Otto von Shtirlits and distinguishes himself for his loyalty and effectiveness.[21] The TV series depicts seventeen moments during the spring of 1945 and focuses on how Shtirlits almost single-handedly exposes a Anglo-American attempt to conclude a separate peace with the Nazis and open a joint front against the Soviet Union.

On the surface, Shtirlits epitomizes the ideal Soviet intelligence worker and articulates a rejection of the sixties masculinity model. Having served the state for most of his life, he displays an ironclad will and superior mental abilities. In many ways, he takes after the 1920s revolutionary heroes because of his asceticism, modesty, and business-like manner. He rarely drinks and never indulges in sexual escapades. His only indulgence is driving his posh Horch automobile at breakneck speed. His restraint aside, Shtirlits exudes sophistication. Like a true Renaissance Man, Shtirlits proficiently discusses philosophy, history, and science in the majority of European languages. Besides being a picture of discipline and refinement, Shtirlits remains a true patriot. Even when surrounded by the riches of the West or the exoticism of faraway lands, the Soviet spy longs for his socialist homeland. In almost all regards, Shtirlits is the antithesis of his sixties predecessors. While Sergei in *Lenin's Guard* struggles to determine how to live and Viktor in *Three Days of Viktor Chernyshev* surrenders himself to everyday tedium, Shtirlits single-handedly saves Kraków from destruction, foils the Germans' plans to develop a nuclear weapon, and ensures that a roving Soviet transmitter remains undetected. In contrast to the Hamlet-like figures of the sixties, Shtirlits at no point displays self-doubt or hesitation. He embodies a masculinity defined by an ability to act rather than contemplate. Shtirlits's mind is as sharp as Sherlock Holmes's, but he uses his intelligence to better serve the state rather than to reflect on his own standing in the world.

Although the Soviet spy remains dispassionately rational in most of his dealings, he is never cruel and often acts with compassion. His benevolence, however, is far different from the emotiveness typical of sixties protagonists. He does not allow emotions to govern his life – rather, he manages them carefully and deploys them strategically. He covertly helps those abused by the Nazi authorities and German civilians unassociated with the regime. Yet his personal life is always secondary for him. During the entire run of the miniseries, Shtirlits recalls his wife only once. Significantly, in the one episode that he remembers her, he flashbacks to a clandestine meeting in Germany during the early 1930s when they could merely glance at each other across the room and could not exchange a single word. In this way, Lioznova establishes that Shtirlits's primary connection is to a homosocial masculine environment rather than a more domestic, intimate one. Moreover, by depicting Stalin as issuing orders directly to Shtirlits, Lioznova revives the "great Soviet family" myth and re-establishes Stalin as the ultimate example of Soviet masculinity. As in the aviator cult, Shtirlits becomes the obedient "favourite son" of the Father of the Peoples. Unlike Sokolov in *Fate of a Man*, who experiences the loss of his wife and children as his defining wartime event, Shtirlits's identifies much more strongly with the patriarchal structure and largely ignores his personal life.

By reducing the role that emotions and intimate connections played in the life of the protagonist, *Seventeen Moments of Spring* constructed a logical and ordered world. Sixties protagonists inhabited an existentialist universe; in contrast, Brezhnev-era productions offered a structured cosmos that allowed men to once again tame and govern their surroundings. The miniseries was set in Germany; nonetheless, it suggested a space in which a community of men were able to exercise their influence. One could as easily imagine neo-imperial government offices in the Stalinist Soviet Union filled with soldiers like Shtirlits whose highest calling consisted of serving the homeland among like-minded men of arms.[22] Furthermore, the third person voice-over that filled gaps in the storyline explicated Shtirlits's inner thoughts, informing the viewer of the background of all other characters, a further demonstration of the low tolerance Brezhnev-era productions had for narrative ambiguity: "Omniscient, ubiquitous, and omnipotent, the voice-over controls the development of the plot, the meaning of History itself, and the actions of the male protagonist."[23] Lioznova was leaving nothing to chance; the voice-over categorically rejected any sort of vagueness in interpretation, leaving viewers to merely observe and internalize the action. Sixties directors wanted audiences to wrestle with questions their heroes' actions raised; Brezhnev-era filmmakers tended much more to provide easily digestible answers.

Although Shtirlits seems to have had little in common with wavering sixties protagonists, historian Stephen Lovell has identified the ways in which the mini-series created an ironic distance from hyperbolic and overly theatrical representations of masculinity. Lovell points out that Shtirlits was, at best, only modestly heroic: "He is a thinker rather than a doer or a talker."[24] Indeed, during the series' heyday, numerous stills captured the spy not in action, but in moments of contemplative calm (Figure E.1). A contemporary viewer's response to the notion that *Seventeen Moments* could be considered a thriller brings forward Shtirlits's ambiguous hero status: "Maybe it was a psychological thriller, maybe a political thriller, maybe not a thriller at all."[25] In Lovell's interpretation, Shtirlits is no Soviet James Bond: there are no sexual exploits, no breathtaking feats of derring-do, no grand finales befitting a spymaster. This reading underscores that the return to aesthetic and ideological conservatism could never be complete, for the spirit of the sixties experiment remained intact.

The myriad Shtirlits-themed jokes reveal the self-consciousness with which the populace approached the country's most famous spy and his celluloid ilk, despite their sincere fondness for the main protagonist. Having been exposed as elements of Stalin's oppressive system, the larger-than-life film heroes could no longer fully regain their cultural

Figure E.1. *Seventeen Moments of Spring* (1974). The supremely
rational and contemplative Shtirlits.

cachet. The two jokes below are representative of the Shtirlits oeuvre
in that they mock the very traits that made Shtirlits a household name:
his staged displays of deductive reasoning, and the show's overdram-
atized sense of suspense:

Shtirlits and Müller go to a sauna. As they undress, Müller notices a
large hammer and sickle on Shtirlits's underwear.

> "Shtirlits, where did you get that?!"
> "In Moscow," Shtirlits answered, then thought to himself: "I hope I
> didn't say too much."
> Shtirlits entered Müller's office, and found him dead on the floor.
> "Must have poisoned himself," he thought as he pensively touched
> the axe in Müller's back.[26]

Although sixties superfluous heroes disappeared from the screen as
such, Shtirlits could not escape their legacy, for they discredited hypermasculine heroics as the sole legitimate expression of Soviet subjectivity.

Figure E.2. V. Vysotskii as the emotive and enraged Hamlet
on the Taganka stage.

Even though sixties protagonists in many ways represented an idiosyncratic phenomenon, their legacy and impact proved enduring.

The authorities' semi-successful push to resurrect large-scale heroes
carrying out epic feats fed into a larger social trend that valorized Slavic
machismo as an authentic expression of masculine identity. The bard,
actor, and poet Vladimir Vysotskii best exemplified this phenomenon
in that he appealed to men of all social strata and political persuasions
by projecting a virility that was by turns vulnerable and aggressive,
emotive and unapologetic. Andrea Lanoux and Helena Goscilo identify
the multiple ways in which Vysotskii's public "roles" typified the lure
of streetwise machismo: "as the cool, tough Gleb Zheglov in Stanislav
Govorukhin's 1979 cult TV police series *The Meeting Place Cannot Be
Changed* (Mesto vstrechi izmenit' nel'zia); as the craggy, gravelly-voiced
alter ego of the intrepid pilots, soldiers, mountain climbers, and prisoners in his songs; and as the hard-drinking, uncompromising iconoclast
married to the Russian-French actress Marina Vlady."[27] But even Vysotskii, the incarnation of traditional Russian machismo, suffered openly

and publicly: his debilitating alcoholism, his three failed marriages, and his spotty employment made him a victim of his own demons rather than a self-possessed hero.[28]

So Vysotskii failed to embody the ideals associated with the New Soviet Man; moreover, he celebrated the less glamorous sides of human personality and experience in his poetry, much like sixties filmmakers did.[29] It is therefore not surprising that despite his impulsive and self-destructive tendencies, Russia's most beloved bard of the 1970s came to be identified with the quintessential symbol of sixties masculinity: Hamlet. Vysotskii played the Danish prince at the Taganka Theater from 1971 to 1980, right up until his death in 1980. As The New York Times reported at the time: "It is more like casting Bob Dylan than Laurence Olivier in the title role. And he is no hesitant, self-doubting Hamlet, but an enraged young man struggling against an evil ruler in an evil time."[30] Vysotskii's fate seemed to prove that the sixties figure of the superfluous man had successfully challenged the revolutionary ethos of Stalinist masculinity. This is not say that Stalinist masculinity stopped occupying space in the public forum; Shtirlits's popularity (ironic jokes notwithstanding) showed that it remained an attractive cultural model. Never again, however, would that model occupy exclusive centre stage in popular culture; role models of all stripes would be questioned thereafter.

On a final note, it is worth pointing out the cyclical nature of the Russian "masculinity project." It is not hard to imagine Putin as the twenty-first-century Shtirlits: emotionally detached, calculated, self-assured, and always two steps ahead of his opponents.[31] Putin's remasculinization of the post-Soviet cultural space demonstrates that Urlanis's 1968 exhortation "Save the men!" remains relevant fifty years later. In the Putin era, Russian men live, on average, thirteen years less than Russian women and their male counterparts in the West. Significantly, the causes for this low life expectancy remain the same as they were in 1968. High morality rates for males between fifteen and sixty-four are due mostly to circulatory diseases and non-natural causes – particularly accidents, poisoning, violence, and injuries that accompany high levels of alcohol consumption.[32] In fact, Russian male life expectancy was lower at the turn of the twenty-first century than it was in the mid-1960s.[33] In this dire context, Putin's "dazzling façade of (hyper)masculine bravado belies deep anxieties and vulnerabilities resulting in political overcompensation."[34] Putin's hypermasculinity as a "scenario of power" has been as meticulously staged and crafted as that of Stalin.[35] However, if the story of the Soviet sixties teaches us anything, it is that even the most carefully maintained hypermasculine myths eventually give way to alternative models of masculinity.

Notes

Introduction

1 B. Urlanis, "Beregite muzhchin!," *Literaturnaia gazeta*, 24 July 1968, 12.

2 Ibid.

3 Larisa Kliachko, "Sil'nyi pol vzyvaet k miloserdiu?," *Literaturnaia gazeta*, 14 August 1968, 12.

4 Ada Baskina, "I zhenshchin beregite. Neskol'ko nebespol'eznykh statisticheskikh spravok," *Literaturnaia gazeta*, 4 September 1968, 11.

5 Some of the (abridged) female readers' responses were published here: "Stroki iz pisem. Mnenia i somnenia," *Literaturnaia gazeta*, 9 October 1968, 12.

6 N. Solntseva and V. Solntsev, "Eshche raz pro 'sil'nyi' i 'slabyi' pol," *Literaturnaia gazeta*, 28 August 1968, 11.

7 M. Barovich, "V nash 'nervnyi vek," *Literaturnaia gazeta*, 9 October 1968, 12.

8 V. Zharko, "Muzhskie konsul'tatsii nuzhny," *Literaturnaia gazeta*, 9 October 1968, 12.

9 G. Osheverov, "Stenka," *Izvestiia*, 18 September 1968, 6.

10 Sharif Husanov, "Stroki iz pisem," *Literaturnaia gazeta*, 9 October 1968, 12.

11 G. El'iashevich, "O chem govorit statistika," *Literaturnaia gazeta*, 9 October 1968, 12.

12 Cartoon by Egor Gorokhov, *Literaturnaia gazeta*, 14 August 1968, 12.

13 *LG* ended the discussion by publishing opinion pieces by a demographer and a doctor, both of whom supported Uralnis's original hypothesis. *Literaturnaia gazeta*, 13 November 1968, 13.

14 Zdravomyslova and Temkina, "The Crisis of Masculinity," 40–61.

15 These and other attendance figures come primarily from cinema yearbooks available for this period. Between 1955 and 1961 a cinema yearbook appeared under the title *Ezhegodnik kino*. After 1964 these figures appeared in a yearbook titled *Ekran*.

16 Grushin, *Chetyre zhizni Rossii*, vol. 1, 454.

17 Ibid., 460.

18 Ibid., 460–1.

19 Roberts, "Beyond 'Crisis' in Understanding Gender Transformation."

20 Alekseeva and Goldberg, *The Thaw Generation*; Bittner, *The Many Lives of Khrushchev's Thaw*; Zubok, *Zhivago's Children*.

21 Raleigh, *Soviet Baby Boomers*; Vail' and Genis, *60-e*.

22 Attwood, Ilič, and Reid, eds., *Women in the Khrushchev Era*.

23 Tsipursky, *Socialist Fun*.

24 Dobson, *Khrushchev's Cold Summer*.

25 Fürst, ed., *Late Stalinist Russia*, 1. See also Fürst, *Stalin's Last Generation*.

26 Jones, ed., *The Dilemmas of De-Stalinization*, 14.

27 Kozlov and Gilburd, *The Thaw*, 27.

28 Vainshtein, "Orange Jackets and Pea Green Pants"; Edele, "Strange Young Men in Stalin's Moscow"; Amerian, "The Fashion Gap"; Zakharova, *S'habiller à la soviétique*.

29 Brusilovskaia, "The Culture of Everyday Life during the Thaw"; Slobin, "Aksenov beyond 'Youth Prose.'"

30 Rajagopalan, *Indian Films in Soviet Cinemas*; Roth-Ey, *Moscow Prime Time*; Evans, *Between Truth and Time*.

31 Koenker, *Club Red*; Gorsuch, *All This Is Your World*.

32 Paul R. Josephson, "Atomic-Powered Communism: Nuclear Culture in the Postwar USSR," *Slavic Review* 55, no. 2 (1996): 297–324; Oldenziel and Zachmann, eds., *Cold War Kitchen*; Susan E. Reid, "The Khrushchev Kitchen: Domesticating the Scientific-Technological Revolution," *Journal of Contemporary History* 40, no. 2 (2005): 289–316; Gerovitch, *Soviet Space Mythologies*.

33 Donald J. Raleigh, *Russia's Sputnik Generation: Soviet Baby Boomers Talk about Their Lives* (Bloomington: Indiana University Press, 2006).

34 Essential here is Anatoly Pinsky's research on Soviet writers whose careers began under Stalin but continued into the post-Stalin era. Pinsky's research shows that although the root of the turn to the individual is found in high Stalinism, it was not until the Thaw that Tvardovskii, Abramov, and others asserted that citizens had the right to search for the truth. See Pinsky's "The Origins of Post-Stalin Individuality" and "The Diaristic Form and Subjectivity under Khrushchev."

35 Literary critic Stanislav Rassadin coined the term in 1960; see Stanislav Rassadin, "Shestidesiatniki: Knigi o molodom sovremennike," *Iunost'*, 12 (1960): 58–62.

36 Sheila Fitzpatrick, "Afterword: The Thaw in Retrospect," in Kozlov and Gilburd, eds., *The Thaw*, 482–91.

37 Kozlov and Gilburd, eds., *The Thaw*, 42.

38 Gorsuch and Koenker eds., *The Socialist Sixties*, 10.

39 Kerr et al., *Industrialism and Industrial Man*; Sorokin, "Mutual Convergence"; Levy, *Modernization and the Structure of Societies*; Galbraith, *The New Industrial State*.

40 Jeremi Suri, "The Rise and Fall of an International Counterculture, 1960–1975," *American Historical Review* 114, no. 1 (2009): 53.

41 Cuordileone, *Manhood and American Political Culture*, 14.

42 Haynes, *New Soviet Man*; Kaganovsky, *How the Soviet Man Was Unmade*.

43 Tartakovskaya, "Constructing Masculinity from the War Spirit"; Popović, "A Generation That Has Squandered Its Men"; Ioffe and White, "Taxi Blues."

44 Holmgren, "Toward an Understanding of Gendered Agency," 537.

45 Sperling, *Sex, Politics, and Putin*; Riabov and Riabova, "The Remasculinization of Russia?"

46 Khrushchev, *Khrushchev in America*, 168.

47 "Programma KPSS, Section V, Part 1," *Pravda*, 30 July 1961, 3.

48 Rossiiskii gosudarstvenyi arkhiv literatury i iskusstva (hereafter RGALI), f. 2936, op. 1, d. 900, ll. 18–19. Gofman delivered his comments in March 1959 during a panel at the Cinematographers' Union on the "Character of the Contemporary Hero in Soviet Cinema."

49 N.S. Khrushchev, "Iz rechi N. S. Khrushcheva na vstreche rukovoditelei partii i pravitel'stva s deiateliami literatury i iskusstva," in Fomin, comp., *Kinematograf ottepeli*, vol. 2, 132.

50 Ibid., l. 92.

51 Kotkin, *Magnetic Mountain*; Hellbeck, *Revolution on My Mind*.

52 Pinsky, "The Diaristic Form," 808.

53 The situation was, of course, different for the victims of Stalinist murderous campaigns, as was made clear in Figes, *The Whisperers*.

54 McCallum, *The Fate of the New Man*, 21.

55 Fraser, *Military Masculinity and Postwar Recovery*, 6.

56 Ibid., 13. For an analysis of the non-martial categories that defined men's postwar identities, see Miller, "Between Creation and Crisis."

57 McCallum, *The Fate of the New Man*, 44.

58 After its publication of Turgenev's work, literary critics traced the roots of the masculine trope to A. Pushkin's *Eugene Onegin* (1825) and Mikhail Lermontov's *A Hero of Our Time* (1840). Gheith, "The Superfluous Man and the Necessary Woman," 229–30.

59 Clardy and Clardy, *The Superfluous Man in Russian Letters*, 13.

60 Thomas Riha, *Readings in Russian Civilization*, vol. 2 (Chicago: University of Chicago Press, 1969), 332.

61 Sloan Wilson, *The Man in the Gray Flannel Suit* (Cambridge, MA: Da Capo Press, 2002), 163.

62	Ibid., 272.
63	Henry Tanner, "Communists in Gray Flannel Suits," *New York Times*, 2 August 1964, p. 11.
64	These films usually featured elaborate Art Deco sets with white telephones as the ultimate status symbol of bourgeois wealth.
65	This is how prominent film critic and director Lindsay Anderson reflected on the state of the British film industry in 1957. See Maschler, *Declaration*, 139.
66	These three postwar film movements gathered initially around cinema journals that featured seminal works of criticism that broke with tradition and called for new approaches to cinema. In Italy, the film journals *Cinema* and *Black & White* (Bianco e Nero) served as the main outlets for future neorealist directors, such as Michelangelo Antonioni, Luchino Visconti, and Giuseppe De Santis. *Sight and Sound* became a platform for the founders of the British New Wave: Lindsay Anderson, Karel Reisz, and Tony Richardson. Similarly, *Cahiers du Cinema* provided a jumping-off point for the French New Wave directors to advance an agenda lambasting the postwar era's big so-called quality films (*cinéma de qualité*). For Soviet moviemakers, *Iskusstvo kino* (Cinema Art) served a similar role.
67	The fact that most neorealist filmmakers associated closely with the Italian Communist Party and the Socialist Party also secured them political legitimacy in the Soviet Union.
68	Quoted in Liehm, *Passion and Defiance*, 59.
69	Shiel, *Italian Neorealism*, 2.
70	Hill, "The Soviet Film Today," 33–52.
71	Grenier, "A Soviet 'New Wave'?," 62.
72	Marshall, "The New Wave in Soviet Cinema," 186.
73	Troianovskii, comp., *Kinematograf ottepeli*, vol. 1, 3.
74	Christie, "Back in the USSR," 42.
75	Work on the global new waves rarely include mention of Soviet productions. See, for instance, Nowell-Smith, *Making Waves*; Gerhardt and Saljoughi, *1968 and Global Cinema*.
76	Woll, *Real Images*; Prokhorov, "The Unknown New Wave: Soviet Cinema of the Sixties," in *Springtime for Soviet Cinema*, 7–28; Bulgakowa, "Cine-Weathers"; Harte, "Marlen Khutsiev's *July Rain*."
77	Steven P. Hill locates the roots of the new wave as early as 1954, and Troianovskii similarly begins the new wave timeline in the mid-1950s. Other scholars, including Lilya Kaganovsky, Vladimir Semerchuk, and Ian Christie, propose that sixties cinema was born with early-1960s features, and as examples offer Marlen Khutsiev's 1962 *Lenin's Guard*, Andrei Tarkovskii's 1962 *Ivan's Childhood*, and Mikhail Romm's 1962 *Nine Days of a Year*. See Kaganovsky, "Postmemory, Countermemory," 237;

Vladimir Semerchuk, "Smena vekh: Na iskhode ottepeli," in Fomin, ed., *Kinematograph ottepeli*, vol. 2, 155.

78 Sellier, *Masculine Singular*.
79 Sorokina, "The Lady Vanishes"; Kaganovsky, "Ways of Seeing"; Dmytryk, "Difficult Cases"; Mikhailova and Lipovetsky, "Flight without Wings"; Roberts, "Re-Viewing Homo Sovieticus"; Taubman, "The Cinema of Kira Muratova."
80 Mazierska, *Masculinities in Polish, Czech and Slovak Cinema*, 216.
81 Bosley Crowther, "Vittorio De Sica's *The Bicycle Thief*, a Drama of Post-War Rome, Arrives at World," *New York Times*, 13 December 1949, 44.
82 Baker, *Masculinity in Fiction and Film*, 32.

1 What Was Stalinist Masculinity and Why Did It Change?

1 The three cinematic versions of the Pavel Korchagin story were: *How the Steel Was Tempered* (Kak zakalialas' stal'), dir. Mark Donskoi (1942); *Pavel Korchagin*, dirs. Aleksandr Alov and Vladimir Naumov (1956); and *How the Steel Was Tempered* (Kak zakalialas' stal'), dir. Nikolai Mashchenko (1973–75).
2 V.M. Pomerantsev, "Ob iskrennosti v literature," *Novyi mir* 12 (1953): 218.
3 Rossiiskii gosudarstvennyi arkhiv literatury i iskusstva (hereafter RGALI), f. 2936, op. 1, d. 123, l. 53.
4 Ibid., l. 79.
5 They were referring to Bernard Borderie's 1961 version: *Les trois mousquetaires: La vengeance de Milady*.
6 RGALI, f. 2936, op. 1, d. 227, l. 24. The comment was made during preparations for the Plenum of the Communist Party's Central Committee on Ideological Issues on 22 March 1963.
7 RGALI, f. 2936, op. 1, d. 917, l. 7.
8 RGALI, f. 2936, op. 1, d. 899, l. 102.
9 Khrushchev, *The Crimes of the Stalin Era*, 57.
10 Ibid., 58.
11 Whitney, comp., *Khrushchev Speaks*, 280.
12 Dobrenko, "Creation Myth and Myth Creation," 259.
13 Groys, *The Total Art of Stalinism*, 63.
14 A.V. Lunacharskii, *Rasskazy o Lenine* (Moscow: Izdatel'stvo politicheskoi literatury, 1985), 15.
15 Franklin, ed., *The Essential Stalin*, 217.
16 Rech' sekretaria TsK VKP(b) A.A. Zhdanova, *"Pervyi s"ezd pisatelei. Stenograficheskii otchet* (Moscow: Ogiz, 1934), 4.
17 Taylor, "A 'Cinema for the Millions,'" 439.

18 Shumiatskii was purged and shot in 1937, having been accused of assembling a group of terrorists from within the cinema industry, who allegedly planned to assassinate Stalin and the Politburo. Miller, "The Purges of Soviet Cinema, 1929–38."

19 Manevich, *Za ekranom*, 154.

20 Leonid Maksimenkov, Introduction, in Bondareva, ed., *Kul'tura i vlast' ot Stalina do Gorbacheva*, 41.

21 Zezina, "S tochki zreniia istorii kinozala," 392.

22 McSmith, *Fear and the Muse Kept Watch*, 156.

23 Fomin, Introduction, in *Kinematograf ottepeli*, vol. 2, 7.

24 Ibid.

25 Zezina, "S tochki zreniia istorii kinozala," 390.

26 For a detailed account of Stalin's involvement in the censorship process, see Mar'iamov, *Kremlevskii tsenzor*.

27 Shumiatskii's transcripts of comments from Stalin, V.M. Molotov, L.M. Kaganovich, and K.E. Voroshilov can be found in *Kinovedcheskie zapiski* 61 (2002): 281–346; and 62 (2003): 115–88, as well as in Bondareva, *Kul'tura i vlast'*, 919–1052.

28 Zezina, "S tochki zreniia istorii kinozala," 392.

29 In 1948, Soviet audiences could choose between thirty-four foreign films and only twenty-one domestic ones; in 1949, the Soviet authorities released twelve Soviet features and twenty-eight foreign ones. See Claire Knight, "Stalin's Trophy Films, 1947–52: A Resource," *KinoKultura* 48 (2015), http://www.kinokultura.com/2015/48-knight.shtml#1.

30 For the economic impact of trophy films, see Laurent, *L'oeil du Kremlin*, 234–9.

31 This contraband included 1,531 American, 906 German, 572 French, and 183 British films. See Kapterev, "Illusionary Spoils," 790.

32 These averages are based on box office data for twelve out of eighty-six trophy films and twenty-six of eighty-nine Soviet features during 1947–52. See Knight, "Stalin's Trophy Films."

33 Fürst, "Swinging across the Iron Curtain," 236.

34 Bulgakowa, "Cine-Weathers," 437.

35 Brodsky, *On Grief and Reason: Essays*, 8–9.

36 Kapterev, "Illusionary Spoils," 807.

37 Sergei Zhuk's research reveals that in 1966 almost 60 per cent of all movies shown in Ukrainian cities were of foreign origin, and 50 per cent were films from the capitalist West. Ten years later, in 1975, almost 90 per cent of the films were foreign and almost 80 per cent were Western ones. See Zhuk, "Hollywood's Insidious Charms," 594.

38 Introduction to Fomin, comp., *Kinematograf ottepeli*, vol. 2, 11.

39 Zezina, "S tochki zreniia istorii kinozala," 398.

40 Lilya Kaganovsky speaks to this phenomenon in terms of "genetic memory," pointing out that filmmakers who came into prominence in the mid- to late 1960s worked through "a trauma that was not their own, that 'belonged' to the previous generation." See Lilya Kaganovsky, "Postmemory, Countermemory: Soviet Cinema of the 1960s," in Gorsuch and Koenker, eds., *The Socialist Sixties*, 237.

41 Troianovskii, ed., *Kinematograf ottepeli*, vol. 1, 172.

42 S. Rostotskii, "Novoe kino," *Iskusstvo kino* 1 (1957): 5.

43 Because Romm's productions unambiguously supported the Stalinist agenda, nearly every film he produced between 1941 and 1951 received the highest state accolades and Stalin's personal goodwill. His two Lenin biopics – *Lenin in October* (Lenin v Oktiabre, 1937) and *Lenin in 1918* (Lenin v 1918 godu, 1939) – set the standard in biographies of Vladimir Il'ich. And his three anti-American propaganda movies defined the genre of Cold War propaganda: *Girl No. 217* (Chelovek No. 217, 1944), *The Russian Question* (Russkii vopros, 1947), and *Secret Mission* (Sekretnaia missiia, 1950).

44 Quoted in Sidorov, *Neobkhodimost' poezii*, 213.

45 Cohen, *An End to Silence*, 177–82.

46 Aleksandra Svidorova, "Fil'm, iz'iatyi iz upotrebleniia," Park kul'tury, *My zdes'*, 15 February 2015, http://www.newswe.com/index.php?go=Pages&in=view&id=8561.

47 His most famous and talented students included A.A. Tarkovskii, V.M. Shukshin, R.D. Chkheidze, G.N. Daneliia, G.A. Panfilov, V.P. Basov, A.N. Mitta, T.E. Abuladze, and I.V. Talankin.

48 Chukhrai attributed so much significance to his wartime experiences that he penned a memoir focusing solely on this period in his life. In the memoir Chukhrai states: "All of my movies have, in some measure, been based on my own experiences at the front." See Chukhrai, *Moia voina*, 271.

49 Ibid., 103.

50 Cohen, *An End to Silence*, 180.

51 Za kruglym stolom, "Ruku, tovarishch uchitel'!," *Iskusstvo kino* 4 (1961): 8.

52 G. Bogemskii, "Ital'ianskoe kino segodnia," *Iskusstvo kino* 6 (1966): 27.

53 M. Romm, *Kak v kino: Ustnye rasskazy* (Moscow: Kinotsentr, 1989), 249–55.

54 Ibid.

55 For the full report see *RGANI*, f. 5, op. 55, d. 142, ll. 96–117.

56 For a more detailed account of Gosfil'mofond's activities during the Thaw years, see Malyshev, *Gosfil'mofond*, 107–52.

57 See Kozovoi, "A Foot in the Door"; A.S. Krymskaia, "K istorii nauchno-obrazovatel'nykh obmenov mezhdu SSSR i SSHA v kontse 1950-kh—1960-e gg.," *Noveishaia istoriia Rossii* 2 (2011): 99–106.

58 Bulgakowa, "Cine-Weathers," 473.
59 Nikolai Virta, *Sovetskoe iskusstvo*, 29 March 1952, 3.
60 Cited in Frankel, *Novy Mir*, 16.
61 V.M. Pomerantsev, "Ob iskrennosti v literature," *Novyi Mir* 12 (1953): 218.
62 Ibid., 229.
63 A. Selivanovskii, "V chem ne 'somnevaetsia' Andrei Platonov," *Literaturnaia gazeta*, 10 June 1931, 3.
64 The number of copies, however, does not tell the whole story. In 1965 the *SE* editorial board included a question in its annual viewers' choice award survey, asking the respondents how many people read each copy they received. The survey indicates that, on average, between four and five people read each copy. In other words, the number of readers was much greater than the official subscription numbers revealed. See RGALI, f. 2936, op. 4, d. 44, l. 4.
65 Director M.K. Kalatozov related how, on a 1966 visit to a Moscow *kolkhoz*, he visited four families and noticed domestic and foreign movie stars' cut-out photographs from *SE* in all four homes. See RGALI, f. 2936, op. 4, d. 44, l. 54.
66 *SE* first reported the total number of votes cast in 1961, when the magazine received 24,000 ballots. See "Itogi nashego konkursa kinofil'mov 1961 goda," *Sovetskii ekran* 10 (1962): 1.
67 Ibid., 2.
68 N. Pizhurina, "Ot imeni 24,000," *Sovetskii ekran* 13 (1962): 2.
69 RGANI, f. 5, op. 55, d. 112, l. 18.
70 Ibid., l. 56.
71 Ibid., l. 105.
72 M. Kuznetsov, "Chto zhe vam nravitsia, Stella i Laura?," *Sovetskii ekran* 2 (1964): 18.
73 Kh.N. Hersonskii, "'Kardiogramma' zritel'nogo zala," *Sovetskii ekran* 8 (1964): 17.
74 V.N. Shubkin, "O konkretnykh issledovanniakh sotsial'nykh protsessov," *Kommunist* 3 (1965): 55.
75 Soviet sociology was born sometime early in 1956, the year in which the Soviet Union for the first time sent a delegation to the World Congress of Sociology. In 1958 a decree of the Praesidium of the USSR Academy of Sciences ordained the formation of the Soviet Sociological Association.
76 As E.A. Weinberg points out: "In addition to internal factors, a major stimulus to the revival of sociology in the USSR came from contact with the more highly developed sociology of Eastern Europe and in particular with Polish sociology." See Weinberg *Sociology in the Soviet Union and Beyond*, 9.
77 Between 1928 and 1932 a small number of sociological studies were conducted to determine the populace's attitudes toward films, moviegoing,

and the movie experience in general. For an overview of the surveys conducted during this period see Kogan, *Kino i zritel'*, 14–22.

78 Batygin, *Rossiiskaia sotsiologiia*, 13.
79 Kogan, *Kino i zritel'*, 29.
80 Ibid., 34.
81 Ibid., 111–14.
82 Ibid., 129–51.
83 Ibid., 134.
84 Ibid., 261.
85 Ibid., 241.
86 Art scholar and critic Lev Roshal' also advocated for studies geared toward finding out not just which demographic groups go to the movies, but also why they choose certain movies over others. See Lev Roshal', "Kinozritel' – kakov on?," *Sovetskii ekran* 23 (1967): 20.
87 The data revealed that the 16–25 year-olds were most likely of all age groups to put themselves in the hero's shoes and that 80 per cent of this demographic contingent strove to emulate their favourite heroes. But the survey results also demonstrated that the movie heroes had a mediated influence on most moviegoers' thoughts and actions.
88 First, "From Spectator to 'Differentiated' Consumer," 317–44.
89 Tribuna zritelia, *Sovetskii ekran* 7 (1963): 13.

2 Being a Dad Is Not for Sissies

1 M. Makliarski, "Trudnosti zhanra," *Iskusstvo Kino* 12 (1959): 109–15.
2 Iu. Khaniutin, "Esli smotret' podriad..." *Iskusstvo Kino* 9 (1959): 65.
3 Iu. Haniutin, "Na ekrane – chelovek," *Literaturnaia gazeta*, 18 April 1959, 2; F. Vigdorova, "Chetyre fil'ma," *Literaturnaia gazeta*, 1 September 1959, 3; Semenov, "Dovol'no slez, ne nado prodolzhat'...," *Krokodil* 6 (1960): 10.
4 Helene Carlbäck concludes that an unwed mother was viewed both as a victim of the situation and as not deserving of pity because she had failed to uphold the sexual mores of society. See Carlbäck, "Lone Motherhood in Soviet Russia," 29.
5 Berger, "Soviet Divorce Laws," 826–9.
6 Helene Carlbäck notes that "the figure for children born out of wedlock in Soviet Russia rose to an average of 24 percent in 1945." See Carlbäck, "Lone Motherhood in Soviet Russia," 26.
7 Nakachi, "A Postwar Sexual Liberation?," 426.
8 For women ages 20 to 29, for example, the ratio of men to women in the population fell from .91 in 1941 to .65 in 1946. See Brainerd, "The Lasting Effect of Sex Ratio Imbalance," 229.
9 Nakachi, "A Postwar Sexual Liberation?," 439.

10 Brainerd, "The Lasting Effect of Sex Ratio Imbalance," 236.

11 Moskoff, "Divorce in the USSR," 421; Peter Juviler, "Marriage and Divorce," *Survey* 48 (1963): 107.

12 Moskoff cites a study conducted in the mid-1960s in Novosibirsk, according to which 10.2 per cent of unskilled female workers and 25.1 per cent of skilled female workers divorced their husbands due to their lack of participation in housework. See E.Z. Danilova, *Sotsial'nye problem truda zhenshchiny-rabotnitsy* (Moscow: Nauka, 1968), 65. The insights about men's desire for independence and male companionship can be found in Iu.A. Korolev, *Brak i razvod. Sovremennye tendentsii* (Moscow: Iuridicheskaia literatura, 1978), 161.

13 Perlman and McKee, "Trends in Family Planning in Russia," 40.

14 Avdeev, Blum and Troitskaya, "The History of Abortion Statistics," 60.

15 Randall, "'Abortion Will Deprive You of Happiness!,'" 26.

16 Ibid., 26 and 28.

17 Chernova, "The Model of 'Soviet' Fatherhood," 39–40.

18 Ibid., 42–3.

19 Carlbäck, "Fatherly Emotions in Soviet Russia," 26–7.

20 Kukhterin, "Fathers and Patriarchs," 81.

21 McCallum, "Man About the House," 334.

22 Ibid., 335.

23 A. Makarenko, "Kniga dlia roditelei," *Krasnaia nov'* 7 (1937): 15, quoted in Clark, *The Soviet Novel*, 115.

24 Il'ia Sel'vinskii, "Na sud sovesti," *Literaturnaia gazeta*, 12 December 1959, 2.

25 V. Karbovskaia, "Osobikh primet net," *Krokodil* 13 (1953): 13. A similar kind of story appeared a few issues later, about a playboy, Sergei Kliuchkov, who described leaving one (pregnant) girlfriend after another in his "little black book" of amorous conquests; L. Fedorova, "Poputnye oshchushcheniia," *Krokodil* 28 (1953): 7.

26 A. Bitnyi, *Krokodil* 34 (1965): 14.

27 V. Dobrovol'skii, *Krokodil* 34 (1957): 7.

28 A. Tsvetkova, *Krokodil* 6 (1965): 7.

29 Helene Carlbäck's research thoughtfully reflects on the competing discourses on the fairness of the 1944 decree vis-à-vis "lone mothers." See Carlbäck, "Lone Mothers and Fatherless Children: Public Discourse on Marriage and Family Law," in *Soviet State and Society under Nikita Khrushchev*, ed. Melanie Ilič and Jeremy Smith (London: Routledge, 2009), 86–103.

30 For the 1950s, articles on "welfare mothers," as opposed to deadbeat dads, are noteworthy for their absence. I did come across an article that featured a mother who had given birth to four children by four different men, all of whom had paid alimony; in fact, the government bonuses

Valentina Mikhailova received as a single mother, combined with alimony payments, totalled an impressive 1,100 rubles. Despite such lar-
gesse, the woman was found to be indifferent to her children's welfare
and showed more interest in courting gentlemen callers.

Aleksandra Brushtein, "Otvetchik dolzhen otvechat'," *Literaturnaia
Gazeta*, 14 January 1950, 2. This story was much more common during the
1930s, when women like Mikhailova were called "alimony huntresses."
See Lauren Kaminsky, "Utopian Visions of Family Life in the Stalin-Era
Soviet Union," *Central European History* 44, no. 1 (2011): 73–83.

31 [Anon.], "Ob ottsakh, brosaiushchi svoi detei," *Pravda*, 29 March 1948, 3.
32 [Anon.], "Na zasedanii kollegii Ministerstva Iustitsii SSSR," *Izvestiia*, 15
    January 1948, 4.
33 Z. Mokhov, "Ravnodushie," *Izvestiia*, 22 October 1954, 2; P. Petreikov,
    "Mnogo bumagi..." *Krokodil* 35 (1955), 5.
34 [Anon.], "Ob ottsakh, brosaiushchi svoi detei," *Pravda*, 29 March 1948, 3.
35 [Anon.], "Ottsy-begletsy i ikh pokrovoteli," *Literaturnaia Gazeta* 2 Decem-
    ber 1952, 2.
36 [Anon.], "Korotko o vazhnom," *Literaturnaia Gazeta* 1 July 1950, 2.
37 A. Barto, "V zashchitu Oli Petrovoi," *Literaturnaia Gazeta*, 22 May 1948, 1;
    E. Shatrov, "Bumazhnyi shchit," *Literaturnaia gazeta*, 19 August 1952, 2; A.
    Latsis, "Beregite Natashu!," *Literaturnaia Gazeta*, 22 August 1953, 3.
38 K.P. Gorshenin, "Delo vsei nashei obshchestvennosti," *Literaturnaia
    Gazeta*, 26 August 1950, 2.
39 H. Nazarov, "Sovershenstvovat' zakonodatel'stvo," *Izvestiia*, 3 August
    1958, 2.
40 L.I. Alekseev, "O sviazi pravovykh i moral'nykh norm," *Sovetskoe gosu-
    darstvo i pravo* 4 (1965): 28–34.
41 E. Serebrovskaia, "Eshche raz pro metrikakh," *Literaturnaia gazeta*, 7 June
    1956, 2.
42 N. Cherepanova, "Otsovskaia ispoved'," *Krokodil* 17 (1961): 4.
43 A. Levshin, "Mal'chik – muzhchina – otets," *Izvestiia*, 25 January 1964, 6.
44 N. Kvashnin, "Vazhnaia storona vospitania," *Izvestiia*, 17 August 1961, 4.
45 L. Kovaleva, "V zhizni i v knizhke," *Literaturnaia gazeta*, 18 March 1961,
    1–2.
46 Some of the films that touch on these topics are *Marina's Fate* (Sud'ba
    Mariny, 1953), *A Big Family* (Bol'shaia semia, 1954), *A Man Is Born*
    (Chelovek rodilsia, 1956), *Until Next Spring* (Do budushchei vesni, 1960),
    Introduction to Life (Vstuplenie, 1962), *I Bought Daddy* (Ia kupil papu,
    1962), *Women* (Zhenshchiny, 1965), *A Man-To-Man Conversation* (Muzh-
    skoi razgovor, 1968), and *Mom Got Married* (Mama vyshla zamuzh, 1970).
47 S. Glukhovskii, "Stsenarii. Krysha i nebo," *Iskusstvo kino* 9 (1961): 27.
48 Anatolii Tarasenkov, "Za zhiznennuiu pravdu," *Iskusstvo kino* 5 (1953): 60.

49 I. Kokoreva, "To, chto ostalos' za kadrom," *Iskusstvo kino* 3 (1954): 92.
50 Ibid., 100–1.
51 L. Sukharevskaia, "O kakikh roliah my mechtaem," *Sovetskaia kul'tura*, 25 November 1954, 2.
52 N. Zorkaia, "O iasnosti tseli," *Iskusstvo kino* 4 (1959): 36.
53 [Anon.], "Perepiska s chitateliami i zriteliami," *Iskusstvo kino* 2 (1957): 157.
54 S. Rozen, "Fil'm ponravilsia..." *Iskusstvo kino* 1 (1957): 118.
55 K. Rotova, "Ego zhiznenyi put," *Krokodil* 3 (1958): 8–9.
56 A. Svobodin, "Krug zhizni," *Iskusstvo kino* 4 (1963): 104.
57 The following review reiterates Svobodin's conclusions about Nina Urgant's character: M. Kuznetsov, "Chelovek uchitsia dobru," *Iskusstvo kino* 3 (1963): 12.
58 E. Kononenko, "Fil'm o liubvi," *Pravda*, 26 February 1966, 4.
59 Ibid.
60 N. Igant'eva, "Nastoiashchee," *Iskusstvo kino* 1 (1964): 83.
61 Claire McCallum observes that in the last decade of Stalinism "the demobilised Soviet soldier came to be represented first and foremost as a father, and the impact that this had on the portrayal of the Soviet family, that arguably had the greatest consequences for the conceptualisation of Soviet idealised masculinity." See McCallum, "The Return: Postwar Masculinity and the Domestic Space in Stalinist Visual Culture, 1945–53," *The Russian Review* 74, no. 1 (2015): 117–43.
62 G. Kremlev, "Kuda denutsia deti?," *Sovetskii ekran* 1 (1964): 8.
63 N. Igant'eva, "Nastoiashchee," *Iskusstvo kino* 1 (1964): 83.
64 Borenstein, *Men without Women*, 4.
65 Ibid., 18.
66 Kaganovsky, *How the Soviet Man Was Unmade*, 4.
67 Ibid., 73.
68 *Vasek Trubachev and His Pals* (Vasek Trubachev i ego tovarishchi, 1955), *On Imperial Ruins* (Na grafskikh razvalinakh, 1957), *Two Feodors* (Dva Fedora, 1958), *Little Andrei* (Andreika, 1958), *Brothers Komarov* (Brat'ia Komarovy, 1961), *Two Men Like Us* (My, dvoe muzhchin, 1961), *My Friend Kol'ka* (Moi drug Kol'ka,1961), *A Girl I Was Friends With* (Devchonka, s kotoroi ia druzhil, 1961), *Merry Tales* (Veselye istorii, 1962), *Little Pavel* (Pavlukha, 1962), *Ivan's Childhood* (Ivanovo detstvo, 1962), *Fearless and Blameless* (Bez strakha i upreka, 1963), *Welcome, or Entry Forbidden to Outsiders* (Dobro pozhalovat', ili postoronnim vkhod vospreshchen, 1964), *Someone's Ringing, Open the Door!* (Zvoniat, otkroite dver'!, 1965), *A Little Girl and Echo* (Devochka i ekho, 1965), *The Sky of Our Childhood* (Nebo nashego detstva, 1966), *A Small Fugitive* (Malen'kiii beglets, 1966), *A Girl on a Ball* (Devochka na share, 1966).
69 Reid, *Khrushchev in Wonderland*, 2.

70 Ibid.
71 Ibid.
72 Budiak ed., *Rossiiskii illiuzion*, 357.
73 Shilova, *I moe kino*, 58.
74 M. Kuznetsov, "Zhil-bil mal'chik," *Iskusstvo Kino* 7 (1960): 28.
75 Ibid., 29.
76 N. Ignat'eva, "Serezha," *Sovetskii ekran* 13 (1960): 12.

3 Fathers versus Sons, or, the Great Soviet Family in Trouble

1 *Lenin's Guard* has received much scholarly attention both because of the political controversy that surrounded it and because of M. Khutsiev's cinematographic genius. See Woll, *Real Images*, 142–50; Khlopliankina, *Zastava Il'icha*; Evgenii Margolit, "Landscape, with Hero," in Prokhorov, ed., *Springtime for Soviet Cinema*, 42–7; "Beskonechnost' Marlena Khutsieva. Kruglyi stol v redaktsii *Kinovedcheskikh zapisok*," *Kinovedcheskie zapiski* 14 (1992): 5–26; Kseniia Kurbatova, "Vremia v obraznoi strukture fil'ma Marlena Khutsieva *Zastava Il'icha*," *Kinovedcheskie zapiski* 68 (2004): 237–63; A.A. Levandovskii, "Posledniaia zastava. Fil'my Marlena Khutsieva *Zastava Il'icha* i *Iiulskii dozhd'* kak istochnik dlia izucheniia ischezaiushchei mental'nosti," in Sekirinskii, ed., *Istoriia strany, istoriia kino*, 240–63; Mark Zak, "Zastava Il'icha," in Budiak, ed., *Rossiiskii illiuzion*, 351–56; and A. Prokhorov, "The Myth of the Great Family in Marlen Khutsiev's *Lenin's Guard* and Mark Osep'ian's *Three Days of Viktor Chernyshev*," in Goscilo and Hashamova, eds., *Cinepaternity*, 29–50.
2 McMillan, *Khrushchev and the Arts*, 154. For a full transcript of N.S. Khrushchev's speech at the 8 March meeting, see *Novyi mir* 6 (1963): 3–34.
3 McMillan, *Khrushchev and the Arts*, 155.
4 Nancy Condee brilliantly points out the irony of Khrushchev's complaining about this film: "If Khrushchev could never fully disentangle himself from the sins of Stalin and reinvent himself as innocent, neither could he succeed in arguing to the younger generation a philosophy of obedience, which he himself had so brilliantly violated." Nancy Condee, "Cultural Codes of the Thaw," in Taubman, Gleason, and Khrushchev, eds., *Nikita Khrushchev*, 166.
5 RGANI, f. 2, op. 1, d. 635, l. 15.
6 Ibid., l. 14.
7 Some examples of this trend are: *The Big Family* (Bol'shaia sem'ia, 1954), *Two Fedors* (Dva Fedora, 1958), *Fate of a Man* (Sud'ba cheloveka, 1959), *Waiting for the Mail* (Zhdite pisem, 1960), *They Were Nineteen* (Im bylo deviatnadtsat', 1960), *Heirs* (Nasledniki, 1960), *When the Trees Were Tall* (Kogda derev'ia byli bol'shimi, 1961), *And What If It's Love?*(A esli eto liubov'?,

1961), *My Friend Kol'ka* (Moi drug Kol'ka, 1961), *Ivan's Childhood* (Ivanovo detstvo, 1962), *Two Men* (My, dvoe muzhchin, 1962), *A Ruined Summer* (Propalo leto, 1963), *Welcome, or Entry Forbidden to Outsiders* (Dobro pozhalovat', ili postoronnim vkhod vospreshchen, 1964), *The Children of Don Quixote* (Deti Don-Kikhota, 1965), *Someone's Ringing, Open the Door!* (Zvoniat, otkroite dver'!, 1965), *Our home* (Nash dom, 1965), *A Man-to-Man Conversation* (Muzhskoi razgovor, 1968), and *We'll Survive Till Monday* (Dozhivem do ponedel'nika, 1968).

8 Clark, *The Soviet Novel*, 114–35.

9 Peter Kenez identifies three films – S. Eisenstein's *Bezhin Meadow* (1937), M.A. Barskaia's *Father and Son* (1937), and A. Stolper's *The Law of Life* (1940) – whose censorship led to a long and loud campaign against the aforementioned filmmakers. These films were denounced for the catch-all indictment of "formalism" and defamation of Soviet realities; all three also portrayed unharmonious relationships between authority figures and their charges, challenging the sanctity of the great Soviet family myth. See Kenez, *Cinema and Soviet Society*, 134–40.

10 At the Twentieth Party Congress, Khrushchev stated that "it is impermissible and foreign to the spirit of Marxism-Leninism to elevate one person, to transform him into a superman possessing supernatural characteristics, akin to those of a god." See Khrushchev, *The Crimes of the Stalin Era*, 3.

11 Clark observes that in post-Stalinist literature, the previously central role of the mentor became increasingly problematic: "But 1956 saw such sweeping denunciations of the old father figure that it was really incumbent on writers to employ positive heroes untainted by close ties to him (a reason in itself, incidentally, for using younger heroes)." Clark, *The Soviet Novel*, 226.

12 Prokhorov, "Soviet Family Melodrama," 210.

13 Peacock, *Innocent Weapons*, 159.

14 Livschiz, "De-Stalinizing Soviet Childhood," 132.

15 LaPierre, *Hooligans in Khrushchev's Russia*, 24–7.

16 Ibid., 12. LaPierre evocatively points out that "hooliganism was caused not so much by dissent, but by drinking to which workers turned to escape the boredom, blur, and bleakness of life in the Soviet factory town." Nonetheless, it must be said that juvenile delinquency was not merely an instance of "moral panic." The crime rates also included grave offences, such as murder, banditism, robbery, sex crimes, and group crimes; the rates for these crimes increased significantly during the 1950s. See Livschiz, "De-Stalinizing Soviet Childhood," 118.

17 Peacock, *Innocent Weapons*, 80. Erica Fraser also documents the unease Soviet military officials felt about the (lack of) the postwar generation's

martial conditioning. See Fraser, *Military Masculinity and Postwar Recovery*, 36–44.

18　Worries about the lack of paternal role models began during the Second World War, when single-mother family units became dominant. By 1943, Soviet observers were suggesting a correlation between adolescent delinquency and paternal absence. Local crime reports seemed to support this assessment, claiming that fatherless children committed the majority of offences. See Kucherenko, *Soviet Street Children and the Second World War*, 16.

19　In 1950, there were just 76.6 men per 100 women in the RSFSR. While the war ultimately had little impact on the marital and fertility careers of Russian women (most women eventually married and had two children on average), the unbalanced sex ratios from the war significantly affected other aspects of family formation, resulting in increased female-headed households, abortion rates, and out-of-wedlock births. See Brainerd, "The Lasting Effect."

20　M. Belakhova, "Syn," *Ogonek* 37 (1963): 12.

21　In 1950 the divorce rate was 0.4 divorces per 1,000 people; ten years later, the incidence rate had risen to 1.3 per 1,000. Sanjian, "Social Problems, Political Issues," 632. See also Juviler, "Cell Mutation in Soviet Society," 42.

22　[Anon.], "V zale, gde Lenin provozglasil Sovetskuiu vlast'," *Pravda*, 16 October 1957, 3.

23　A. Kanevskii, "Semeinaia estafeta," *Krokodil* 18 (1963): 6.

24　V. Kataev, "Nash molodoi sovremennik," *Pravda*, 15 April 1958, 4.

25　L. Kabo, "K trudovoi zhizni," *Literaturnaia gazeta*, 28 June 1955, 2.

26　Quoted in Fisher, *Patterns for Soviet Youth*, 262.

27　K.E. Voroshilov, "XX s'ezd Kommunisticheskoi partii Sovetskogo Soiuza: Rech' tovarsicha K. E. Voroshilova," *Pravda*, 21 February 1956, 6.

28　K. Rotov, "Iskusstvo i zhizn'," *Krokodil* 17 (1956): 4.

29　Fleurs, "Education Reform in Moscow Secondary Schools," 7.

30　This law has a long history. Pilot programs began as early as 1954. Although the law never achieved the desired results, for it faced a great deal of opposition from teachers, parents, and factory personnel alike, Khrushchev continued pushing the professionalization of the school system throughout his term. For key work on this subject, see two dissertations: Fleurs, "Education Reform"; and Edward Sharp, "School Reform during the Khrushchev Period: A Radical Attempt to Re-Make Soviet Social and Economic Structures" (University of Michigan, 1995).

31　Fleurs, "Education Reform," 2.

32　N.S. Khrushchev, "Vospityvat' aktivnykh i soznatel'nykh stroitelei kommunisticheskogo obshchestva. Rech' tovarishcha N. S. Khrushcheva na XIII s'ezde VLKSM 18 aprelia 1958 goda," *Pravda*, 19 April 1958, 1.

33　Ibid.

34 "Zakon ob ukreplenii sviazi shkoly s zhizn'iu i o dal'neishem razvitii sistemy narodnogo obrazovania v SSSR," *Pravda*, 25 December 1958, 1.

35 E. Gorokhov, "Student-diplomnik u okulista," *Krokodil* 17 (1959): 11.

36 For an earlier acerbic characterization of young men as lazy see G. Val'k, "Mal'chik-pal'chik," *Krokodil* 24 (1958): 6. This cartoon features a strapping young lad leisurely transporting a single wood log while his elderly dad does the brunt of the chopping.

37 D. Zaslavskii, "Dar molodosti," *Krokodil* 29 (1958): 2–3.

38 E. Shukaev, "Menia na periferiiu?," *Krokodil* 10 (1963): 5.

39 V. Nemtsov, "Chuzhie vetri," *Sovetskaia kul'tura*, 2 July 1959, 2.

40 V. Nemtsov, "Mysli o vospitanii," *Sovetskaia kul'tura*, 26 November 1960, 2.

41 Fürst, "The Arrival of Spring?," 150.

42 Ibid., 136.

43 LaPierre, *Hooligans*, 11.

44 "Doklad tovarishcha L.F. Il'icheva," *Literaturnaia gazeta*, 19 June 1963, 3.

45 K. Nevler, "Poet samoreklamov," *Krokodil* 5 (1963): 2.

46 "Doklad tovarishcha L.F. Il'icheva," *Literaturnaia gazeta*, 19 June 1963, 3.

47 I. Semenov, *Krokodil* 6 (1963): cover.

48 "Rech' tovarishcha N. S. Khrushcheva na mitinge, posviashchenom vstreche kosmonavtov Valentiny Tereshkovoi i Valeriia Bykovskogo," *Sovetskaia kul'tura*, 23 June 1963, 3.

49 "Literatura sotsialisticheskogo realizma vsegda shla ruka ob ruku s revolutsiei," *Pravda*, 12 May 1963, 4.

50 K.A. Fedin, "Sovetskaia literatura v stroitel'stve kommunisticheskogo obshchestva," *Sovetskaia kul'tura*, 23 May 1967, 2.

51 E. Vinokurov, "Ne opozdavshie rodit'sia," *Literaturnaia gazeta*, 18 October 1967, 5.

52 Brian LaPierre observes that "with these measures, the hardline stance on hooliganism, which existed under the Khrushchev regime in the 1960s, was solidified and strengthened. See LaPierre, *Hooligans*, 199.

53 "The Decree of the Presidium of the Supreme Soviet of the USSR: On Strengthening the Liability for Hooliganism," *Pravda*, 28 July 1966, 2.

54 See Bonnell, *Iconography of Power*.

55 Michaela Pohl shows that the Virgin Lands project was especially tough to navigate for female volunteers because of "hunger and shortages, disease and high accident rates, ubiquitous violence, consistently lower pay and less satisfying jobs than men." See Pohl, "Women and Girls in the Virgin Lands," in Attwood, Reid and Ilič, eds., *Women in the Khrushchev Era*, 71.

56 [Anon.], "Obsuzhenie p'esy N. Pogodina 'My vtroem pokhali na tselinu'," *Literaturnaia gazeta*, 5 January 1956, 2.

57 R. Iurenev, "Ikh pervyi podvig," *Sovetskaia kul'tura*, 5 May 1956, 4.

58 N. Klado, "Razmyshleniia o fil'me 'Gorizont'," *Sovetskaia kul'tura*, 10 March 1962, 3.

59 V. Liubimova, "Vospitanie vysokikh chuvstv," *Sovetskaia kul'tura*, 3 April 1956, 3–4.

60 V. Shalunovskii, "Veselyi novogodnii karnaval," *Sovetskaia kul'tura*, 27 December 1956, 2.

61 Z. Papernyi, "Komediia mozhet byt' smeshnoi," *Literaturnaia gazeta*, 5 January 1957, 2.

62 Liudmila Grabenko, "Za kadrom: Iurii Belov," *Bul'var Gordona*, 27 July 2010, http://bulvar.com.ua/gazeta/archive/s30_64041/6307.html.

63 Zriteli o kinokartine "Karnaval'naia noch'," *Sovetskaia kul'tura*, 10 January 1957, 2.

64 L. Maliukova, "Idi i smotri. Elem Klimov," *Novaia gazeta*, 30 October 2003, http://2003.novayagazeta.ru/nomer/2003/81n/n81n-s35.shtml.

65 A. Zorkin, "Komediia, delo ser'eznoe," *Sovetskaia kul'tura*, 10 October 1964, 3.

66 Iu. Haniutin, "Oshibka tovarishcha Dynina," *Literaturnaia gazeta*, 13 June 1964, 3.

67 Maliukova, "Idi i smotri."

68 Scriptwriter D.Ia. Khrabrovitskii initially envisioned this film to be about a test pilot who broke the sound barrier. However, Chukhrai thought the movie was doomed after a consultation at the Zhukovskii Academy regarding the movie's accuracy vis-à-vis the technical aspects of breaking the sound barrier. Chukhrai almost abandoned the film, but the crew working on the project and the studio's administration urged him to proceed with filming. While the filming continued, the script was improvised from one scene to the next.

69 As Clark notes, Stalin never stinted on the affection he showered on his "pets" (*pitomtsi*). In a short story about pilots titled "The Teacher and the Students," Stalin exudes "fatherly warmth" whenever he met the pilots. A 1937 editorial in *Literaturnaia gazeta* went so far as to imply that Stalin's "warmth" was potent enough to protect the pilots against the Arctic temperatures. Stalin displayed fatherly concern through his actions: he would see off the pilots before their flights, and welcome them back, and if one of the pilots died, Stalin would serve as his pallbearer. See, Clark, *The Soviet Novel*, 126–7; and Bergman, "Valerii Chkalov."

70 Boris Polevoi, *Povest' o nastoiashchem cheloveke* (Moscow: Sovetskii pisatel', 1949), 26.

71 Ibid.

72 P. Pavlenko, "Poema o sovetskom cheloveke," *Pravda*, 23 November 1948, 3.

73 Polevoi, *Povest'*, 27.

74 Pavlenko, "Poema," 3.

75 Ibid.
76 Chukhrai, *Moe kino*, 142.
77 The equivalent of this Russian saying is "You can't make omelets without breaking eggs."
78 Chukhrai, *Moe kino*, 145.
79 RGALI f. 2936 op. 1, d. 457, l. 8.
80 Ibid., ll. 34–5.
81 Ibid., l. 102.
82 Johnson, *Khrushchev and the Arts*, 154.
83 N.N. Chushkin, *Gamlet-Kachalov* (Moscow, 1966), 309, quoted in Mendel, "Hamlet and Soviet Humanism," 733.
84 I. Vertsman, "K problemam 'Gamleta,'" in *Shekspirovskii sbornik* (Moscow, 1961), 129, quoted in Mendel, "Hamlet," 734.
85 RGANI, f. 5, op. 55, d. 41, l. 77.
86 Grigorii Kozintsev, *Nash sovremennik. Villiam Shekspir* (Moscow, 1966), 306, quoted in Mendel, "Hamlet," 743.
87 RGALI, f. 2468, op. 5, d. 46, l. 13.
88 Ibid., l. 33.
89 N.S. Khrushchev, "Molodye stroiteli kommunizma, vysoko nesite znamia Lenina," *Pravda*, 21 April 1962, 1.
90 Gibian, "Themes in Recent Soviet Russian Literature," 427.
91 Chudak and Chudakova, "Sovremennaia povest' i iumor."
92 Slobin, "Aksenov beyond 'Youth Prose,'" 51.
93 Anna Latynina, "Epitafiia shestidesiatnikam: Poslednii roman Vasiliia Aksenova," *Novyi mir* 2 (2010): 153–60.
94 Many of the youth publicly expressed attitudes that clearly distinguished them from the rest of the literary establishment. See, for instance, a questionnaire published in *Voprosy literatury* 9 (1962): 123–33.
95 Zubok, *Zhivago's Children*, 153.
96 The details of Khrushchev's meeting with the intellectuals on 7–8 March 1963 are available in M. Romm's memoirs. See M. Romm, *Kak v kino. Ustnye rasskazy* (Nizhnii Novgorod: DEKOM, 2003).
97 Johnson, *Khrushchev and the Arts*, 164.
98 The Soviet press reported that this film was sent abroad to represent the achievements of Soviet cinema. For instance, it was one of the films sent to Turkmenistan to mark the tenth anniversary of Russian culture in that Central Asian republic. Also, Lebedev made it to Sofia for a festival celebrating up-and-coming Soviet directors.
99 N. Cherkasov, "Golos epokhi," *Literaturnaia gazeta*, 15 February 1966, 1.
100 See S. Pavlova, "Legenda o pervom bakhshi," *Sovetskaia kul'tura*, 14 December 1965, 1; "Bratskoe rukopozhatie," *Sovetskaia kul'tura*, 5 April 1966, 4, R. Iurenev, "O nashikh sovremennikakh," *Pravda*, 4 May 1966,

6; L. Pogozheva, "Esli ty chelovek – vstan' i idi..." *Sovetskaia kul'tura*, 11 December 1965, 4.

101 RGALI, f. 2936, op. 1, d. 917, 17.

102 Johnson, *Khrushchev and the Arts*, 154.

4 The Trouble with Women

1 Christine Varga-Harris points out that contemporary fiction, like film, turned men into victims of women's blind obedience to consumerist impulses. See Varga-Harris, *Stories of House and Home*, 95–8.

2 B. Gal'diaeva, "Kazhdomu svoe," *Krokodil* 16 (1960): 13.

3 R. Kalkopola, "V gorod na uchebu..." *Krokodil* 20 (1956): 8–9.

4 Borenstein, *Men Without Women*.

5 Wylie, *Generation of Vipers*, 218.

6 Ibid., 49–50.

7 Ibid., 217.

8 Ibid., 206.

9 Ibid., 200.

10 Varga-Harris, *Stories of House and Home*, 11.

11 Speech at a Kremlin reception for cotton growers, TASS, 20 February 1958. The quotation appears in *Soviet World Outlook: A Handbook of Communist Statements* (Washington, D.C.: Department of State Publication, 1959), 137.

12 Goldman, "The Reluctant Consumer," 367.

13 Chapman, "Real Wages in the Soviet Union," 147.

14 I. Semenova, "Velikoe pereselenie narodov," *Krokodil* 22 (1964): 8–9.

15 Pomerantsev's comments are quoted in Zubkova, *Russia After the War*, 176.

16 Quoted in Susan E. Reid, "The Khrushchev Kitchen: Domesticating the Scientific-Technological Revolution," *Journal of Contemporary History* 40, no. 2 (2005): 295.

17 Bogdanova, "The Soviet Consumer," 116.

18 Field, *Private Life and Communist Morality*, 6.

19 Quoted in Varga-Harris, *Stories of House and Home*, 85.

20 Field's book on communist morality cited above makes clear just how messy and nuanced the contestation of moral issues was during this period, particularly in the realm of the most personal affairs: marriage, divorce, abortion, and the upbringing of children.

21 Castillo, *Cold War on the Home Front*; Oldenziel and Zachmann, eds., *Cold War Kitchen*.

22 Reid, "Cold War in the Kitchen," 220–1.

23 Varga-Harris, *Stories of House and Home*, 85.

24 Reid, "Cold War in the Kitchen," 242.

25 Ibid., 245.

26 At regular intervals *Krokodil* published short stories about husbands who ruined their marriages by being misanthropes. They viewed their wives as housewives and housekeepers, not partners in love and life. See, for instance, S. Narin'iani, "Bazarich," *Krokodil* 1 (1958): 4–5, L. Iordanov, "Meshchanka," *Krokodil* 29 (1961): 10; A. Nikol'skii, "Kak lovil meshchanina," *Krokodil* 5 (1964): 4–5.

27 Boris Leo, "Zhenikh s pridanym," *Krokodil* 19 (1955): 14.

28 Boris Leo, *Krokodil* 5 (1960): 14.

29 Iu. Cherepanova, "Polubila s pervogo vzgliada," *Krokodil* 36 (1963): 11.

30 Iu. Ganfa, "Ellochiny trofei," *Krokodil* 2 (1963): 10.

31 [Anon.], "Kak Mar'ia Ivanovna rukovodila uchrezhdeniem, rukovoditelem kotorogo shchitalsia ee muzh," *Krokodil* 23 (1956): 16.

32 B. Savkov, *Krokodil* 22 (1964), cover page.

33 Varvara Karbovskaia, "Simochka," *Krokodil* 19 (1958): 5.

34 F. Samukas, *Krokodil* 19 (1960): 16.

35 B. Sakova, *Krokodil* 5 (1967): 4.

36 K. Eliseev, "Priemnye ispytania nachalis'," *Krokodil* 18 (1958): 4.

37 N. Khalatov, "Rasti, Murzilka!" *Iskusstvo kino* 4 (1957): 106.

38 Iu. Fedorova, "Mama smotrit skvoz' pal'tsy," *Krokodil* 5 (1962): 7.

39 A. Kanevskii, "Zabotlivaia mamasha," *Krokodil* 1 (1964): 3.

40 Plant, *Mom*, 33.

41 Ibid., 46.

42 Oever, *Mama's Boy*, 7–8.

43 Ibid., 8.

44 Ibid., 9.

45 Schrand, "Soviet 'Civic-Minded Women' in the 1930s."

46 Rojavin and Harte, eds., *Women in Soviet Film*, 5.

47 Some examples of this genre were blockbusters; others failed to attract a large following. Nonetheless, together they form a significant post-Stalinist cinematic trend. *How They Met* (Oni vstrechalis' v puti, 1957), *My Home* (Dom v kotorom ia zhivu, 1957), *The City Sparks a Fire* (Gorod zazhigaet ogni, 1958), *My Dear Fellow* (Dorogoi Moi Chelovek, 1958), *Ballad of a Soldier* (Ballada o soldate, 1959), *Fate of a Man* (Sud'ba chelovka, 1959), *A Simple Story* (Prostaia istoriia, 1960), *Clear Skies* (Chistoe Nebo, 1961), *The Gals* (Devchata, 1961), *Flooding* (Polovod'e, 1963), *A True Story* (Nepridumanaia istoriia, 1964), *The Light of a Distant Star* (*Svet dalekoi zvezdoi*, 1965), *Our Home* (Nash dom, 1965), *Three Poplars in Pliushcikha* (Tri topolia na Pliushchikhe, 1968).

48 I. Kokoreva, "Pervyi festival' sovetskikh fil'mov v Bel'gii," *Iskusstvo kino* 8 (1956): 108. According to Soviet reports the film was also

enthusiastically received when it debuted in France. See M. Shalashnikov, "Nedelia sovetskikh fil'mov vo Frantsii," *Sovetskaia kul'tura*, 12 December 1955, 4.

49　G. L'vovskii, "Lektsii s primakoi," *Sovetskaia kul'tura*, 28 April 1956, 4.

50　N. Klado, "Chelovekovedenie – glavnaia zadacha iskusstva," *Iskusstvo kino* 12 (1955): 27.

51　"Kinozriteli o khudozhestvennom masterstve," *Iskusstvo kino* 3 (1956): 83.

52　M. Iof'ev, "Obrazy trebuiut siuzhetov," *Iskusstvo kino* 2 (1956): 54–8.

53　Iu. Shevkunenko, "Akter i geroi," *Sovetskaia kul'tura*, 2 August 1956, 4.

54　Klado, "Chelovekovedenie," 28.

55　L. Pogozheva, "Fil'm o schast'e," *Sovetskaia kul'tura*, 20 October 1955, 4.

56　N. Lordkipanidze, "Svoi vzgliad," *Iskusstvo kino* 4 (1962): 10.

57　G. Medvedev, "Chto sluchilos' s Kuz'moi Iordanovym?" *Sovetskii ekran* 1 (1962): 8.

58　G. Kapralov, "Odinochestvo – iskliucheno," *Sovetskii ekran* 6 (1962): 13.

59　V. Pogostina, "Stat' chelovekom," *Iskusstvo kino* 3 (1965): 40.

60　V. Korobtsov, N. Kozhin, R. Artamonov, and V. Nikolaev, "Trudnoe, ne-skoroe, schast'e," *Izvestiia*, 16 February 1965, 4.

61　Pogostina, "Stat' chelovekom," 39.

62　I. Kokoreva, "V krugu melkikh chustv," *Izvestiia*, 29 October 1959, 10.

63　G. Mdivani, "Pokolenie geroev," *Iskusstvo kino* 1 (1959): 10.

64　[Anon.], "Posmotrev novuiu kartinu. Zriteli obsuzhdaiut fil'm 'Raznye sud'by,'" *Sovetskaia kul'tura*, 25 October 1956, 3.

65　All these questions are raised in a review penned by three Moscow State University students. See S. Kotenko, E. Pereslegina, and G. Glaskina, "Sud'by molodykh liudei," *Izvestiia*, 11 October 1956, 3.

66　[Anon.], "Posmotrev novuiu kartinu," 3.

67　M. Turovskaia, "Da i net," *Iskusstvo kino* 12 (1957): 15.

68　RGANI, f. 5, op. 36, d. 80, l. 81.

69　Condee. "Veronika Fuses Out," 173–83.

70　Ibid., 12.

71　Anninskii, *Shestidesiatniki i my*, 40.

72　Shilova, *I moe kino*, 55.

73　Woll, *The Cranes Are Flying*, 77.

74　Ibid.

75　Shilova, *I moe kino*, 57.

76　*It Happened in Penkovo* (Delo bylo v Pen'kove, 1957), *Walking the Streets of Moscow* (Ia shagaiu po Moskve, 1963), *I Am Twenty* (Mne dvadtsat' let, 1964), *A Chap Like Him* (Zhivet' takoi paren', 1964), *A Long, Happy Life* (Dolgaia schastlivaia zhizn', 1966), *One More Time about Love* (Eshche raz pro Liubov, 1967), *Four Pages of a Young Man's Life* (Chetyre stranitsy od-noi molodoi zhizni, 1967), *To Love* (Liubit', 1968).

77	[Anon.], "Glazami storonnego nabliudatelia," *Moskovskii komsomolets*, 17 July 1954, 2.
78	V. Dorofeev, "Geroi v sovremennoi Sovetskoi literature," *Komsomol'skaia pravda*, 23 October 1954, 4.
79	Iu. Surovtsev, "Trudnye puti," *Literaturnaia gazeta*, 27 July 1954, 2.
80	A. Dement'ev, "Vernye poiski," *Iskusstvo kino* 4 (1956): 9.
81	R. Iurenev, "Chuzhaia rodnia," *Moskovskaia pravda*, 21 January 1956, 5.
82	A. Petrosian, "O dogmatizme v kritike," *Znamia* 8 (1955): 192.
83	E.S. Grebenshchikov, poster for *Noisy Day* (Moscow: Reklamfil'm, 1960).
84	SK-Novosti (2002), interview with Georgii Natansov, "'Shumnii Den'" i drugie," https://www.film.ru/articles/shumnyy-den-i-drugie.
85	V. Merimanov, "Shumnii Den'," *Sovetskii ekran* 2 (1961): 6.
86	Iu. Borev, "Veseloe prikluchenie," *Literaturnaia Gazeta*, 3 January 1959, 3. Another reviewer declared the plot of the film to be "uncomplicated" (*nezamyslovat*), reflecting the "naturalness" of the situation. See N. Krushakov, "Poleznyi 'kinovitamin'," *Izvestiia*, 13 July 1963, 6.
87	An. Vartanov, "So znakom 'plius'," *Iskusstvo kino* 9 (1963): 49.
88	It is no surprise that the few sixties movies that feature successful romantic connections eschew urban settings. Examples include *Honeymoon* (Medovyj mesiats, 1956), *Heights* (Vysota, 1957), *Spring on Zarechnaya Street* (Vesna na Zarechnoi ulitse, 1957), *The Gals* (Devchata, 1961), *Alioshka's Romance* (Aleshkina liubov', 1960), *Shore Leave* (Uvol'nenie na bereg, 1962).

5 Our Friend the Atom?

1	During the Thaw there was no lack of movies featuring scientist as protagonists or revolving around scientific issues: *Journeys and Destinies* (Puti i sud'by) by Iakov Bazelian (1955), *Honeymoon* (Medovyi mesiats) by Nadezhda Koshverova (1956), *Researchers* (Iskateli) by Mikhail Shapiro (1957), *The Man from Planet Earth* (Chelovek s planety Zemlia) by Boris Buneev (1958), *A Sleepless Night* (Bessonnaia noch') by Isidor Annenskii (1960), *Spring Storms* (Vesennie grozy) by Nikolai Figurovskii (1960), *Kangaroo Court* (Sud sumashedshikh) by Grigorii Roshal' (1961), *Battle Along the Road* (Bitva v puti) by Vladimir Basov (1961), *Nine Days of a Year* (Deviat dnei odnogo goda) by Mikhail Romm (1962), *Academician from Ascania* (Akademik iz Askanii) by Vladimir Gerasimov (1962), *The Barrier of Uncertainty* (Bar'er neizvestnosti) by Nikita Kurikhin (1962), *Flag Station* (Polustanok) by Boris Barnet (1963), *The Conquerors of Heaven* (Im pokoriaetsia nebo) by Tat'iana Lioznova (1963), *Everything Is Left to the People* (Vse ostaetsia liudiam) by Georgii Natanson (1963), *Winter Oak* (Zimnii dub) by M. Kozhin (1963), *A Gunshot in the Fog* (Vystrel v tumane) by Anatolii Bobrovskii and Aleksandr Seryi (1964), *The Easy Life* (Legkaia zhizn') by Veniamin Dorman (1964), *Traces in the Ocean* (Sled v okeane) by Oleg Nikolaevskii (1964), *Into the Storm* (Idu na grozu) by Sergei Mikaelian (1965), *Ballet Star* (Zvezda baleta) by Aleksei Mishurin (1965), *Lebedev Versus Lebedev* (Lebedev protiv Lebedeva) by Genrikh Gabai (1965), *Avdot'ia Pavlovna* by Aleksandr Muratov and Valerii Isakov (1966), *The Ashen Disease* (Seraia bolezn') by Iakov Segel' (1966), *Leaf Fall* (Listopad) by Otar Ioseliani (1966), *Hi, It's Me!* (Zdravstvui, eto ia!) by Frunze Dovlatian (1966), *They Live Next Door* (Oni zhivut riadom) by Grigorii Roshal' (1967), *The Mysterious Wall* (Tainstvennaia stena) by Irina Povolotskaia and Mikhail Sadkovich (1967), *They Called Him Robert* (Ego zvali Robert) by Il'ia Ol'shvanger (1967), *The Merchant of Air* (Prodavets vozdukha) by Vladimir Riabtsev (1967), *Off-Season* (Mertvii sezon) by Sava Kulish (1968).

2 The Soviet intelligentsia can be divided into two main categories: the creative (*tvorcheskaia*) and scientific-technical (*nauchno-tekhnicheskaia*). The former group included those employed in the arts, while the latter consisted of scientists, researchers, and engineers.

3 Quoted in Gerovitch, "'New Soviet Man' inside Machine," 136.

4 Stites, *Russian Popular Culture*, 145.

5 Raleigh, trans. and ed., *Russia's Sputnik Generation*, 167.

6 Grushin, *Chetyre zhizni Rossii*, vol. 1, 403.

7 Quoted in Powell, "The Effectiveness of Soviet Anti-Religious Propaganda," 371–2.

8 V. Vladin, "O tom kak pisat' ob uchennykh voobshche i o molodykh fizikakh v chastnosti," *Literaturnaia gazeta*, 15 February 1967, 16.

9 Slava Gerovitch and Iina Kohonen have already discussed the ambiguous cultural status that Soviet science held in this time period. They point to the fact that the official cult of science did not offer a single, one-dimensional narrative. See Gerovitch, "'New Soviet Man' inside Machine"; Kohonen, "The Space Race and Soviet Utopian Thinking," 127.

10 Significantly, reflecting on their own experience during the sixties in their memoirs, scientists also recall occupying multiple and contradictory positions vis-à-vis their masculinity. Erica Fraser's research indicates that the tales they tell "locate them as simultaneously powerless, constantly surveilled by the state and othered by men in the military institutions ... and nearly deified as superior beings, armed with the knowledge and technical expertise to design weapons that could destroy the world." Fraser, *Military Masculinity*, 19.

11 Romm's film won the main award at the Karlovy Vary film festival in Czechoslovakia in 1962, received honorary diplomas at festivals in San Francisco (1962) and Melbourne (1965), and earned a Polish Critics' Award in the "Best Foreign Film" category in 1962.

12 *Storm* was a two-part film and each part attracted 20 million viewers.

13 *Nine Days* escaped the censors' kiss of death because of M. Romm's influence in the industry, while *Storm* avoided being placed on the censorship shelf because an already acclaimed novel served as the basis for the script. *Rainbow* and *Robert*, however, were the work of inexperienced directors who based their films on original scripts and were therefore much more vulnerable to party meddling.

14 As Marx famously proclaimed: "The hand-mill produces a society with the feudal lord; the steam-mill, society with the industrial capitalist." See Karl Marx, *The Poverty of Philosophy* (Moscow: Progress, 1971), 56.

15 Pollock, *Stalin and the Soviet Science Wars*, 3.

16 The five most relevant instances of this trend are *Defiant* (Vstrechnyi) by Fridrikh Ermler and Sergei Iutkevich (1932), *A Special Case* (Chastnyi sluchai) by Il'ia Trauberg (1933), *The Dark Gorge* (Chernaia past') by Aleksandr Razumnyi (1935), *Party Card* (Partiinyi billet) by Ivan Pyr'ev (1936), and *Engineer Kochin's Mistake* (Oshibka inzhenera Kochina) by Aleksandr Macheret (1939).

17 Fateev, *Obraz vraga v Sovetskoi propagande*, 77–85.

18 Nikolai Krementsov's book makes it clear that both the play and the film took their inspiration from true events surrounding two Soviet scientists, N.G. Kliueva and G.I. Roskin. See Krementsov, *The Cure*; and Esakov and Levina, *Delo KR*.

19 Jeffrey Brooks notes: "Whereas *Pravda* devoted only seventeen lead editorials to science and technology from 1921 and 1927, it allotted fifty-four from 1928 through 1932, and eighty-four from 1933 through 1939. The newspaper's size remained roughly six pages, but space given to science and technology tripled from three pages a month from 1921 through 1927 to nine from 1928 through 1939." See Brooks, *Thank You, Comrade Stalin!*, 100.

20 See Bergman, "Valerii Chkalov"; and Clark, "The Stalinist Myth of the Great Soviet Family," in *The Soviet Novel*, 114–35.

21 McCannon, "Positive Heroes at the Pole," 353.

22 Josephson, "'Projects of the Century,'" 538.

23 Cited in Z. Berebeshkina, *Problema sovesti v Marksistsko-Leninskoi etike* (Moscow: Izd. VPShi AON pri TSK KPSS, 1963), 88.

24 Boobbyer, *Conscience, Dissent, and Reform*, 64.

25 Quoted in Marsh, *Soviet Fiction Since Stalin*, 218.

26 Ibid.

27 For more on Voznesenskii's poem "Oza," see Marsh, "Soviet Fiction and the Nuclear Debate," 256.

28 Vesa Oittinen, "Introduction," in "The Philosophy of Evald Il'enkov," ed. Vesa Oittinen, special issue, *Studies in East European Thought* 57, no. 3 (2005): 226.

29 Susan Costanzo, "The 1959 *Liriki-Fiziki* Debate: Going Public with the Private?," in Siegelbaum, ed., *Borders of Socialism*, 251–68.

30 Quoted in Marsh, *Soviet Fiction since Stalin*, 213.

31 K. Rotova, "Budushchee v predstavlenii Vovy Ivanova," *Krokodil* 35 (1958): 8–9.

32 "Zakon ob ukreplenii sviazi shkoly s zhizn'iu i o dal'neishem razvitii sistemy narodnogo obrazovania v SSSR," *Pravda*, 25 December 1958, 1.

33 N. Martynenko, *Krokodil* 5 (1960): 15.

34 B. Brainina, "Vernyi kurs, vernoe napravlenie," *Voprosy literatury* 1 (1965): 69.

35 Although the making of the film began in 1961, the scriptwriter, Daniil Habrovitskii, recalls that he began working on a script about physicists three years prior to filming. See D. Habrovitskii, "Daniil Habrovitskii rasskazyvaet...," Ofitsial'nyi sait narodnogo artista L'va Durova, http:// www.levdurov.ru/show_arhive.php?&id=1147.

36 I. Mikhailov, "Nash sovremennik," *Molot* (Rostov-on-Don), 28 March 1962, 4.

37 A. Zorkii, "O fil'me 'Deviat dnei odnogo goda'," *Birobidzhanskaia pravda*, 5 April 1962, 2.

38 V. Liukov and Iu. Panov, "Eto li gorizonty?" *Oktiabr'* 5 (1962): 186.

39 I. Chicherov, "Po-novomu o novom," *Voprosy literatury* 12 (1962): 50.

40 L. Pogozheva, "Poltora chasa razmyshlenii," *Iskusstvo kino* 4 (1962): 3.

41 *Into the Storm* was based on D.A. Granin's extremely popular 1961 novel of the same title; Granin also co-authored the script with the director. The book enjoyed great popularity with readers and critics alike, becoming a staple in literature courses. The novel is still taught in Russian classrooms as one of the Soviet classics.

42 M. Zak, "Idti k tseli," *Iskusstvo kino* 2 (1965): 17.

43 G. Iungval'd-Khil'kevich, "Fil'm o robote," *Sovetskii ekran* 8 (1966): 5.

44 G. Iungval'd-Khil'kevich, *Za kadrom* (Moscow: Tsentrpoligraf, 2000), 69–73.

45 Georgii Kapralov, "Kak sazdavat' intellektual'nye fil'my," Ofitsial'nyi sait narodnogo artista L'va Durova, http://www.levdurov.ru/show_arhive.php?&id=1150.

46 V. Orlov, "Atomy i liudi," *Pravda*, 20 March 1962, 4.

47 In his discussion of how the depiction of man within the environment was transformed, film critic Evgenii Margolit concluded that during the Thaw nature was not fighting with humans; it simply did not notice them. Despite its indifference to humans, it consistently overpowered them, effortlessly foiling their plans to bring the environment under man's control. See Margolit, "Chelovek v peizazhe," in V. Troianovskii, comp., *Kinematograf ottepeli*, vol. 1, 99–117. See also Margolit, "Landscape, with Hero," in Prokhorov, ed., *Springtime for Soviet Cinema*, 29–50.

48 Peter Vail' and Aleksandr Genis, *60-e. Mir Sovetskogo cheloveka* (Moscow: Novoe Literaturnoe obozrenie, 2001), 105.

6 De-Heroization and the Pan-European Masculinity Crisis

1 This two-part film sold nearly 28 million tickets upon its release.

2 On a symbolic level, Annie Girardot was ideal for this conversation because she starred in Luchino Visconti's 1960 motion picture *Rocco and His Brothers* (Rocco e suoi fratelli), notable for its graphic and gut-wrenching scenes of violence and murder. This film would likely have been familiar to Soviet citizens who lived in major metropolitan areas.

3 A. Karaganov, "Geroi. Zritel'. Zamysel." *Sovetskaia kul'tura*, 18 April 1963, 2.

4 N. Abramov, "'Eksperimental'noe'? Net, antichelovechnoe!," *Sovetskii ekran* 7 (1963): 18.

5 M. Turovskaia, "Eshche o "rasserzhennykh," *Iskusstvo kino* 12 (1960): 136–9; Editorial board op-ed, "Pobezhdaet pravda," *Iskusstvo kino* 2 (1961): 3.

6 I discuss some of these collaborative trends in the introduction and chapter 1. On the history of Soviet co-productions and other cultural collaboration, see Michaels, "Mikhail Kalatozov's *The Red Tent*; Siefert, "Soviet Cinematic Internationalism"; Kozovoi, "A Foot in The Door."

7 John Osborne, *Look Back in Anger: A Play in Three Acts* (Woodstock: The Dramatic Publishing Company, 1957), 69.

8 The term de-heroization first received widespread currency in connection with criticisms of V.A. Nekrasov's first book, *In the Trenches of Stalingrad*. But because Stalin intervened to award Nekrasov a Stalin Prize for literature in 1947, the term largely fell out of use until 1963. The June 1963 Plenum of the CPSU Central Committee, which announced a war against bourgeois ideology, breathed new life into the term. Throughout the 1960s and '70s, critics resorted to it when criticizing novels and motion pictures that presented historic events and contemporaneity in a documentary, unembellished fashion.

9 Sergei Gerasimov, "Iskusstvo bez grima," *Pravda*, 27 September, 6.

10 The June 1963 Plenum of the CPSU Central Committee announced renewed vigilance against bourgeois ideology, with art being called upon to act as the party's main tool against foreign threats. See L.F. Il'ichev, *Osnovnye zadachi ideologicheskoi raboty partii. Doklad na plenume tsentralnogo komiteta KPSS, 18 iiunia 1963 goda* (Moscow: Izdatel'stvo politicheskoi literatury, 1963).

11 RGALI f. 2936, op. 1, d. 227, l. 18.

12 I.A. Pyr'ev, "Po puti, ukazannomu partiei," *Sovetskii ekran* 9 (1963): 1.

13 Quoted in Raymond F. Betts, *Europe in Retrospect: A Brief History of the Past Two Hundred Years* (Lexington: D.C. Heath, 1979), 191.

14 RGANI, f. 5, op. 55, d. 41, l. 77.

15 "Nightmare and Flight," *Partisan Review* 12, no. 2 (1945), reprinted in *Essays in Understanding, 1930–1954*, ed. Jerome Kohn (Harcourt Brace, 1994), pp. 133–5.

16 Novell-Smith, *Making Waves*, 120.

17 Hames, *The Czechoslovak New Wave*, 2nd ed., 7.

18 These films usually featured white telephones as the ultimate bourgeois status symbol.

19 This is how prominent film critic and director Lindsay Anderson reflected on the state of the British film industry in 1957. See Maschler, *Declaration*, 139.

20 Marcus, *Italian Film in the Light of Neorealism*, 23.

21 Mario Verdone, *Storia del cinema italiano* (Rome: Tascabili Economici Newton, 1995), 43.

22 For a broad consideration of issues of Italian history in a range of films, see Dalle Vacche, *The Body in the Mirror*.

23 Luzzi, "Romantic Allegory," 71.

24 Besides Vittorio De Sica, Roberto Rossellini, and Giuseppe De Santis, Free Cinema creators drew their inspiration from John Ford (his humanism), Humphrey Jennings (his focus on the everyday in his wartime documentaries), and Jean Vigo (his lyrical and surrealist cinematography of interwar years).

25 Maschler, *Declaration*, 141.

26 Ibid., 142.

27 The British New Wave is the label conventionally given to a series of films released between 1959 and 1963. Here is the series in full: *Room at the Top* (Jack Clayton, 1959), *Look Back in Anger* (Tony Richardson, 1959), *The Entertainer* (Tony Richardson, 1960), *Saturday Night and Sunday Morning* (Karel Reisz, 1960), *A Taste of Honey* (Tony Richardson, 1961), *A Kind of Loving* (John Schlesinger, 1962), *The Loneliness of the Long Distance Runner* (Tony Richardson, 1962), *This Sporting Life* (Lindsay Anderson, 1963), *Billy Liar* (John Schlesinger, 1963).

28 Katerina Clark, "Socialist Realism in Soviet Literature," in *The Routledge Companion to Russian Literature*, ed. Neil Cornwell (London: Routledge, 2001), 182.

29 RGALI, f. 2936, op.1, d. 152, ll. 14–15.

30 Fogler, ed., *Wajda Films*, 13.

31 From a transcript of a roundtable discussion titled "Nikto bol'she ne sdelaet ni *Pepel i almaz* ni *Tishinu i krik*: Kinematograf Vostochnoi Evropy – proshchanie s proshlym," *Kinovedcheskie zapiski* 71 (2005): 35–51.

32 Pomerantsev began his essay with following diagnosis and question: "Sincerity. This is exactly what, in my view, is lacking in some books and plays. And one must ask, how can one be sincere?"

33 I.I. Anisimov filed the report on 16 August 1954, to P.N. Pospelov, a secretary of the Communist Party Central Committee. See RGANI f. 5, op. 17, d. 454, ll. 103–4.

34 Baranczak, "Before the Thaw."

35 For a more detailed description of the Polish School see Haltof, *Polish National Cinema*, 74–6.

36 Grenier, "Berlin, Karlovy-Vary, Venice," 26.

37 During the decade preceding the start of the German offensive, the Soviet government encouraged artists to depict a triumphant war in which the Red Army suffers minimal losses. Blustering slogans, repeated *ad nauseam* beginning in 1935, assured citizens that war would happen on foreign soil (*na chuzhoi territorii*), would be carried out with thunderous force (*moguchim molnienosnym udarom*), and would be won with little (Soviet) blood spilt (*maloi krov'iu*). Between 1935 and the beginning of the war in 1941, the Stalinist propaganda machine inundated Soviet citizens with songs, plays, and films that depicted war as child's play. In fact, commenting on one particularly naive war play, a critic soberly commented: "Wars look like that only in children's war games." E.L. Dzigan's 1938 motion picture *If War Comes Tomorrow* (*Esli zavtra voina*) is typical of the film genre that emerged during this time.

38 Khrushchev, *The Crimes of the Stalin Era*, 36–43.

39 Ibid., 37–8.

40 Bondarchuk's film was an adaptation of the Mikhail Sholokhov classic novel of the same title. The novel was published in 1957.

41 Jerzy Stefan Stawiński wrote the script based on his novel of the same title. Stawiński himself survived in the sewers as a soldier of the Home Army (Armia Krajowa).

42 Qouted in Falkowska, *Andrzej Wajda*, 49.

43 Fogler, *Wajda Films*, 50.

44 For a more detailed description of the treatment of Soviet POWs after the Second World War see Edele, *Soviet Veterans of World War II*, 102–28.

45 The passage the madman quotes is from Canto XVIII, in which Dante describes the lowest two circles of Hell as reserved for sinners who commit conscious fraud or treachery. The flatterers are steeped in human excrement, which represents the dishonesty they produced.

46 Bosley Crowther, "Screen: Wartime Poland," *New York Times*, 10 May 1961, 52.

47 Coates, *The Red and the White*, 119.

48 The most celebrated examples of the wave include Jack Clayton's *Room at the Top*, Tony Richardson's *Look Back in Anger* and *The Loneliness of the Long Distance Runner*, Karel Reisz's *Saturday Night and Sunday Morning*, Lindsay Anderson's *This Sporting Life*, and John Schlesinger's *Billy Liar*.

49 The British New Wave had roots in the period's literature and theatre. During the late 1950s the British literary and theatrical scene was taken over by the "angry young men," who rejected those institutions that held a sociopolitical and cultural monopoly over British life. The monarchy, the Anglican Church, Parliament, and (beginning in the 1920s) the BBC had had a decisive impact on British identity, and a group of postwar intellectuals and artists challenged the undisputed power of these establishments by ridiculing them as antiquated and out-of-touch. See Williamson, *The Temper of the Times*, 89.

50 Sandbrook, *Never Had It So Good*, 140.

51 RGANI, f. 2, op. 1, d. 635, l. 106.

52 As historian Arthur Marwick points out, Allen Sillitoe's 1958 novel *Saturday Night and Sunday Morning*, on which Reisz's script was based, contained many more graphic scenes and gratuitous obscenity. See Marwick, *"Room at the Top."*

53 Balakian, "The Flight from Innocence," 262.

54 M. Papava, "Razgovor cherez desiatiletie," *Iskusstvo kino* 6 (1968): 8.

55 In his essay comparing Osep'ian's *Three Days* with Khutsiev's *Lenin's Guard*, Alexander Prokhorov writes that Osep'ian "parodies Khutsiev's picture, calling attention to the crisis of the Great Soviet Family mythology as it was redefined during the Thaw." See Goscilo and Hashamova, eds., *Cinepaternity*, 29–50.

56 Allan Sillitoe, *Saturday Night and Sunday Morning* (New York: Plume, 1958), 136.

57 Kalliney, "Cities of Affluence."

58 RGALI, f. 2936, op. 4, d. 522, l. 79.

59 Khutsiev's first two motion pictures – *Spring on Zarechnaia Street* (Vesna na zarechnoi ulitse) in 1956, and *Two Fedors* (Dva Fedora) in 1959 – also faced censure for their dark depictions of Soviet realities and imitation of the neorealist style.

60 N. Zorkaia, "Vokrug kartiny 'Iul'skii dozd'," *Iskusstvo kino* 2 (1968): 27–8.

61 I. Pyr'ev, "Tvorit s narodom dlia naroda," *Iskusstvo kino* 2 (1963): 2.

62 RGANI, f. 2, op. 1, d. 635, l. 137.

63 R. Iurenev, "Esli govorit otkrovenno. Otkrytoe pis'mo kinorezhisseru M. Khutsievu," *Sovetskaia kul'tura*, 29 August 1967, 3.

64 When asked about persistently casting the woman's perspective as central, Antonioni said: "It seems to me that female psychology is a finer

filter for reality than male psychology. Anyway, women are less hypocritical by nature than men, therefore more interesting." Quoted in Cameron, "Michelangelo Antonioni," 41.

65 Harte, "Marlen Khutsiev's *July Rain*," 139.
66 Iurenev, "Esli govorit otkrovenno," 4.
67 RGALI, f. 2936, op. 4, d. 147, ll. 42–3.
68 Ibid., 54.
69 Ibid., 22.
70 Ibid., 17.
71 Ibid., 33.
72 Liehm, *Closely Watched Films*, 251.
73 Mazierska, *Masculinities in Polish, Czech and Slovak Cinema*, 33.
74 Hanáková, "The Construction of Normality," 152–5.
75 František, "The Czech Difference."
76 Liehm, *Closely Watched Films*, 312.
77 Ibid., 305.
78 Riazanov discusses the entire episode of the film's official banishment in his autobiography. See his *Nepodvedennye itogi*, 122–37.
79 RGANI, f. 5, op. 36, d. 138, ll. 7–8.
80 Afanas'eva and Afiani, comps., *Ideologicheskie komissii TsK KPSS, 1958-1964*, 469.
81 *Forty-First, The Cranes Are Flying, Ballad of a Soldier, Ivan's Childhood, Nine Days of a Year*, and *Lenin's Guard* all won prizes abroad and departed from the strict interpretations of socialist realism, establishing a unique perspective on Soviet realities.
82 RGALI, f. 2936, op. 1, d. 123, l. 61. Pogozheva directed her comments at V.A. Kochetov, a conservative writer and editor of the conformist journal *Oktiabr'*, who argued that artistic intellectuals should completely disregard the commentary coming from abroad. He insisted that criticism from the bourgeois camp indicated the socialist camp's success.
83 Mikhail Romm, *Kak v kino: Ustnye rasskazy* (Moscow: Dekom, 2003), 219.

Epilogue

1 E. Surkov, "Tsena pravdy," *Iskusstvo kino* 2 (1965): 20.
2 A. Obraztsova, "Tvorcheskii portret. Mikhail Ul'ianov," *Sovetskii ekran* 4 (1965): 3.
3 Kh.N. Khersonskii, "Proverka zhizn'iu. Nash magnitofon v zritel'nom zale doma kul'tury kolkhoza im. Kirova," *Sovetskii ekran* 4 (1965): 5.
4 Ibid.

5 Anninskii, *Shestidesiatniki i my*, 168. Similar discussions were conducted after a closed viewing of the film among the members of the Cinematographic Union. RGALI, f. 2936, op. 1, d. 525, ll. 1–73.

6 Ibid.

7 A month later, on 25 March 1966, another thirteen members of the scientific-technical and creative intelligentsia wrote to the Presidium of the Communist Party to express support for the original letter and signatories. Both letters were shared with the foreign press. See documents no. 10 and no. 13 in Artizov, ed., *Reabilitatsiia*.

8 Sergei Khrushchev noted that his retired father became so distressed over the idea of rehabilitating Stalin that he began to write an expose of Stalinism, which evolved into his memoirs. Nikita Khrushchev thought that Brezhnev insisted on Stalin's rehabilitation because he wanted to be seen as occupying the armchair of "the most brilliant leader of all times and peoples" rather than the restless "corn promoter" (*kukuruznik*). See Khrushchev, ed., *Memoirs of Nikita Khrushchev*, vol. 1, 715–16.

9 Roy Medvedev argues that the official rehabilitation never took place because the leadership of the Polish, Hungarian, and Italian Communist Parties refused to take part. See Medvedev, *On Soviet Dissent*, 26–8.

10 Bacon and Sandle, eds., *Brezhnev Reconsidered*, 150.

11 Golovskoi, *Kinematograf semidesiatykh*, 124.

12 *Samizdat* publications existed under Khrushchev, but they proliferated under Brezhnev even as the regime applied sharper measures against such dissident activities.

13 Golovskoi, *Kinematograf semidesiatykh*, 353.

14 Faraday, *Revolt of the Filmmakers*, 87.

15 Prokhorova, "The Post-Utopian Body Politic," 133.

16 Golovskoi, *Kinematograf semidesiatykh*, 197.

17 Bushnell, "The 'New Soviet Man' Turns Pessimist," 186.

18 Bushnell remarked on the optimism of the 1960s: "This New Soviet Man was proud of his country's accomplishments, confident that the Soviet Union was *the* rising power in the world, convinced that the Soviet Union's rapid economic advances were being translated into a rising level of personal well-being, and certain that the Soviet system provided unlimited personal opportunities, especially for the young." Ibid., 182.

19 Prokhorova, "The Post-Utopian Body Politic," 133.

20 Ibid.

21 Like James Bond, Shtirlits/Isaev played the protagonist in thirteen of Semenov's novels stretching from 1966 (*Password Unnecessary* [Parol' ne nuzhen]) to 1990 (*Otchaianie* [Desperation]).

22 Here I echo Stephen Lovell's observation that "Much of what *Seventeen Moments* communicates on the workings of the Nazi elite might be more applicable to the Soviet *nomenklatura* of the Brezhnev era." See Lovell, "In Search of an Ending," 310.

23 Prokhorova, "The Post-Utopian Body Politic," 136.

24 Lovell, "In Search of an Ending," 312.

25 Quoted in ibid., 310.

26 Baudin, "Le phénomène de la série culte."

27 Helena Goscilo and Andrea Lanoux, introduction to *Gender and National Identity in Twentieth-Century Russian Culture* (Dekalb: Northern Illinois University Press, 2006), 19.

28 Rosneck, "Vladimir Vysotsky," 324–35.

29 Qualin, "Laughing at Carnival Mirrors."

30 Hedrick Smith, "Modern 'Hamlet' Stirs Moscow Stage," *New York Times*, 29 February 1972, 26.

31 The Russian *Esquire* has also pointed to the (intentional?) similarity between Putin and Shtirlits. Alexander Galperin, "Putting on Putin," *Columbia Journalism Review* 46, no. 6 (2008): 10–11.

32 David M. Adamson and Julie DaVanzo, "Russia's Demographic 'Crisis': How Real Is It?" (Santa Monica, CA: RAND Corporation, 1997): 3–4.

33 Julie DaVanzo and Clifford A. Grammich, "Dire Demographics: Population Trends in the Russian Federation" (Santa Monica, CA: RAND Corporation, 2001): xiii.

34 Novitskaya, "Patriotism, Sentiment, and Male Hysteria," 302–4.

35 Wood, "Hypermasculinity as a Scenario of Power."

Bibliography

Archives

Apparat of the Central Committee of the Communist Party of the USSR, Fond 5
2468 M. Gor'kii Moscow Film Studio (Moskovskaia kinostudiia im. M. Gor'kogo), Fond 2468
Russian State Archive of Contemporary History (Rossiiskii gosudarstvennyi arkhiv noveishei istorii)
Russian State Archive of Literature and Art (Rossiiskii gosudarstvennyi arkhiv literatury i iskusstva)
USSR Cinematographers' Union (Soiuz kinematografistov SSSR), Fond 2936

Document Collections

Afanas'eva, E.S., and V.Iu Afiani, comps. *Ideologicheskie komissii TsK KPSS 1958-64. Dokumenty*. Moscow: Rosspen, 1998.
– eds. *Apparat TsK KPSS i kul'tura, 1953–1957. Dokumenty*. Moscow: Rosspen, 2001.
Artizov, Andrei, comp. *Reabilitatsiia. Kak eto bylo. Dokumenty Prezidiuma TsK KPSS i drugie materialy*, vol. 2: *Fevral' 1956–nachalo vos'midesiatykh godov*. Moscow: Materik, 2003.
Bondareva, G.L. *Kul'tura i vlast' ot Stalina do Gorbacheva. Kremlevskii kinoteatr, 1928–1953*. Moscow: Rosspen, 2005.
Fomin, V.I., comp. *Kinematograf ottepeli*, vol. 2. Moscow: Materik, 1998.
Franklin, Bruce, ed. *The Essential Stalin: Major Theoretical Writings, 1905–52*. Garden City: Anchor Books, 1972.
Grushin, B.A. *Chetyre zhizni Rossii v zerkale oprosov obshchestvennogo mneniia*, vol. 1: *Zhizn' 1-aia. Epokha Khrushcheva*. Moscow: Progress-Traditsiia, 2001.

Mikhailov, V.P., comp. *Zapreshchennye fil'my. Dokumenty, svidetel'stva, kommentarii*. Moscow: Nauchno-issledovatel'skii institut kinoiskusstva, 1993.

Poliakov, Iu.A. ed. *Naselenie Rossii v XX veke. Istoricheskie ocherki, 1960–1979*, vol. 3. Moscow: Rosspen, 2005.

Troianovskii, V.A., comp. *Kinematograf ottepeli*, vol. 1. Moscow: Materik, 1996.

Whitney, Thomas P., comp. *Khrushchev Speaks: Selected Speeches, Articles, and Press Conferences, 1949–1961*. Ann Arbor: University of Michigan Press, 1963.

Newspapers and Journals

Pravda (Moscow)
Iskusstvo kino
Komsomol'skaia pravda (Moscow)
Krokodil
Literaturnaia gazeta
Izvestiia
Novyi mir
Oktiabr' (Moscow) *Sovetskaia kul'tura Sovetskii ekran Sovetskoe iskusstvo*
The New York Times

Filmography

A Person Is Born (Chelovek rodilsia), dir. Vasilii Ordynskii (1957)
A Soldier's Father (Otets soldata), dir. Rezo Chkheidze (1964)
A Traveler with Baggage (Puteshestvennik s bagazhom), dir. Il'ia Frez (1965)
Alien Kin (Chuzhaia rodnia), dir. M. Shveitser (1955)
An Easy Life (Legkaia zhizn'), dir. Veniamin Dorman (1964)
An Unfinished Story (Neokonchennaia povest'), dir. Fridrikh Ermler (1955)
And What If It's Love? (A esli eto liubov'?), dir. Iu. Raizman (1961)
Big Family (Bol'shaia sem'ia), dir. Iosif Kheifits (1954)
Blood Relations (Rodnaia krov'), dir. M. Ershov (1963)
Carnival Night (Karnaval'naia Noch'), dir. El'dar Riazanov (1956)
Chairman (Predsedatel'), dir. A. Saltykov (1964)
Children of Don Quixote (Deti Don Kikhota), dir. Evgenii Karelov (1965)
Clear Skies (Chistoe nebo), dir. G. Chukhrai (1961)
The Cranes Are Flying (Letiat zhuravli), dir. M. Kalatozov (1957)
Different Fates (Raznye Sud'by), dir. Leonid Lukov (1956)
Fate of a Man (Sud'ba cheloveka), dir. S. Bondarchuk (1959)
Forty-first (Sorok pervyi), dir. G. Chukhrai (1956)

Four Pages of a Young Man's Life (Chetyre stranitsy odnoi molodoi zhizni), dir.
Rezo Esadze (1967)
Hamlet (Gamlet), dir. G. Koznintsev (1964)
How the Steel Was Tempered (Kak zakalialas' stal'), dir. Mark Donskoi (1942)
How the Steel Was Tempered (Kak zakalialas' stal'), dir. Nikolai Mashchenko
(1973–5)
I Bought Dad (Ia kupil papu), dir. Il'ia Frez (1963)
Into the Storm (Idu na grozu), dir. S. G. Mikaelian (1965)
Introduction to Life (Vstuplenie), dir. Igor' Talankin (1962)
Ivan's Childhood (Ivanovo detstvo) dir. Andrei Tarkovskii (1962)
Journalist (Zhurnalist), dir. S. Gerasimov (1967)
July Rain (Iul'skii dozhd'), dir. M. Khutsiev (1966)
Kanal (Kanał), dir. A. Wajda (1959)
Lenin's Guard (Zastava Il'icha), dir. M. Khutsiev (1963)
Life Passed Him By (Zhizn' proshla mimo), dir. Vladimir Basov (1959)
Little Sergei (Serezha), dirs. G. Daneliia and I. Talankin (1960)
Man from the First Century (Muz z prvního století), dir. O. Lipský (1961)
Man from Nowhere (Chelovek niotkuda), dir. E. Riazanov (1961)
Marina's Fate (Sud'ba Mariny), dirs. Viktor Ivchenko and Isaak Shmaruk (1953)
Nine Days of a Year (Deviat' dnei odnogo goda), dir. M. Romm (1961)
Noisy day (Shumnyi den'), dir. G. Natanson (1960)
Pavel Korchagin, dirs. Aleksandr Alov and Vladimir Naumov (1956)
Rainbow Formula (Formula radugi), dir. G. E. Iungval'd-Khil'kevich (1966)
Saturday Night and Sunday Morning, dir. Karel Reisz (1960)
They Called Him Robert (Ego zvali Robert), dir. I. S. Ol'shvanger (1967)
Three Plus Two (Tri plius' dva), dir. Genrikh Oganisian (1963)
Trust Me, Folks! (Ver'te mne, liudi!), dirs. I. Gurin and V. Berenshtein (1964)
Two Fedors (Dva Fedora), dir. M. Khutsiev (1958)
We Are Two Men (My, dvoe muzhchin), dir. Iurii Lysenko (1962)
Welcome, or No Trespassing (Dobro pozhalovat', ili postoronnim vkhod
vospreshchen), dir. Elem Klimov (1964)
When the Trees Were Tall (Kogda derev'ia byli bol'shimi), dir. L. Kulidzhanov
(1961)
Women (Zhenshchiny), dir. Pavel Liubimov (1966)

Published Memoirs and Other Personal Accounts

Adzhubei, Aleksei. *Te desiat' let.* Moscow: Sovietskaia Rossiia, 1989.
Anninskii, Lev. *Shestidesiatniki i my. Kinematograf stavshii i ne stavshii istoriei.*
Moscow: Kinotsentr, 1991.
Budiak, L.M., ed. *Rossiiskii illiuzion.* Moscow: Materik, 2003.
Chukhrai, Grigorii Naumovich. *Moe kino.* Moscow: Algoritm, 2002.

– *Moia voina*. Moscow: Algoritm, 2001.

Iungval'd-Khil'kevich, Georgii. *Za kadrom*. Moscow: Tsentrpoligraf, 2000.

Khrushchev, N.S. *Khrushchev in America*. New York: Crosscurrent Press, 1960.

Khrushchev, Sergei, ed. *Memoirs of Nikita Khrushchev*, vol. 1: *Commissar. 1918–1945*. University Park: Pennsylvania State University Press, 2004.

Liehm, Antonín J. *Closely Watched Films: The Czechoslovak Experience*. White Plains: International Arts and Sciences Press, 1974.

Manevich, Iosif. *Za ekranom. Razroznennye listki zapisannykh naspekh razdumii nad proshlym*. Moscow: Novoe izdatel'stvo, 2006.

Maschler, Tom, ed. *Declaration*. New York: Dutton, 1958.

Raleigh, Donald J., ed. *Russia's Sputnik Generation: Soviet Baby Boomers Talk about Their Lives*. Bloomington: Indiana University Press, 2006.

Riazanov, El'dar. *Nepodvedennye itogi*. Moscow: Vagrius, 2000.

Romm, Mikhail. *Kak v kino: Ustnye rasskazy*. Moscow: Kinotsentr, 1989.

Shilova, Irina. *I moe kino. Piatidesiatye, shestidesiatye, semidesiatye*. Moscow: NIIK Kinovedcheskie zapiski, 1993.

Sidorov, Evgenii. *Neobkhodimost' poezii. kritika, publitsistika, pamiat'*. Moscow: Geleos, 2005.

Secondary Sources (Monographs and Dissertations)

Aksiutin, Iurii. *Khrushchevskaia ottepel' i obshchestvennye nastroeniia v SSSR v 1953–1964 gg*. Moscow: Rosspen, 2004.

Alekseeva, L., and Paul Goldberg. *The Thaw Generation: Coming of Age in the Post-Stalin Era*. Boston: Little, Brown, 1990.

Ashwin, Sarah, ed. *Gender, State, and Society in Soviet and Post-Soviet Russia*. New York: Routledge, 2000.

Attwood, Lynne, ed. *Red Women on the Silver Screen: Soviet Women and Cinema from the Beginning to the End of the Communist Era*. London: Pandora Press, 1993.

Attwood, Lynn, Susan Emily Reid, and Melanie Ilič, eds. *Women in the Khrushchev Era*. New York: Palgrave Macmillan, 2004.

Bacon, Edwin, and Mark Sandle, eds. *Brezhnev Reconsidered*. New York: Palgrave Macmillan, 2002.

Baker, Brian. *Masculinity in Fiction and Film: Representing Men in Popular Genres 1945–2000*. London: Continuum, 2006.

Batygin, G.S. *Rossiiskaia sotsiologiia shestidesiatykh godov v vospominaniiakh i dokumentakh*. Saint Petersburg: Institut sotsiologii RAN, 1999.

Betts, Raymond F. *Europe in Retrospect: A Brief History of the Past Two Hundred Years*. Lexington: D.C. Heath, 1979.

Bittner, Stephen V. *The Many Lives of Khrushchev's Thaw: Experience and Memory in Moscow's Arbat*. Ithaca: Cornell University Press, 2008.

Bonnell, Victoria. *Iconography of Power: Soviet Political Posters under Lenin and Stalin*. Berkeley: University of California Press, 1999.

Boobbyer, Philip. *Conscience, Dissent, and Reform in Soviet Russia*. New York: Routledge, 2005.

Borenstein, Eliot. *Men without Women: Masculinity and Revolution in Russian Fiction, 1917–1929*. Durham: Duke University Press, 2000.

Brodsky, Joseph. *On Grief and Reason: Essays*. New York: Farrar, Straus and Giroux, 1995.

Brooks, Jeffrey. *Thank You, Comrade Stalin! Soviet Public Culture from Revolution to Cold War*. Princeton: Princeton University Press, 2000.

Castillo, Greg. *Cold War on the Home Front: The Soft Power of Midcentury Design*. Minneapolis: University of Minnesota Press, 2010.

Clardy, Jesse V., and Betty S. Clardy. *The Superfluous Man in Russian Letters*. Washington, D.C.: University Press of America, 1980.

Clark, Katerina. *The Soviet Novel: History as Ritual*. Bloomington: Indiana University Press, 2000.

Coates, Paul. *The Red and the White: The Cinema of People's Poland*. New York: Wallflower Press, 2005.

Cohen, Stephen F. *An End to Silence: Uncensored Opinion in the Soviet Union*. New York: W.W. Norton, 1982.

Cuordileone, K.A. *Manhood and American Political Culture in the Cold War*. New York: Routledge, 2005.

Dalle Vacche, Angela. *The Body in the Mirror: Shapes of History in Italian Cinema*. Princeton: Princeton University Press, 1992.

Danilova, E.Z. *Sotsial'nye problem truda zhenshchiny-rabotnitsy*. Moscow: Nauka, 1968.

Dobson, Miriam. *Khrushchev's Cold Summer: Gulag Returnees, Crime, and the Fate of Reform after Stalin*. Ithaca: Cornell University Press, 2009.

Edele, Mark. *Soviet Veterans of the Second World War: A Popular Movement in an Authoritarian Society 1941–1991*. Oxford: Oxford University Press, 2008.

Esakov, Vladimir Dmitrievich, and Elena Solomonovna Levina. *Delo KR. Sudy chesti v ideologii i praktike poslevoennogo stalinizma*. Moscow: Institut rossiiskoi istorii RAN, 2001.

Evans, Christine Elaine. *Between Truth and Time: A History of Soviet Central Television*. New Haven: Yale University Press, 2016.

Falkowska, Janina. *Andrzej Wajda: History, Politics, and Nostalgia in Polish Cinema*. New York: Berghahn Books, 2007.

Faraday, George. *Revolt of the Filmmakers: The Struggle for Artistic Autonomy and the Fall of the Soviet Film Industry*. University Park: Pennsylvania State University Press, 2000.

Fateev, A.V. *Obraz vraga v Sovetskoi propagande, 1945–1954 gg*. Moscow: Rossiiskaia akademiia nauk, 1999.

Field, Deborah A. *Private Life and Communist Morality in Khrushchev's Russia.*
    New York: Peter Lang, 2007.
Figes, Orlando. *The Whisperers: Private Life in Stalin's Russia.* New York:
    Metropolitan Books, 2007.
Fisher, Ralph Talcott, Jr. *Pattern for Soviet Youth: A Study of the Congresses of the
    Komsomol, 1918–54.* New York: Columbia University Press, 1959.
Fleurs, Loretta Dawn. "Education Reform in Moscow Secondary Schools,
    1958–1964." PhD diss., Princeton University, 1999.
Fogler, Janusz, ed. *Wajda Films.* Warsaw: Art and Film Publishers, 1996.
Frankel, Edith Rogovin. *Novy Mir: A Case Study in the Politics of Literature,
    1952–58.* Cambridge: Cambridge University Press, 1981.
Fraser, Erica. *Military Masculinity and Postwar Recovery in the Soviet Union.*
    Toronto: University of Toronto Press, 2019.
Fürst, Juliane. *Stalin's Last Generation: Soviet Post-War Youth and the Emergence
    of Mature Socialism.* Oxford: Oxford University Press, 2012.
– ed. *Late Stalinist Russia: Society between Reconstruction and Reinvention.* New
    York: Routledge, 2009.
Galbraith, J.K. *The New Industrial State.* Boston: Houghton Mifflin, 1967.
Gerhardt, Christina, and Sara Saljoughi. *1968 and Global Cinema.* Detroit:
    Wayne State University Press, 2018.
Gerovitch, Slava. *Soviet Space Mythologies: Public Images, Private Memories, and
    the Making of a Cultural Identity.* Pittsburgh: University of Pittsburgh Press,
    2015.
Golovskoi, Valerii. *Kinematograf semidesiatykh. Mezhdu ottepel'iu i glasnost'iu.*
    Moscow: Materik, 2004.
Gorsuch, Anne. *All This Is Your World: Soviet Tourism at Home and Abroad after
    Stalin.* Oxford: Oxford University Press, 2013.
Gorsuch, Anne E., and Diane P. Koenker, eds. *The Socialist Sixties: Crossing
    Borders in the Second World.* Bloomington: Indiana University Press, 2013.
Goscilo, Helena, and Yana Hashamova, eds. *Cinepaternity: Fathers and Sons in
    Soviet and Post- Soviet Film.* Bloomington: Indiana University Press, 2010.
Groys, Boris. *The Total Art of Stalinism: Avant-Garde, Aesthetic Dictatorship, and
    Beyond.* Princeton: Princeton University Press, 1992.
Gromov, E.S. *Vremia, Geroi, Zritel'.* Moscow: Izd-vo TsK VLKSM Molodaia
    gvardiia, 1965.
Haltof, Marek. *Polish National Cinema.* New York: Berghahn, 2002.
Hames, Peter. *The Czechoslovak New Wave.* London: Wallflower Press, 2005.
Haynes, John. *New Soviet Man: Gender and Masculinity in Stalinist Soviet
    Cinema.* Manchester: Manchester University Press, 2003.
Hellbeck, Jochen. *Revolution on My Mind: Writing a Diary under Stalin.*
    Cambridge, MA: Harvard University Press, 2006.

Kaganovsky, Lilya. *How the Soviet Man Was Unmade: Cultural Fantasy and Male Subjectivity under Stalin.* Pittsburgh: University of Pittsburgh Press, 2008.

Kenez, Peter. *Cinema and Soviet Society from the Revolution to the Death of Stalin.* London: I.B. Tauris, 2001.

Kerr, Clark, John T. Dunlop, Frederick Harbison, and Charles Myers. *Industrialism and Industrial Man: The Problems of Labor and Management in Economic Growth.* Cambridge, MA: Harvard University Press, 1960.

Kharkhordin, Oleg. *The Collective and the Individual in Russia: A Study of Practices.* Berkeley: University of California Press, 1999.

Khlopliankina, Tatiana. *Zastava Il'icha: Sud'ba fil'ma.* Moscow: Kinotsentr, 1990.

Khrushchev, Nikita Sergeevich. *The Crimes of the Stalin Era: Special Report to the 20th Congress of the Communist Party of the Soviet Union.* New York: New Leader, 1962.

Koenker, Diane. *Club Red: Vacation Travel and the Soviet Dream.* Ithaca: Cornell University Press, 2013.

Kogan, L.N. *Kino i zritel'. Opyt sotsiologicheskogo issledovaniia.* Moscow: Iskusstvo, 1968.

Korolev, Iu.A. *Brak i razvod: Sovremennye tendentsii.* Moscow: Iuridicheskaia literatura, 1978.

Kotkin, Stephen. *Magnetic Mountain: Stalinism as a Civilization.* Berkeley: University of California Press, 1995.

Kozintsev, G.M. *Nash sovremennik Viliam Shekspir.* Lenigrad: Iskusstvo, 1966.

Kozlov, Denis. *The Readers of Novyi Mir: Coming to Terms with the Stalinist Past.* Cambridge, MA: Harvard University Press, 2013.

Kozlov, Denis, and Eleonory Gilburd, eds. *The Thaw: Soviet Society and Culture during the 1950s and 1960s.* Toronto: University of Toronto Press, 2013.

Krementsov, Nikolai. *The Cure: A Story of Cancer and Politics from the Annals of the Cold War.* Chicago: University of Chicago Press, 2002.

Kucherenko, Olga. *Soviet Street Children and the Second World War: Welfare and Social Control under Stalin.* London: Bloomsbury Press, 2016.

Lanoux, Andrea, and Helena Goscilo, eds. *Gender and National Identity in Twentieth-Century Russian Culture.* DeKalb: Northern Illinois University Press, 2006.

LaPierre, Brian. *Hooligans in Khrushchev's Russia: Defining, Policing, and Producing Deviance during the Thaw.* Madison: University of Wisconsin Press, 2012.

Laurent, Natacha. *L'oeil du Kremlin. Cinéma et censure en URSS sous Staline, 1928–1953.* Toulouse: Privat, 2000.

Levy, Marion. *Modernization and the Structure of Societies.* Princeton: Princeton University Press, 1966.

Liehm, Mira. *Passion and Defiance: Film in Italy from 1942 to the Present.* Berkeley: University of California Press, 1984.

Lunacharskii, A.V. *Rasskazy o Lenine.* Moscow: Izdatel'stvo politicheskoi literatury, 1985.

Malyshev, V.S. *Gosfil'mofond. Zemlianichnaia poliana.* Moscow: Pashkov dom, 2005.

Marcus, Millicent Joy. *Italian Film in the Light of Neorealism.* Princeton: Princeton University Press, 1986.

Mar'iamov, Grigorii. *Kremlevskii tsenzor. Stalin smotrit kino.* Moscow: Konfederatsiia soiuzov kinematografistov kino tsentr, 1992.

Marsh, Rosalind J. *Soviet Fiction Since Stalin: Science, Politics, and Literature.* London: Croom Helm, 1986.

Mazierska, Ewa. *Masculinities in Polish, Czech, and Slovak Cinema: Black Peters and Men of Marble.* New York: Berghahn Books, 2008.

McCallum, Claire. *The Fate of the New Man: Representing and Reconstructing Masculinity in Soviet Visual Culture, 1945–1965.* DeKalb: Northern Illinois University Press, 2018.

McMillan, Priscilla Johnson. *Khrushchev and the Arts: The Politics of Soviet Culture, 1962–64.* Cambridge, MA: MIT Press, 1965.

McSmith, Andy. *Fear and the Muse Kept Watch: The Russian Masters from Akhmatova and Pasternak to Shostakovich and Eisenstein under Stalin.* New York: New Press, 2015.

– *On Soviet Dissent.* New York: Columbia University Press, 1980.

Miller, Brandon Gray. "Between Creation and Crisis: Soviet Masculinities, Consumption, and Bodies after Stalin." PhD diss., Michigan State University, 2013.

Nowell-Smith, Geoffrey. *Making Waves: New Cinemas of the 1960s.* New York: Bloomsbury, 2013.

Oever, Roel van den. *Mama's Boy: Momism and Homophobia in Postwar American Culture.* New York: Palgrave Macmillan, 2012.

Oldenziel, Ruth, and Karin Zachmann, eds. *Cold War Kitchen: Americanization, Technology, and European Users.* Cambridge, MA: MIT Press, 2009.

Peacock, Margaret. *Innocent Weapons: The Soviet and American Politics of Childhood in the Cold War.* Chapel Hill: University of North Carolina Press, 2014.

Plant, Rebecca Jo. *Mom: The Transformation of Motherhood in Modern America.* Chicago: University of Chicago Press, 2010.

Pollock, Ethan. *Stalin and the Soviet Science Wars.* Princeton: Princeton University Press, 2006.

Prokhorov, Aleksandr, ed. *Springtime for Soviet Cinema: Re/Viewing the 1960s.* Pittsburgh: Pittsburgh Russian Film Symposium, 2001.

– *Unasledovannyi diskurs. Paradigmy Stalinskoi kul'tury v literature i kinematografe ottepeli.* Saint Petersburg: Akademicheskii proekt, 2007.

Rajagopalan, Sudha. *Indian Films in Soviet Cinemas: The Culture of Movie-Going after Stalin.* Bloomington: Indiana University Press, 2008.

Raleigh, Donald. *Soviet Baby Boomers: An Oral History of Russia's Cold War Generation*. Oxford: Oxford University Press, 2011.

– *Russia's Sputnik Generation: Soviet Baby Boomers Talk about Their Lives*. Bloomington: Indiana University Press, 2006.

Reid, Susan. *Khrushchev in Wonderland: The Pioneer Palace in Moscow's Lenin Hills, 1962*. Pittsburgh: Center for Russian and East European Studies, University of Pittsburgh, 2002.

Riha, Thomas. *Readings in Russian Civilization*, vol. 2. Chicago: University of Chicago Press, 1969.

Rojavin, Marina, and Tim Harte, eds. *Women in Soviet Film: The Thaw and Post-Thaw Periods*. New York: Routledge, 2017.

Roth-Ey, Kristin. *Moscow Prime Time: How the Soviet Union Built the Media Empire That Lost the Cultural Cold War*. Ithaca: Cornell University Press, 2011.

Sandbrook, Dominic. *Never Had It So Good: A History of Britain from Suez to the Beatles*. London: Little, Brown, 2005.

Sekirinskii, S.S., ed. *Istoriia strany, istoriia kino*. Moscow: Znak, 2004.

Sellier, Geneviève. *Masculine Singular: French New Wave Cinema*. Durham: Duke University Press, 2008.

Sharp, Edward. "School Reform during the Khrushchev Period: A Radical Attempt to Re-Make Soviet Social and Economic Structures." PhD diss., University of Michigan, 1995.

Shiel, Mark. *Italian Neorealism: Rebuilding the Cinematic City*. London: Wallflower Press, 2006.

Siegelbaum, Lewis H., ed. *Borders of Socialism: Private Spheres of Soviet Russia*. New York: Palgrave Macmillan, 2006.

Spechler, Dina. *Permitted Dissent in the USSR: Novy Mir and the Soviet Regime*. New York: Praeger, 1982.

Sperling, Valerie. *Sex, Politics, and Putin: Political Legitimacy in Russia*. Oxford: Oxford University Press, 2014.

Stites, Richard. *Russian Popular Culture: Entertainment and Society Since 1900*. Cambridge: Cambridge University Press, 1992.

Taubman, William. *Khrushchev: The Man and His Era*. New York: W.W. Norton, 2003.

Taubman, William, Abbot Gleason, and Sergei Khrushchev, eds. *Nikita Khrushchev*. New Haven: Yale University Press, 2000.

Tsipursky, Gleb. *Socialist Fun: Youth, Consumption, and State-Sponsored Popular Culture in the Soviet Union, 1945–1970*. Pittsburgh: University of Pittsburgh Press, 2016.

Vail', Petr, and Aleksandr Genis. *60-e. Mir Sovetskogo cheloveka*. Ann Arbor: Ardis, 1988.

Varga-Harris, Christine. *Stories of House and Home: Soviet Apartment Life during the Khrushchev Years*. Ithaca: Cornell University Press, 2015.

Weinberg, Elizabeth Ann. *Sociology in the Soviet Union and Beyond: Social Enquiry and Social Change*. Burlington: Ashgate, 2004.

Widdis, Emma. *Visions of a New Land: Soviet Film from the Revolution to the Second World War*. New Haven: Yale University Press, 2003.

Williamson, Bill. *The Temper of the Times: British Society Since World War II*. Oxford: B. Blackwell, 1990.

Woll, Josephine. *The Cranes Are Flying*. London: I.B. Tauris, 2003.

– *Real Images: Soviet Cinema and the Thaw*. London: I.B. Tauris, 2000.

Wylie, Philip. *Generation of Vipers: In Which the Author Rails against Congress, President, Professors, Motherhood, Businessmen, and Other Matters American*. Champaign, IL: Dalkey Archive Press, 1996.

Youngblood, Denise J. *Russian War Films: On the Cinema Front, 1914–2005*. Lawrence: University Press of Kansas, 2007.

Zakharova, Larissa. *S'habiller à la soviétique. La mode et le Dégel en URSS*. Paris: CNRS Éditions, 2011.

Zhuk, Sergei. *Rock and Roll in the Rocket City: The West, Identity, and Ideology in Soviet Dniepropetrovsk, 1960–1985*. Baltimore: Johns Hopkins University Press, 2017.

Zubkova, E.Iu. *Russia after the War: Hopes, Illusions, and Disappointments, 1945–1957*. Armonk: M.E. Sharpe, 1998.

Zubok, V.M. *Zhivago's Children: The Last Russian Intelligentsia*. Cambridge: Belknap Press, 2009.

Secondary Sources (Articles and Essays)

Adamson, David M., and Julie DaVanzo. "Russia's Demographic 'Crisis': How Real Is It?," 1–5. Santa Monica, CA: RAND Corporation, 1997.

Amerian, Stephanie. "The Fashion Gap: The Cold War Politics of American and Soviet Fashion, 1945–1959." *Journal of Historical Research in Marketing* 8, no. 1 (2016): 65–82.

Atwood, Lynne. "Gender Angst in Russian Society and Cinema in the Post-Stalin Era." In *Russian Cultural Studies: An Introduction*, edited by Catriona Kelly and David Sheperd, 352–67. Oxford: Oxford University Press, 1998.

Avdeev, Alexandre, Alain Blum, and Irina Troitskaya. "The History of Abortion Statistics in Russia and the USSR from 1900 to 1991." *Population: An English Selection* 7 (1995): 39–66.

Balakian, Nona. "The Flight from Innocence: England's Newest Literary Generation." *Books Abroad* 33, no. 3 (1959): 261–70.

Baranczak, Stanislaw. "Before the Thaw: The Beginning of Dissent in Postwar Polish Literature and the Case of Adam Wazyk's *A Poem for Adults*." *Eastern European Politics and Societies* 3, no. 1 (1989): 4–21.

Baudin, Rodolphe. "Le phénomène de la série culte en contexte soviétique et post-soviétique. L'exemple de Semnadcat' mgnovenij vesny." *Cahiers du monde russe* 42, no. 1 (2001): 49–70.

Berger, Michael D. "Soviet Divorce Laws and the Role of the Russian Family." *Brigham Young University Law Review* no. 3 (1986): 821–33.

Bergman, Jay. "Valerii Chkalov: Soviet Pilot as New Soviet Man." *Journal of Contemporary History* 33, no. 1 (1998): 135–52.

Bernstein, Laurie. "Communist Custodial Contests: Adoption Rulings in the USSR after the Second World War." *Journal of Social History* 34, no. 4 (2001): 843–61.

Bogdanova, Elena. "The Soviet Consumer: More Than Just a Soviet Man." In *Communism and Consumerism: The Soviet Alternative to the Affluent Society*, edited by Timo Vihavainen and Elena Bogdanova, 113–38. Leiden: Brill, 2015.

Brainerd, Elizabeth. "The Lasting Effect of Sex Ratio Imbalance on Marriage and Family: Evidence from World War II in Russia." *Review of Economics and Statistics* 99, no. 2 (2017): 229–42.

Brusilovskaia, Lidiia. "The Culture of Everyday Life during the Thaw." *Russian Studies in History* 48, no. 1 (2009): 10–32.

Bulgakowa, Oksana. "Cine-Weathers: Soviet Thaw Cinema in the International Context." In *Thaw: Soviet Society and Culture during the 1950s and 1960s*, edited by Denis Kozlov and Eleonory Gilburd, 436–81. Toronto: University of Toronto Press, 2014.

– "Vocal Changes: Marlon Brando, Innokenti Smoktunovsky, and the Sound of the 1950s." In *Sound, Speech, Music in Soviet and Post-Soviet Cinema*, edited by Lilya Kaganovsky and Masha Salazkina, 145–62. Bloomington: Indiana University Press, 2008.

Bushnell, John. "The 'New Soviet Man' Turns Pessimist." In *The Soviet Union Since Stalin*, edited by Stephen F. Cohen, Alexander Rabinowitch, and Robert Sharlet, 179–99. Bloomington: Indiana University Press, 1980.

Cameron, Ian. "Michaelangelo Antonioni." *Film Quarterly* 16, no. 1 (1962): 1–58.

Carlbäck, Helene. "Fatherly Emotions in Soviet Russia." *Baltic Worlds* 1–2 (2017): 20–9.

– "Lone Motherhood in Soviet Russia in the Mid-20th Century – in a European Context." In *And They Lived Happily Ever After: Norms and Everyday Practices of Family and Parenthood in Russia and Central Europe*, edited by Helene Carlbäck, Yulia Gradskova, and Zhanna Kravchenko, 25–46. Budapest: CEU Press, 2012.

– "Lone Mothers and Fatherless Children: Public Discourse on Marriage and Family Law." In *Soviet State and Society under Nikita Khrushchev*, edited by Melanie Ilič and Jeremy Smith, 86–103. London: Routledge, 2009.

Chapman, Janet G. "Real Wages in the Soviet Union, 1928–1952." *Review of Economics and Statistics* 36, no. 2 (1954): 134–56.

Chernova, Zhanna. "The Model of 'Soviet' Fatherhood." *Russian Studies in History* 51, no. 2 (2012): 35–62.

Christie, Ian. "Back in the USSR." *Film Comment* 36, no. 6 (November–December 2000): 39–42.

Chudak, Aleksandr, and Marietta Chudakova. "Sovremennaia povest' i iumor." *Novyi mir* 7 (1967): 222–32.

Clark, Katerina. "Socialist Realism in Soviet Literature." In *The Routledge Companion to Russian Literature*, edited by Neil Cornwell, 174–84. London: Routledge, 2001.

Condee, Nancy. "Veronika Fuses Out: Rape and Medium Specificity in *The Cranes Are Flying*." *Studies in Russian and Soviet Cinema* 3, no. 2 (2009): 173–83.

Costanzo, Susan. "The 1959 *Liriki–Fiziki* Debate: Going Public with the Private?" In *Borders of Socialism: Private Spheres of Soviet Russia*, edited by L.H. Siegelbaum, 251–68. New York: Palgrave Macmillan, 2006.

DaVanzo, Julie, and Clifford A. Grammich. "Dire Demographics: Population Trends in the Russian Federation," 1–102. Santa Monica: RAND Corporation, 2001.

DeBlasio, Alyssa. "The New-Year Film as a Genre of Post-War Russian Cinema." *Studies in Russian and Soviet Cinema* 2, no. 1 (2008): 43–61.

Dmytryk, Olena. "Difficult Cases: Communist Morality, Gender, and Embodiment in Thaw Cinema." *Studies in Russian and Soviet Cinema* 11, no. 1 (2017): 3–19.

Dobrenko, Evgeny. "Creation Myth and Myth Creation in Stalinist Cinema." *Studies in Russian and Soviet Cinema* 1, no. 3 (2007): 239–64.

Edele, Mark. "Strange Young Men in Stalin's Moscow: The Birth and Life of the Stiliagi, 1945–1953." *Jahrbücher für Geschichte Osteuropas* 50, no. 1. (2002): 37–61.

First, Joshua. "From Spectator to 'Differentiated' Consumer: Film Audience Research in the Era of Developed Socialism, 1965–80." *Kritika* 9 (2008): 317–44.

František, Daniel. "The Czech Difference." In *Politics, Art, and Commitment in the East European Cinema*, edited by David W. Paul, 49–56. London: Macmillan, 1983.

Fraser, Erica. "Masculinity in the Personal Narratives of Soviet Nuclear Physicists." *Aspasia* 8, no.1 (2014): 45–63.

– "Yuri Gagarin and Celebrity Masculinity in Soviet Culture." In *Gender, Sexuality, and the Cold War*, edited by Philip E. Muehlenbeck, 270–89. Nashville: Vanderbilt University Press, 2017.

Fürst, Juliane. "The Arrival of Spring? Changes and Continuities in Soviet Youth Culture and Policy between Stalin and Khrushchev." In *The Dilemmas of De-Stalinization*, edited by Polly Jones, 135–53. New York: Routledge, 2006.

– "Swinging across the Iron Curtain and Moscow's Summer of Love: How Western Youth Culture Went East." In *Transnational Histories of Youth in the Twentieth Century*, edited by R.I. Jobs and D.M. Pomfret, 236–59. London: Palgrave Macmillan, 2015.

Gerovitch, Slava. "'New Soviet Man' inside Machine: Human Engineering, Spacecraft Design, and the Construction of Communism." *Osiris* 22, no. 1 (2007): 135–57.

Gheith, Jehanne M. "The Superfluous Man and the Necessary Woman: A 'Re-Vision.'" *Russian Review* 55, no. 2 (1996): 226–44.

Gibian, George. "Themes in Recent Soviet Russian Literature." *Slavic Review* 23, no. 3 (1964): 420–31.

Goldman Marshall I. "The Reluctant Consumer and Economic Fluctuations in the Soviet Union." *Journal of Political Economy* 73, no. 4 (1965): 366–80.

Grenier, Cynthia. "Berlin, Karlovy-Vary, Venice." *Film Quarterly* 14, no. 2 (1960): 24–9.

Grenier, Richard. "A Soviet 'New Wave'?" *Commentary* 72, no. 1 (1981): 62–7.

Hanáková, Petra. "The Construction of Normality: The Lineage of Male Figures in Contemporary Czech Cinema." In *Mediale Welten in Tschechien nach 1898. Genderkonstructionen und Codes des Plebejismus*, edited by Uta Röhrborn, 149–59. Munich: Kubon and Sagner, 2005.

Harte, Tim. "Marlen Khutsiev's *July Rain*, Cultural Liberation, and a New Soviet Woman." In *Women in Soviet Film: The Thaw and Post-Thaw Periods*, edited by Marina Rojavin and Tim Harte, 137–54. London: Routledge, 2018.

Hill, Steven P. "The Soviet Film Today." *Film Quarterly* 20, no. 4 (1967): 33–52.

Hoffmann, David L. "Mothers in the Motherland: Stalinist Pronatalism in Its Pan-European Context." *Journal of Social History* 34, no. 1 (2000): 35–54.

Holmgren, Beth. "Toward an Understanding of Gendered Agency in Contemporary Russia." *Signs* 38, no. 3 (2013): 535–42.

Ioffe, Dennis G., and Frederick H. White. "Taxi Blues: The Anxiety of Soviet Masculinity." *Journal of European Studies* 44, no. 3 (2014): 263–80.

Jones, Polly, ed. *The Dilemmas of De-Stalinization: Negotiating Cultural and Social Change in the Khrushchev Era*. New York: Routledge, 2009.

Josephson, Paul R. "'Projects of the Century' in Soviet History: Large-Scale Technologies from Lenin to Gorbachev." *Technology and Culture* 36, no. 3 (1995): 519–59.

– "Atomic-Powered Communism: Nuclear Culture in the Postwar USSR." *Slavic Review* 55, no. 2 (1996): 297–324.

Juviler, Peter H. "Cell Mutation in Soviet Society: The Family." In *Soviet Society and Culture: Essays in Honor of Vera S. Dunham*, edited by Terry L. Thompson and Richard Sheldon, 37–56. Boulder: Westview Press, 1988.

Kaganovsky, Lilya. "Postmemory, Counter-Memory: Soviet Cinema of the 1960s." In *The Socialist Sixties: Crossing Borders in the Second World*, edited by Anne Gorsuch and Diane P. Koenker, 235–50. Bloomington: Indiana University Press, 2013.

– "Ways of Seeing: On Kira Muratova's *Brief Encounters* and Larisa Shepit'ko's *Wings*." *Russian Review* 71, no. 3 (2012): 482–99.

Kalliney, Peter. "Cities of Affluence: Masculinity, Class, and the Angry Young Men." *Modern Fiction Studies* 47, no. 1 (2001): 92–116.

Kapterev, Sergei. "Illusionary Spoils: Soviet Attitudes towards American Cinema during the Early Cold War." *Kritika* 10, no. 4 (2009): 779–807.

Knight, Claire "Stalin's Trophy Films, 1947–52: A Resource." *KinoKultura* 48 (2015), http://www.kinokultura.com/2015/48-knight.shtml#1.

Kohonen, Iina. "The Space Race and Soviet Utopian Thinking." *Sociological Review* 57, no. 1 (2009): 114–31.

Kozovoi, Andrei. "A Foot in The Door: The Lacy–Zarubin Agreement and Soviet–American Film Diplomacy during the Khrushchev Era, 1953–1963." *Historical Journal of Film, Radio and Television* 36, no. 1 (2016): 21–39.

Krymskaia A.S. "K istorii nauchno-obrazovatel'nykh obmenov mezhdu SSSR i SSHA v kontse 1950-kh – 1960-e gg." *Noveishaia istoriia Rossii* 2 (2011): 99–106.

Kukhterin, Sergei. "Fathers and Patriarchs in Communist and Post-Communist Russia." In *Gender, State, and Society in Soviet and Post-Soviet Russia*, edited by Sarah Ashwin, 71–89. London: Routledge, 2000.

Latynina, Anna. "Epitafiia shestidesiatnikam. Poslednii roman Vasiliia Aksenova." *Novyi mir* 2 (2010): 153–60.

Livschiz, Ann. "De-Stalinizing Soviet Childhood: The Quest for Moral Re-Birth, 1953–58." In *The Dilemmas of De-Stalinization: Negotiating Cultural and Social Change in the Khrushchev Era*, edited by Polly Jones, 117–34. New York: Routledge, 2006.

Lovell, Stephen. "In Search of an Ending: *Seventeen Moments* and the Seventies." In *The Socialist Sixties: Crossing Borders in the Second World*, edited by Anne E. Gorsuch and Diane P. Koenker, 303–21. Bloomington: Indiana University Press, 2013.

Luzzi, Joseph. "Romantic Allegory, Postwar Film, and the Question of Italy." *Modern Language Quarterly* 68 (2007): 53–85.

Marsh, Rosalind J. "Soviet Fiction and the Nuclear Debate." *Soviet Studies* 38, no. 2 (1986): 248–70.

Marshall, Herbert. "The New Wave in Soviet Cinema." In *The Red Screen: Politics, Society, Art in Soviet Cinema*, edited by Anna Lawton, 175–91. London: Routledge, 1992.

Marwick, Arthur. "*Room at the Top, Saturday Night and Sunday Morning*, and the 'Cultural Revolution' in Britain." *Journal of Contemporary History* 19, no. 1 (1984): 127–52.

McCallum, Claire E. "Man about the House: Male Domesticity and Fatherhood in Soviet Visual Satire under Khrushchev." In *The Palgrave Handbook of Women and Gender in Twentieth- Century Russia and the Soviet Union*, edited by Melanie Ilič, 331–47. London: Palgrave Macmillan, 2017.

– "The Return: Postwar Masculinity and the Domestic Space in Stalinist Visual Culture, 1945–53." *The Russian Review* 74, no. 1 (2015): 117–43.

McCannon, John. "Positive Heroes at the Pole: Celebrity Status, Socialist-Realist Ideals, and the Soviet Myth of the Arctic, 1932–39." *Russian Review* 56, no. 3 (1997): 346–65.

Mendel, Arthur P. "Hamlet and Soviet Humanism." *Slavic Review* 30, no. 4 (1971): 733–47.

Michaels, Paula A. "Mikhail Kalatozov's *The Red Tent*: A Case Study in International Coproduction across the Iron Curtain." *Historical Journal of Film, Radio and Television* 26, no. 3 (2006): 311–25.

Mikhailova, Tatiana, and Mark Lipovetsky. "Flight without Wings: The Subjectivity of a Female War Veteran in Larisa Shepit'ko's *Wings* (1966)." In *Embracing Arms: Cultural Representation of Slavic and Balkan Women in War*, edited by Helena Goscilo and Yana Hashamova, 81–106. Budapest: CEU Press, 2012.

Miller, Brandon Gray. "The New Soviet *Narkoman*: Drugs and Youth in Post-Stalinist Russia." *REGION: Regional Studies of Russia, Eastern Europe, and Central Asia* 4, no. 1 (2015): 45–69.

Miller, Jamie. "The Purges of Soviet Cinema, 1929–38." *Studies in Russian and Soviet Cinema* 1, no. 1 (2007): 5–26.

Moskoff, William. "Divorce in the USSR." *Journal of Marriage and Family* 45, no. 2 (1983): 219–25.

Nakachi, Mie. "N.S. Khrushchev and the 1944 Soviet Family Law: Politics, Reproduction, and Language." *East European Politics and Societies* 20, no. 1 (2006): 40–68.

– "A Postwar Sexual Liberation? The Gendered Experience of the Soviet Union's Great Patriotic War." *Cahiers du Monde Russe* 52, nos. 2–3 (2011): 423–40.

Novitskaya, Alexandra. "Patriotism, Sentiment, and Male Hysteria: Putin's Masculinity Politics and the Persecution of Non-Heterosexual Russians." *NORMA* 12, nos. 3–4 (2017): 302–18.

Perlman, Francesca, and Martin McKee. "Trends in Family Planning in Russia, 1994–2003." *Perspectives on Sexual and Reproductive Health* 41, no. 1 (2009): 40–50.

Bibliography

Pinsky, Anatoly. "The Diaristic Form and Subjectivity under Khrushchev."
    Slavic Review 73, no. 4 (2014): 805–27.
– "The Origins of Post-Stalin Individuality: Aleksandr Tvardovskii and the
    Evolution of 1930s Soviet Romanticism." *Russian Review* 76, no. 3 (2017):
    458–83.
Pollock, Ethan. "'Real Men Go to the Bania': Postwar Soviet Masculinities and
    the Bathhouse.' *Kritika* 11, no. 1 (2010): 47–76.
Popović, Dunja. "A Generation That Has Squandered Its Men: The Late Soviet
    Crisis of Masculinity in the Poetry of Sergei Gandlevskii." *Russian Review* 70
    (2011): 663–76.
Powell, David. "The Effectiveness of Soviet Anti-Religious Propaganda."
    Public Opinion Quarterly 31, no. 3 (1967): 366–80.
Prokhorov, Alexander. "The Adolescent and the Child in the Cinema of the
    Thaw." *Studies in Russian and Soviet Cinema* 1, no. 2 (2007): 115–29.
– "Soviet Family Melodrama of the 1940s and 1950s: From *Wait for Me* to *The
    Cranes Are Flying*." In *Imitations of Life: Two Centuries of Melodrama in Russia*,
    edited by Louise McReynolds and Joan Neuberger, 208–31. Durham: Duke
    University Press, 2002.
Prokhorova, Elena. "The Post-Utopian Body Politic: Masculinity and the
    Crisis of National Identity in the Brezhnev-Era TV Miniseries." In *Gender
    and National Identity in Twentieth-Century Russian Culture*, edited by Helena
    Goscilo and Andrea Lanoux, 131–50. DeKalb: Northern Illinois University
    Press, 2006.
Qualin, Anthony. "Laughing at Carnival Mirrors: The Comic Songs of
    Vladimir Vysockij and Soviet Power." *Russian Literature* 74, no. 1 (2013):
    185–205.
Randall, Amy E. "'Abortion Will Deprive You of Happiness!': Soviet
    Reproductive Politics in the Post-Stalin Era." *Journal of Women's History* 23,
    no. 3 (2011): 13–38.
Rassadin, Stanislav. "Shestidesiatniki: Knigi o molodom sovremennike."
    Iunost' 12 (1960): 58–62.
Reid, Susan E. "Cold War in the Kitchen: Gender and the De-Stalinization of
    Consumer Taste in the Soviet Union under Khrushchev." *Slavic Review* 61,
    no. 2 (2002): 211–52.
– "The Khrushchev Kitchen: Domesticating the Scientific-Technological
    Revolution." *Journal of Contemporary History* 40, no. 2 (2005): 289–316.
Riabov, Oleg, and Tatiana Riabova. "The Remasculinization of Russia?
    Gender, Nationalism, and the Legitimation of Power under Vladimir
    Putin." *Problems of Post-Communism* 61, no. 2 (2014): 23–35.
Roberts, Graham. "Re-Viewing Homo Sovieticus: The Representation of
    the Male Body in the Films of Kira Muratova." *New Cinemas: Journal of
    Contemporary Film* 1, no. 2 (2002): 113–19.

Roberts, Mary Louise. "Beyond 'Crisis' in Understanding Gender Transformation." *Gender and History* 28, no. 2 (2016): 358–66.

Rosneck, Karen. "Vladimir Vysotsky." In *Russian Poets of the Soviet Era*, edited by Karen Rosneck, 324–35. Detroit: Gale, 2011.

Sanjian, Andrea Stevenson. "Social Problems, Political Issues: Marriage and Divorce in the USSR." *Soviet Studies* 43, no. 4 (1991): 629–49.

Schrand, Thomas G. "Soviet 'Civic-Minded Women' in the 1930s: Gender, Class, and Industrialization in a Socialist Society." *Journal of Women's History* 11, no. 3 (1999): 126–50.

Siefert, Marsha. "Soviet Cinematic Internationalism and Socialist Film Making, 1955–1972." In *Socialist Internationalism in the Cold War: Exploring the Second World*, edited by Patryk Babiracki and Austin Jersild, 161–93. New York: Palgrave Macmillan, 2016.

Slobin, Greta N. "Aksenov beyond 'Youth Prose:' Subversion through Popular Culture." *Slavic and East European Journal* 31, no. 1 (1987): 50–64.

Smirnova, Michelle. "Multiple Masculinities: Gender Performativity in Soviet Political Humor." *Men and Masculinities* 20, no. 2 (2017): 204–29.

Sorokin, P.A. "Mutual Convergence of the United States and the USSR to the Mixed Sociocultural Type." *International Journal of Comparative Sociology* 1, no. 2 (1960): 143–76.

Sorokina, Anastasia. "The Lady Vanishes: Soviet Censorship, Socialist Realism, and the Disappearance of Larisa Shepitko." *Film Matters* 8, no. 3 (2017): 21–7.

Stiazhkina, Elena. "The 'Petty-Bourgeois Woman' and the 'Soulless Philistine': Gendered Aspects of the History of Soviet Everyday Life from the Mid-1960s to the Mid-1980s." *Russian Studies in History* 51, no. 2 (2012): 63–97.

Suri, Jeremi. "AHR Forum: The Rise and Fall of an International Counterculture, 1960–1975." *American Historical Review* 114, no. 1 (2009): 45–68.

Tartakovskaya, Irina. "Constructing Masculinity from the War Spirit." In *Collective Memories in War*, edited by Elena Rozhdestvenskaya et al., 163–75. London: Routledge, 2015.

Taubman, Jane A. "The Cinema of Kira Muratova." *Russian Review* 52, no. 3 (1993): 367–81.

Taylor, Richard. "A 'Cinema for the Millions': Soviet Socialist Realism and the Problem of Film Comedy." *Journal of Contemporary History* 18, no. 3 (1983): 439–61.

Vainshtein, Olga. "Orange Jackets and Pea Green Pants: The Fashion of *Stilyagi* in Soviet Postwar Culture." *Fashion Theory* 22, no. 2 (2018): 167–85.

Wood, Elizabeth A. "Hypermasculinity as a Scenario of Power." *International Feminist Journal of Politics* 18, no. 3 (2016): 329–50.

Zdravomyslova, Elena, and Anna Temkina. "The Crisis of Masculinity in Late Soviet Discourse." *Russian Social Science Review* 54, no. 1 (2013): 40–61.

Zezina, Mariia. "S tochki zreniia istorii kinozala. Kinoprokat i massovoi zritel' v gody ottepeli." In *Istoriia strany, istoriia kino*, edited by S.S. Sekirinskii, 390–402. Moscow: Znak, 2004.

Zhuk, Sergei. "Hollywood's Insidious Charms: The Impact of American Cinema and Television on the Soviet Union during the Cold War." *Cold War History* 14, no. 4 (2014): 593–617.

Index